The Seduction of Modern Spain

The Seduction of Modern Spain

The Female Body and the Francoist Body Politic

Aurora G. Morcillo

Lewisburg
Bucknell University Press

Associated University Presses
2010 Eastpark Boulevard
Cranbury, NJ 08512

The paper used in this publication meets the requirements of the American National Standard for Permanence of Paper for Printed Library Materials Z39.48-1984.

Library of Congress Cataloging-in-Publication Data

Morcillo, Aurora G.
The seduction of modern Spain : the female body and the Francoist body politic / Aurora G. Morcillo.
p. cm.
Includes bibliographical references and index.
ISBN 978-0-8387-5753-6 (alk. paper)
1. Women—Spain—Social conditions—20th century. 2. Sex role—Spain—History—20th century. 3. Body image—Spain—History—20th century. 4. Spain—Politics and government—1939–1975. 5. Francoism. I. Title.
HQ1692.M668 2010
305.48′86100904—dc22

2009043747

PRINTED IN THE UNITED STATES OF AMERICA

Para mis padres, Aurora y Manuel
Por todo. Siempre.

[S]*eduction alone is radically opposed to anatomy as destiny.* Seduction breaks the distinctive sexualization of bodies and the inevitable phallic economy that results.

—Jean Baudrillard, *Seduction*

With lowered eyes we tried to protect you from our **feminine seduction.**

—Ana Rosetti, *Yesterday*

Contents

Acknowledgments

This book has been in gestation for seven years and many colleagues, friends, and family have supported me through the labor and delivery. Thank you to Carolyn Boyd for reading the very early drafts and providing continuous support and encouragement; to my colleagues at the History Department at Florida International University, especially Darden Pyron who provided useful and constructive criticism, and specially to David and Sasha Cook who read the entire first draft and nourished my intellect with advice and my body with delicious tapas and vinito. To the Women's Studies Writing Group at FIU, specially to Lynn Barrett, Asunción Gómez, Pascale Becel, Ana Roca, María Aysa, Sarah Mahler, Vrushali Patil, Alexandra Cornelius Dialo, Tara Kay, Chantalle Verna, Kirsten Wood, and Laurie Shrage.

Thank you to my maestros/as and colleagues on the other side of the Atlantic: Mary Nash, Paul Preston, Cinta Ramblado, Margarita Birriel, Mónica Moreno, Ana Aguado, Fatina Sadiqi, Elena Hernández Sandoica, Octavio Ruiz Manjón, Fernando Martínez, Sofia Rodríguez, Oscar Rodríguez, to all of them for their encouragement and wisdom. My students have been a source of inspiration and intellectual wonder both in History and Women's Studies: Julio Capo, Brian Pekel, Gema Junco, Ashley Mateiro, Jennifer Sheran, Joseph Holbrook.

Thank you to my friends: Ana María Bidegain, Margaret McCaffery , María del Mar Logroño, and Paula de la Cruz Fernández for their loving friendship and loyalty. Thank you to my family, my parents Manuel and Aurora to whom I dedicate this book; my sister Emilia from whom I learned about how to be a good feminist; my brother José Manuel from whom I have learned what being brave means. To all of them for their continuous unconditional love and support from afar in my hometown, Granada, where every summer they shower me with love and renew my passion for history. They all teamed up behind José

Antonio in preparing the illustrations for this book and their efforts are most appreciated. To June Pilsitz for her eagle eye and Charles Bleiker for his poetic gift, both read every single line and edited masterfully different drafts of the manuscript. Thank you to the anonymous readers for their constructive feedback and a very special thanks to Christine Retz. And finally, I am most thankful to my husband Chuck and my son Carlos who are my emotional compass and refuge always.

Archives Consulted

- Archivo General de la Administración, Alcalá de Henares
- Biblioteca Nacional de España
- Hemeroteca Municipal de Madrid
- Archivo Histórico Provincial de Granada
- Archivo Histórico de la Universidad de Granada
- Hemeroteca de Filosofía y Letras, Universidad de Granada
- Hemeroteca Municipal de Granada, Casa de los Tiros
- Filmoteca Nacional
- Vatican Archives on line

Research Awards

This research has received funding from:

- Program of Cultural Cooperation between US universities and Spanish Ministry of Culture at The University of Minnesota in 2000;
- Provost Summer Research Award at Florida International University (FIU) in 2004
- Dean's of Arts and Sciences at FIU in 2005.

The Seduction of Modern Spain

Introduction: Gendered Metaphors

> Against the white sand, the contours of my father's body were well defined, emphasized its existence, an independent, solid existence in a world where everything was liquid, where the blue of the sea melted into the blue of the sky with nothing between. This independent existence was to become the outer world, the world of my father, of land, country, religion, language, moral codes. It was to become the world around me. A world made of male bodies in which my female body lived.
>
> —Nawal El Saadawi, *A Daughter of Isis*

OUR OWN BODIES PROVIDE THE BASIS FOR AN EXTENSIVE ARRAY OF ontological metaphors.[1] These metaphors we live by help us recognize phenomena in our world in terms that we can understand on the basis of our own motivations, actions, and characteristics. Viewing something abstract in human terms has an explanatory power that makes sense to most people.[2]

This book is about the symbolic relationship between the Spanish body politic during the dictatorship of Francisco Franco (1939–75) and the allegorical female body of the nation. It is also about the metaphorical use of gender imagery in political discourse in the transition from the early period of autarky in the 1940s to the "consumerism" and "aperturismo" (literally meaning opening) that ensued in the late 1950s and 1960s. For purposes of this study, the ontological metaphor is that of the gendered nation. The concept of "nation" turns into the physical figure of a "woman" with all the attendant qualities—nurturing, vulnerability, fertility.

The main focus in my interpretation of gender politics during the later phase of Franco's dictatorship is the centrality of corporeal gendered metaphors in the regime's rhetorical framework, rooted in the ideology of "organic democracy." Within this organic, biological metaphor of the nation, women's bodies played a central role in the political imagination, and the control of those bodies was inherently essential to the "bio-power" the regime tried to sustain toward its end. In this way, the metaphorical and the actual interacted in ways that were not predicted by the ruling regime.

In this book, I attempt to show how sexuality and gender play a major role in defining the political and social structures that controlled Spanish life after the Civil War. Between 1939, the year identified as "Año de la Victoria" (year of victory) and 1975, the year Franco died, gender relations were defined according to the National Catholic values inspired in the Golden Age and Counter-Reformation.

Franco's Spain in the 1950s is a particularly interesting case study because it combines church doctrine of the sixteenth and seventeenth centuries and pseudoscientific treatises from the nineteenth century to indoctrinate a generation of Spaniards. The ongoing tension in the book, then, is between the regime's attempt to control and discipline women's bodies in the service of its National Catholic ideals, and the economic and social changes that threatened and weakened that control. In the narrative, I examine, utilizing the body as the ontological metaphor, the technologies of control Francoism deployed in the transition from autarky to consumerism. This period of transition from autarky to consumerism is a good example of what Homi Bhabha calls an "in between moment," when the regime tried to stabilize gender relations to maintain its Catholic foundations in the context of onrushing economic transformation.[3] In Spain, the Franco's regime attempted to recast the image of the liberated woman put forth by the Second Republic, as a pious, motherly, and utterly devoted "True Catholic Woman." But cloaking her in the costumes and customs of old only made her reemergence that more striking. The consumerist economy that Spain gradually adopted in the 1950s and 1960s opened the way to this new, modern, Western woman; a sexualized consumer flaunting herself in front of the official doctrine of "True Catholic Womanhood."[4] This woman of the magazine ads and movie screens seduced a new generation of Spaniards into thinking that life held more for them than the austerity of their recent past, the severity of their strict Catholic heritage, and the social straitjacket of Francoist doctrine.

The transition to this new model of womanhood gives us the opportunity to problematize the concept of modernity. As the image of the pious, obedient Catholic woman gave way to the rebellious, carefree, and sexually adventurous consumer, the official, masculine image of the state became muted. What started as a ripple in the social fabric of Spain under Franco—women in short dresses—ended in a tidal wave of eroticism following his death.

Popular media has been an underrated force in the shaping of modern nations. We think of propaganda as war posters and political cartoons, not soap ads and radio plays. But the new forms of media (i.e., magazines, cinema, television) that gave us these subversive diversions, I argue, played as much of a role in shaping the political landscape of countries like Spain as the heavy-handed efforts of state ministries.[5] We can see in real time how the images of women's bodies change during this epoch. This physical transformation is not solely a Spanish phenomenon but one smuggled into the country from the United States and the emerging Western European democracies under the guise of economic development. With increased trade pacts and security treaties with the democratic West, and the development of a tourist industry supported largely by foreigners, Franco's government was compelled to loosen its hold on the moral propaganda used to legitimize itself in the early days of the regime.

Why the Body?

Some conceptualization of embodiment is crucial to giving structure to a feminist historical analysis of Francoism. Leslie Adelson reminds us that a "[h]istory without bodies is unimaginable."[6] A historical concept of the body will help us map historical continuities and ruptures.[7] Women's bodies are at the same time "real" physical organisms and the loci of historically specific cultural inscriptions of femininity.

National Catholic ideology fostered what I have called *True Catholic Womanhood*[8] based on the cultural construction of Castilian Catholic identity in the 1490s and 1500s. The corporeal nature of women dominated conduct manuals like Juan Luis Vives's *The Instruction of the Christian Woman* (1523) or Fray Luis de León's *La perfecta casada* (1583). Their virtue was rooted in their ability to preserve their modesty.[9] In the New Spain, dawning after 1939, the Golden Age virtues—piety, purity, and domesticity—were revived by the state and administered by the Women's Section of Falange.[10]

Young women must prepare themselves to become *angels of the home,* winning the respect of humankind by preserving their physical and spiritual virginity. "[I]n a woman, no one requires eloquence or talent or wisdom or professional skills or admiration of the republic or justice or generosity; no one asks anything of her but chastity."[11]

Vives's work is significant beyond the Spanish cultural realm. Translated into most European languages, its Christian principles became the cultural capital for Western European female respectability in the early modern and modern era.[12]

The cultural feminine emerges in the somatic metaphors of the regime's official discourse. The organic language of the Francoist body politic lends itself to analysis from a gender perspective to understand the relationship between the cultural feminine and the body politic. Furthermore, the analysis of Francoist somatic metaphors unveils its gendered nature and helps us understand women's place within the body politic. When nation, gender, and sexuality intersect, the body becomes an important expression of the national and political identity.

Catholic principles are at the center of the somatization of the Francoist political language largely because Catholicism constituted the axis around which Franco legitimized his hold on power during the Cold War. The regime looked back with nostalgia to 1492 as the point in history when the Spanish ethos was forged by the Catholic Monarchs' conclusion of the *Reconquista.* The Spanish Civil War represented in Francoist recollection the twentieth-century crusade against the anti-Spain. Franco's image—forged during the Civil War and publicized after 1939—was that of the iron surgeon, cutting out the cancer of chaos and anarchy created by the "inorganic democracy" of the lay and anti-Spanish Republic. The official propaganda proclaimed the caudillo's leading role in bringing the country back to its time-honored natural form of government: the traditional Catholic monarchy. After the Allies' victory in World War II, Franco launched a new political formula called *organic democracy* that legitimized him in power in the context of the Cold War. National Catholicism became the ideological substratum of organic democracy that allowed Francoist longevity until 1975.

The pursuit of organic democracy began immediately. The regime's institutionalization took shape during the Civil War. Implicit was the notion of a mystic body politic resulting from a symbolic union between the national body and the state with the sanction of Spanish Catholic traditions. The notion of organic democracy was not new. It goes back to the Golden Age political discourse that the regime revived to legitimize itself in power. Spanish organicist tradition, rooted in the works of baroque Counter-Reformation scholars, fits perfectly within the authoritarian Francoist model—having as its main objective a divinely sanctioned order in which each individual plays a predetermined and immutable role. As in the baroque period, National Catholicism made Franco head of the state (a role assigned to the king in the early modern period) and strong supporter of the Catholic Church as in the Counter-Reformation era. In turn, the Catholic Church lent legitimacy to the regime, and corporeal wholeness, by acting as its heart and soul.

As early as the fifteenth century and even more so during the Golden Age and Council of Trent, Spanish intellectuals established a strong correlation between carnal body and body politic. During the sixteenth and seventeenth centuries the body became the object of a continuous "metaphorization" around political, social, and literary aspects.[13] This is typical of the Golden Age's highly analogical system of thought. The universe or macrocosm, the human body or microcosm, and the Republic's body all revolve in concentric orbits, connected to each other by the pull of their gravities. The human body becomes the measure of everything.[14] The "organicist" theory is mostly conservative because it tends to institute a political and social order of divine origin in which each individual has its immutable place and performs its duty. This orientation is central to the rise of the centralized modern state, and it is based on the notion of divine right—an idea borrowed from the Counter-Reformation. The king becomes the sustenance of the Catholic Church, which is the "head, heart and soul of the Republic." Jurists and political theorists of the sixteenth and seventeenth centuries constantly used the corporeal metaphor of the "sick Republic" and in this sense it is not surprising that medical scholars like Jerónimo Merola or Cristóbal Pérez de Herrera wrote medical treatises about how to heal the Republic's sick body.[15] While the unity of the Republic depends on the head of the state (the monarch), the unity of the Church derives from the Pauline concept of mystic body in which Christ is the head of the Church and the baptized followers the body. The mystic body became particularly significant during this time in Spain. This was the time of the Council of Trent, when Spain under Philip II closed herself off and relied more and more on the concept of *limpieza de sangre* as the organic way to belong to the Republic and establish a clear distinction between old and new Christians.

It is my contention that in the late Francoist period the regime showed a neo-baroque quality and National Catholicism lent ideological cohesion to the dictatorship in its last two decades. I utilize here the concept of neo-baroque. This aspires to be a documented narrative on the ways in which the baroque and Francoism were ideologically, politically, and religiously close. I study the thesis of Maravall on the culture of the baroque, specifically an article he published in 1956 to describe the baroque mystic body politic that I apply to study the regime's state apparatus. Moreover, this is my "branding" of the Francoist regime as a neo-baroque apparatus. I believe that my use of gender analysis allows an understanding of the politics and dynamics of power beyond traditional periodizations (bringing into the conversation early modern and modern scholars). Gender as a category of analysis also illustrates how the regime drew on traditional Counter-Reformation values to perpetuate gendered politics.

The neo-baroque is understood here as the clearest expression of the postmodernism fully developed in the transition to democracy and already in the making in the 1950s and 1960s. The study of sexual relations and the metaphorical utilization of the female body in political discourse helps us measure not only the level of fragmentation that the regime experienced with the advent of consumerism but also facilitates a better understanding of gender relations in the political realignment in the democratic transition.

This book is divided into six chapters. In chapter 1, *The Anatomy of Francoist Power,* I examine the somatic metaphors utilized by politicians and theorists by applying Michel Foucault's concept of bio-power, which the regime exercised through the discursive constitution of the body in the school system, the army, and the medical profession. National Catholicism, the ideological substratum of the Francoist dictatorship, proclaimed its commitment to restore the order destroyed by the Second Republic characterized in official propaganda as an "inorganic democracy." After the Allies' victory in World War II, Franco launched a new political formula called organic democracy that legitimized him in power in the context of the Cold War until 1975. The religious discourse elaborated by the official propaganda resorted to the Counter-Reformation "mystic body politic." The parallelism between the baroque and the Francoist regime are many—hence I characterize the Francoist National Catholic state as neo-baroque, particularly when studied from a gender perspective. Chapter 2, *(De)limiting Women's True Nature,* focuses on the definition of femininity afforded by Spanish intellectuals and moralists at the turn of the twentieth century, its redefinition with the conflict of the Spanish Civil War, and the advent of Francoist National Catholic values.

In chapter 3, *Fallen Women: Public Morality in Transition,* and chapter 4, *Perfect Wives and Mothers,* I examine the Francoist legislation regulating sexuality and public morality. Men's and women's bodies became indispensable members ("limbs") of the Francoist mystic body politic; men were to be soldiers and producers, and women political and biological reproductive mothers. In order to unveil the importance of the wife's body as an essential means to construct Spanish women's national identity, I first examine in this chapter the religious discourse and its legal translation, and second, popular conduct manuals published under the regime. Marriage, in this context, was more a politically charged venture than a social event. In chapter 3 my argument is a legal, economic, and cultural one. From a legal perspective Spain under Franco legalized prostitution as a buffer against Spanish men and their virgin brides; an entire industry grew up with many willing (exploited) workers during a time of scarcity and hunger. The rest of Europe and the United States regarded as backward (and immoral) the institution of legalized prostitution. Spain is ambivalent about legalized prostitution but makes the Faustian compromise because it believes that the ends—pure women and satisfied men—justify the means. The Patronato de Protección de la Mujer (Institute for the Protection of Women) was in charge of rehabilitating fallen women in their convent/prison centers.[16] With the advent of consumerism and the international rehabilitation of Franco's regime, Spain wanted to join the rest of the civilized world and therefore outlawed prostitution in 1956. From an economic perspective, prostitution also provided jobs for poor women and solace for men who were struggling in postwar Spain; prostitution was also a commodity to sell to the growing number of outsiders (e.g., US sailors) visiting Spain from Europe and the United States, at a time when Spain had very little else to sell. Women's bodies became a commodity to be bought and sold at market prices. They could even be exported to the brothels of North Africa. The highly sexualized flamenco dancer, Mérimée's *Carmen,* dark mysterious eyes, hot temper, intense physicality, became the archetype and the packaging for this commodity for the flourishing tourist industry under the slogan "España es diferente" (Spain is Different).

Chapter 4 focuses on the regulation of the good women's bodies; bodies turned also into commodities, made more valuable by the large number of fallen women in their midst. Their scarcity during the postwar years brings them a higher price in terms of marriage and prestige in the new social hierarchy. This polarization of femininity in the Spanish imagination has its roots in the long history of Spain. The archetypal fallen women are a mix of the exotic invaders, the other "queer Spain" (Greeks and Romans, Carthaginians, Arabs and Jews, and of course Gypsies or Roma) that make up Spain's pagan past. The archetype "Catholic" women represent the purity and enlightenment of the Christian reconquest of the Iberian Peninsula and the expulsion of the darker forces that had inhabited Spain for most of its history. True Catholic womanhood in the official discourse expected good women to remain pure and to remind the world why Christianity has prevailed over the immorality and wantonness of past, non-Christian civilizations. The Franco Regime was exploiting this myth of two women in order to keep control over a fractious, diverse population.

By creating and taking advantage of this popularized dichotomy, the regime is admitting that Spain is not a pure, Christian country, but one of a complex heritage and ethnicity. While the brothel doors were shutting officially in 1956, highly sexualized images from movies and magazines were flying in the window, undermining the "good" women that the Franco regime spent so much effort to control. Franco was fighting a losing battle against the tide of modernization, and the conception of women that the official propaganda so calculatingly tried to manipulate for his own political ends is coming back to haunt him.

Chapter 5, *Modern Women's Docile Bodies,* analyses the nationalization of men's and women's bodies by the Francoist regime through the Women's Section of Falange. Until 1977 Spanish Falangist women had an exclusive official mandate to mold women's bodies. This longevity, over its Nazi sisters, offers us the opportunity to examine the effect of modernization and consumerism on the Francoist regime's discourse on domesticity and its struggle to maintain it in the late Francoist period. I apply a Foucauldian reading to the Law of Physical Education issued in December 1961, as well as the legislation issued by the Ministry of Labor from a gender perspective. The remaining chapters of *The Seduction of Modern Spain* focus on the counter-discourses produced as a result of the transition to the consumer economy after the economic and military agreements with the

United States with the 1953 Pact of Madrid. The study of the media (press, radio, and television) and movie industry of this period is particularly helpful in illustrating how ads and films shaped and contested the regime's vision of modernity and gender roles. In March of 1965 *National Geographic* published a special report on "The Changing Face of Spain." The writer Bart McDowell, accompanied by his wife and the magazine's photographer Albert Moldvay, introduce the American audience to the most stereotypical image of Spain—one in tune with the regime's new tourist slogan "Spain is Different" coined by the Ministry of Press and Propaganda led by Manuel Fraga Iribarne.

Chapter 6, *Strangers in the Dark,* focuses on the cinematographic occasion as an embodied experience. I am particularly interested in the transitional period from autarky to consumerism inaugurated in the 1950s and further developed in the 1960s. This period in the film industry is known as the *New Spanish Cinema* under the administration of José María García Escudero. The *New Spanish Cinema* may be considered the anteroom to the cultural transition to democracy after Franco's death.

The Cold War facilitated rapprochement of the United States with the Pact of Madrid in 1953. In the 1960s consumerism and international anticommunist politics inaugurated in Spain a timid cultural aperturismo (opening), which in turn led to a redefinition of the regime's purpose and the safeguard of its foundations. Cinema represented the best medium to reach international approval. Far from doing away with censorship, the regime issued more precise regulations in 1963, ending the existing random policy in place until that moment. The new regulations provided room for the production of two versions of every film made in Spain: one censored for national consumption, the other uncut for international markets. It was through censors' mutilation of women's cinematic bodies that the regime made the distinction between those two versions of every film. Censors' cuts responded not only to their mandate to preserve Spanish women's virginal innocence but also to protect the National Catholic integrity of the nation's political and Christian body as a whole. These tasks became most important in the transition to the consumer economy in the 1950s and 1960s when the regime underwent a process of aperturismo in cultural circles that permeated social gender relations and eventually led to the regime's demise. Cultural censorship became the regime's crusade in peacetime and women's bodies its conduit. In this chapter, I include a personal interview with screen star Aurora Bautista and compare her work with that of Sara Montiel, the Spanish Marilyn Monroe.

I examine the film *La Tía Tula* directed by Miguel Picazo in 1964 under the auspices of the New Spanish Cinema. I view this film as an excellent example of the neo-baroque/postmodern Almodóvar's exploration of the economy of desire, and the antecedent of the phenomenon known as "destape" in the post-Franco transition to democracy. The reading of women's cinematic bodies in *Tardofranquismo* might shed some light on the way gender relations were redefined in the transition to democracy. *La Tía Tula* offers us the opportunity to look at the economy of desire in the later stage of Francoism.

Marsha Kinder points out how the New Spanish Cinema of the 1960s highlights the contrast between "the neo-realist Italian cinema and Hollywood escape to excessive pleasures." Spanish filmmakers recaptured the artistic license that played with the tension between crude reality and frivolous overindulgence. This artistic ability had been present in the works of Golden Age writers like Cervantes, Lope de Vega, Calderón de la Barca, and Quevedo. This "baroque-like" contrast between realistic depiction and false idealization became particularly vivid in Francoist Spain in the transition from autarky to consumerism. Sara Montiel as María Luján in *El último cuplé* and Aurora Bautista's Tula embodied in the screen this neo-baroque quality that will be carried on in extreme fashion in the post-Franco Spanish cinema. I use here the definition of neo-baroque proposed by Alejandro Valeri: "Neo-baroque is associated with post-modernity due to its ability to establish a continuity with the past by appropriating the baroque aesthetics."[17] Neo-baroque receives the category of aesthetic movement that could even replace the postmodern concept in the Spanish-speaking context. We assist in the loss of integrity and unity to give way to instability and multidimensionality in the transitional period of the 1950s and 1960s undergone by Francoism. The constant malleability of the regime in the last two decades of existence will prepare the terrain for the transitional period to democracy in the immediate post-Francoist era. The transition to democracy was a period characterized by mass culture under a strict, though eventually futile, official control.[18] From the excessiveness of postwar historical melodramas that exemplified the most traditional kitsch, the cinema of the 1960s inaugurates the kitsch of the consumer society. While the erotic site in autarkic cinema resided not on the skin but on the garments worn by female stars from the 1940s to the 1960s, there was no more natural way to excite eroticism and seduction than to undress the female body after the dictator was gone.

In the conclusion, I demonstrate how the somatic metaphors used by Franco's official propaganda shed light on the ideological nature of the regime. I conclude that the baroque and Francoism were ideologically, politically, and religiously close, and hence I interpret the Francoist regime ideologically and culturally as neo-baroque, particularly when examined from a gender perspective.

National Catholicism turned into the means to revive a Counter-Reformation of sorts: the redemption of those who lost the war presented in official propaganda as a crusade against those whom the regime branded as anti-Spanish. The religious overtones of National Catholicism helped the regime to reenter the international scene through the backdoor as the *other* within Europe. Spain was different in the official slogan to attract tourists. The official propaganda showed how Spain had been the "sentinel of the West" since the Middle Ages; then against Islam and in the late 1950s against Soviet Communism.

Gender relations were bound up with this discourse that made somatic metaphors and women's bodies in particular the crux of the equation. The incognita was whether Spain was worthy of entering modernity in the same way as the rest of Western Europe. In conclusion, this book attempts to explore the concept of modernity. Spain's modernization happened, like in the rest of Europe, but the way this modernization came about was different. Furthermore, it is important to elaborate the concept of modernization as an improvement in social and gender relations. As a matter of fact what I show in the epilogue is how modernization did not necessarily mean liberation for women, who, in a Faustian bargain changed one set of limitations under the conformity of dictatorship for the conformity of the consumer culture.

1
The Anatomy of Francoist Power

> The Army is the nation's backbone. It unites, sustains, and supports the whole. The vital and sacred values of the Fatherland run through its marrow. It is neither the leading thinking head nor any of the other limbs that organically constitute [the country], but the backbone that holds them together. If broken the [nation's] body would turn into a wreck.[1]
>
> —Francisco Franco (1951)

> [T]he sea, having turned into a lake, links you to the other shore, as the fetus is tied to the mother's blood-engorged womb, the umbilical cord between them coiling like a long sinuous strip of *serpentine.*[2]
>
> Juan Goytisolo, *Count Julian* (1976)

FRANCOIST NATIONAL CATHOLIC DISCOURSE REGARDED THE LAY Second Republic as the manifestation of "inorganic democracy," namely heresy and materialism. By contrast, the new pseudofascist state, born in the aftermath of the Spanish Civil War and led by the army with Franco as commander-in-chief, was presented as a Catholic "organic democracy." Organic democracy meant the reassertion of Catholic values as the driving force of the new state in the context of the Cold War. These values, his propagandists proposed, were able to grow naturally once the cancer of the Second Republic had been cut out by the Iron Surgeon—another image ascribed to Franco.

Organic democracy could trace its genealogical and ideological roots back to the Golden Age concept of the body politic illustrated in Jerónimo Merola's *República original sacada del cuerpo humano* (1587). By reaching back to the boneyard of Spain's by now distant glorious past to construct his political ideology, Franco tried to create a new mystic body politic. This reincarnation of Golden Age Spanish doctrine was further legitimized by

Figure 1. Detail of "Alegoria de Franco y la Cruzada," mural painting in the Archivo Histórico Militar in Madrid. Franco is portrayed as a medieval knight wearing shining armor and holding a sword in which reflects the phallic symbol of his anthropocentric regime. Courtesy of Archivo Oronoz.

the Church in such writings as Pius XII's encyclical *Mystici Corporis Christi* (1943), the *regenerationist* discourses developed in Spain after 1898, and the medicalization of political discourse in the context of eugenics.

Intellectuals like Joaquin Costa (1846–1911) and Angel Ganivet (1865–98), of the so-called Generation of 98, had previously looked for solutions to Spain's long-held national identity crisis. Philosopher José Ortega y Gasset (1883–1955) inherited the pessimistic political and philosophical outlook of the Generation of 98 believing that Spain was living an extreme case of what he called "historical invertebration" in the early 1920s. In his work *Invertebrate Spain* (1921), he wrote passionately about the Spanish ethos, the country's historical decadence, and political crisis. Suggestions and prescriptions to heal the motherland's ailing body came from moralists, politicians, and intellectuals.[3] The medical doctor's professional appraisal of the political events was a modern addition to those voices. One of these voices was Antonio Vallejo Nágera (1889–1960). Dr. Vallejo Nágera was a leading psychiatrist during the Second Republic, who, well protected under the rank of lieutenant in the army, had no problem expressing publicly his antidemocratic political beliefs. In the tradition of Costa, Ganivet, or Ortega y Gasset, Nágera believed Spain's political tribulations were the result of the degenerative decline of the once "virile Hispanic race."[4] For him philosophers and politicians' "concoctions had barely stung the pachyderm-like skin of the racial body."[5]

The common denominator in these elements that constitute organic democracy is Catholicism. The exploitation of religious doctrine and history that National Catholicism provided under Francoism became crucial for the longevity of a regime that lasted beyond most people's expectations, and in the shadow of the postwar modernization of Western Europe. Franco, to silence his internal critics, could point to tradition and religion to make the case that Spain was special, and had its own destiny to follow, separate from that of the rest of Western Europe.

At the same time Franco was arguing internally for a Spanish particularism, he was also emphasizing western democracies shared a common Cold War enemy: Communism. This postwar obsession of the West offered Spain an opportunity to rehabilitate itself, and to recast its image in a more heroic and holy light. In looking for the substance and the style to compel Spain into a new golden age of Catholicism, Franco looked backward to the more glorious past. No other time was more glorious for Spain than the Counter-Reformation, known as the Golden Age in intellectual circles. The Counter-Reformation, ushered in during the age of the baroque (the great populist reaffirmation of Catholic doctrine), offered a template for the Francoist political reinvention. Franco was drawn to the accessibility, mysticism, and visceral power of baroque thought and style. It fit well with his own image as a holy warrior and his modern construction of a gendered body politic emerging out of an organic democracy. By clothing itself in the ornate regalia of the Counter-Reformation, the Francoist regime ushered in a neobaroque revival.

Francoism's Neo-baroque Design

The institutional quest for Spain's organic Christian democracy started with the establishment of the Cortes in 1942, a body that provided, in Stanley Payne's words "a covering of legitimization and support to the regime."[6] Following close behind was the Law of Succession of 1947 that proclaimed Spain a kingdom and established the Council of the Realm under Franco's life Regency. These legal texts were to complete previous legislation. First, the 1938 *Labor Charter (Fuero del Trabajo)* modeled after the 1927 Italian fascist *Carta di Lavoro* and the doctrine of Pius XI's encyclical *Quadragesimo Anno* (1931).

In 1945 the *Spaniards' Charter (Fuero de los Españoles)* was introduced as a bill of rights of sorts for the Spanish citizens. A Referendum Law, also in 1945, complemented the Spaniards' Charter—this was later corroborated with the Law of the Fundamental Principles of the National Movement issued in 1958 and published a year later as Fundamental Laws of the State in the Official Bulletin of the State. The Organic Law of the State of 1967 completed the institutionalization.

The caudillo's anti-Communism in international forums was well received as he presented himself as the *Sentinel of the West* against the Soviet Union. The regime's propaganda vindicated the Civil War as its national crusade against Communism. Subsequently, the world conveniently forgot Hitler and Mussolini's support for the Francoist cause during the Spanish Civil War. National Catholicism facilitated the regime's international rehabilitation with its new organic democracy formula. A political discourse imbued with western Christendom righteousness was built into the new mystic body politic of Francoism. The regime's religious trappings validated Franco's power inside and outside of Spain in 1953 with the signing of two major diplomatic agreements: First, the *Pact of Madrid* that signaled the beginning of relations between the United States and Spain consisting of economic aid and the establishment of American military bases on Spanish soil and second, the Concordat with the Vatican that revealed to the world Spain as the spearhead of Catholicism in the West. With the Concordat of 1953 the Catholic Church consolidated its power in the areas of Spanish education and public morality.

Religious discourse contributed to the feeling of a culture of excessive emotion and religious symbolism. Religious symbolism was even more oppressive in the midst of a culture of poverty. The hunger, disease, and fear rampant in the 1940s lingered into the 1950s. American powdered milk was much needed in a country dominated by *estraperlo* (black market goods) and where ration books were withdrawn from public circulation only in 1952.

Franco needed to reestablish some political balance to satisfy the international scrutiny. In the second half of the 1950s, he tried to play both sides, appeasing his base while also liberalizing his policies for the outside world. He commissioned the General Secretary of the Movement, José Luis Arrese, to revise the Party Statutes and elaborate three legislative projects: a Law of the Fundamental Principles of the State, an Organic Law of the Movement, and an Organizational Law of the Government. Such action was a vote of confidence for the Falange to elaborate what came to be considered the "Constitution" of the Regime. He also reshaped the cabinet (in 1957), establishing the presence of Opus Dei in the government and the application of liberal economic policies, along with the monarchy, as the formula for succession. The cabinet launched two important measures to accommodate the regime to the unavoidable political and economic modernization of the times: first, the proclamation of the Law of the Fundamental Principles of the State in 1958, and second, the Stabilization Plan of 1959. Both measures defined the political and economic boundaries that would favor the arrival of consumerism.

The three drafts of the Law of the Fundamental Principles of the State elaborated by Arrese's commission made no reference to the monarchy, as prescribed by the Law of Succession of 1947. On the contrary, they emphasized the movement's political significance and strengthened the power of the National Council and the General Secretary of FET y de las JONS. Both leadership and succession to the regime remained vague. Predictably, criticisms came from all fronts: army, Church, and Opus Dei. The non-Falangist members of the cabinet regarded Arrese's proposal as a Falangist coup de main and rejected it entirely.[7] Monarchists objected particularly to the exclusion of any mention of the crown, and the Church hierarchy declared the proposals "in disagreement with pontifical doctrine" and complained that they had no roots in "Spanish tradition, but in totalitarian regimes of certain other countries after the First World War."[8] At this point, Franco shelved the Falangist proposal and accepted those presented by cabinet member Laureano López Rodó and also endorsed by Carrero Blanco (Franco's right hand). López Rodó wrote the final document that was approved in the Cortes on May 19, 1958. The new version of the Principles of the Movement was conceived as the "Constitution" of the regime, although the spirit of the 1936 uprising remained. The old twenty-six falangist principles of the National Movement were replaced by twelve, fully sanitized of any overtly fascist language. These twelve points affirmed patriotism, unity, peace, Catholicism, the family as pillar of society, and representation through the syndicates and the municipalities. Principle two defined Spain as one nation, whose unique faith was Catholicism: "It is the core honor of the Spanish Nation to obey God's laws, in accordance with the Roman Catholic Church doctrine, the only true one; such faith is *inseparable from the national conscience, faith which inspires our legislation* (my emphasis).[9] In National Catholic Spain, the family remained the pillar of social relations, along with the syndicate and municipal authorities. This corporativist social order sustained the so-called "traditional social and representative Catholic monarchy."[10] Political participation was allowed only through the family, the syndicate, and the municipality, and "any other political organizations outside of this representative system will be considered illegal."[11] The regime enacted an "organic democracy" based on what scholar Juan Linz calls a *limited pluralism.*[12] Limited not only politically but also econimcally.

The political facelift intended to attract international recognition of the regime was desperately needed in the midst of the misery lingering from the 1940s known as the Hunger Years. The economic penury at the turn of the 1950s is described in jarring detail in Richard Wright's travelogue *Pagan Spain.* Wright chronicles his travels in the country on two separate occasions, 1954 and 1955. His eyewitness narrative is much more than the typical travel diary of an exotic place; it is an incisive look at an oppressed population from a writer who had known such oppression his entire life. Food rationing ended officially in 1952 and two years later Wright still saw children begging in the streets and women selling their bodies to feed their children. Prostitution, as we will see in chapter 3, was rampant in Spain during the 1940s and 1950s. The regime maintained a policy of toleration toward prostitution in the 1940s and appointed the Patronato de Protección de la Mujer (Board for the Protection of Women) in 1942 to regulate public morality. Male sexual initiation required the existence of brothels. Prostitutes had to register with the government and get periodical health exams to continue working. The double moral standard was rooted in the baroque concept of unavoidable sin. The prostitute (bad, corrupted, and dispensable) leached out men's malignant, carnal lust so that good women (pure and marriageable) were safe to walk the streets. Writer Carmen Martín Gaite's work *Usos amorosos en la postguerra* reveals how in the code of courtship a woman who wanted to get married should avoid being critical, avoid analyzing things, and not fail to smile on a regular basis.[13] According to conduct manuals men disliked serious or sad women who were considered unfeminine. There also existed a double standard with respect to sex between men and women. Men could not come to the marriage bed clumsy and inexperienced, whereas for women virginity was a must. The moral double standard was redefined as we will see in the following chapters with the urbanization of the country in the 1960s.

The Falangist Women's Section's discourse on womanhood represents the ultimate example of *cursilería*. Middle-class señoritas, as Martín Gaite explains, suffered from an acute case of "ñoñez"—a sort of dripping, whining, affected infantile behavior. Raised to become wives and devout mothers, their only objective in life was to be as nonthreatening as possible to male authority. Their physical appearance had to be impeccable even if this meant living above their means. *Cursilería* for young women became the ticket to success and the "nuevos ricos" class that emerged from *estraperlo* lavished in the "camp" social etiquette of the time.

To this end the new curriculum to develop national spirit in female students included more lessons and activities related to domestic chores and social etiquette. The lessons required more hours than those for male students. According to the new curriculum prescribed by Law of Secondary Education of 1953, the study of domestic matters was essential to women's proper training as part of their patriotic duty to the fatherland. Girls' instruction included a synthesis of the political indoctrination, physical education, and home economics (enseñanzas del hogar). The program for the first three grades cultivated the female national spirit by training girls in family and social norms, physical education, sewing, and music. The fourth, fifth, and sixth grades added to these subjects a program of cooking, home economics, and infant care.[14]

Like in the early modern period, circumspection, order, and hygiene composed the essence of the Catholic ideal woman.[15]

Eventually the regime's stiffness stirred resentment and embarrassment, even among the children of those who fought in the war for Franco. Based on an obsolete baroque code of behavior and beliefs, Franco's personal rule hid behind the national and religious façade of National Catholicism. Francoism, with its grandiose edicts based on a long gone imperial past, quickly became a caricature of itself. The result was a neo-baroque kitsch regime, so stale and obsolete that not only the opposition but the regime's own offspring began distancing themselves from its image.[16] The Spanish term *cursi* is sometimes used to replace the term kitsch. However, Maravall explains that kitsch always is the collective human category while cursi refers to the individual. Noël Valis's recent study on *The Culture of Cursilería* also indicates the distinction between the two terms. "*Kitsch* seems to be a post-modern form of *cursilería*" she says, "it is not coincidental or surprising that "lo cursi" should re-emerge as kitsch or even camp in the post-Franco era, for the *movida* years in the 1980s more often than not vamped as pastiche or parody the culture of Francoism itself (or its remains) as quintessentially *cursi.*[17]

The official Catholic discourse of the regime did not appeal to the young generations raised within the values of the Second Vatican Council. Not only the old reds but also the regime's offspring were to shake its foundations in the mid 1950s until the regime's demise. As Gregorio Cámara Villar puts it: "[T]hat ridiculous, antiquated fascism which was imposed in our childhood with memorization, textbooks, and a good measure of slaps on the hands while our thin diet was supplemented with powdered milk and American cheese, has a lot to do with the mentality and attitudes that today constitute the physical micro- and macromosaic of the diverse powers and forms of Spanish life."[18]

This period of transition became a period of turmoil loaded with potential for change. University students joined workers in the anti-Francoist movement orchestrated by the clandestine Spanish Communist Party in small cells all over the country. Several labor strikes took place in the major urban centers: Madrid, Barcelona, as well as the Basque region. The unrest in 1956 led to the resignation of Joaquín Ruiz Giménez, minister of education, who had initiated a timid liberalization of the academic world. The regime purged several professors. In 1960 the secretary general of the International Commission of Jurists visited Spain to monitor their trials. A year later Italian professor Silverio Coppa of the Rome Bar acted as an observer of the Commission at the trial in Madrid of Professor Enrique Tierno Galván of the University of Salamanca and eight other academics.[19] In 1962 Leslie Munro, secretary general of the Commission, wrote the introduction of the report issued by the international observers: "The Commission is animated by the sincere wish that the brave and spirited people of Spain with their splendid history and culture, should move towards freedom and prosperity in the European Community."[20] The body politic was in crisis. The regime's version of Catholicism that cloaked and legitimized the caudillo's power was based on an obsolete yet functional authoritarian rule based on organic democracy. It was precisely the Catholic trappings of the regime that made its brand of democracy "organic," meaning natural.

George Mosse reminds us how Nazis attempted to establish a "new religion with elements of mysticism and liturgical rites."[21] In the Spanish case Catholicism provided the regime with a rich mystical patrimony. The insistence of the regime's propaganda in looking back to the Golden Age manifested itself in a spectacle of power charged with sham Catholic *rites.* For Richard Wright the Spanish nation was a most complex and unsettling "sacred state."

> In Spain there was no lay, no secular life. Spain was a holy nation, a sacred state— . . . the boundaries of Spanish religiosity went *beyond* the Church. . . .
>
> For a long time my own Westernness proved a veritable stumbling block to my seeing the truth that stared me in the face. The cold fact was: *Spain was not yet even Christian!* It had never been converted, not to Protestantism, not even to *Catholicism* itself![22]

National Catholicism intended to sustain and strengthen Spain's eternal mystic body politic. The members must assume their place and duty in the social and political order inaugurated by the new massive culture of consumption. In this mystic corpus, gender remained crucial to perpetuate the power dynamics. Duties were clearly defined along gender and class lines and sanctified by the Church. Men's and women's bodies were indispensable members ("limbs") of the Francoist mystic body politic; men as soldiers and producers, and women as political and biological reproductive mothers. In Brenan's words: "religion in Spain, except in the brief period of the Carmelite mystics, has been an affair of ritual and observance, heavy with taboos and seeking neither intellectual nor imaginative expression."[23]

The neo-baroque nature of the regime is most evident when we examine the intellectual debate in the 1950s and 1960s. Looking back to the 1500s proved to be fruitful in analyzing the Francoist power structure and its repression of dissidence. Enrique Tierno Galván was one of the most important intellectuals of the late period of Francoism and a key political figure of the transition as mayor of the nation's capital, Madrid. Known as the "Old Professor," he declared at the end of his days that his intellectual work helped him in his political struggle. In the early 1950s he was professor of Political Law at the University of Murcia and in the academic year 1953–54 took a position at the University of Salamanca where he launched a new publication, *Boletín Informativo de la Cátedra de Derecho Político de la Universidad de Salamanca.* In the pages of the bulletin, Tierno and other progressive intellectuals engaged in discussions about Spain's imperial past, the Golden Age. The baroque would come to be in this period for Tierno the means to criticize the regime covertly. In *Notas sobre el Barroco* (*Notes about the Baroque*), published in Murcia in 1954, he proposes a parallel between these two historical junctures of Spain.

While far removed in time, the baroque and Francoism were ideologically, politically, and above all religiously close. The baroque became a pretext to show the official culture that the most important subject to study was that of the glorious imperial past, but underneath was the opportunity to engage in a veiled critique of the regime's foundations using a cryptic intellectual extrapolation.[24] Raul Morodo wrote in 1966: "During many years in our country in the same way that happens in those countries based on non-liberal ideologies, the political reality was approached 'cryptically.' Especially the political writer would look for the historical evasion or subterfuges and baroque formulas with an obscure language to criticize the existent status. Baroque mentality was spread out because baroque ambiguity was less compromising than direct criticism."[25] *Notas sobre el Barroco* focuses on the baroque's religiously charged world vision, on the idea that is the foundation and lends coherence and legitimacy to Francoism. The baroque consists in a constant quest for balance between nature and grace. Religious elements impregnated life in Spain during the sixteenth and seventeenth centuries, reflecting the nation's history as birthplace of the Counter-Reformation. Grace must prevail over instinctive nature. All sinners may find their way into the baroque community by repenting in order to gain the grace of redemption. In the same way the vanquished after the Spanish Civil War were to be reprogrammed to redeem themselves from their anti-Spanish conduct and to gain grace within the regime. In 1939 the state General Secretariat of Prisons issued a weekly publication called *Redención* (*Redemption*). Its main objective was "to shape the political consciousness of prisoners in accordance with the political and social goals of the New State." This was the only publication allowed in the penitentiary system. It was a means of propaganda with a printing of 24,000 copies. The publication eventually became the only line of communication between the prisoners and the utterly bureaucratic judicial system. Prisoners would send letters to the editor requesting information on the status of their cases.

In 1956, Spanish scholar José Antonio Maravall recaptured the metaphor of the body politic and added the notion of mysticism and messianic nature of the nation's leader. That year the regime had confronted the most serious university crisis. Maravall was a respected scholar, a literary critic, and specialist of early modern literature and history. In an article entitled "La idea de cuerpo místico en España antes de Erasmo" ("The idea of the mystic body in Spain before Erasmus"), Maravall highlighted how religion had infused Spanish politics since the Middle Ages culminating in the 1492 Reconquest of Spain by Isabella and Ferdinand under the banner of Catholicism. The body politic was defined in this piece as the marker of unity versus multiplicity and as the sign of order born from that unity. "According to thirteenth-century jurist San Raimundo Peñafort" says Maravall, "*ius universitatis consistit in uno.*" In his examination of the idea of mystic body as applied to the political body, Maravall provided as evidence several medieval Spanish texts published under the reign of Alfonso X including the *Partidas* and *Flores de Filosofía.*[26] The centralization of power in the hands of a single leader who rules over all the nation's subjects is conceived as everyone (leader and subjects) being members of a single political "corpus." It also establishes a tangible and permanent status to all individuals who are regulated and normalized, turning power into a measurable endeavor. The position of each subject in medieval society was immutable; they were kept under surveillance from above, and below.

Maravall's concept of the political, medieval mystic body inherent to Spanish political order was artfully refurbished in corporatist Francoist Spain. The emotional element congruent with totalitarian politics turns the political experience into a religious one. In 1975 Maravall published an important study entitled *La cultura del Barroco. Análisis de una estructura histórica* (*The Culture of the Baroque. Analysis of a Historical Structure*).[27] He defined baroque as a cultural process, as a historical structure rather than simply an art form of the past. When he examined the historical situation of Spain in the late sixteenth and seventeenth centuries he unveiled a conservative Catholic mass culture under Phillip II, a culture highly controlled, urbanized.

According to Maravall seventeenth-century culture in Europe was charged with a strong centralized power. "[T]he culture of the baroque was an operative means to exercise control over preconceived men, to make them behave among themselves and in relation to the community and the political power according to the rules of the strong political principles of the times. In other words, *baroque is a set of cultural means of very diverse nature, gathered and articulated to manipulate men adequately to maintain them within the social system in place*" (my emphasis).[28]

The baroque reflects the period's religious tensions (Catholic versus Protestant); a new and more expansive worldview based on science and exploration; and the growth of absolutist monarchies. Maravall points out the important development in the area of the human science. Precise and pragmatic knowledge of the citizenry to be controlled is of utmost importance for the modern State—what Foucault calls bio-power as discussed above. In Maravall's view, pragmatism dominated the Baroque.

As in the baroque, the Francoist predisposition to dominate and manipulate human behavior (individually and collectively) leads to the identification between conduct and morality. There is a boom in the publication of manuals to indoctrinate young people in the right way, the moral way, the Christian way to conduct themselves in the New Spain. As Maravall points out, for the baroque the result (in Francoist Spain too) is the reduction of the individual to a "pragmatic prototype." The baroque established an "engineering of humanity" based on statistics inaugurating the modern age of bio-power.

Mystici Corporis Christi

In a speech in 1961 during a journey to Andalucia, Franco reiterated the indisputable union of Church and state under his aegis:

> We are all children of God, we are spiritual men, our rule is God's law . . . Our National Movement has come to unite the national element, which was threatened, with the social, but beneath the power of the spiritual, or the law of God. . . .

> [T]he union of Church and State, their collaboration in their respective functions, can bring nothing but good to society, the Church and the world.[29]

After the Allies' victory over Nazi Germany and Fascist Italy in 1945 it seemed Western democracies had won the struggle against fascism. But, the Cold War created a new polarized political scene between Western capitalist values and Soviet Communist ideals. It was at this moment that Francoism sought the opportunity to reinvent himself.

A close reading of the Church doctrine on the relation between religion and government will help us unveil the Spanish organic democracy's theoretical foundation. Leonine doctrine informed Pius XII's revision of the Church tradition on the relation between government and religion. Leo XIII's doctrine was the late nineteenth-century Church's response to "sectarian liberalism." It was a profound criticism of the liberal pillars: "freedom of religion" and the "separation of Church and State." For Leo XIII these principles threatened Catholic dogma and its political implications. According to Church dogma the state is part of a "moral universe," subject to the law of God; and society, in the end, is part of the Christian economy, subject as well to the law of Christ.[30] The premise guiding the Pope's argument is that Catholicism is the only true faith.[31] It is in the encyclical *Immortale Dei* in which Leo XIII clearly explains the Christian way of living as the fundamental basis of societies, meaning that it is the wisdom of the Gospel that ought to be the inspiration of human culture and civilization. The pontiff saw liberalism as a blasphemous doctrine because it enshrined human law and the will of the people. In Leonine doctrine, worldly matters must be subjected to the law of God, which always prevails over the will of the people. Never should a government rule against moral Christian law utilizing what Leo XIII called the fallacious idea of "separation of church and state." In religious terms the primary mission of the government was to guarantee the freedom of the Church and facilitate its Christian ministry; because religion, according to Leonine doctrine, is not created by government but by the Church.[32]

Whenever Catholic nations were under siege from materialist liberalism, Leo XIII justified vigorous state intervention to impose the true religion. Therefore, the officers involved in the military uprising in Spain on July 18, 1936 regarded it as an imperative to save the true Christian values of the nation, Christian values they believed the Constitution of 1931 had trampled upon when it explicitly declared the separation of church and state. Moreover, on July 1, 1937 the Church hierarchy issued a collective pastoral letter lending their support to the so-called crusade against the Reds.[33] Francisco Franco's victory in 1939 restored to the Catholic Church its social and cultural privileges, eroded during the Second Republic.

By the mid 1950s the Francoist regime was regarded as one of the best examples of the Leonine ideal Catholic state. Pius XII (1939–58) reconsidered Leo XIII's doctrine on the issue of religion and government relations and further elaborated the dogma of the infallibility of the papacy, which helped settle the notion of absolute truth deriving from his authority as head of the Catholic Church, not just on religious but on secular matters as well. There is no question this became a priority in the historical context that Pius XII faced: the rise of totalitarianism, the Holocaust, the Second World War, and the unfolding of the Cold War.

Spain had always been a dear Catholic state in the heart of the pontiff. Franco's final victory in the Spanish Civil War on April 1, 1939 came about only a month after Pius XII's proclamation as Pope. The following day the monarchist daily *ABC* published a telegram from the Pope congratulating Franco on his victory: "Raising our heart to the Lord, we sincerely thank Your Excellency, [for] the desired Catholic victory [in] Spain. We pray for this dearest country, that once peace is reached, it may revive with new strength its old Christian traditions, which made it so great. We send effusively to Your Excellency deep feelings, and our apostolic blessing to the noble Spanish people."[34] During World War II the Pope maintained formal relations with all the belligerents. This no doubt led later to serious criticism toward his pontificate for not having spoken out against the Nazi persecution of the Jews and not doing enough to protect them within Italy. Then after the war Pius XII was openly alarmed by the resurgence of Communism in the world and fostered the growth of Catholic Action groups to strengthen the Catholic influence in civil society. In 1949 he excommunicated Italian Catholics who joined the Communist party.[35]

Franco shared with Pius XII a visceral anti-Communism that the dictator traced back to the Civil War, the conflict was presented to the world in the 1950s as a crusade against atheist communism. The international rehabilitation of the regime was completed when the United Nations welcomed Spain in 1955. Certainly, the rise to power of the highly conservative secular order Opus Dei in the 1950s with its significant role in the implementation of the Stabilization Plan of 1959 and the Development Plans in the early sixties turned Opus Dei into the Catholic think tank that orchestrated the economic takeoff on the regime's behalf. Founded by Monseñor Javier Escrivá de Balaguer in 1928, Opus Dei encouraged its members to bring Christian values into their everyday lives. Known as the technocrats, these men took over the university chairs and the CSIC (National Research Council) and occupied the most important economic seats in Franco's cabinets in 1951 and 1957. Opus Dei received official endorsement from the Vatican in 1947 with the *Provida Mater,* a papal document that established the new legal secular institutes as part of the Church lay orders.

During his pontificate Pius XII reopened Leo XIII's discussion on the relationship between the government and religion. Historically immersed in the twentieth century, Pius XII faced the emergence of a global society and therefore the need for an "official community of nations." The pontiff confronted political globalization in contrast to Leo XIII's nineteenth-century reality of escalating nationalisms. The fundamental theoretical principle that guided Pius XII's doctrine revolved around the safeguarding of *unity* and *peace.* Like Leo XIII, he emphasized the subjection of state power to Christian moral order—as imperative for peace. His main concern was the justification of the use of coercive secular power against error and evil. The issue of tolerance or intolerance is at the heart of Pius XII's doctrine. What were the duties of government in a divided and sinful world? According to the Pope, the particular circumstances a Catholic jurist may confront must be to decide whether to lean toward tolerance or intolerance of error and evil. The Catholic jurist must always keep in mind the ultimate goal: the preservation of unity and peace. Therefore, tolerance is not a mandate but rather "tolerance and intolerance are alternative modes of legal action each finding its justification in the same set of principles" and subject to the particular circumstances.[36]

Because Communism was the incarnation of atheism and was equated with heresy, the Francoist regime's discourse on repressing any political dissidence was regarded as its duty as a Catholic state of "legal intolerance" of non-Catholic values. The Catholic Church found in the New Spain, born in 1939, its champion. The new Spaniard was to be a fusion of old and new Christian values. Hence, Catholicism became inextricably united to national identity: to be Spaniard one must be nothing else but Catholic. In this way the Church and the state entered an indissoluble matrimony becoming one flesh, a political mystical body of sorts.

In religious language, Jesus is the Church's head, and the faithful constitute her body. In the same manner, the relation between the sexes mirrors the hierarchy of the Church body. Pius XI's encyclical *Casti Connubii* (1930) on the dignity of Christian matrimony prescribed that the sexes could only encounter each other within marriage. "Married women" according to the encyclical, "ought to be subjected to their husbands, as they are subjected to the Lord; because the man is the head of the woman as Christ is the head of the Church."[37] National Catholic discourse enacted a symbolic indissoluble union between state and Church becoming "one flesh." This notion meant the incorporation of the mystic body politic concept that epitomized the Church's body as described in Pius XII's encyclical *Mystici Corporis Christi* (1943). "We intend to speak of the riches stored up in this Church which Christ purchased with His own Blood."[38] The organic nature of the Church had been advanced by Leo XIII as Pius himself acknowledged:

> That the Church is a body is frequently asserted in the Sacred Scriptures. "Christ," says the Apostle "is the Head of the Body of the Church." If the Church is a body, it must be an unbroken unity, according to those words of Paul: "Though many, we are one body in Christ." But it is not enough that the Body of the Church should be an unbroken unity; it must also be something definite and perceptible to the senses as Our predecessor of happy memory, Leo XIII, in his Encyclical *Santis Cognitum* asserts: "the Church is visible because she is a body. Hence they err in a matter of divine truth, who imagine the Church to be invisible, intangible, a something merely "pneumatological" as they say, by which many Christian communities, though they differ from each other in their profession of faith, are untied by an invisible bond.[39]

The unbroken unity proclaimed in the papal text was also adopted and promoted by the Francoist state apparatus from the very beginning, and it would become the key to the doctrinal basis of organic democracy with the advent of the Cold War. In the official propaganda the Spanish nation had been purchased with the blood of those led by Franco in the Civil War, the savior who delivered Spain from atheist Communism.

With the death of Pius XII on October 9, 1958, Spain lost one of its most eminent international allies. The election of Cardinal Angelo Giuseppe Roncalli as Pope John XXIII opened a new chapter of tolerance toward modern liberalism for the Catholic Church in general and a realignment of forces within the Spanish Catholic hierarchy in particular. John XXIII's most important accomplishment was the launching of the Second Vatican Council in October 1962. The spirit of goodwill and openness that guided the Council debates had been laid out in the encyclical *Mater et Magistra* issued by the Pope in 1961. Referring to his predecessors' doctrines from Leo XIII's *Rerum Novarum* and Pius XI's *Quadragesimo Anno,* John XXIII remarks in his encyclical, "Our purpose, therefore, is not merely to commemorate in a fitting manner the Leonine encyclical, but also to confirm and make more specific the teaching of our predecessors, and to determine clearly the mind of the Church on the new and important problems of the day."[40] Certainly one of the central issues discussed was the right to humane conditions for industrial and agricultural workers and the responsibility of Christian governments toward the poor, which included providing decent living wages for their work.[41] John XXIII based this argument on the very idea of the smooth functioning of the "Mystical Body of Christ." "The Church has always emphasized that this obligation of helping those who are in misery and want should be felt most strongly by Catholics, in view of the fact that they are members of the Mystical Body of Christ. 'In this we have known the charity of God,' says St. John, "because he has laid down his life for us; and we ought to lay down our lives for the brethren. He that hath the substance of this world and shall see his brother in need and shall shut up his bowels from him; how doth the charity of God abide in him?"[42]

Likewise in his goal to bring up to date the relation between the Spanish regime and the Church principles, the pontiff sent a message to the Bishop of Barcelona Modrego y Casaus in September 1961 that lamented the brutality of the Spanish Civil War and refrained from calling it a "Crusade."[43] The groundbreaking document issued by the Pope in 1963 was the encyclical *Pacem in Terris.* The Pope advocated in this document for peaceful coexistence and tolerance, freedom of speech, freedom of communication and association as well as the right of people to choose those who govern them. Likewise, the document condemned societies that repressed these rights and the freedom of language and culture of ethnic minorities. Spanish liberal Catholics felt the encyclical was referring to Spain in particular. The Spanish Church hierarchy and the regime were silent about the message from the Vatican and hoped for change when John XXIII died two months after the publication of the document. Paul VI, successor in the pontificate, presided over the Second Vatican Council until its closure in 1965. The document that summarized the spirit of the council was the 1968 encyclical *Humanae Vitae.*

The Vatican had assembled the council to confront and find answers to a world moving rapidly toward secularization. In the case of Spain, this move started with the emergent consumer economy and meant the crumbling of National Catholicism as a viable prop for Franco's absolute power. The council had questioned the legitimacy of National Catholicism. However, change was unavoidable. The spirit of aggiornamento guided the new *Spanish Episcopal Conference* (*Conferencia Episcopal Española* CEE) established in 1966 to replace the *Junta de Metropolitanos* functioning since 1923. The generational gap between the hierarchy and the priesthood was most evident. Even within the high Church hierarchy there were new voices such as Bishop Vicente Enrique y Tarancón who distanced themselves from the older generation of bishops who felt they owed Franco the restoration of order and the end to the fierce anticlericalism of the 1930s.

Although there was a new openness in the area of political affairs and labor relations (particularly with the Catholic Action organization of workers' strikes and resistance to the regime), the issues concerning family, marriage, and sexuality remained unquestionable from the Church perspective.[44] Changes in the area of gender relations and women's bodies would take place at the symbolic level in the mass media.

Hispanic Eugenics

The third element in the organic democracy formula is the early twentieth-century responses to the crisis of 1898 and the regime's appropriation and transformation of regenerationist discourses along with the baroque organicist legacy. Indeed, as in the Catholic discourse somatic metaphors were deliberate in the writings of Spanish intellectuals and politicians throughout the nineteenth and early twentieth centuries when they pondered the origins and destiny of the Spanish nation in the aftermath of the Spanish-American War of 1898.

As a member of the "regenerationist" movement at the turn of the twentieth century, Joaquín Costa (1844–1911)[45] attempted to find new formulas to refurbish national pride after the Spanish-American War. Costa resorted to medical metaphors when analyzing Spanish social and political realities during this time. The nation, conceived of as a sick female body, required careful attention to restore her health. Costa proposed a "legal dictatorship" as a healthy alternative. He emphasized the need for a new strong political figure, a caudillo; to take matters into his own hands and come to the aid of the sick mother country. He advocated the advent of a "surgeon with an iron hand." "[W]e need," Costa remarked, "in charge of government Bismarcks implanted in Saint Francis of Assisi types."[46] This hybrid autocrat/soldier/spiritual healer that Costa dreamt of had to be more saint than Bismarck. General Primo de Rivera's dictatorship aspired to embody Costa's political ideals when he assumed power in 1923 with the support of King Alfonso XIII. The general was fond of quoting Joaquín Costa but his dictatorship could not bring Spain to health. After failing attempts to resolve the centuries'-long problems of the country in 1931 the Second Republic was inaugurated by popular vote on April 14.

Philosopher José Ortega y Gasset (1883–1955) inherited the pessimistic political and philosophical outlook of the Generation of '98. Ortega believed that Spain was living an extreme case of what he called "historical invertebration" in the early 1920s. In his work *Invertebrate Spain,* he wrote passionately about the Spanish ethos, the country's historical decadence, and political crisis. One of Ortega's most read political and social statements (along with the sequel *The Revolt of the Masses*), *Invertebrate Spain* was first published in 1921 and reedited several times in Spanish. An English version appeared in 1937 in the United States with a foreword by Mildred Adams. According to Ortega, "[a] nation is a human mass which is organized and given structure by a minority of chosen individuals. . . . This is a natural law, and as important in the biology of social bodies as is in the law of densities in physics."[47] "A nation," he explained, "when the mass refuses to be mass—that is to say, when it refuses to follow the leading minority—the nation goes to pieces, society is dismembered, and social chaos results. The people as a people are des-articulated and become invertebrate."[48]

The somatic metaphors utilized in *Invertebrate Spain* to explain the country's historical decadence are many. The core of the problem is, according to Ortega y Gasset, the fact that in

Spain "the illness is not confined to the political life; it is society itself that is sick. It is the head and the heart of almost every Spaniard which is ailing."[49] Ortega argued that there was no specific point in history when Spain had begun her decline. For him Spain "had a defective embryology."[50] He was very blatant in his diagnosis for change. Only a strong authority would redirect the historical course of Spain's destiny. But change for the better would only be possible after much suffering in "[Spain's] own flesh"[51] so that the masses learn they need to be submissive to the select minority.

Ortega y Gasset's ideas had a tremendous impact on Ernesto Giménez Caballero (1899–1988), the first major proponent of fascism in Spain. "*Invertebrate Spain*" he declared, "was for me almost a book of devotions . . . a kind of intellectual dogma that I humbly respected and revered."[52] In 1919 Giménez Caballero graduated in philology from the University of Madrid and initiated graduate studies in philosophy under Ortega's mentorship. What eventually would distance the student from the master would be Caballero's strong nationalism versus Ortega's awe for Europeanization. Spain's defective embryology, according to Ortega, constituted the country's tragedy that began with the Visigoths. For him the Franks were of superior genetic stock and the way to modernize Spain would be to imitate the accomplishments and ethos of northern European countries. Giménez Caballero profoundly disagreed with his mentor on this point. During the first years of Primo de Rivera's dictatorship, Caballero struggled to resolve the conflict between his unconditional nationalism and devotion to Spain and his recognition, like Ortega's, of the country's backwardness. Caballero did not accept Ortega's praise of the Franks and contempt for the Visigoths' heritage, because this in the pupil's eyes made Spain's recovery impossible. Giménez Caballero became disillusioned with German nationalism and rejected German philosophy and the infatuation some Spanish scholars had with it. Instead, he praised Italian fascism and believed that it was the answer to Spain's political problems. He did not see, however, the dictatorship of Primo de Rivera solving anything. For him Spain at the time "rested, got fat, and fanned herself."[53] After drawing this caricature of Spain he continued by describing Mussolini's Italy in the following terms: "Today's Italy punishes as unique sins quietude, the lack of ardor, silence, irony and fat bellies . . . Mussolini exercises his people as he does his muscles: trying to get in condition. His politics are those of a trainer. Hence this enormous, sportive feeling of Italy's, where life is invigorating works done on a diet and hard discipline."[54]

The juxtaposition of the images of "fat" effeminate Spain versus a masculine "athletic" Italy says much about the gendered nature of the fascist cult of the body as well as the identification of the effeminate with the negative versus the masculine with the powerful in political discourse. Giménez Caballero fully ascribed himself to fascist ideology in an editorial entitled "Letter to a Comrade of Young Spain." He felt it was crucial to elaborate a Spanish form of fascism. "A people who do not find their own proper formula of fascism," he remarked, "are a people without inspiration, without character, without substance."[55] The solid man represented in Italian futurism, cubism, or high modernism would be the architect of the new athletic Spain. This soldier, man, dictator, or iron surgeon, is the ultimate representation of the Hobbesian artificial man, or man-machine that mirrors the body politic[56]—a hypermasculine body politic.

According to Douglas Foard, Giménez Caballero played the role of a "Spanish D'Annunzio." He opened the way for the founders of the political parties that embodied Spanish fascism: Ramiro Ledesma Ramos and José Antonio Primo de Rivera, son of the dictator and founder of Falange Española Tradicionalista in 1933. Foard reminds us how "[b]oth Ledesma and José Antonio would eventually win conspicuous places in the official pantheon of Franco's Spain."[57]

Falange Española Tradicionalista meant to provide the Orteguian political elite of a few young men, half soldiers-half monks, to accomplish the desired recovery of ailing Spain. "Man is the system;" declared José Antonio in his introduction to the Spanish edition of Mussolini's *La Dottrina del fascismo* (1932), "this is one of the profound human truths which fascism has brought to light again."[58] As Joaquin Costa did decades before, José Antonio strongly proposed the advent of the hero who would lead Spain into a healthy political state. The Francoist masculine ideal aspired to be a combination of monk and soldier and Franco incarnated such a combination, becoming by process of elimination the "leader," the "hero," the "redeemer"; the order of all these factors would not alter the product: a dictatorial rule that lasted for almost forty years.

In the official propaganda Franco became the iron surgeon in charge to restore health to the agonizing body politic at the turn of the twentieth century. He incarnated the savior who delivered

Spain from the evil secularizing Second Republic. Certainly, the ultimate sacrifice took place in the Civil War characterized in the Francoist discourse as a crusade against the so-called godless Reds. This understanding anointed as true Spaniards those who gave their lives for the "right" Spain and therefore the only ones entitled to be active members of the new political body. The bloodletting of sick motherland in the Civil War ushered in a New Spain, a new nation whose foundations were well rooted in Catholic traditions and that would count on divine sanction as we have seen above.

Blood constituted precisely the life-giving foundation of the restored Spanish organic nation. In order to be an active member of the new body politic a blood offering was required. Those who died in the front for the Nationalist cause were declared martyrs who spilled their blood for the mother country.[59] Blood as a means to gain membership in the national community goes back to the Catholic Monarchs' forging of Spain as a nation and the promulgation of the *estatutos de limpieza de sangre* (statutes of pure blood) to establish old Christian ancestry, in a time when Jews and Muslims were forced to leave the country or convert. The *estatutos de limpieza de sangre* introduced the organic concept of the national body as well as the connection between racial purity and religious faith. Francoism looked back with nostalgia to 1492 as Spain's historical apex. The civil war characterization as a crusade against the Reds—modern infidels—emulated the medieval reconquista led by the Catholic monarchs.

The new Francoist state issued a *sui generis limpieza de sangre* for the citizens to belong to the new national community after 1939. A look at psychiatrist Antonio Vallejo Nágera's (1889–1960) prolific writing[60] on the subject of racial regeneration is extremely important to assess the organic nature of the political discourse under Francoism. Vallejo Nágera had studied medicine in Valladolid and did his internship at the asylum of that city. Upon graduation he joined the Army Medical Corps in 1910. Like Franco, he made his military career in Africa, but in contrast to the caudillo's front service Vallejo functioned inside the bureaucratic strand. Military headquarters sent him in 1918 to the Spanish embassy in Berlin as part of the military commission. As member of one of WWI's neutral nations, Nágera visited German concentration camps. While in Germany, he also visited hospitals and asylums, taking the opportunity to get to know firsthand the works of leading German psychiatrists. Dr. Ernst Kretschmer's work had a lifelong impact on the Spanish doctor. Particularly interesting to him was Kretschmer's thesis of the direct correlation between body type and temperament.

During the 1920s Nágera acquired a great deal of power within academic circles. In 1928 he entered the National Academy of Medicine and a year later he was appointed director of the Army Psychiatric Hospital in Cienpozuelos, near Madrid. It was during these years that he elaborated an uncouth theory that explained Spain's crisis. In the same vein as Costa, Ganivet, or Ortega y Gasset, Nágera found Spain's political tribulations were the result of the degenerative decline of the once "virile Hispanic race."[61] For him the philosophers and politicians' "concoctions had barely stung the pachyderm-like skin of the racial body."[62]

In the preamble of his work *Eugenesia de la Hispanidad y regeneración de la raza* (*Hispanic Eugenics and the Regeneration of the Race*) published in 1937 in the throes of the civil war, Dr. Antonio Vallejo Nágera declared "It would be a shame that the blood generously spilled at the fatherland's altar would not give rise to the nucleus of racial virtues and, in a terrain irrigated so costly, weed would take over."[63]

With *Eugenesia de la Hispanidad,* Nágera proposed a program of regeneration of the racial body. The text represents a clear example of how the regime partially designed its bio-power over the Spanish population well before the civil war had concluded. Nágera signed the prologue to *Eugenesia de la Hispanidad* in Madrid in March 1936, three months before the military uprising. "To better plan" he writes, "the means and objectives of a eugenic national policy, we must arrive to precise conclusions about our knowledge of the laws of biological inheritance. We must study the demographic conditions of the country and take also into account the cultural idiosyncrasies that have a conscious or unconscious influence on the people."[64] Nágera explained in this work how the regeneration of the masses only was possible by programming the population for individual self-regeneration. His assessment and recommendations had a more serious relevance to the everyday lives of those who lost the war, as we will see below. As one of the most acclaimed psychiatrists of the period his works were received not as mere philosophical elucidations but rather as scientifically proven truths that warranted drastic political action.

Following German psychiatrist Ernst Kretschmer's work, Nágera believed in the union and synchronization of body and spirit. For him environmental conditions as much as genetics determined the final phenotype. Personality and biopsychiatric constitution were to be balanced.[65] "The purpose of racial hygiene," he declared, "is to obtain perfect genotypes by manufacturing *ideal phenotypes.*" This would only be possible when the individual was "constantly immersed in an atmosphere of *supersaturated* morality."[66] The racial policy, in Nágera's judgment hence, had to be programmed to better the phenotype, not to maintain a seemingly superior genotype devoid of any moral values, which had to be necessarily Catholic. "Currently, there exists in all nations a collective state of mental illness . . . It has disappeared from the collective consciousness the ideas of God, Fatherland and Family that have such a strong influence on people. Religious values have been uprooted from the masses without being replaced by something that might elevate human ethics. The concepts of hierarchy and social discipline have been razed. *The entire emotional frame of civilization is ruined or decaying.*"[67]

Like Ortega y Gasset, Nágera proposes as the only solution the action of a "select minority driven by reason." This minority, in his view, was not only to resolve the problem of a degenerate race by procreating prolifically healthy ideal phenotypes, but those few would purify the sins of *cainismo.*[68] The concept of race afforded by Nágera was as follows:

> We agree with Spengler, what is important is a strong race which integrates the volk or nation. A strong race in body and spirit as we have repeated so many times. When we talk about race we refer to the Hispanic race, to the Iberian genotype, that in the present moment has experienced the most diverse mixes due to the contact and relation with other peoples. From our racist [*sic*] point of view, we are more interested in the spiritual values of the race that allowed us to civilize vast lands and have an intellectual impact in the world. Hence our concept of race is fused with the concept of "Hispanidad." . . . We must not give any relevance to the facial angle or the color of the skin, because what we call race is not just made up of the biological elements . . . but rather by those elements that are the light of the spirit: thought and language.[69]

The family was to be the basic cell of the new society. Nágera published a series of articles in the daily press that were compiled in 1938 into a small book entitled *Política racial del Nuevo Estado* (*Racial Policy of the New State*). In these short essays he proposed practical actions to be undertaken by the new totalitarian state to increase birthrates by creating incentives to encourage earlier marriages and at the same time penalize those who remained selfishly single. Nágera condemned Marxist Malthusianism, pointing to the contraceptive propaganda initiated during the Second Republic with the publication of literature on birth control and family planning and the distribution of pamphlets such as the one called "Huelga de los vientres" (Wombs' Strike). He proposed the promulgation of a law of Social Assistance and Welfare that would contemplate a social security for life, illness, and disability to better implement a state-run racial policy. Therefore, the most serious national enemy after the war was Malthusianism[70] pure and simple. Dr. Nágera enlightened his readers with what he presented as sound scientific facts: "Anti-Malthusian champions will scrupulously provide statistics proving how the children are more intelligent and healthy after the fifth child. Many will talk about the sad future of the only child, and certainly, I studied some time ago the only child neurosis, and had pointed out how early dementia and schizophrenia is common among only-children."[71]

These essays were written for the general public so the author did not feel he needed to back any of his affirmations with bibliographic annotations. He presented himself a "racial hygienist" and was simply "putting on paper his deep thoughts on these issues" guided by, as he explained in the prologue, "Patriotism and a deep felt moral responsibility before God."[72] For him the most powerful racial "disinfectant" was religion. The "deep re-Christianization of society" was certainly to translate from his perspective into a dramatic increase of the birthrates. In addition, to facilitate a natalist policy, Nágera proposed to develop a nuptial policy based on the penalization of those who remained single. Since what he calls the "family-home will be the cell of the new Spain" a sound nuptial policy must be based on three pillars: "pre-marital counseling, fighting female and male sterilization with the punishment of clandestine and therapeutic abortion; and finally fighting the single status by encouraging marriages before age 25."[73]

Since as he put it "decrepit parents engendered weak offspring" it was important to encourage young people to start a home early following the model applied in Italy by Mussolini, which Nágera considered very successful. Some of the incentives mentioned in his essay included affordable housing, brides' trousseaux provided by the state, inexpensive furniture to be paid in installments, tax breaks for married men thirty and younger, and finally the nationalist option to give a premium to those young couples who married on a national holiday.[74] Vallejo Nágera acknowledged the cases of those who remained single due to "timidity or an inferiority complex." He considered these cases a good example of individuals who were "schizophrenic, paranoids, or psychopaths"—in sum, unable to adapt. For those he qualified as licentious, it was better not to get married if they had no intention to rectify their ill behavior.[75] "It is the responsibility of every good citizen, conscious of the moral responsibility of his historical destiny, to form a family, if he is healthy. The bachelor in general, is a bad patriot and bad citizen, or a sick individual. Those bachelors must consider very seriously their duties before God, the Fatherland, and the State, and they will corroborate my assertion. Religious vocation or ideological motivations of sublime category may justify for an individual to remain single, in very rare cases. *The ideal citizen in the New Spain will be married and a prolific parent.*"[76]

Those who deviated from the prescriptive Catholic norm were categorized as mentally disturbed. Only those individuals who complied with the New State precepts were to enjoy the benefits of the social services established around the policies highlighted by Vallejo Nágera. He proposed to implement a serious campaign against social and political "hysteria and neurasthenia," ignited as a result of democracy incarnated in the Second Republic. Hysteria and neurasthenia were the offspring of a materialist and decadent civilization, according to Vallejo Nágera. Here he pointed out how he did not intend to set a scientific doctrine, but rather "plant fertile seeds for the race; therefore if in some aspects we might deviate from the psychiatric orthodoxy, our sin must be forgiven, due to the good intention in our part."[77] Nágera proposes a careful application of a hierarchical professional distribution that allocates each individual to the task, trade, or profession that better suits him according always to his social station. The advice is to follow on the parental steps: the son of a doctor would be a doctor, the son of a plumber a plumber. "Professional orientation will have an effect on the wellbeing of the Race. It will decrease the number of neurasthenics and hysterics, since professional failure leads to a complex of inferiority, and consequently in finding refuge in illness. Both hysteria and neurasthenia are miasmas that degenerate the race."[78]

The *Fuero del Trabajo* (Labor Charter) issued in 1938 proclaimed the end of class struggle and established the corporate structure of the labor force with the establishment of vertical syndicalism in which owners and workers had to work and cooperate with each other. In addition, gender distinction guided the labor charter that proclaimed women were "liberated" from factory work and established by law their national duty to be confined to the home. Nágera's considered professional "distribution" a therapeutic way to avoid mental illness, and believed in the extreme-right idea that class was being based on the working-class complex of inferiority that led to a jealousy and hatred of the wealthy. Social justice should be the work of religious charity or a despotic government.

But conflict and violence were unavoidable. Their roots, according to Vallejo Nágera, were present in the very beginnings of the human race. Original sin had for him a symbolic meaning since in his view Adam and Eve must have transmitted a shortfall to their progeny. One finds the type of congenital pervert in the first human generation incarnated by Cain versus Abel; the former being the evil, the latter the amiable and fair prototype.[79] It is this inherited flaw, explained in religious and providential terms, that Nágera will use to create his "scientific" explanation of the vanquished after the Civil War. Those men and women defeated by the Francoist self-proclaimed Abels of the Spanish race were the offspring of Cain. In the midsummer of 1938, Vallejo Nágera, head of the Psychiatric Services of the Army stationed in Burgos, received a telegram from General Francisco Franco that read:

> In response to your petition of 10th of the current proposing the creation of a Department of Psychological Research whose main objective will be to study the bio-psychological roots of Marxism, I declare that in accordance with your mentioned proposal, I authorize the creation of the said department. The funding for this enterprise will come from the general budget assigned to that inspection, and the personnel that offer services in it will be the physician that voluntarily and without pay wants to perform this task. It could be military personnel if necessary.—I make this decision known to you to arrange and report to me those doctors that must be militarized so that the Department is functioning immediately.[80]

The Department of Psychological Research was closed in October 1939. The results of the research performed on the prison population were published in two medical journals: *Revista Médica Española* (*Medical Spanish Review*) and *Revista Española de Cirugía y Medicina de Guerra* (*Spanish Journal of Surgery and War Medicine*). The results confirmed Nágera's predictions. The enemy lacked any sense of morality, a brute devoid of any kind of humanity. As historian Ricard Vinyes puts it: "finally they [the nationalists] had in their hands the archetype of evil, the idea of evil in pure form" sustained by what was presented as objective scientific research.[81] Moreover, being that the hypothesis confirmed and derived from the ultra-Catholic fervor, the therapy proposed must follow Christian moral reeducation of those willing to redeem themselves. Segregation and purge of the ominous sins were part of that therapeutic process of reinsertion into the New Spain. This therapy was concomitant with Nágera's belief that it was not mere genetics but the environment that determined the ideal phenotype. The concept of Hispanic racial purity was not a matter of skin color but rather the conquest of the spiritual values present in the most glorious past of our ancestors—the Golden Age, the age of the mystics, of the Counter-Reformation *Propaganda Fide.* "We must start a fervent hygienic fight against the morbid germs that rot our Hispanic race to lead her to the most wretched degeneration. It is *not simply a matter of returning to the humanist values of the fifteenth and sixteenth centuries.* We must restore those values to people's everyday so that we cleanse morally the environment."[82]

Like many contemporaries Nágera viewed the Counter-Reformation as a referent point in the past to regenerate the social body in the new Francoist Spain. His service to the New Spain was highly compensated with a promotion to colonel for his exemplary dedication to the fatherland. As part of his responsibilities in the years following the end of the war he was in charge of writing the scientific reports about the legal responsibilities of those sentenced to death.

Vallejo Nágera was forty-seven years old when the Civil War started. He continued to enjoy the respect of the scientific community not only in Spain but internationally. In 1950 he presided over the First International Psychiatry Congress celebrated in Paris. It was still a time of conflict and polarization—Cold War.

"Change is Here to Stay": Consumer Economy

With the transition from autarky to consumerism in the late 1950s and 1960s, the regime confronted the challenge of maintaining the status quo while veiling the institutional apparatus with organic democratic principles. The unavoidable process of urbanization and the population displacements due to tourism and emigration led to a new historical structure in itself. Intellectuals in exile, as well as those inside Spain, maintained heated debates about the Spanish essence and historical purpose.

The new consumerist society, inaugurated with the *Stabilization Plan* of 1959 and deepening with the 1960s development plans, changed the social landscape and furthered the identity crisis of the regime's foundational values. Indeed, consumerism and a timid social liberalization came to further complicate this crisis and contestation the regime was suffering. Spanish society was economically devastated at the beginning of the 1950s. Between 1951 and 1955 the Spanish population increased from 28,094,612 to 29,055,535.[83] Only 38 percent of Spanish homes had running water. In cities of more than 50,000 inhabitants that percentage raised to 74 percent while in the rural areas it was only 13 percent. A full bathroom or one with a shower existed only in 9 percent of Spanish homes.[84] From the perspective of public health there was still a high incidence of tuberculosis. In the winter of 1951 influenza took the lives of 10,000 people. Between 1956 and 1960 the population growth went from 29,300,860 to 30,303,040. During the next five years the population increased to 31, 339,100 people. The total number of people who died due to tuberculosis in 1964 was 7,794; while typhus took the life of 7,497 people. Influenza was the cause of death resulting in the dramatic figure of 548,201 fatalities in 1964.[85]

Tourism began to take off in the 1950s. In 1953, 1,700,000 tourists visited Spain and 4,200,000 had come to Spain by 1959, most of them during the summer months.[86]

In 1964, 498,203 Spaniards migrated to the big cities. About 232,883 of those were women. Barcelona received 144,075 immigrants of whom 64,929 were women. Of the total immigrant population 86,070 were single men and women in their twenties. Madrid absorbed 58,102 immigrants of whom 27,199 were women. Valencia received 41,638 and Vizcaya 38,486. One of the most interesting figures provided by the state statistics was the number of illiterate emigrants. The official definition of an illiterate person was a fourteen-year-old person who could not read or write. There were 20,149 illiterate emigrants the state accounted for in 1964.

The economic changes led to a series of Global Sociology Studies conducted by Catholic private philanthropic foundations to aid the government in the orchestration and implementation of the development plans in the 1960s. If the 1940s were called the "hunger years" the 1960s will be known as the "economic miracle" years.

The FOESSA foundation (Fomento de Estudios Sociales y Socialogía Aplicada) was established in 1965. Spain echoed the United States' commitment to implement policies to fight poverty. President Johnson, in his address to Congress on May 1, 1966, explained that his new policy ("The War on Poverty") supported the need to generate statistics and social indicators to help appraise the needs in the area of education and health. In Spain the social Catholic impulse of the Second Vatican Council led to the support of the Church in the quest to better the economic situation of the masses. At the beginning of 1960 Cáritas Española published three volumes that were the result of the Church-promoted CCB (*Comunicación Cristiana de Bienes* or *Christian Communication of Wealth*) to identify the Spanish social reality. These early studies identified six problems or needs in the Spanish social fabric: diet, health, education, housing, labor; and a miscellaneous category called "social community."[87] The studies conducted in the second half of the 1960s by the FOESSA foundation gathered the work of prominent academics in Spain and approached the research with impartiality. However, in the early studies there was no discussion or questioning of the political situation of the country. The sociological studies were presented as mere aids to the state economic policies. Chapter five of the 1970 report, entitled "vida política y asociativa," was censored and the volume was published without it yet the table of contents remained unchanged.[88] Only in 1976 after the death of the dictator would FOESSA publish any data about the political affairs.[89] FOESSA published four major sociological reports, which had a tremendous impact on the development plans to identify economic as well as social indicators. These documents have been excellent sources for the analysis of the transition from autarky to consumerism because their approach to development is far from purely economic. Instead, it emphasized the need to pay attention to social welfare.

With urbanization and the rural exodus to big cities there was a rise of middle-class families who were able to buy their first

Seat 600 automobile and purchase their domestic appliances through credit. In 1964 there was a fleet of 299,968 official vehicles, of which 126,967 were private cars and 112,063 motorcycles. The most important transformation within the household was the television set, although it arrived in Spain considerably later than in other European countries. Broadcasting started on October 28, 1956. In 1960 only 1 percent of Spanish homes had a TV; in 1964, 13 percent; and in 1966, 32 percent. In 1966 the percentages of consumer goods in Spanish households included: radio, 82 percent; washing machine, 36 percent; television set, 32 percent; refrigerator; 28 percent; bicycle, 15 percent; car, 12 percent; record player, 12 percent; motor bike, 11 percent; and 10 percent lacked any of these consumer goods. A timid sign of economic betterment showed in the number of telephones and cars Spaniards began to own. The number of telephones went from 327,000 in 1940 to 981,000 in 1954. Gerald Brenan would comment on the number of people listed in the phone book when he visited the country in 1949: "There are less people in the telephone book for the whole Andalusia than for the Swindon and Gloucester area."[90]

The number of homes with telephones rose from 12 to 23 percent between 1960 and 1966. In 1948 only 19 per 1,000 had a telephone in Spain; 50 of every 1,000 inhabitants had a telephone in 1958; and 80 per 1,000 in 1965.[91]

Logically the ownership of these items depended on socioeconomic status and was aligned along the urban/rural divide. For example 22 percent of the urban workers owned refrigera-

Telephones Per 1000 Inhabitants in Different European Countries 1948–1965

Country	1948	1958	1960	1963	1965
Belgium	70	114	124	147	156
France	54	83	95	111	117
Italy	22	61	74	95	105
Spain	**19**	**50**	**53**	**67**	**80**
Portugal	15	38	45	54	57
Greece	—	16	21	42	50
Yugoslavia	6	12	14	17	19

Source: Fundación FOESSA, *Informe Sociológico sobre la situación social de España,* (Madrid: Editorial de Euroamérica, 1966), 75.

tors versus only 6 percent of the peasant middle class. Among the urban middle class, 29 percent owned a TV set versus 11 percent of the peasant middle class. With regard to laundry machines, only 4 percent of the peasant lower class had one versus 80 percent of the urban upper class. This is an interesting figure since most middle-class families had a maid. An interesting indicator is the number of record players: only 1 percent of the peasant lower class versus 40 percent of the urban upper class. This last figure is the result of the expansion of the entertainment industry.

The bicycle was the means of transportation for the lower classes, whose income in 1965 ranged from 2,500 pts to 4,000 pts per month. Those whose income was 8,500 to 14,500 pts per month owned a motor bike instead; the total percentage being 20 percent. Ownership of a refrigerator, TV, car, record player, and laundry machine constituted the essential consumer goods to display upper-socioeconomic status in the mid 1960s.[92]

The number of homes with a car in 1960 was 4 percent while six years later it increased to 12 percent. Having a car is the most important indicator of the move from a transitional economy to a consumer mass society. Having an automobile means a change in different aspects of social interaction that the FOESSA study enumerated as follows:

a) Rationalization of the distribution of urban space for housing. Decongestion of the urban conglomerates
b) Change in the geographical mobility patterns and the working location
c) Change in the family relations, shopping, scheduling of leisure time
d) Possibility of more autonomy for young people who become even more independent from the parental authority
e) Emergence of new problems: higher cost of means of communication, traffic ordinance, noise, accidents, pollution[93]

The increment on the fleet of vehicles was a direct consequence of the rise of the per capita income—from 257,000 vehicles in 1953 to almost 2 million in 1964. The most important increase happened in private vehicle ownership, which in 1965 was 21 per 1,000 inhabitants.[94]

The Fundación FOESSA published *Estudios Sociológicos sobre la situación social de España 1975* in 1976. There was an important change in the title from "Report" to "Studies." The former two reports had been directed by Amando de Miguel, who was a professor in Sociology at the University of Valencia. The "Studies" produced in 1975 were, however, the result of the work of several teams of researchers in charge of the different chapters, which gave the final product a more diverse approach and methodologies.

The introduction to the "Studies" showed a more critical analysis of the regime in the aftermath of Franco's death. In the introduction to the new Studies, entitled "Los nuevos españoles. Introducción a un informe," the coordinator of the different study groups, Professor Luis González Seara, quoted Ortega y Gasset's somatic description of a changing political situation like the one Spain was facing in 1975. In 1918 José Ortega had published an article entitled "La verdadera cuestión española" in the Madrid daily *El sol.* "If there has been a serious prospect for change of our public establishment, it is now mostly due to necessity rather than mere whim. Rather than imposing on the Spanish body politic alien legislative trends, it is of the essence to avoid the absurd attempt to preserve under a heavy musculature the skeleton of a child . . . In the last thirty years, Spanish society has profoundly transformed itself. Let's try to equip it with a new public structure."[95]

Since Ortega wrote these sentences Spain had experienced several dictatorships, the Second Republic, the Civil War, a Francoist imperialist and autarkic period, a Francoist technocratic and development period, a Francoist period of "aperturismo"; and a newly established monarchy. Nonetheless, and in spite of all those changes, Professor Luis González Seara thought Ortega's words had the same pervasiveness and practical sense. "How it is this possible?" He posed that it was "due to what Antonio Machado called the 'macizo de la raza,' a Hispanic caste, a political elite resorting to diverse ideological discourses and props. But now there are indicators that seem to show, for the first time, the erosion of that 'racial core' due to external influences and internal movements and certainly these profound changes deserve to be studied and put into perspective."[96]

According to González Seara, the great changes undergone in Spain must not be examined just from a materialist point of view; it is important to see the transformation of the cultural values of that "racial core": the middle classes, the bourgeoisie, the working mass, all of them with a strong attachment to traditional practices, fear of change, reliance on strong authority and superstitious attitudes toward public institutions. Members of this social conglomerate were peasants, workers, middle classes, intellectuals, clergy, and a large part of the army. All these groups, González Seara affirmed, had lived accepting their fate with resignation because they believed there must always be "rich and poor"[97] and the motto "someone else will succeed me that will make my actions praiseworthy" and usually that other would be a liberal, Mason, or Communist. Given these circumstances, González Seara believed any deviation from such social conglomerate at the service of the hegemonic oligarchy had been historically almost impossible. "The attempts to transform this "dried-up country" into a modern society have been weakened at every turn. Therefore, now that the erosion is finally evident it is essential to examine the elements prompting it. The "racial core" has been based on a rural structure that now has become an urban society; massive rural exodus is the new sign of Spanish landscape.[98] Conservatism has deep roots in rural life; an anti-urban sentiment is not exclusive to Spain or Europe but also exists in America. González Seara points out that in the United States, for example, from "Thomas Jefferson to Frank Lloyd Wright, from Emerson to William James, intellectuals had shown a special aversion to urban life as a site of corruption, decadence and demoralization."[99] Urbanization was extremely fast in the 1960s in Spain. More than 50 percent of Spanish population lived in cities of more than 20,000 inhabitants—higher than the figures for Italy and France.

The urbanization of the country affected public religiosity as defined by National Catholicism. Since the Concordat of 1953, Spanish society was better off economically. Although secular organizations such as Catholic Action and Opus Dei had positions in the state apparatus, there would be an increasing intellectual reaction against the Church's control over scientific, educational, and cultural areas as well as a strong secularization of way of life and the decisive transformation of the Catholic Church with the Second Vatican Council. Hence, some factions of Spanish Church hierarchy drifted apart from the regime, initiating a moderate opposition, and to a certain extent claimed some independence from the regime. National Catholicism is repudiated by the Church hierarchy with figures as important as Cardinal Enrique Tarancón, pushing democratization from the synod itself.

Meanwhile, important elements of National Catholicism persist: Spain was officially a Catholic country according to the Fundamental Laws of the Regime issued in 1958; canonic marriage remained in place without any chance to even discuss divorce. Formal education remained under the control of the Catholic Church and its schools received subsidies and official protection; cultural censorship of cinema and television remained strong under the control of Catholic values. The instruction of Catholic religion, political indoctrination, and physical education, which were known among the student body as the "three Marys," remained strong. There were still many National Catholic vestiges but the Catholic Church's democratization and the process of secularization were instrumental in triggering the end of a regime that were hanging on to Trent and the baroque spectacle of the Inquisition.[100]

After the Allies' victory in World War II, Franco unveiled a new political philosophy called organic democracy, which was to legitimize him in power for the next three decades. Supporting organic democracy were the strong pillars of National Catholicism. Together Church and state worked to turn back the clock to an earlier Golden Age political discourse known as Tacitismo. Tacitismo fit well with the authoritarian Francoist model, having as its main principle the establishment of a divinely sanctioned order in which each individual plays a predetermined and immutable role.

This baroque-age discourse, infused with somatic metaphors, were then liberally borrowed by the new regime: National Catholicism proclaimed Franco as head of the state (a role assigned to the king in the early modern period) and (as in the Counter-Reformation era) the backbone of the Catholic Church. In turn, the Catholic Church lent legitimacy to the regime as its heart and soul. Mixed in with the somatic metaphors were heroic images of Spain's early days. As Paul Preston points out, Franco, the caudillo, became "the medieval warrior-crusader, defender of the faith and restorer of Spanish national greatness, with his relationship to the Church as an important plank in the theatrical panoply."[101]

Therefore, I characterized the Francoist regime's cultural, social, and political nature as neo-baroque, in line with the theoretical proposal of José Antonio Maravall for the early modern period in his work, *La cultura del Barroco.* When examined from a gender perspective the baroque and the Francoist regime are culturally, politically, and socially closed. The dictatorship created artificial men and women, the latter at the center of the modernization process through the commodification of their bodies in marriage and motherhood. In the next chapters we will unveil the regime's technologies of control of women's bodies to fit into the Francoist organic democratic agenda.

2

(De)limiting Women's True Nature: Writing Women's Bodies onto Francoist Body Politic

> BERNARDA: *In this house you will do as I tell you. You can't run telling tales to your father now. Needle and thread for the woman, whip and mule for the man. That's how it is for people born to certain obligations.*
>
> —*The House of Bernarda Alba,* (1936)[1]

THE FRANCOIST RECOVERY OF TRADITION WAS FUNDAMENTALLY gendered and meant the articulation of what I have called "True Catholic Womanhood."[2] National Catholic ideology informed a repressive sexual discourse based on the imposition of Christian family values as the pillar of social and gender relations. The regime's notion of physical and moral female purity and piety were carefully wrapped up in a formula of domesticity sanctified by the Catholic Church since the Council of Trent. This chapter focuses on the cultural construction of gender relations under Francoism. Specifically, I examine how the official discourse on women's nature fused Catholic values rooted in the baroque period with pseudoscientific beliefs on womanhood from the turn of the twentieth century. The fusion between science and religious discourses lent a veneer of modernity to the official design of the "New Woman" embodied in the Falange's Women's Section (Sección Femenina de Falange) members.[3]

For the purpose of this study it is important to look back to the *loci communes*[4] on womanhood in the official Francoist discourse rooted in the sixteenth and seventeenth centuries' cultural legacy. This will allow us to see diachronically how Francoism banked its gender ideology on notions of womanhood rooted in early modern European medical and religious discourses.[5] The neo-baroque nature of the regime was fundamentally gendered.

The Early Modern Period's Notions of Woman

As we have shown in chapter 1, the Catholic Spanish ethos was forged in medieval times. Throughout the Middle Ages, Iberia was a site of encounter with a cultural *other* (incarnated in the Moors) whose identity was defined along a perceived unnatural sexuality, a sexuality that transgressed Christian orthodoxy. As Gregory S. Hutcheson and Josiah Blackmore point out, medieval Iberia, in the European context, was the land of heterodoxies embodied by the infidels that struck at the very heart of Christian theology.[6] The Reconquista meant the confrontation within the Iberian soil of these two different worldviews (Christian versus non-Christian) and, in the final analysis, led to the construction and imposition of a monolithic Spanish Catholic culture with the conquest of Granada in 1492.[7] This Spanish Catholic identity did away with a cultural synchronicity of sorts among Christian, Muslims, and Jews. Spanish historian Américo Castro's (1885–1972)[8] proposal of the idea of *convivencia*[9] of the three cultures, coined early in the twentieth century, challenged the pretended eternal Catholic identity at the heart of Francoist ideology.[10] National Catholicism reread Spain's historical past, and this new interpretation imposed a Catholic heterosexual imperative.

National Catholic ideology fostered what I have called True Catholic Womanhood[11] based on the cultural construction of Castilian Catholic identity in the 1490s and 1500s. Juan Luis Vives's *The Instruction of the Christian Woman* (1523) represents one major work whose dicta on women's virtue, piety, and domesticity Francoism revived. Vives wrote this manual for Mary Tudor of England and later it was translated into every major European language. Conversely, in the seventeenth century writer María de Zayas y Sotomayor[12] narrated sexually explicit experiences through her female characters in her *Novelas amorosas y ejemplares* (*The Enchantments of Love,* 1637), followed by another volume entitled *Desengaños amorosos* (*The Disenchantments of Love,* 1647) as a way of reclaiming the female body's power over the patriarchal sex. Zayas's two volumes were printed between 1637 and 1814, and translated into French, English, German, and Dutch. The close discourse analysis of

Juan Luis Vives and María de Zayas's works reveals the two sides of the coin when it comes to evaluating the Spanish cultural geography of the female body. Finally, I will examine the work of Fray Benito Jerónimo Feijóo y Montenegro (1676–1764) in the eighteenth century to sum up the Spanish approach to woman's nature in early modern Spanish intellectual tradition

Juan Luis Vives (1492–1540) was born in Valencia in a well-to-do Jewish converso merchant family. He never admitted his Jewish upbringing in his writings even though his father and mother were victims of the Inquisition's violence. His father was executed in 1524, but in the mother's case the story turns into a sort of horror tale. Her name was Blanquina March Maçana, daughter of a family of jurists. Although she escaped the Inquisition and died of the plague in 1508, twenty years later her remains were exhumed and burned at the stake after a sinister trial.[13] These events illustrate the highly corporeal nature of religious practice in the early modern period.[14] It might also explain Vives's emphasis on the somatic roots of spiritual purity and his determination to detach himself from any doubt about his Christian beliefs. He studied and worked in England along with humanists such as Thomas Linacre, John Fisher, William Latimer, and Thomas More. Although Vives had an opportunity to return to Spain, he would not accept the chair of Latin philology at the University of Alcalá, replacing Antonio de Nebrija, for fear of the Inquisition.

Queen Catherine of Aragon, first wife of Henry VIII, commissioned Vives to write a manual on the instruction of girls. This work not only discusses the education of women in three stages of their lives—unmarried, married, and widowed—it also deals with the social status of women and their moral instruction. The corporeal nature of women dominates the three books in which the work is divided. The main goal is the preservation of chastity in all stages of life: before marriage, for wives, and for widows. Vives follows Saint Augustine's dictum in *De Sancta Virginitate (On Holy Virginity)* and defines virginity as "integrity of the mind, which extends also to the body, integrity free of all corruption and contamination."[15] Women must preserve an "angelic mind" and guard themselves against impure thoughts. "She is unchaste," Vives asserts, "who even without engaging in an illicit sexual act desires it."[16] Young women must prepare themselves to become *angels of the home,* winning the respect of all humankind by preserving their physical and spiritual virginity. Those who took little care of their chastity deserved the worst calamities to overcome them, certainly more so than unchaste men: "For many things are required of a man: wisdom, eloquence, knowledge of political affairs, talent, memory, some trade to live by, justice, liberality, magnanimity, and other qualities that it would take a long time to rehearse. If some of these are lacking, he seems to have less blame as long as some are present. But in a woman, no one requires eloquence or talent or wisdom or professional skills or admiration of the republic or justice or generosity; no one asks anything of her but chastity."[17]

Women's single asset of chastity equates to the many male virtues. Vives weaved female pure souls into a spiritual cocoon to envelop their untouchable bodies. The angels of the home that Vives depicted in his work in the Spanish Renaissance remained dormant until Francoism brought Spanish women face to face with their true nature. But Vives's work is significant beyond the Spanish cultural realm. Translated into most European languages, these Christian values became the cultural capital for female respectability in the early modern and modern era in Western European countries. Certainly, Vives's beliefs resonate in Victorian ideals of female virtue such as purity and piety.

In chapter 7, Juan Luis Vives discusses "How the Young Woman Will Treat her Body." Frequent fasts will be beneficial, especially before marriage. "Let her nourishment be light, plain and not highly seasoned." "Their drink will be clear water," Vives says, "because it is well known that the next step after Bacchus, father of intemperance, is that which leads to unlawful lust."[18] Only when the stomach does not tolerate water does Vives prescribe beer as an alternative libation because it "not only is good for restraining sexual passion, lust, and wantonness of the body, but it also promotes most robust health."[19] Quoting St. Jerome, Juan Luis Vives declares that it is better that the health of the body be at risk rather than that of the soul. "It is preferable that the stomach be in pain rather than the mind; better to rule the body than be a slave to it, to falter in one's steps rather than in one's chastity."[20]

The body is the instrument to achieve salvation. Not only must young women abstain from foods that incite lust but also from every stimulus of their senses "that excites our internal organs, such as unguents, perfumes, conversations and the sight of men."[21] Cleanliness is of utmost importance. A young woman must be neat and spotless. The cleanliness of the body is nothing but the reflection of the cleanliness of the soul. A young lady must never be idle. Vives explains, "One of the principle remedies against love is that Cupid's arrow does not catch us idle and unoccupied."[22] Devotion to their prayers and domestic duties must be the sole occupations of the Christian woman. "What a shameful thing to see a woman not with her basket of wool but at the gaming board, rolling knuckle-bones instead of the spindle, throwing dice instead of spinning the shuttle, dealing out playing cards instead of battening the wool or reading her prayer book."[23]

Interesting are those chapters that Vives devoted to women's "adornment" and in particular their use of cosmetics. For him masquerade and deception guided the woman who hid her true self behind artificial makeover. "It seems to me," Vives declares, "that wishing to attract a man with makeup is the same as trying to do so with a mask. Just as you attracted him in this disguise, so will you drive him away when you are unmasked."[24] Further into the chapter, Vives even justifies his point by comparing the purchase of a slave to the acquisition of a wife. "Who has reached that point of madness that when he is going to buy a slave or a horse he prefers that they be shown to him touched up for sale rather than in their natural state? We do this in the purchase of slaves and beasts of burden; will we not do the same with wives?"[25]

In the last chapter written for unmarried women and entitled "On Seeking a Spouse," Vives clearly describes women as animals by quoting Catalan poet Pere Torroella, who had compared some women to she-wolves. It is for this reason that Vives believed that parents must be entirely responsible for the choice of a spouse for the young lady, since God instituted marriage so that offspring would be holy and pure. Those women who sought men's attentions and favor were of the worst variety. "It cannot be estimated how great part of our youth is corrupted by this type of—shall I call her a woman or a stinking corpse? I cannot even mention such squandering of life without a feeling of disgust. . . . Thus, love for that type of woman is very much like the potions of that famed witch Circe, by which they say she turned men into wild beasts.[26]

Vives's language is rooted in a long Western Christian tradition that coupled female nature with evil. There are several examples of misogynist works in Spanish literature from the Middle Ages to the 1600s. Some include Fray Francesc Eiximenis's (1340–1410) *Llibre de les dones* (*Book on Women*); Alfonso Martínez de Toledo, archpriest of Talavera's *Corvacho, Reprobación del Amor Mundano* (1498); Queen's Isabella's favorite poet Fray Iñigo de Mendoza's *Coplas en Vituperio de las malas hembras* (*Couplets in Vituperation of Evil Women*); and Fernando de Rojas's *Celestina. Tragicomedia de Calisto y Melibea* (1502). Rojas's work was translated into all European languages and reprinted some sixty times, becoming one of the most read and popular texts of the sixteenth century. In all these works, the female body is a symbolic vehicle, a transcoder to convey sin and virtue on both the individual and collective levels in the 1490s, a time of great social and political anxiety, a time in which a female monarch, Queen Isabella, was in power. The fifteenth century saw the proliferation of medical language in the political discourse with the publication of health guides, surgical handbooks, and hygienic manuals to educate the public. It is in the fifteenth century with the birth of the clinic, in Foucauldian terms, that there is a proliferation of writings dealing with corporeality, sexual well-being; an age in which bio-power is born. Michael Solomon addresses the misogynist discourses in early modern Spain in his study of Alfonso Martinez de Toledo's *Arcipreste de Talavera* (1438) and Jaume Roig's *Espill,* o *Libre de les dones* (*Book of the women*), the former a priest, the latter a physician from Valencia.[27] Solomon reminds us of the close connection between misogynist discourses in these texts and medical language.

Misogynist discourses were contested by other voices such as seventeenth-century writer María de Zayas y Sotomayor (1590–1661?). In her novella *The Disenchantments of Love* (1647) we read: "See now ladies the example of women of the past whether you find within you the strength to trust men, even your husbands. You will come to the realization that the man who says he loves you, in reality detests you, the one who praises you, in reality will sell you out, the one that shows more admiration, will disdain you the most, and the one who displays longing for you, in the end will kill you. . . . Death to men!, because we owe less to them than to ourselves."[28] Zayas's zeal to unveil the gendered injustices of her time leads some scholars to identify in her a "conservative feminist."[29] According to Alicia Yllera, Zayas's main goal is to defend women's honor, blaming men for women's sexual misconduct. "What may husband, father, brother, and any suitor expect from a lady who is despised, lacks what she needs, and never received a little respect or praise?—Only misfortune. For God's sake, how trusting men are today; not worried that a woman might do any mischief! They think that just close watch and keeping them under lock is enough to prevent women's misconduct. But they mislead themselves [men]. *Love women, touch them, and give them what they lack. Don't lock them and guard them* [my emphasis]. For [women] will guard and protect themselves, out of virtue not obligation."[30]

María de Zayas acknowledged the sexual needs of women. Those abandoned by their husbands are not guilty of the sin of adultery but rather their husbands are because of their conjugal neglect. Zayas reclaims the female body, turning it into the woman's possession, not their male guardian's. Like Vives, she defends chaste honesty as the most precious virtue but in opposition to him, only when it is guarded out of women's free will, not obligation. What makes Zayas's arguments stronger is the fact the she is a woman herself. According to Marina Brownlee, "In her writing, Zayas is concerned both with new emerging forms of writing, and with the desire to expose the social conditions that produced them." She calls for a return to the idealized gender relations of the Catholic Monarchs' era.[31] That was certainly a golden past of imperial splendor based on a zealous repression of political (meaning religious and cultural) dissent.

Zayesque narrative exemplified fluidity of sex and gender roles in baroque Spain and consequently heightened sociopolitical fear. Through her short stories Zayas discloses the decay of the empire. The topics discussed in her narrative include rape, torture, dismemberment, male and female cross-dressing, lesbian desire, and male homosexuality; all of them topics considered to be inappropriate for a woman to write about.[32] However, as Brownlee points out, the real talent of Zayas is to navigate between sensationalism and exemplary story telling. She moves from the Renaissance exemplary text to the baroque excess.[33]

By the 1700s the debate about the relation between the sexes and the nature of women entered the circles of enlightened thinkers who inaugurated the modern rationalist approach to the war of the sexes. One of the most important figures of the Spanish Enlightenment was Father Benito Jerónimo Feijóo y Montenegro born in 1676 into a noble family in a little hamlet called Casdemiro in Galicia, the northwestern region of Spain. Benito Feijóo entered the Benedictine order when he was fourteen years old and devoted himself to a monastic life of study, becoming a doctor in theology and professor for forty years. Identified by some as the "Spanish Voltaire" due to his revolutionary ideas, Feijóo was a man of reason and skepticism but within the limits of his faith. In 1786, shortly after his death, his writings were translated into different languages. One of the most important works written by Feijóo was the *Teatro Crítico Universal,* an eight-volume opus divided into *Discursos* (treatises) written between 1726 and 1740. In line with the encyclopedic style of the times, the themes in these volumes range from politics, philosophy, and history to literature and theology. Treatise XVI, *Defensa de la Mujer* (In Woman's Defense), of the first volume was published in 1726. His attempt to turn the "woman question" into a scientific discussion represents a novelty for when and where he wrote. Feijóo wrote this rebuttal in favor of women in response to previous male diatribes against them. Referring to Huarte de San Juan's *Examen de ingenios para las ciencias* (1576) proving the mental inferiority of women,[34] Feijóo points out how "many have no problem in calling the female an imperfect animal and even a monstrous one, asserting that nature at the time of generation always intends to create a male, and only by mistake, of matter or ability, a female is produced."[35] He addresses Aristotelian theory of matter and form reelaborated by Saint Thomas Aquinas, who explained the embryonic difference by saying that God insufflated the soul at the fortieth day of gestation in the male embryos and at the eightieth in the female. To these ideas Feijóo responds: "Oh venerable doctor! From this we could infer that nature takes on its own decay—Since the species cannot live without the accord of both sexes. We could also conclude that human nature produces more failures than perfection, since it is certain that there are more women than men."[36] Feijóo clearly indicates how some of the many authors who write about women's inferiority, in fact, are promiscuous in their behavior and in general bears no respect for them. "Scathing against women," he asserts, "many times, if not always, goes hand in hand with a disorderly [sexual] inclination towards them."[37] When Feijóo discusses the theological implications of these physical flaws imposed on women, he refers to the platonic theory of transmigration of women's souls who could not enter heaven directly but only after incarnating into male bodies. "The same physical defects that deem women imperfect animals lead to another theological error, refuted by St. Augustine (lib.22 de *Civitate Dei,* c. 17). To those authors who declare that in the Universal Resurrection women must achieve perfection because they are naturally imperfect, all women will transform into men; so that grace will correct nature's error."[38]

Feijóo clearly states that his intention is not "to plead for advantages" for women but rather "to seek equality" between the sexes. In order to accomplish his goal he addresses the conventional qualities allotted to each sex. According to Feijóo's recollection, male qualities were robustness, perseverance, and prudence, and female qualities beauty, docility, and simplicity. The theologian analyzes them one by one in his attempt to prove their equal social value. "Robustness, which is a body's gift, can be counter-weighted with beauty, equally a physical attribute," he says, but when pondering which one of the two should prevail Feijóo chooses strength over beauty. "Because War, Agriculture, and Mechanics are the three pillars that sustain the Republic; men's strength becomes essential. [However] from women's beauty, I do not know what important product one might obtain, but maybe by accident."[39] For Feijóo strength has an essential impact on reason while beauty reins over will, and hence he considers both qualities equally important for the constitution of human nature but of different value when it comes to consider the good of the Republic. Feijóo counterbalanced men's perseverance and forethought with women's submissiveness and humble character. In the same way as Luis Vives,[40] Feijóo praised women's modesty as their most valuable trait. "Modesty is such a precious trait in [women] that even when they die they do not lose it. Certainly, Plinio points out that the corpses of drowned men float face up while those of women's do face down: *as if nature respected the modesty of dead female bodies.*[41]

Although this statement proves he is a man of his times with regard to the value of women's modesty, Feijóo's defense of women's ability to reason is apparent when discussing their intelligence with regard to men. It is on this point that he uncovered the flaws in the interpretation of those thinkers who despised women's intelligence. Feijóo considered those "superficial men who only see women destined to perform domestic chores and hence infer they cannot do anything else."[42] Women's inability to engage in abstract thinking was not the result of a different intelligence between the sexes but rather, according to Feijóo, the product of different training and application of the sexes. Feijóo also discusses the physical explanations given by those "superficial men" to validate women's low intellect and categorically concludes: "I affirm there is no physical justification."

How these values became ingrained in the Spanish psyche to permeate the gendered imaginary is the focus of this book. Female nature was reinscribed onto the Francoist body politic following the eternal feminine values debated for centuries. Francoism did not invent sexism; it just perfected it to legitimize authoritarian rule in the midst of turmoil after the Spanish civil war, first, and later during the Cold War. It is precisely the gendered overtones of the National Catholic discourse that lends a neo-baroque character to the social and political relations, making them natural. Religion and gender naturalized the authoritarian dictatorship, transforming it into an organic democracy.

The new Francoist Spain, much in the same way as in the baroque period, confronted the angst derived from the postwar reconstruction. As in the apex of the Reconquista, the New Spain dawning in 1939 much needed to establish a clear distinction between the true and eternal Catholic values versus the lay anathema of the Second Republic. Blood had been spilled in a crusade against modern infidels: the Reds. Many bodies had been sacrificed and the nation needed to regenerate itself. In the new Francoist Spain, women's bodies turned into the vessels needed in national reconstruction. Women were given a national purpose; as mothers they would have to devote themselves to their natural task, procreate for the patria, in body and soul. Certainly, domesticity would be the most precious virtue of the new woman under Francoism. This is an interesting approach for the purpose of our study of Francoist official discourse on gender relations. Joaquin Costa, a most significant representative of the *regenaracionismo* in the nineteenth century, will resort to medical language to discuss the political crisis ensuing after 1898; he coined the metaphor of the "Iron Surgeon"—saving the ill body of the motherland.

Modern Times: Angels of the Home

Nineteenth-century nationalist iconography of the nation represented Spain as a mother afflicted by the political conflict infecting Spanish social relations, aggravated by a profound antagonism between the haves and have-nots. Spanish Republican press of the mid-1800s epitomized Spain as a wretched matron. Scholar José Alvarez Junco[43] points to the War of Independence against the Napoleonic invasion (1808–14)[44] as the moment of "invention" of our *madre patria.*[45] Literally meaning mother fatherland, la madre patria conveys a hermaphrodite-like essence of the Spanish nation; mater and pater involved in the unfolding of Spanish destiny.

Inherent to nineteenth-century Spanish republicanism was regional separatism, adding to the problem of an integrated and indivisible organic concept of Spain. For traditionalists there was no room for Republican federalism, regarded as a mutilation of the motherland's body. Moreover, the organic concept of the nation as female represented the motherland as a damsel in distress in need of a manly hero to come to her rescue.

The individual became a scientific object of study to better serve the national body. Heavily rooted in anatomical appraisals were nineteenth-century studies on racial distinctions, sexual deviation, and gender differences.[46] Defining the sexual pervert implied a "normal" sexed being.[47] At a time when some women started to question their restricted place in society, male intellectuals in the medical and biological sciences began to rationalize traditional sex roles as based in anatomy and physiology.[48]

A new pseudoscientific discipline called phrenology studied the configuration of the skull to determine the level of development in individuals. Dr. Franz Joseph Gall (1758–1828) was the pioneer in this area of studies. He presented a report in 1808 to the Institute de France that was later published under the title *Recherches sur le système nerveux en général, et sur celui du cerveau en particulier* (Paris, 1809). Ten years later, Dr. Gall completed his first study with a second work entitled *Anatomie et physiologie du système nerveux* (Paris 1810–19).[49] According to Dr. Gall, women's smaller skull, and according to the German physiologist T. Bischoff, their lighter-weight brain proved female intellectual inferiority when compared to those of men. P. J. Moebus, professor of neuropathology and psychiatry in Leipzig, supported these ideas. In Spain, Carmen de Burgos Seguí translated these works into Spanish in a book called *La inferioridad mental de la mujer* (Valencia, n.d.). "Many female characteristics are very similar to those of the beasts; mainly the lack of a mind of their own. Since the beginning of times they have functions like that, hence the human race would be stagnated in its original state if there were only women."[50]

A commonplace opinion about women in the nineteenth century was that due to their fragile nature they were ill most of their lives. The source of these physical dysfunctions resided in women's sexual organs that drove them mentally, physically, and morally. While men were driven by their brain, women were slaves of their uterus. A. Jimeno wrote along these lines in 1882:

> There exists in women a center of sensibility that constitutes undoubtedly the base for their physical and moral character—their sexual organs.
>
> The power of that apparatus is magnificent, always sensitive and always excitable. It is there where all the fancies live, from the most

exquisite and delicate to those ridiculous and extravagant; it is there where their inclinations exist; it is there where the attributes of the fair sex become alive; it presides over all of her functions.[51]

Women were regarded as fragile creatures, captives of their internal organs and suffering from periodic sickness with menstruation, pregnancy, and menopause.[52] The belief was that such physical obstacles were precisely what made it impossible for women to enter the public male sphere. If women were allowed to go beyond their natural duties, as feminists of the time proposed, the traditionalists feared the human race was in danger of extinction. In an editorial entitled "Las mujeres y el darwinismo" published in the journal *España Moderna* in 1895, the author Pero Pérez translated an article by R. Kossman predicting the deterioration of the human species beyond repair. "If we agree with Darwinian principles . . . we cannot deny that changes in politics and economic life derived from the erasure of men's and women's roles will have repercussions on the systems of both."[53]

In the late 1860s Spanish medical journal *Siglo Médico* published some articles by J. M. Otero in which the author discussed the differences between the sexes on the basis of biological distinctions. For Otero social and natural orders must be not only in sync but also scientifically demonstrable. In his article "Brief Considerations about the Physiological Differences between Woman and Man" ("Breves consideraciones fisiológicas diferenciales entre la mujer y el hombre") Otero explained: "Notice that in general women are shorter than men; they are not as vigorous physically or intellectually. Woman's figure is rounder and better finished . . . Women do not have beards, which gives them a special and youthful charm, their voice is full of harmony and enchantment, their walk coordinated, their moves languid and graceful; everything has been done for her to seduce, to please, to console, never to rule."[54] Women's biological destiny was motherhood and their means to achieve it seduction. They were creatures trapped in their bodies' defective functioning. Spanish physicians followed their European colleagues' lead: all women's pathologies, whether physical or psychological, were rooted in the uterus. Otero's Freudian appraisal prevailed from the end of the 1800s on: "The kind of action that the uterus plays in women's constitution is at least as essential, as the one the nervous system operates since both seem to be closely connected."[55]

The biological determinism impregnating the medical discourse made it almost logical to exclude women from any kind of physical or intellectual work. Those from the popular classes did not fit into this description. At the turn of the twentieth century illiteracy was rampant among the popular classes, reaching 70 percent among women. As early as the 1840s, liberal thinkers of the Institución Libre de Enseñanza (Free Institution of Learning), were firm believers that education was the key to modernization and achieving equal footing with Europe. As part of the discussion of who had the right to be educated, the "woman question" remained central. Did women deserve an education? And if so, what kind of education and for what purpose? The whole idea of educating a human being considered by most as inferior intellectually and ruled by her uterus both physiologically and emotionally at the end of the 1800s had, no doubt, a strong bearing on these considerations. Universal access to education meant democratization, an effort to minimize the gap between the haves and have-nots and for the first time incorporated the woman question into the debate in the pedagogical conferences celebrated in Spain in 1882 and 1892. Coeducation and the right of women to practice a profession were recognized at this point.

Although 91 percent of the female population was still illiterate in 1870, there were a number of well-educated women who became successful writers and defended the rights of women to earn an education along with men and practice a profession. Some of those women were Cecilia Böhl de Faber, Concepción Arenal, and Rosalía de Castro.

Concepción Arenal (1820–93) (who had attended law school disguised as a man in the early 1840s) was a self-taught social reformer, and certainly considered as one of the founding mothers of Spanish feminism in the nineteenth century. She worked to make the penitentiary system a place where the inmates were reformed rather than punished. As an expert in penal law she followed the thoughts of reformer Pedro Dorado Montero. She authored several books including *Beneficence, Philanthropy, and Charity* (*Beneficencia, filantropía y caridad,* 1861), *Penitentiary Studies* (*Estudios penitenciarios,* 1877), and *The Woman of the Future* (*La mujer del porvenir* (1884). She died in Vigo in 1893.

The Woman of the Future is a short but profound feminist statement. Particularly interesting here is to examine her response to Dr. Gall's studies on the inferiority of women based on his studies on brain weight and size differences between men and women. Arenal points out how Dr. Gall identified the frontal occipital diameter, larger in women because, he said, this is the physiological site of love for her children. However, the rest of her skull is smaller than man's; to this statement Arenal answered in the following terms: "If it were necessary the equality of [skull's] volume to perform with equal power, the inferiority of women would be in all areas. Her senses would be clumsier, and in accordance to Gall's capacity categorization, her circumspection would be inferior as would be her sense of location, her love for property, her sense of justice, her disposition for the arts etc . . . But nothing like this transpires: Women in most abilities are equal to men and their intellectual differences begin where their different education starts. Indeed their teachers soon realize the difference between boys' and girls' talent, and if there is any it is in favor of girls, who are more docile and in general more precocious."[56]

The other major feminist in nineteenth-century Spain, Emilia Pardo Bazán (1852–1921), advocated in public forums for the right of women to receive instruction. Pardo Bazán wrote several novels of great success and is considered the leading figure of naturalism in Spain along with Leopoldo Alas Clarín. One of the ways in which she expressed her feminist ideas was through newspaper articles and essays. Some of these were published in English in the London periodical *Fortnightly Review* and in Spain in the magazine *Nuevo Teatro Crítico.* For Pardo Bazán, married and a mother of three children, it was a mistake to reduce women's destiny to the reproductive function. She ended by separating from her husband and having a romantic and intellectual partnership with Benito Pérez Galdós, the great Spanish figure of literary Realism.

Like Arenal, Pardo Bazán emphasized the need to educate women to be able to break out of the straitjacket they were put in—marriage and motherhood. Educating Spanish women would lead to a betterment of society and Spain in general according to Pardo Bazán. But illiteracy remained extremely high among the Spanish lower class and particularly among women in the first three decades of the twentieth century. The proclamation of the Second Republic on April 14, 1931, signaled the serious commitment on the part of the intellectual elites to accomplish true social equality by educating the masses. The campaign on literacy to educate women led by the Republican government had some good results. Ultra-Catholic conservative thought was deeply anti-intellectual in general and when it came to women the combination of intellect/femininity was anathema.

The cornerstone of the new constitution of 1931 was to proclaim the separation of Church and state and the implementation henceforth of legislation inspired by lay democratic values rather than Catholic obscurantism. Certainly, women's lives had been defined around the religious and scientific given of female modesty and biological determinism. Women were expected to follow their Christian destiny by becoming good wives and mothers. As socialist feminist Margarita Nelken pointed out in her work *Mujer y sociedad* (1921), university women were for the most part a rara avis in Spanish society.

A number of Spanish intellectuals, physicians, and philosophers in the 1920s and 1930s embarked on the definition of the female body as a way to reach an understanding of women's nature and their role in politics and society. The shift from religious to pseudoscientific explanations of women's nature occupies a central place in the discourse of modernity. Philosophers such as José Ortega y Gasset and physicians such as Gregorio Marañón engage the discussion of female nature from a rational rather than moral or religious approach. The Second Republic (1931–39) granted the vote to women under the progressive constitution of 1931 that declared the separation of Church and state. Many traditional interests were overturned. Monarchists, Catholics, army, business, and latifundia owners were deeply dissatisfied. Women's suffrage was discussed in parliament under the rubric of democratic equality. True democracy could only be possible with the implementation of universal suffrage. During the first three decades of the twentieth century, the feminist movement was still weak in Spain. Lawyer and MP Clara Campoamor (1888–1972), as a member of the Republican Radical Party, was the only politician who truly believed in the importance of universal suffrage. In 1935 she published her political memoirs, *Mi Pecado Mortal. El Voto Femenino y Yo,* a reflection on her role as the key figure in the struggle to include women's suffrage in the constitution of 1931. Her determination led to her subsequent political ostracism and exclusion from the list of representatives in the elections of 1936. Even the left was against female suffrage. They worried about the right taking advantage of an inexperienced electorate. This fear was seemingly confirmed in 1933 when the right-wing coalition CEDA won the elections that inaugurated the so-called Black Biennium (Bienio Negro). But the Popular Front victory in the elections of 1936 did not lead to praising the female electorate. The only Republican reform that survived the civil war was universal suffrage.[57]

Philosophers and intellectuals elevated to worship the inferiority of the so-called fair sex. The left perceived the notion of handing women the power to vote as a threat. A majority of working-class women in the 1930s were illiterate. The women of the middle and upper classes were under the control of their husbands, fathers, or spiritual counselors. Spanish women as a whole lacked political experience. Participation in public issues was, for a few working-class women, through trade unions and through Church charities and associations and clubs created by middle-class women. Science came to the aid of traditional Catholicism to reinforce gender hierarchy. Luis López Ballesteros translated Freud's works into Spanish between 1922 and 1934.

Margarita Nelken, however, saw the ability to partake in the urban landscape at the turn of the twentieth century as a greater emancipation for the middle-class woman. Only by conquering the city streets, the boulevards, cafés, cinemas, and clubs would women gain access to higher education or paid employment as well. Physical exercise and hygiene dominated the intellectual minds of the 1920s and in this context Nelken wrote: "The symbol for us [middle-class women] resides in that footing [*sic*], that morning walk, elastic step, rhythmic body covered by a loose outfit of our young women who these warm early spring days come out for hygienic reasons."[58] The incursion of women into the urban landscape is loaded with behavioral codes on how to manifest respectable femininity that end up welcoming the female body as display and adornment rather than co-actor with men in the making of the public sphere. Elizabeth Munson points out: "[s]implistically, the nineteenth-century liberal rights of individuals were transformed for women into the right to consume and the choice to wear whatever one pleased. Consumerism itself was a politicized activity because it evolved into a key element in the identity of female citizenship."[59] This is crucial to understanding how, in the transition from autarky to consumerism in 1950s and 1960s, the Francoist regime had to turn reproducer mothers into consumers. The advertising in magazines and the avalanche of Hollywood movies established the display of the female body. After Franco's death the rights of female citizens in the immediate post-Franco era turn into the right to be consumers and the right to take off their clothes.

José Ortega y Gasset's *Estudios sobre el amor* (sixteenth edition) was published in 1966. One of the most important Spanish philosophers at the beginning of the twentieth century, Ortega first wrote on this topic in German, and the first Spanish translation came out in 1940. As in Plato's *Symposium*, it is through the discussion of love that human nature, and the female body in particular, comes under Ortega's consideration. For half a century his ideas about female identity and morphology were prevalent, being, as they were, cloaked with a pseudoscientific veneer. With *Estudios sobre el amor* he embraced Western philosophical tradition on womanhood. For Ortega, "woman was first of all for man a prey—a body that can be seized."[60] He passionately explained his position on the historical "biological mission" not of the mother, wife, sister, or daughter, but of what he calls the "human female" ("hembra humana"). For Ortega, it is women's biological being and their ability to excite men that is the force in history, for "if the woman does not seduce the man he will not choose her."[61] For Ortega, women's right to vote or to gain an academic degree is not the way to help them influence history. "*There is no other force in human condition stronger than the biological force that women possess which is to attract men with accuracy and efficiency* [my emphasis]. Nature has made this the most powerful means of selection and a sublime force to modify and perfect the species."[62] For Ortega y Gasset, while men's worth is the product of their actions, women's worth is based in their inner essence, their "being." It was precisely their female essence not their actions that attracted men. Hence, females' role in history resides, according to Ortega, in their passive existence. "Everything women do," declares Ortega, "they do it without doing it, simply by being there: glowing."[63] He sees women's value to come not just from their roles as mothers, wives, sisters, or daughters, but rather from their spiritual essence, inseparable from their biological being. For the Spanish philosopher the living body is not just matter but rather the incarnation of the soul. "[The body] is flesh, and flesh is sensibility, expression. [Her] hands, cheeks, full-lips always convey something; they are essentially sign, spirit's shell, revelation of what we call psyche. Corporeality is holy because of its transcendental mission: personify the spirit."[64]

Ortega's dictum about women's historical purpose not only highlights their biological destiny but shows the philosopher's belief in women's somatic historicity. Moreover, by emphasizing women's purpose to attract men and hence incite them to action, Ortega points very clearly to the heterosexual imperative as essential historical force and woman's maternal role as unavoidable.

In order to understand from a scientific point of view the relation of the sexes, physicians like Roberto Nóvoa Santos (1885–1933) or Gregorio Marañón (1887–1960) wrote in the 1930s about transsexuality, bisexuality, and heterosexuality. In doing so they embarked upon the definition of normalcy versus deviation (what in religious discourse would be good versus evil). In his essay on the biological position of women entitled *La mujer, nuestro sexto sentido y otros esbozos* (1928) Nóvoa Santos declared how those women who were exceptionally intelligent and original did not represent the female archetype. They were a "monstrosity" he said, with secondary male sexual characteristics.[65] He defined these individuals as biopathological types suffering a somatic or spiritual inversion.

The publication of a new edition of Gregorio Marañón's complete works in the late 1960s revived his 1920s and 1930s work on sexuality and women's nature. Marañón had returned to Spain in 1942 after a brief exile in Paris escaping the horrors of the Spanish Civil War, and developed a successful career under the dictatorship of Franco. In 1958 in the midst of the university crisis initiated two years earlier, Marañón was appointed president of the newly inaugurated Spanish Center for Biological Research.

In "Educación sexual y diferenciación social" ("Sexual education and social distinction") Gregorio Marañón reminded us of Aristophanes' speech in Plato's *Symposium* to explain what he called the "relativity of sex": "It is well known, that for him [Aristophanes] in the beginning men were two halves and three categories: some male from the sun, some females from the earth, and some androgynous, half male/half female from the moon. Jupiter, to punish their insolence, divided them into two halves as an egg—says Plato—cut by a thread; and since then, each half seek its opposite, its other half, 'its half orange' as we Spaniards say. And this is love. The halves of mixed men are the *normal* (my emphasis) men of today."[66] Marañón explained how "double men" or "double women" "attained great expansion in Plato's times" and the natural love was not heterosexual but homosexual. Nonetheless, Marañón considered this a monstrous aberration of nature. In tune with the Christian heterosexual imperative notion, he explained that "just because an aberrant form of love is biologically possible does not mean it is normal."[67] Marañón believed "the fruits of sexual sins grew in every climate," but also asserted that each climate produced different kinds. For him the Spanish case presented both advantages and disadvantages. However, he concluded "passions and anomalies are here [Spain] developed with much more simplicity" and there were three reasons for this. First of all, a deeply felt and widely spread Catholicism and moral Catholic values among Spaniards; second, the influence of Muslim ideas about the home and women's place in it; and third, Spanish temperament very much in tune with those other people of our *same race and climate.* For Marañón: "To construct their moral values Spaniards have combined principles from Catholicism and Islam: Spanish women must stay at home, like Islam prescribes, but alone and for ever, as the Christians see it; and Spanish men, polygamous like Muslims, but always outside the home. With such freedom, that particularly in those cities and villages in Southern Spain, every man walking freely on the street is entitled, and almost obliged, to gawk and remark on every woman's physique that he encounters. And he does this boldly and with no reproof. Therefore, we must concur that the result of this hybrid Muslim-Christian morality has favored females very little."[68] The immanence of historical and cultural determinism explained the moral double standard Spanish women had to endure. In Marañón's estimation, it is this hybridism in Spanish mores that leads to the development of what he calls male "donjuanismo" as intrinsic to Spanish heterosexism.

Gregorio Marañón studied sexuality from a clinical perspective and explored not only the heterosexual relations but expressed openly his interest in the different symptoms both psychological and somatic of what he called intersexuality. "There is a human morphological state known as hermaphrodite in whom both anatomical sexual traits appear combined: masculine and feminine. There is also a psychological state, homosexuality, in which the complete inversion of *normal sexual behavior exists*" (my emphasis).[69]

For Marañón the sexual inversion was more common among women than men. For males, adolescence represented the "critical" stage of intersexuality as they developed into *manly men;* but for women the intersexual quest began with puberty and became more prevalent as they grew older, being almost exclusively a woman's problem by the time they reached menopause. "Almost all female existence is a slow puberty dominated by crisis," Marañón declares. Only the onset of menstruation represents a significant step in women's maturity because it signals what he called "their primary sexual function" not other than motherhood. Women remain sexually apt until their midfifties and then the slow decay of menopause is unleashed. Marañón described the physician as the new machinist of the human engine[70] —an expert who had also the moral authority and responsibility to guide the uneducated public.

The "normal" female body was the foundation for the psychological and social definitions of woman-as-mother in the writings of these physicians. It was precisely this maternal body that remained the focal point defining Spanish women's national liabilities under Francoism. Furthermore, this maternal body had to remain chaste after marriage. Women's adultery became more than a sin and was severely punished by the Francoist state. The wife's body was the repository of male honor, and its surveillance guaranteed the legitimacy of the offspring. But this was about to change with the advent of consumerism and the arrival of tourists by the millions. A new female identity emerged in the late 1950s and fully developed in the 1960s.

The Many "New Women" of Spain

Women's bodies continued to be the site of contention as the regime was welcomed into the Western orbit with the United States' help. Like in the early modern period, piety, circumspection, order, and hygiene composed the essence of the Catholic ideal woman in the 1950s and 1960s.[71] The last two decades of Franco's regime gave birth to contested discourses on women's bodies and their social role in a growing economy in need of skilled labor. In order to confront the changing social reality, the state approved the reform of the civil code in 1958. This reform was intended to amend the legal status of women, ruled since 1938 by the civil code of 1889. The regime implemented further reforms with the sponsorship of the Women's Section of Falange that led to the *Law of Political and Professional Rights for Women* passed in July 1961.[72] However, women's identity in the transition from autarky to consumerism was to remain faithful to the Christian script duality virgin/whore. This binary was further complicated with the sharp class inequalities that the regime continued to perpetuate. In her novel *The Backroom* (*El cuarto de atrás*) published in 1978 Carmen Martín Gaite resorts to the oneiric style to unfold the polarized womanhood imposed in Francoist society:

> In the anaesthetized postwar world, between servings of that compote of words and music—carefully cooked up and dished out by the composers of boleros and the comrades of the Women's Section—to lull engaged couples being herded toward a marriage without problems, to

> shore up beliefs and bring beatific smiles to people's lips, a dark wind came up sometimes unexpectedly, in the voice of Concha Piquer, in the stories her songs told. *Stories of girls who were not at all like the ones we knew who were never to enjoy the tender affection of the peaceable home and fireside that set us respectable young ladies to dreaming—girls drifting on the fringes of society, unprotected by the law. These women had no first or last names. They filed past with no identity, involved in conflicts stemming from their not having one, aggressively raising their nicknames as a shield to protect themselves: Lily, Gypsy, Nightingale, the Fifty Thousand Peseta Girl. They had provocative and defenseless bodies, and as the finishing touch, beautiful faces with dark circles under the eyes.*[73] [my emphasis]

The folk songs in the voice of iconic *copla*'s singer Concha Piquer (1908–90) provided afternoon-snack entertainment to middle-class Señoritas, who like Gaite's, for a brief moment took a glimpse into their counterparts' lives: "In these stories of Conchita's [Piquer] the light of the moon shown on the betrayals, stabbings, cheap kisses, tears of rage and fear. A rhetoric that today is trite and stale, but that in those days was meant to serve the revulsive, as an undermining of the foundations of happiness that the propagandists of hope endeavor to reinforce. Those women who staggered through life and did not bid their intended goodnight at their front door at 9:30 on the dot made people uneasy, because they hinted at the existence of a world where fidelity and eternal values had not won the day. They were the rubble left by the war. . . . A passion such as that was forbidden us sensible, decent young ladies of the New Spain."[74] During the postwar and well into the 1960s the only respectable option for a young woman other than marriage was to enter a convent. Becoming a nun was a source of pride for the family. Lucia Graves remembers in *A Woman Unknown* how celebrated such an occasion was in their local milkman's daughter's decision to become a nun in the mid 1950s, not only because of the pious connotations and high social regard but because it represented "the only free decision a woman could take": "When the girl in the dairy shop opposite our flat in Palma decided to become a nun, she stopped pouring milk into the tin cans at the counter and retired to the back of the shop for a while, to avoid contact with the outside world, until her novitiate began. . . . She had become an almost supernatural creature, an untouchable person whom one could not criticize for giving up her duty for the Spanish nation (which was to become a submissive wife and a devoted mother of as many children as God would send her) because she had retired from this world to marry God and wear His wedding ring."[75] Nuns had a very important role in the social services to the state. They became prisons' wardens, teachers, and nurses along with their lay counterparts, the members of the Women's Section of Falange. Their work fitted in the symbiotic union between Church and state during Francoism. They were instrumental in shaping the identity of the official True Catholic Womanhood with the implementation of the 1950s new National Catholic high school curriculum. The new curriculum designed to develop national spirit in middle-class girls included lessons and activities related to domestic chores and social etiquette. The lessons required more hours than those for male students. According to the new curriculum prescribed by the Law of Secondary Education of 1953, the study of domestic matters was essential to women's proper training as part of their patriotic duty to the fatherland. Girls' instruction included a synthesis of the political indoctrination, physical education, and home economics (enseñanzas del hogar). The program for the first three grades cultivated the female national spirit by training girls in family and social norms, physical education, sewing, and music. The fourth, fifth, and sixth grades added to these subjects a program of cooking, home economics, and infant care.[76] Lucia Graves remembers reading with her school friend Francisca the text in their history book entitled *The Holy Land of Spain: An Exaltation of our National History:* "'The National Crusade saved our Homeland from the wicked enemy' and 'Generalissimo Franco is Head of the Spanish State and Head of Falange. He achieved the sacred unification of our Catholic Fatherland.'"[77]

The history teacher, Señorita Mercedes, belonged to the Women's Section and was also in charge of imparting physical education. Twice a week the girls would wear their gymnastics uniforms—white shirts and dark blue bloomers: "the movements had to convey a military precision: arms up and open, legs apart, one two, open, close, open, close! But we also had to smile, to project the inner joy of living in Franco's Peace."[78] In Lucia's eyes, Francisca was perfect. She had the smoothest olive skin she had ever seen, dark eyes, and black wavy hair. Already a little bride to be wearing like most girls of her age at the time a gold ring with one of her milk teeth mounted as a pearl, which complemented her pearl earrings, and a gold chain with a crucifix around her delicate neck. Lucía Graves explains: "Francisca was the epitome of the middle-class girl of the fifties, the product clearly aimed at by our textbooks and the Spanish educational system of the time: she was tidy, obedient, helpful, deeply religious and in due course would no doubt be willing to fit into the domestic role into which all Spanish girls were destined, that of marrying, slavishly looking after their husbands, having as many children as God would send them, and bringing them up to be patriotic (right-wing) [*sic*] and religious (Catholic) [*sic*]."[79]

Women's visible contribution to the national endeavor resided in their building harmonious homes. To this end, the curriculum contained several lessons devoted to "order" in the first, second, and third grades that referred to the arrangement and tidiness of both the household (the bathroom, the living room, or the kitchen), and the immediate physical environment of the student in the classroom: her desk, her books, her notes. Order was understood as harmony, balance, and softness, circumscribed within the private sphere. Because the family reflected Francoist society as a whole, order within the family in the physical aspect represented a metaphor for the political order the regime aspired to impose.[80] A few lessons were dedicated to silence as a virtue, discussing when it was appropriate to talk in different social settings (at the dinner table, in the classroom), and posing several questions for study, such as: Is laughter good? When could a lady sneeze? What is the importance of overcoming pain? What should a lady never touch? What would people think of a cheeky girl?[81]

An entire lesson was dedicated to the ways in which girls should correct their "bad character" and arrogance.[82] With these lessons Spanish women learned the most important feminine virtues: being kind, submissive, tidy, clean, and quiet. The fact that all these issues were included in the curriculum the government enacted for the formation of the national spirit of female students in the 1950s clearly evidenced the state desire to perpetuate True Catholic Womanhood, under consumerism as much as under autarky.

Implicit in all the tasks, teachings, and sermons of the Women's Section of the Falange, Carmen Martin Gaite's character remembers in *The Backroom,* was the fear of remaining a spinster. The postwar rhetoric spouted in Falangists' discourse was aimed at discrediting any kind of feminist tendencies from the Second Republic and emphasizing the self-sacrificing silent heroism of marriage and motherhood. "All the harangues that our instructors and female comrades subjected us to in those inhospitable buildings, reminiscent at once of airplane hangars and popular movie houses, where I grudgingly did my Social Service, sewing hems, doing gymnastics, and playing basketball, all turned around to have the same aim: to get us to accept, with pride and joy, with a steadfastness that nothing could discourage . . . our status as strong women."[83] Lucía Graves remembers her father saying, "The Patriarchal social system is behind all our problems" as he chopped vegetables in their Majorcan kitchen.[84] Following on the tradition of Romantic travelers, Robert Graves had fallen in love with Spain in 1929 and established permanent residence in Majorca in 1946. Like Graves, Gerald Brenan and African-American writer Richard Wright lived in and visited Spain as tourists and observed how Francoism perpetuated a highly gendered society rooted in Catholic ancestral traditions during the 1950s and 1960s. They represent good examples of the outsider's gaze on the Spanish process of modernization in general and the resulting remapping of gender relations.

In his visit to the Sanctuary of Montserrat outside of Barcelona, Richard Wright resorted to Freudian metaphors to describe the topography. The description afforded by Wright not only described the physical landscape but the cultural topography of Spain in the early 1950s when the regime went into the conversion from autarky to consumerism. Gender relations were dominated by Catholic beliefs, which propped up the regime into the 1970s. The women of Spain were to fit the schizophrenic polarity of virgin/whore. The patriarchal symbolism is evident in Wright's description of the Virgin of Montserrat: "Bathed in an effulgence of indirect golden light was a wooden image of a woman seated upon a throne of gold. The right and left sides of the statue were bounded by two phallic-looking uprights with oblong, smooth, extended heads. The statue was about three feet high, gracefully carved, black of face, and held within its plastic ensemble a kind of quite, expectant tension. The facial features seemed a blend of the Roman and the Oriental; the nose was aquiline. Seated upon the woman's lap and seeming to gaze in the same direction that the woman was gazing, was a baby whose features resembled those of the woman. The infant possessed that same attitude of quiet, tense expectancy."[85] This description encapsulates the patriarchal order of things; motherhood enshrined and guarded by the phallic order. Moreover the fact that the Virgin of Montserrat is black and has hybrid features of Roman and Oriental background makes a clear reference to the place of Spain in the margins of European psyche as the bridge between Europe and Africa; Western Christian values and Orientalism. As we will see in the following chapters, the social polarization encouraged by National Catholicism affected class, gender, and regional lines. The polarization between the victorious versus the vanquished after the civil war permeated other realms: the good versus the bad women; the rich versus the poor; the industrious regions like Catalonia or the Basque countries versus the exotic ludic South dominated by passion and poverty. These sharp contrasts with the rest of Europe became so palpable and vivid in Wright's narrative. "No neat, simple dialectical diagnosis of class relations could clarify the reality that had flooded upon me," he remarked. "Frankly, I had not been prepared for what I had encountered. . . . Spain was baffling; it looked and seemed Western, but did not act or feel Western."[86] Richard Wright described Spain as a "holy nation, a sacred state." "All was religion in Spain" he remarked, but in his analysis the boundaries of Spanish religiosity went beyond the Church. "Spain was not yet even Christian." Wright came to the conclusion that "somehow the pagan streams of influence flowing from the Goths, the Greeks, the Jews, the Romans, the Iberians, and the Moors lingered strongly and vitally on, flourishing under the draperies of the twentieth century. An early and victorious Catholicism, itself burdened with deep traits of paganism that it had sought vainly to digest, had here in Spain been sucked into the maw of a paganism buried deep in the hearts of the people. *And the nature and function of Catholicism had enabled that paganism to remain intact. And today Spanish Catholicism boasted that it was the most perfect and purest Catholicism in all the world* [my emphasis]."[87] Wright rejected the metaphysical assumptions of the Catholic Church in Spain endorsed by the Francoist regime because he rejected what he called "surrealistic" condition of the people of Spain as the normal lot of man, and that for him was inconceivable in a modern Western world. So in the final analysis Spain was not Western; it was exoticized and eroticized. Francoism was well prepared to play this trump card in the transition to consumerism. National Catholicism was the card to play. Again religious trappings saved the day with Opus Dei as the new leadership in government to guide the economic development plans inaugurated with American dollars. The Ministry of Information Tourism and Propaganda under Manuel Fraga Iribarne coined the most famous slogan to attract visitors "Spain is Different." And this promise brought millions of outsiders. Spain was also much cheaper to visit than any other European country.

The tourist industry had grown immensely since Richard Wright's visit in the early fifties. In March of 1965 *National Geographic* published a special report entitled "The Changing Face of Old Spain." The writer Bart McDowell, accompanied by his wife and the magazine photographer Albert Moldvay, introduced the American audience to the most stereotypical image of Spain, one in tune with the regime's new tourist slogan, "Spain is Different," coined by the Ministry of Information and Tourism led by Manuel Fraga Iribarne. The magazine's cover (fig. 2) shows a woman dressed in flamenco attire frozen in a dance pose—her leg thrown back in the air almost touching her head. The image of Spain epitomized in this woman's contortion emulates the regime's political warps as well. McDowell informed his readers how in 1965 Spain expected 15 million visitors, equal to half of the population of the country at the time.[88] The photographs that illustrate the text are of good quality for the period. One of the pictures exemplifying the booming tourist industry shows three Swedish women tourists wearing bikinis on the beach. Spanish women and especially men were drawn to the seaside spectacle of free-flowing bodies[89] in an environment in which, as in the case of the body politic, gender relations were couched in aphorisms that appealed to the sanctity of men's and women's bodies destined to procreate for the nation.

The exotic subtext in the *National Geographic* story was based on a long tradition of Romantics' eyewitness tales of a seductive Spain. From Washington Irving's *Tales of the Alhambra* (1851) to Prosper Mérimée's novella *Carmen* (1845), which became widely popularized by his fellow countryman Georges Bizet's operatic version in 1875 the female stereotype into twentieth-century European/Western psyche was prolonged.

The new generation of Spaniards raised in the 1950s welcomed the masses of tourists who provided them with the opportunity to learn as much about these strangers as about themselves. "I saw the beaches fill with pale human flesh during the day," remembers Lucía Graves of the time she lived in Majorca, "until there was not a square inch on which to sit. . . . I saw where I lived was taken over by the tourists."[90] The main square became the center where all the tourists gravitated at night while the Spanish families retired to their homes where they would sit at night at the front of the houses and talk with the neighbors. Young foreigners—Scandinavian, British, or German—outnumbered the Spanish people in the main plaza at night in the summer tourist towns. Spanish girls were not allowed out after a

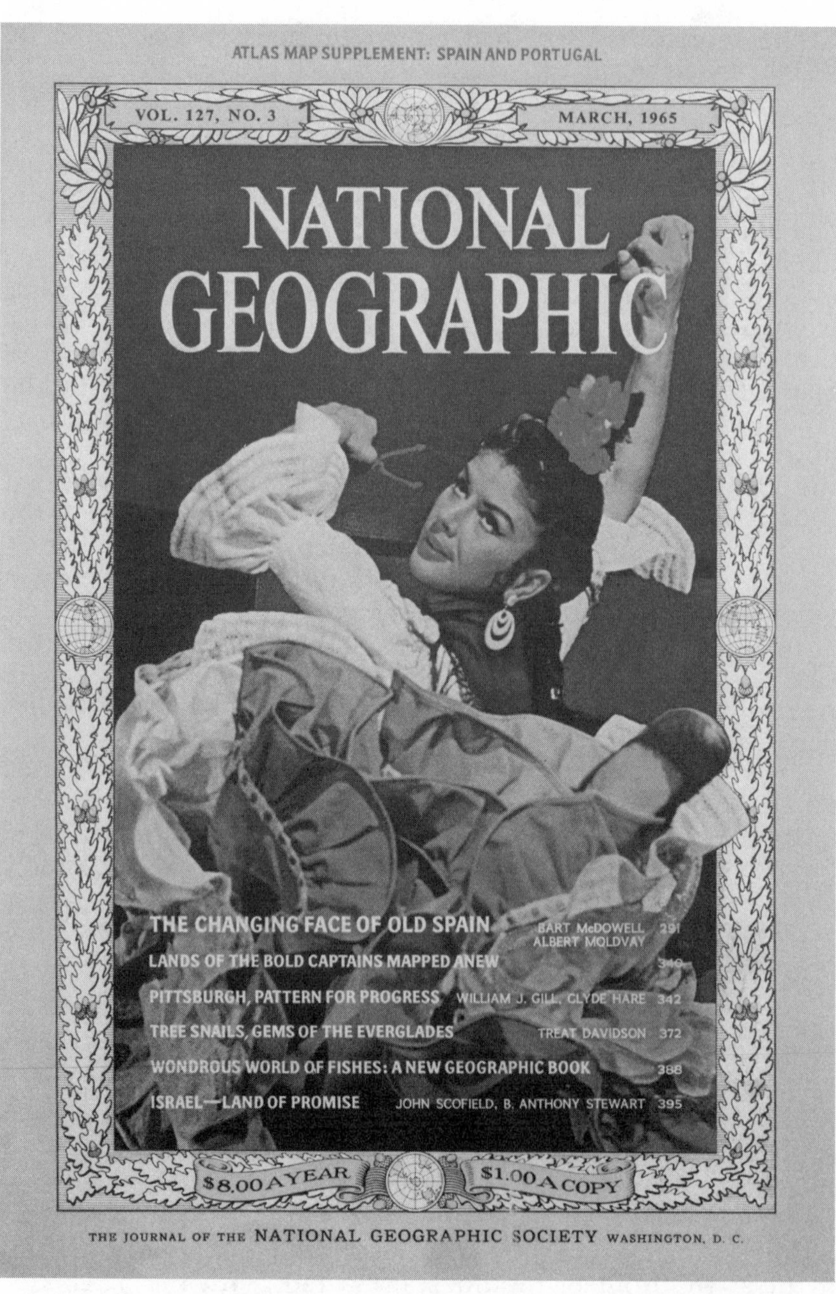

Figure 2. Cover of *National Geographic,* March 1965. Courtesy of *National Geographic.*

certain hour. Their boyfriends would take them home and then they would go back to meet a foreign girl to party and possibly have sex. "The large majority of Spanish girls had been brought up to guard themselves against any sexual advances of their *novios* before marriage. They had been taught that *la decencia* was the most important asset in a woman. . . . It had to be projected in their physical appearance, their social behavior, their gestures, their language, and a tight control over their sexuality."[91] When liberated foreign girls arrived, Spanish men viewed this as a more attractive option than the old-fashioned brothel initiation. The Spanish girl conscious of her boyfriend's sexual encounters with these foreign women, all called *suecas,* did not consider them like the prostitutes. They had names and might even fall in love with their men. Some indeed married them. "While Toni was making love to the Swedish girl in her hotel room, his *novia,* would be remembering how he had looked at her that morning . . . saying so much without speaking, without touching her, and she too would feel desire for him."[92]

After the war Francisco Franco declared his social and political goals to journalist Manuel Aznar. The caudillo expected Spanish people to realize one of their new patriotic tasks—that of attaining a population of forty million Spaniards.[93] Women's national duty at this juncture was to produce as many children as possible for the fatherland. The female political persona was defined by biological destiny: motherhood. By enforcing pro-family policies, the state aspired to control the population. Bodies turned into power-exchange tokens under the totalitarian economy. Bodies were tantamount to state political control. Catholic conservative values informed the regime's public morality enforced upon Spaniards through official censorship, imprisonment, repression, and torture.

The consumerist economy that Spain gradually adopted in the 1950s and 1960s opened the way to the new modern Western woman, a sexualized consumer, leaving behind the official ideal of "True Catholic Womanhood."[94] At the end of Franco's rule, Spain had done much to ready itself for integration back into the whole of Europe. The 1950s and 1960s represent an in-between moment in which cultural inscriptions of femininity—what Catholic womanhood had meant up until then—suffered a transformation that can be traced in women's bodies. Women's bodies therefore are not only physical organisms but rather the loci of historical meaning.

In exploring the Francoist bio-power it is important to look at the relation between women's bodies and the state.[95] Francoist mystic body politic discussed in chapter 1 squarely falls into the Foucauldian category of pastoral power. Foucault examines *politics* applying the idea of the pastor-sovereign, a king, or judge-shepherd of the human flock. Franco the savior is the shepherd whose power is guided by four preestablished objectives: providing sustenance, watching over them on a daily basis, ensuring their salvation, and investing in the control of the individual behavior for the common good.[96] This is the kind of power introduced in the West by Christianity that took the ecclesiastical form of pastorate. This is the kind of power described in the mystic body of Christ (the Church) and emulated by the Francoist body politic. The formation of such "governmentality," Foucault reminds us, took shape in the sixteenth and seventeenth centuries, the baroque period that Maravall described as a historical structure in itself. For gender relations, as we will see in the following chapters, meant the establishment of national duties that defined femininity within the boundaries of marriage and motherhood. Through the fulfillment of these duties women partook in the creation of organic democracy. But there were multiple conceptual contradictions born out of the economic takeoff. The women of Spain were too many to fit into the straitjacket of the official True Catholic Womanhood.

Richard Wright devoted a short and poignant chapter to Spanish women's nature that encapsulates the multiple paradoxes posed by Spain to the outsider's eye. Wright believed Spanish men had built a state, but the pillar of society in Spain was "in the hearts and minds and habits and love and devotion of its women." The anchor being their maternal instinct,

> they are lithe-limbed women who whirl and clack their castanets and stomp their heels and make of an otherwise dull nation an exciting and human spectacle; women who plow the fields; who wash clothes in country streams; who drive the oxen-drawn carts; who satisfy their men and nurse their babies; and who, at the beginning and at the end of the day, creep forward and kneel humbly before the weeping Virgins in the dim and drafty cathedrals; *long-suffering and enduring women* who follow their hot-eyed men into war and peace when they understand nothing of the causes of war and peace; *desperately practical women who sleep with strange men* for food while their babies coo or cry in nearby cribs; *undernourished skinny women* who flee the chill of their concrete houses to sit on curbstones and mend tattered clothing in the sun's wan light; *despairing women* who send

lunch boxes to their daughters who work in the warehouses; *old lonely women* who weep at the memory of their sons and daughters who have gone off to seek their destinies in the cold, strange world; *silly women who sleep half of the day and pay their maids five dollars a month and who primp themselves long and lovingly before their mirrors so that they can walk arm in arm with five other women down the Ramblas* and not impair their respectability; *Lesbian women* living their quiet secluded lives within the shadows of cathedrals where they go to confess and make their atonements; *blind women* who sit on street corners in rain or sun and sell lottery tickets; *bold-eyed women* who begin staring at you ten feet away and whose eyes hold yours until you are abreast of them; women who ask men to their beds without a flicker of shame; *shy little women* who swab the tile floors on their knees and whose frightened eyes beseech you not to soil the floor that they have so meticulously cleaned; *beautiful, rouged; jeweled women* drinking cognac in bars who will tell you with a sweet, sad smile that they cannot read or write; *ugly women* with black-and-blue marks on their arms from the embrace of drunken sailors; *hard-faced women* who are willing to escape loneliness by cooking; working, whoring, and dying for a man; *frail, dry little women* who sell candies and sunflower seed and almonds, and who sometimes die while sitting in their wooden stalls; *fat and frightened women* who, when they see the black hearse drawn by two magnificent black horses with purple plumes on their heads, cross themselves and throw a kiss from their index fingers to the Virgin of their devotion; *tall, long-limbed women* who stride down the street lifting up their big feet and planting them down with the assurance of men; *solemn, vindictive women* who stand gossiping in the middle of the street with elbows akimbo; *young devout women* who have husbands who are hopelessly ill and who stifle their deepest physical needs while their hair whitens before they are thirty—yes, all of those and more are the women of Spain, the heart of Spain. . . .[97]

The destinies of the many women of Spain—self-effacing, assertive, bold, shy, devout, poor, rich, lesbian or not—were about to take a dramatic turn in the 1950s and 1960s. The last act of the regime was about to begin and women's dissatisfaction with the patriarchal arrangements of the regime had a lot to do with its demise.

3

Fallen Women: Public Morality in Transition

ON JANUARY 9, 1951, BARCELONA WELCOMED THE SAILORS OF THE United States Sixth Fleet with open arms. With their distinctive white hats floating on a sea of humanity in the city's Barrio Chino, they brought economic prosperity to the city in general, and an economic boon to the prostitutes who saw their price soar from the 15¢ paid at the officially sanctioned brothels to the $5 per client they could make "independently." The sailors were generous and even took them shopping, a practice that became popular with the flood of American dollars. When the American fleet arrived in Barcelona harbor, shady hotels would admit under age girls as long as an American escorted them.[1]

Popular songs by renowned composer Rafael de León romanticized this underworld. Immortalized by Concha Piquer during the 1940s and 1950s,[2] they told tales of fallen women in love with blond, green-eyed foreigners.[3] In one of these songs, *Tattoo,* Piquer sang about a prostitute who wanders from tavern to tavern in pursuit of a lost lover—a sailor, blond like beer, who arrived on a foreign ship.[4] This song demonstrates the humanity of these women, prostitutes with a golden heart, a considerably more sympathetic image than the official portrayal. The regime's propaganda presented the prostitute as the nemesis of the honest woman, a relationship that symbolized in the larger context the fraudulent, fallen Second Republic versus the virtuous and victorious dictatorship of Franco—pagan versus Catholic Spain.

Catholicism imbued political discourse with only one purpose: to regenerate the whorish body politic of the Second Republic. The regime practiced a policy of controlled leniency toward prostitution that lasted until 1956. Later, by the decree of March 3, 1956, the Francoist regime declared prostitution illegal and joined the international community in the fight against it. To pu-

Figure 3. ***Visita al barrio chino*** **by Francesc Catalá Roca, 1952. Courtesy Museo de Arte Contemporáneo Reina Sofia.**

rify the nation's body, the regime established the *Patronato de Protección de la Mujer* (*Foundation for the Protection of Women*) in 1941. The foundation's task was further strengthened by the law of December 20, 1952, and the decree abolishing prostitution in 1956. Steeped in Catholic values, this agency carried out the state's task of surveillance and rehabilitation of the prostitute's body and soul.

Religious values shaped the regime's penal and health systems with regard to prostitution—a reinterpretation of old 1500s Counter-Reformation mentality.[5] Only penance restored virginal integrity to the soul—integrity lost in the prostitute's body. Mary Magdalene, the repentant whore par excellence, had risen to sainthood through penance. Penance, as in the Golden Age, represented an opportunity to refashion the self to fit into the straitjacket of Catholic dogma during Francoism.

Franco's regime during the first decade was truly ambivalent about the practice of prostitution. On the one hand, it saw prostitution as a necessary evil—a healthy outlet for natural male desires. This image of the sexually potent man fit with the regime's promotion of itself as virile and masculine. The thinking went that if these strong men did not have the prostitute's body as a barrier, they would surely defile the pure and chaste bodies of their fiancées—True Catholic Women and the future mothers of the New Spain. Officially sanctioned, this moral double standard (allowing prostitution but demonizing the prostitute) developed into a dysfunctional sexuality disguised under the appearance of Christian purity and normalcy.

The most important shift in social mores taking place after the Francoist victory was the criminalization of other sexual behaviors. The regime reformed the penal code in 1944 and enacted a series of laws dealing with "sexual indecency" immediately after the Civil War. By the law of January 24, 1941, abortion was declared illegal. Subsequently the law of March 12, 1942 prosecuted adultery, infanticide, and abandonment of the conjugal home and family obligations. The Francoist penal system also introduced new laws against sexual and moral immodesty, suicide, and assault in addition to enacting harsh punishments for theft and vandalism.[6] According to the report drafted by Supreme Court Prosecutor Blas Pérez González in 1942:

> The desertion and neglect of family obligations causes much social damage and peril. The new legal order will allow Prosecutors to achieve—with the help of government authorities and the Police—better results. It is for this reason that a thoughtful deliberation about the scope of these procedures is necessary, particularly the Law of abandonment of family.
>
> . . .
>
> The definition of crime is very broad. Whereas moral or legal obligations are violated, either by action or omission, there will be a crime that must be prosecuted with force. It won't be necessary for the dam-

age to be done. It will suffice the mere consideration of risk that the crime may happen to implement the full penalty agreed on.[7]

Crime was broadly defined, particularly when referring to issues as slippery as decorum and public morality. In 1941 Prosecutor Blas Pérez González identified economic penury as the direct cause of the "lack of decency and perversion of minors." "The frivolity that has infiltrated our customs fosters the deterioration of female modesty disguised under the term *modernity;* it leads our young women to improper behavior (in their dress-code, in frequenting certain kind of shows and cabarets, in encouraging solitary promiscuity, and in the abuse of alcohol and tobacco)."[8] Gerald Brenan too offers his own observation of prostitution in Málaga during his trip in 1949: "A few yards further on one comes to the taverns, crowded with soldiers, sailors and the less monastic sort of prostitute," he observes, "while the long narrow street on the right, which connects the market place with the popular quarter, is given up to houses of assignation. These have greatly helped to spread extramarital relations between the sexes, since all a young woman has to do is to step sideways into an open doorway, where she will find her lover awaiting her and a bedroom at the disposal for a trifling sum."[9] The explanation to this situation according to Brennan was that "poverty and strained circumstances to be found in almost all classes has weakened female morality and increased the number of people who prey on it." Brenan does not comment on men's moral behavior and simply mentions how their Spanish friend Rosario points out to him where to find one of the professional bawds who arrange with the male passengers of trains and buses arriving in town a private encounter with one of those fallen women.[10] The Brenans saw only misery the rest of their trip through Andalusia in sharp contrast with the capital, Lucena, a small southern town in the mountains.

We wandered about the town, depressed by the awful poverty and misery. The women in particular horrified us. In all the side streets one could see them, dressed in rags that had been women's clothes—potato sacks, scraps of army blanket, moldering remains of soldier greatcoats—with their legs and faces caked with dirt which they no longer trouble to wash off. The babies they carry were pinched and emaciated and even the young marriageable girls were in no better way, but walk the streets in the same strips of cloth fastened together with safety pins which the married women wore. Were these

> Spaniards, we asked? Were these members of that proud and modest race for whom twelve years ago even a stockingless leg was regarded as an iniquity? No, they were a pariah class, though of the family of ordinary day laborers, a class who, I was told, never entered a Church or married or baptized their children because they could not either pay the priest's fees or cover their bodies sufficiently.[11]

Brenan believed Spain was suffering from "shell shock." He described Madrid as "the observation-point in a centrally organized prison"—the eye of a panopticon in Foucauldian terms.[12] One of the instruments the regime utilized for the surveillance of public morality would be the *Patronato de Protección de la Mujer or Foundation for the Protection of Women* established in 1941.

Report on Public Morality for the Foundation for the Protection of Women

To address the state's obligations with regard to public morality, the regime established, under the Ministry of Justice, the *Patronato de Protección de la Mujer* (*Foundation for the Protection of Women*) by the decree of November 6, 1941. Four months later, on March 25, 1942, Esteban Bilbao, minister of Justice, presided over the inaugural ceremony. The minister officially appointed a permanent commission with Carmen Polo de Franco, the caudillo's wife, as honorary president. Catholic values guided the rationale behind the Foundation in issues of public morality. To tolerate immoral practices "in the streets, coffee houses, beaches, sporting events, plays and movie theaters, ballrooms, books, and magazines," endangered and perverted people's sense of right and wrong. The highly impressionistic young were considered the most vulnerable; unable to discern between good and evil.[13]

As in the Golden Age, the period of Francoism opted for tolerance and regulation of prostitution rather than abolition. This tolerance was rooted in the interpretation of Augustinian dictum: "Suppress from society public women and you will fill everything with vices. Place these women in equal standing with honest women and you will find everything turning impure and hideous."[14]

The social realignment that followed the Francoist victory in 1939 meant not only restoration but actualization of Counter-Reformation hierarchical power. The formula applied by the

Francoist state to solve the problem of prostitution was a clear renewal of the baroque outlook on this matter: Francoism restored adherence to Catholic orthodoxy as the political and economic law of the land. In the image of the inquisitorial implementation of the Council of Trent (1545–63) directives, Catholic dogma transformed social relations into religious occasions compounding everyday concerns in the New Spain.[15] Indeed, women's chastity as prescribed in texts such as Juan Luis Vives's *The Instruction of the Christian Woman* (1523) and Fray Luis de León's *The Perfect Wife (La perfecta casada)* (1583) became the most valued female virtue under Francoism. As Mary Elizabeth Perry points out "the unchaste woman posed not only a threat to social order but a real danger to the salvation of men's souls."[16] To exercise control over women's chaste bodies three social institutions were established in the early modern period that were perfected during the nineteenth century: the brothel, the Magdalene house, and the prison.[17] These institutions remained at the center of Francoist public policy as a means of regulating morality. Since the Middle Ages, the brothel had been officially authorized in Spain; it served the community by containing prostitutes physically and legally and preventing them from polluting the social fabric. Public houses were regarded as the lesser vice, helping to prevent the more heinous sins of incest and homosexuality. To perpetuate this moral double standard, another institution, the reform prison, was added to the brothel in the early modern era: state and religious reform prisons with the function to reprogram bad women (repentant or not) and turn them into good individuals.[18] The Catholic moral system dominated the social order in new National Catholic Spain. The regime hastened to purge the vanquished population for the sake of political stability and religious purity. It also renewed the so-called Magdalene houses, church-run shelters for repentant women.

The scientific discourse that developed during the nineteenth century further complemented this religious sanitation inaugurated with Francoist victory.[19] Since the nineteenth century, new scientific discourses depicted prostitutes as *degenerates,* the product of predetermined organic fatalism, rather than morally *fallen sinners.* Prostitution turned into pathology due to its association with the underworld of delinquency and substance abuse that made prostitutes easy targets of study. The prostitute was not only physically unfit but mentally ill; she was placed under the rubric of social deviant.[20]

Franco's responsibility, as head of the state, was to orchestrate a zealous surveillance of public morality and to prevent the spreading of libertine behaviors that led to venereal diseases and ultimately racial degeneration. Francoist power became ubiquitous by imposing a "culture of fear" through the glorification of the caudillo, a tight censorship of personal and public morality in the hands of the Catholic Church, and the incarceration and repression of dissidents by state police. Francoism strengthened the existing law of *vagos y maleantes* (vagrants and criminals) of August 1933 with laws of May 4, 1948, July 15, 1954, and April 24, 1958. This legislation penalized not only any beggar or apparently homeless person but also persecuted individuals regarded as a threat to public moral order. Homosexuals, prostitutes, and their procurers were arrested and placed in prisons or asylums.

Morality and criminality were fused under Francoist law. The penal system was built around the penance and redemption philosophy—or what scholars have labeled its "penitentiary universe."[21] The Ministry of Justice published *Redemption,* a newspaper for the prisoner population. The name clearly reflected the religious overtones of the penitentiary system.[22]

The opening remarks of the 1943 *Report on the Status of Public Morality in Spain* were infused with these messianic ideas:

> Immorality in any of its forms is a deep aggression to the *physical life* and integrity of the Fatherland, because there exists the closest relationship between public morality and the sound foundations of the family. The more immorality there is the many more single people and fewer children will be born within marriage and wretched public health will prevail. The defense of morality is more important than the defense of territorial borders.[23]

Upon its induction, the Foundation's permanent commission conducted a survey that gathered information from its newly established local offices and police departments on the status of public morality in Spanish towns and cities. The two major concerns with regard to public morality were of a religious and health nature. Catholic authorities issued pastoral letters and guidelines on dress code and public behavior. This increased focus by the government on issues of morality also led to the establishment of national health dispensaries to tend to postwar disease morbidity—typhus, tuberculosis, venereal diseases, and dermatologic infections. Gerald Brenan saw still in 1949 the effects of the war on the bodies of people on the streets. "The number of cripples; every few yards one meets a one-armed or a one-legged man. Some have no legs at all and creep along on all fours, wearing a sort of boot on their hands. For example, a chambermaid in our hotel tells me that she is a widow who supports her three children and both her parents. Her father cannot work because he has no legs. . . . He was a railway man and an engine ran over them. . . . [W]hat is really shocking is that although foreign exchange is freely used to buy the most expensive cars none is spent on artificial limbs."[24]

Those cripples were the living wounded, the vanquished that populated the public spaces along with the prostitutes, embodiments of political and moral debacle. If the vanquished were the incarnation of political evil, prostitutes were the embodiment of moral degeneration. In contrast to the integral, closed, virginal body of the bride, the prostitute's body was presented as an open sore on the public body politic. She was a threat not only because she enticed good men to fall from grace, but also because she literally infected the Spanish citizenry with disease. Contagious diseases were a real threat to the regeneration of postwar Spain.

Postwar propaganda presented the Second Republic as a period of decay and infestation. "Spain as a Christian State is compelled to uphold high standards of faith and morality. Without these norms the very essence of our people would be destroyed as it was temporarily shattered in the recent past the spiritual unity of our nation."[25]

The fallen nation after the Civil War was likened to a fallen woman. Spain had sinned like a prostitute. After the purge and bloodletting of the Civil War "she" had to repent to regain her virginal integrity. The Foundation's task was most urgent in the midst of the extreme poverty faced by the majority of the population in the immediate years following the Civil War. Such devastation led Madrid's local government (order of May 30, 1941) to open a shelter for homeless people known as the "Parque de Mendigos" (Beggars' Park). In this shelter the Foundation for the Protection of Women implemented its regimen of social purification. According to the 1943 Foundation's report on public morality, in the park were crammed between 1,500 to 1,700 men, women, and children whose ages ranged from infants to elderly over seventy years old. Because the prisons were crowded with war prisoners, the government had to utilize what had been an old slaughterhouse and turned it into a concentration camplike shelter, with improvised miserable living areas: barracks, a stable, and a barn. Eight hundred women and children were jampacked into the barracks with no separation of quarters or privacy of any kind. Sanitation conditions were precarious at best. Latrines in the stables were poorly outfitted and became sources of infection. Some of the men living in the stables did not have beds to sleep in so they had to occupy the mangers where they fit only in the fetal position, and lay on the hay with no blankets to cover themselves. In fact most of the homeless living there did not have clothes of their own, and wore just tattered garments. Women had no underwear and a few men had only a blanket to cover their naked bodies. The extreme weather conditions made the problems more acute. During the day the inmates had to stand in an open cement esplanade with no trees or covered area to protect them from the elements. According to the official Foundation's report, 828 inmates died between April 1941 and May 1942. Some froze to death in the barracks. Infectious diseases like skin ulcers and tuberculosis were rampant among the starving population.[26] From the Foundation's jaundiced perspective, the most severe and urgent problem to tackle, was the immoral behavior among the inmates.

> The all encompassing dissipation in the Parque de Mendigos [Beggars' Park] was enormous; *but logically it could not be any other way in a place where there co-existed miserable men, women, and children with no education or religious principles.* These are idle people, half naked with no separation between the sexes but at bed time and this rule is rarely observed. There have been reports of men entering the women's pavilion due to the inadequate number of guards. But the worst of all is that the park was a site for the perversion of children and young girls housed there because they had been picked up by the police begging in the streets but they have turned into something worse than just beggars [my emphasis].[27]

To address the moral dilemma the Foundation for the Protection of Women sent a number of their newly trained women guards to investigate the situation with respect to the park's female inmates. According to the report, by the end of 1943 there were only two hundred women and two children who remained living at the park. Fifty-nine women had been confined to the Foundation's centers and two hundred more were sent to live with relatives that promised to safeguard their honesty.[28]

It was the redemption of *fallen women* that was the most important task assigned to the Foundation for the Protection of Women. Several convent wards and prisons were designated to incarcerate those women who fell under the category of "promiscuous" or "at risk" of losing their virtue. To facilitate this process, a female Guard Corps (Cuerpo de Celadoras) was established to watch over public morality. It was specifically charged with making sure that these women did not backslide once they had served their time and fulfilled their penance. A key element to redemption was public humiliation. By openly acknowledging through confession their sinful past, repentant prostitutes were able to refashion themselves and reenter society.

The tasks of the female guardians involved the surveillance of women's moral behavior. They watched over public transportation and public spaces for incidents of immorality. Among their duties was providing the Foundation information about the family environment surrounding young girls and supervising the transfer of these girls to state funded centers.

Those women interested in joining this moral all female police force had to be at least thirty years old and be able to pass a training course established by order of June 6, 1942. The faculty of the School of Family and Social Training sponsored by the High Council of the Women's Association of Catholic Action took charge of the instruction. Several priests assisted in the instruction as well: for religion, José Collado and Alejandro Martínez Gil; for morals, José García Goldaraz; for psychology, Máximo Yurramendi; for hygiene and medicine, Francisco Javier Echalecu; and for legal issues, José Rodríguez Soler. The women teachers were in charge of those subjects pertaining to behavioral discipline and adjustment: for correctional pedagogy, Miss Elisa Barraquer attorney; for work methods, Miss María Sabater; for behavioral improvement, Miss Ana d'Herouville; and for evaluation, Miss María Sabater and Miss Sara Alvarez Valdés.[29]

Forty-two women applied to the program during the first year, of whom twenty-five were selected to finish the intensive five-month instruction. The curriculum consisted of 108 hours divided into 30 hours of religious instruction, 18 of moral instruction, 15 of psychology and education, 9 of social hygiene, 18 of what they called "medicine," and 18 hours of labor legislation and general legal training.[30] Once these theoretical lectures were completed the trainees had 72 hours of practical training divided in equal increments of 18 hours in the areas of "Correctional pedagogy," "Work methods," "Behavioral adjustment," and "Assessment."

The students were also supposed to fulfill a total of 144 practicum hours (8 hours per week) in sites such as: "Anti-Tuberculosis Clinics," "Anti-Venereal Clinics," "Prenatal Centers," "Psychiatric Centers," "Delinquent Children's Center," "Our Lady of Refuge Shelter," and "Professional Counseling." In addition, some students conducted survey questionnaires at state institutions such as the Minors Foundation, Minors Court, Foundation for the Protection of Women itself, and the Puente de Vallecas Center located outside Madrid.

The Foundation's guardians collaborated with the police and church authorities in matters of redemption. The state's so-called repentant houses (*casas de arrepentidas*) raised masonry walls to protect brides' and wives' virginal integrity. Around them another symbolic high wall stood; that made from the bodies of the so-called fallen women.

The Foundation for the Protection of Women relied on the guidance and material infrastructure that religious orders provided.[31] Female religious orders came to the aid of the state in the disciplining of prisoners in general and fallen women in particular. The three most important female orders involved in the Foundation for the Protection of Women's disciplinarian role had been part of the Spanish Christian regenerative landscape since the 1800s: Sisters Adoratrices, Oblates, and Sisters of the Good Shepherd. Since the mid-nineteenth century, they had provided in their convents correctional facilities for women who had lost their chastity or found themselves "at risk."[32]

Likewise, the Foundation relied on the counsel of some of the senior members of the judicial system such as Council of Minors Tutelage Court and the Foundation for the Protection of Women. During the first nine months of its establishment in 1942–43, the Foundation for the Protection of Women reported to have assisted 427 young women, 213 of whom were detained in their correctional facilities.[33]

The Foundation paid 4 pesetas per day for the women's care, and a little more for centers keeping single pregnant women. Villa Sacramento, for example, was a center created exclusively to tend to expectant mothers who were allowed to stay after their delivery to "bond with their babies." The goal was to reeducate these young single mothers in the Christian values of motherhood. According to the report, most of the women who entered Villa Sacramento were former servants who had been seduced or raped by their boyfriends or employers. Many were turned in after trying to abort their pregnancies. In the center they worked as seamstresses for no pay.

The religious nature of the regime made it mandatory to provide baptism certificates for all public bureaucratic dealings, from marriage to enrolling in school to obtaining a passport or a driver's license. In plenary session on July 24, 1942, the Foundation approved the norms guiding the imprisonment of fallen women or those "at risk" in its rehabilitation asylums. Each inmate was issued a personal file containing the following: a police report, a written statement from the Foundation's officer to verify authenticity, a declaration of the woman herself and one by her parents or guardians, birth and baptism certificates, and an official medical report.[34] This documentation allowed the Foundation bureaucracy to separate those to be "preserved" from those who had to be "reformed." Their minimum stay was two years and their files were reviewed annually. Those who had proven their religious zeal and contrition were more likely to return to their families. However, the guard in charge of each particular case had the last word in determining whether they would be freed or detained even longer. Once outside, the repentant women had to report periodically to the officials and the guard that had taken care of her case: failure to comply meant reentering the asylum.

The Foundation conducted a nation wide survey about the state of public morality. With the support of the National Security Secretariat, the Foundation collected information from police departments and the Foundation's provincial branches. The report showed a decrease in the national birthrate, and described the public morality in the slums, and the state of delinquency. The information from the police departments differed from that submitted by the Foundation's branches, which were controlled by religious authorities with a more prudish approach to conduct. The questionnaire requested information about the number of public and clandestine brothels, number of rooms reported per house, and number of registered, as apposed to clandestine, prostitutes in each province. The questionnaire also requested a list of entertainment centers—cabarets, teahouses, and dancing halls—that women of "questionable reputation" frequented. Several questions sought information about the activities of minors in the area: the number of minors (under eighteen years old) attending theaters and cinemas; minors involved in corruption reports, abortions,[35] and infanticides, as well as abandoned children and the number of single mothers assisted in provinces' maternal clinics. The last part of the survey concerned the infrastructure that served the purpose of redemption: the number of institutions to reform fallen women, entities established to moralize the community, and their budgets. The last two questions asked for an estimation of the status of public morality and possible solutions to each particular situation.[36]

This was no scientific study, and showed in many cases the personal biases of either the police or the Foundation's members. In addition, Barcelona and Zaragoza established their own independent associations to monitor public Christian decorum. The *Liga Española contra la Pública Inmoralidad* (Spanish League against Public Immorality) in Barcelona and the *Bloque contra la Pública Inmoralidad* (The Bloc against Public Immorality) in Zaragoza added their voices to the report. Made up of prominent figures in these important urban settings, these two associations reported to the Foundation for the Protection of Women their meticulous appraisal of social propriety. Each respondent had a different definition of public morality. For the chief of police from Avila: "Immorality, in the broad sense of the word, is understood as: blasphemous and foul language; non compliance of law abiding dominical rest; the disintegration of Spanish Christian family life, shift from the home to centers of entertainment: casinos, cinemas, taverns etc. . . . and above all the relaxation of proper values publicly apparent in young people's behavior in walks, gardens, streets and plazas, as well as the women's indecent clothes and attitudes in public sports and gatherings."[37]

The reports from the chief commissaries from Albacete, Alicante, Burgos, Cáceres, Huelva, Huesca, Lérida, Segovia, Teruel, and Zaragoza considered the state of public morality to be "good" in their provinces. Many more reported the status of public decorum in their areas to be "bad" or "not so good" including: Barcelona, Zaragoza, Almería, Castellón, Pamplona, Badajoz, Baleares, Cádiz, Córdoba, and Vizcaya. The report from Jeréz de la Frontera, for example, highlighted the fact that births out of wedlock or couples "living in sin" was common among the upper classes. La Coruña emphasized the rural custom of accepting the young women who had children out of wedlock. Fathers were not known or avoided responsibilities in both regions, leaving mothers alone to fend for themselves and their children. In many cases the lower-class single mothers had to prostitute themselves to make ends meet.

The report from Badajoz lamented that "in spite of police surveillance there are a great number of domestic servants and young widows from the war who, some because they are promiscuous, others because they have no alternative source of income, practice clandestine prostitution in their own homes or rent out rooms. Therefore, we may affirm that prostitution is least practiced in authorized brothels."[38]

Certainly, the Civil War created a web of misery for those women who lost their husbands or parents. The repressive state apparatus affected them in two ways: Some went to prison to pay for the crimes of their relatives; others had to prostitute themselves to survive in a labor market that favored the victors over the vanquished. Total public humiliation, either serving time in jail or registering in a public brothel, was the penance many poor women paid for survival. They inhabited bodies that belonged to the regime.

Most domestic servants were expected to "fall" after they suffered sexual harassment and rape from their employers. The report from Palencia stated that 25 percent of those girls working as domestic servants were not registered prostitutes in that province. In the same way, the factory girl was considered "at risk." The Foundation for the Protection of Women monitored, and in many cases locked up, servants and factory girls to shield them against sin—their own or that of those who would inflict it upon them.

According to police reports, single mothers were to be found mostly in the rural areas and among the urban lower classes. Interestingly, they identified a lower number of pregnancies and abortions in areas where there was a more "promiscuous lifestyle" than in the more conservative regions where birth control practices were less well known. Their explanation to this paradox was that only promiscuous women would know about avoiding unwanted pregnancies. A decent woman would not even try to seek information.

The report also identified several causes behind moral deterioration. The consequences of the war along with economic hardship figured among the main reasons: "Women still young, widows of red soldiers, or wives of those imprisoned or fugitive look into prostitution as the means to survive themselves and their offspring. Illegitimate unions, concubine arrangements, and intimate encounters take place in the slums with a certain regularity that does not shame anyone. Misery leads to condoning everything, even when there is no real misery. This is the case of many families that live off *estraperlo* [black market] of food and tobacco."[39] Estraperlo was the "sole thriving industry" in Spain, wrote Brenan. The motto of the dictatorship was "pan y justicia" (bread and justice) and people said "We have seen his [Franco's] justice, and we don't like it, but we haven't seen his bread."[40] However severe the misery Spain was experiencing in the 1940s, in the eyes of the moralists and the police writing official reports such as the Foundation's, the real source of the problem was that these were morally flawed individuals who suffered from a lack of religious education, parental neglect, and just longed for the purely material. Their problems were made more difficult by the lack of adequate housing, which created a large number of homeless people especially women, children, and elderly. Brenan tells us that in the southern town of Churriana twenty families were living in a barn divided up by cane partitions in portions of about ten feet per family. There they would live, sleep, and cook. Brenan explains the reason for such overcrowding was the low wages, which do not allow any working-class family to pay an economical rent, and the government and local authorities did not make any grants.[41] Without shelter and food these morally fragile women were easy prey to those wishing to dishonor them.

The Foundation's report proposed some solutions including the "evangelization" and "*españolización*" of the promiscuous masses: strengthening their religious instruction, closing down dancing halls, making parents accountable for any moral neglect of their children, and creating more punitive institutions and centers to reprogram fallen people. These recommendations focused on instilling better control mechanisms within the individual—what Foucault would call "technologies of the self." The report also included a few suggestions to address the economic crisis caused by the war. It advocated lowering the cost of living, creating more affordable housing, giving economic help to young, abandoned women, and fighting crime and corruption.

In order to fight the damage caused by modern vices, Zaragoza and Barcelona enlisted a number of conscientious, pious, and law-abiding citizens into the new order. The Bloque contra la Pública Inmoralidad (The Bloc against the Public Immorality) in Zaragoza was established in1941 with the blessing of the bishop of this region. The membership came from the Association of Parents and the different branches of Catholic Action. The first actions taken by the Bloc concerned the surveillance of movie theaters where, in the report's words, "couples with no modesty whatsoever indulge in their carnal instinct under almost complete darkness."[41] In order to solve this problem the Bloc worked to enforce the regulation issued by the Ministry of Interior about installing dim lights in the theaters to monitor the behavior of lovers. Other public places were also under surveillance by members of the Bloc. "We have closed all the clandestine dance halls.

Also closed were those that although legal did not comply with the current regulations. We have limited their hours of operation, allowing some to open only on holidays. . . . We were very successful in our summer campaign. We have established separate use of public swimming pools for men and women and always wearing the legally established swimming suit."[43]

The most serious problem the Bloc faced was prostitution. Because of "the irreparable damage it inflicts upon soul and body," they raided the streets, rounding up prostitutes, women between fifteen and twenty years of age who were unable to work in the regulated bawdy houses. According to the report, 90 percent of these girls suffered from contagious diseases. These women crowded the Adoratrices and Oblates congregations' convents and the Bloc planned to raise some funds to build a pavilion to expand the shelter space. Three hundred and ninety of those women categorized as "recalcitrant prostitutes" were sent to prison where they received catechism from Missionary Ladies and nuns. The Bloc against Public Immorality established a draconian surveillance over the urban landscape.

> The Bloc has opened its headquarters in a section of the Civil Governor building. We open every day from noon till one and from six till seven in the afternoons. Daily the Executive Board convenes to deal with the different issues at hand—every day more to solve. Likewise, in attendance are the officer from the General Police Corps and two agents of the Armed Police appointed for this duty to report about the jobs assigned to them the previous day. There is a retired Civil Guard officer in charge of the files and to file police reports and sanctions. Membership cards are issued with previous submission of a parish priest's recommendation. The local dailies *Amanecer* and *El Noticiero* and the local radio station have been extremely cooperative as means of propaganda.[44]

As in Zaragoza, Barcelona had the Liga Española contra la Pública Inmoralidad (Spanish League against Public Immorality). Founded in 1941, the league was "to collaborate with the authorities in public morality matters." Some of the actions undertaken by the League included campaigns to monitor modesty in dress codes and "anti-blasphemy," as well as the surveillance of beaches. Its members belonged to Young Spanish Catholic Action, Marian Congregations, and the Women's Section of Falange. The League sent a report to the Foundation for the Protection of Women describing the state of affairs in Barcelona. Their report highlighted the corruption of customs in the metropolitan area of Barcelona. Particularly disastrous was the influence of entertainment centers such as ballrooms and cinemas. The most dramatic assertion in the report had to do with the increase in clandestine prostitution. The League started a directory of illicit places that included: 39 ballrooms, 31 cabarets, 118 meublés,[45] 113 brothels, 11 beaches, 16 bathhouses, 3 public swimming pools, 12 dance studios, 9 acting and 6 singing studios, 12 amusement barracks, and 27 picnic areas.[46]

The Barrio Chino (China Town) had been notorious for corruption, crime, and prostitution since the turn of the twentieth century. Its proximity to the harbor and labyrinthlike design, along with the entertainment centers, hostels, and brothels made this district the nucleus of crime in Barcelona. Prostitution continued to be the most profitable industry in Barcelona. Brothels were packed and the prices were very low. The women known as *pajilleras* would masturbate clients for a small fee. They acted in dark movie theaters and their fees were between 1 and 5 pesetas (1 to 5 cents) depending on their age and experience. Movie theaters tolerated them because they brought in clients for the cinema and extra income in the way of tips for the ushers. Some of these ushers provided the clients for a commission. They would pick any man who entered the theater alone and seat them where the pajilleras worked. Movie theaters benefited from this sex commerce because a large number of young men not old enough to frequent brothels took advantage of these clandestine services. Occasionally, some of these women would have intercourse with their clients in the restrooms for extra money.[47]

In the 1940s, Barcelona's police prosecuted a new crime known as "gatera." This was the term used for a particular kind of prostitution also associated with theft. There were few police reports because men did not want to make public their use of prostitution. A police report of 1945 reads:

> Last Thursday 4 January 1945 around 15:00 hours while walking down the Rambla Santa Monica in this city a woman approached him and proposed to introduce him to a young woman to have sexual relations. He accepted and followed her to Mina Street number 4 and another woman came in with whom he had intercourse. He hanged his clothes on the room's coat rack. Afterward he paid ten pesetas to this woman and three pesetas to the one he met on the street. Yesterday when he returned to his village where he lives he noticed 10,000 pesetas missing from inside an envelope he was carrying in the inside pocket of his coat. The envelope contained still another 9,000 pesetas. He did not notice immediately the theft because the enve-

lope was still in his pocket when he left and only when he re-counted the money at home in the village he realized part of the money had been stolen. He suspects these women stole his money while he was having sex with one of them. He described the one he met in la Rambla as follows: average height, around 35 to 40 years old, straight black hair picked up, lively eyes, a little chubby, wearing a greenish coat or dress with a light colored apron, and wearing espadrilles. The woman he had sex with was of average height or rather short, black or brown hair picked up, she spoke Castilian with no regional accent he could appreciate, black eyes and very poorly dressed, her underwear was black, she also wore espadrilles and looked about 30 years old.[48]

This case illustrates the utter misery in postwar Spain. In Barcelona many homeless, like those in Madrid, wandered naked with only newspapers covering their sick bodies. Many had their heads shaved to get rid of lice. Hunger and disease led to unannounced death in the corners of half-demolished buildings. According to a summary of the court number 4 in Barcelona "On Mediodia Street num. 5, third floor, a building with no doors and virtually in ruins without any furniture or any other things because is completely empty. Upon entering to the left there is a dead body of a woman of around 30 years of age, in fetal position. She does not present any sign of violence. Dressed poorly in a black suit, brown stockings and grey espadrilles, her head shaved. After searching her clothes there is not documentation or anything else to be found. She begged during the day and slept where she was found."[49] The horrific postwar reality presented amidst the urban ruins not only adult indigents but also the remains of fetuses. Some of the women who decided to carry their full-term pregnancies would sell their children to survive. According to a criminal sentence on December 2, 1946, on July 30, 1945, twenty-two-year-old Carmen G. gave birth to a girl in the Clinical Hospital. The baby was registered with the names Francisca María del Carmen. When Juana C., a friend of Carmen's who sold cigarettes on the street, found out about the birth she agreed with the mother and a third woman, Victoria B., to find an unknown lady to sell the baby. Carmen received 475 pesetas and gave Juana and Victoria 25 pesetas each as a commission. The whereabouts of the baby or if her life was in danger were unknown afterwards.[50]

The Foundation for the Protection of Women's report on public morality provides some figures pertaining to the public morality, prostitution, single mothers, and number of children abandoned as well as the number of infanticides and abortions city by city. In 1943 in Barcelona there were 105 authorized brothels, a total of 1,144 registered and about 5,600 clandestine prostitutes. More than 3,000 single mothers were attended to that year in the official clinics. Since 1939, sixty-two children were abandoned, 12 infanticides reported, and 73 abortions occurred. The report indicated how the number of abortions had increased since the government introduced its penalization. Particularly high are the figures sent in from Oviedo in the northern region of Asturias reporting a total of 576 children abandoned in 1942, the year the survey was done. "According to the police there were no infanticides or abortions recorded this year. But the provincial Junta noted that the maternity clinic there treated 112 women, single and married, from the entire county between January and October 1942.This figure represents only 5 percent of those who did not go to the clinic in the same ten-months period; data that in a year translates into the following: 134 for the twelve months, that being 5 percent of the total number, point at a total of around 2,600 abortions per year."[51]

This number is extremely high and stands out from the reports of the rest of the country that recorded no abortions or, if they mentioned any, presented them as just a few isolated cases. In Valencia, for example, where the document reported 1,130 prostitutes, there were only two infanticides and one abortion reported in the year. This indicates the frequency of clandestine abortions under the regime. Most of the reports blamed the modern lifestyle and urban settings—movie theaters and dance halls especially. But the most mentioned reason behind delinquency and prostitution is the desire for material extravagance rather the misery most of the population suffered in the postwar years. For the town of Palencia, the report pointed to the domestic servants and factory workers as women at risk for becoming prostitutes and stated that they started a registry of names of women who fell "prey to evil ways."

The Foundation for the Protection of Women published a substantial number of personal files opened to those women who entered the Magdalene houses under its institutional supervision. These personal files give us a profile of the women who were imprisoned. Most of them were teenagers classified under the rubric of "abandoned" or "in need of protection against a hostile environment." Some were truly selling themselves to survive, while others were simply orphaned after the war but were not necessarily prostitutes. Many of these young girls had been raped by a family member or an acquaintance and immediately turned in to the Magdalene houses by their own relatives or guardians to save them from further falling into "the bad life." Some of these young women's files show the official surveillance of public morality. Any young woman who had the misfortune to be poor and alone ran the risk of being incarcerated.

File number 45 tells the story of a seventeen-year-old girl from Madrid registered in the Oblates convent. During the war, while living with her relatives, she suffered beatings from the hands of her own father. She escaped this domestic violence and joined the militia, offering her services to wash and mend other soldiers' clothes. She lived in squalor and ate from the garbage most of the time. After a soldier raped her she fell into prostitution. She was arrested and put under the Foundation's custody.[52] Another eighteen-year-old girl from Gijon in northern Spain was turned in to the Foundation by the officers of the provincial branch. Apparently she had been "seduced" by a doctor when she went for a health checkup. The provincial branch of the Foundation confined her for this reason and for being away from her parents. File number 457 tells the story of an eighteen-year-old girl from Cáceres "despoiled" by her brother-in-law. As a result, she moved to Madrid and requested to be locked up in a Magdalene house to escape this man's harassment.[53]

File number 204 was registered at the Adoratrices Convent in Madrid. This file belongs to a seventeen-year-old girl "picked up because she was abandoned." The records also indicate she was "well educated and apparently with no penal history." Free movement was not tolerated for a woman alone in those days, as was the case of File number 334, placed at the convent of the Adoratrices in Madrid: "Nineteen-years-old from Almería [city in the southern region of Andalucia]. When the nationalist forces freed that region, she left with a foreign legion soldier that eventually abandoned her. She went back home and then left again to look for her boyfriend that she said was in Getafe [outside Madrid]. She was arrested by the police that turned her in to the Foundation of Protection of Women. She behaves very well in this school."[54]

Certainly prevention was a very important task for the Foundation. Any woman alone would be at risk to fall into disgrace or even worse would turn into a temptation for others. Her own body if unguarded could turn into her own enemy. Hence, the official policing of her actions was essential to preserve not just her moral integrity but social order and decorum. The Foundation assumed the national and patriotic task of preventing and preserving not only the spiritual health but also the physical health of the country with a thorough campaign against the spread of venereal disease. Surveillance was of the essence. Surveillance of others and oneself, what Foucault calls pastoral power. Self-monitoring was indispensable if the regime was to succeed in its political and moral purifying quest. And so it is not surprising to read in some of these files that a few of these women would turn themselves in. Mostly, however, it was the surveillance of others, as in the case of file number 181, a sixteen-year-old girl from Madrid who was turned in by her own parents "because of her being incorrigible," that kept the regime pure. In another case, a sixteen-year-old girl, also from Madrid, ran away from her foster home and was arrested by the police on her way to Barcelona. She was declared to have had a boyfriend but "not to have fallen," and then registered in the convent of the School of the Good Shepherd "to correct her adventurous spirit."[55] In file number 410 a seventeen-year-old girl from Madrid, who "lived with her relatives, was reported by them because she was seeing a married man. They brought her against her will to the Foundation to prevent her from falling."[56] In file number 354 we learn about a motherless seventeen-year-old girl from Cuenca who was sexually abused by her father who abandoned her and a younger brother. She reported the abuse to the Civil Guard who advised her to stay in the house until she sold her furniture. She and her brother lived with what they made for a little while and then they parted for two different villages. The young girl arrived in Madrid and found herself forsaken, and eventually fell into the "bad life." Later she found a job as domestic servant and the lady, "feeling sorry for her," placed her in the hands of the Foundation, arguing that if she were confined in the convent she "might resolve, even in part, her disgrace with adequate correction."[57] To correct, to prevent from falling; that was the purpose of the Foundation for the Protection of Women. The Foundation's writings emphasized the defense of Christian family values: "We may affirm in absolute terms that there exists an almost perfect correspondence between a country's public morality and the inner strength of the family, because almost all of lust manifestations jeopardize the order and aims of marriage and the education of the offspring. Therefore, we infer necessarily that it is public immorality that constitutes the most direct and essential injury against the fatherland's prosperity and existence."[58]

The Foundation pointed out that the moral order was the domain of both the civil and the religious authorities and the Foundation was "the State organ in charge of: the surveillance and safeguarding of public morality; the protection of women in danger, and the redemption of the fallen, mainly minors." They considered their obligations to be the following:

a) to inform the government about the de facto status of public morality
b) To submit basic guidelines that must guide the policy for moral sanitation and defense of morality
c) To implement, as the government's instrument, the moralizing mission as well as the defense of the victims of vice in four ways: helping the Church in its redeeming social mission; sponsoring those social institutions created for this purpose; guiding the authorities; and undertaking the responsibilities when there is a void[59]

It was through the "durable and effective regeneration of fallen women and the preservation of those in danger" that the Foundation saw its patriotic role to regenerate the motherland as well. In order to better redeem these young women the Foundation expected them to work in the houses and prisons where they served sentences for a minimum of two years. Their meager wages were used to pay for their stay in these institutions. Once the Foundation decided they had regained the trust of society, some of these young women found work as domestic servants, and very few would get married or join the nunnery.

As practical recommendations, the Foundation proposed in its conclusions surveillance of cinemas and dance halls as well as the zealous censorship of films and print material to "severely reprimand those who did not observe public decorum, demanding they provide personal identification to the authorities" who might stop them on the street. Couples not providing the proper identification who were found just holding hands in public risked being arrested. In addition, the Foundation encouraged the implementation of missionary campaigns in hospitals and correction centers.

The Fight against Venereal Diseases

In the nineteenth century, European states led campaigns to regulate prostitution in order to control the spread of venereal diseases.[60] The Spanish government established a kind of "customs police" to monitor public morality. This police force was charged with the task of repressing acts and words that offended honesty, religion, and morality. Hence, not only physical but also moral sanitation became the state priority.

In addition to religious and public order concerns, the state sought to prevent the expansion of venereal diseases with the establishment of clinics to monitor prostitutes' health. The state issued a health report card for those women who voluntarily registered and worked in the authorized brothels between 1939 and 1956. Every two weeks a state-certified physician examined those women and, if "clean," authorized them to continue working. Otherwise they were required to stay in the hospital for treatment. The prostitute's body in this context represents a social sarcoma. The official clinics, where every two weeks the registered prostitutes received clearance to go back to work, created a false sense of control over the spread of venereal diseases. The clients were not subject to any kind of medical control and in turn the doctors' wives ran the risk of being infected. By the turn of the twentieth century the medical and legal establishments were divided between abolitionism and regimentation to address the ongoing problem of prostitution.[61] Spanish abolitionists were clearly against what they saw as a paternalistic, unjust, immorality of those in favor of regulating prostitution. They saw the regulation as ineffective because it did not deal with the high number of clandestine prostitutes, and because the periodic medical checks did not include the men who frequented brothels. In addition to these two major problems there were infrastructural deficiencies: not enough physicians or hospital beds available, and poorly equipped facilities. Abolitionists also addressed legal considerations of prostitution such as equality before the law. They highlighted the fact that regulation violated the right of the prostitute over her own body. Recognizing property rights as sacred, they argued the ownership of one's own body was the most sacred right of all. Regimentation was also, in their view, a violation of the individual's freedom—these women were submitted to tight control of their acts and were forbidden the right to determine their own private behavior, their right to be immoral if they wished. For abolitionists, an individual's own moral behavior should be the subject of legal scrutiny and punishment only when it was inflicted upon another person against his/her will. In other words it was all right to punish rape, deception and intimidation as any delinquent act associated with prostitution, but not to punish prostitution when it represented the free exchange between consenting parties. Finally, abolitionist jurists found regulation to infringe upon the right of equality along gender and class lines. While sexual trade was punished in women it was not censored in men. They also highlighted the class bias in this regulation law because it targeted only the poor prostitute while the rich courtesan remained unpunished.

Abolitionists accused the state of moral depredation and of exploiting the material revenues produced by the international sex market. On the other hand it was the materialist argument that was most emphasized by those in favor of regulating prostitution. They viewed regulation as a necessity in the modern market economy. The state had to assure the quality control of the merchandise, prostitutes. The market economy turned sex workers into commodities more than ever and human trafficking flourished. In order to better control the illegal kidnapping and trafficking of women into the sex industry, a series of international agreements established the monitoring of prostitution and crime associated with it in each European country.

In 1956 Dr. Tomás Caro Patón published his memoirs and reflections on his thirty-seven-year experience as a state doctor fighting venereal diseases and treating prostitutes.[62] Caro Patón's book was a strong endorsement of abolitionism at the time the regime was drafting a law making prostitution illegal. Caro Patón opens the book with a powerful image: that of a prostitute as martyr.

> Shortly after I entered the Anti-venereal Campaign as head of a rural clinic, they brought me a wounded prostitute. Some youngsters had followed and threw stones at her causing an injury in her forehead. The wound was bleeding profusely, an artery had been broken and intermittent jets of blood pumped at the rhythmic impulses of her heart beat. I had to perform a ligature and suture, and then proceeded to put a circular dressing resembling a crown. Under the bandage her straight bobbed bloody hair fell. The poor woman, blood-spattered, pale, her eyes ajar showing some tears, she did not groan, did not say anything, she was motionless like a statue. It was hot; the window was open and the blinds down, and outside the youngsters still shouting angrily: "Die you bitch!" . . . And I looked at her sad figure; she seemed to be the picture of martyrdom.[63]

Dr. José García Cuesta launched the abolitionist campaign in Spain in the early 1950s as a result of his experience with prostitutes in the Hospital of San Juan de Dios in Granada. Caro Patón provides a sketched profile of the 112 prostitutes he attended in his first year in the clinic. All of them were poor women who worked in the public brothels and had to pass the medical check-up every two weeks to be able to go back to work. Paton emphasized the precarious conditions that led these women to practice prostitution: 76 per cent were orphans, 52 percent illiterate and 20 percent mothers.[64] For Caro Patón the prostitute could be redeemed because of her religious fervor. To this the doctor made clear the need to economically support these women to reinsert themselves into society working in an honest job and not having to depend on their pimps. It was imperative to prosecute the exploitative network of people who profited from their misery—men and women with no scruples. "The brothel," he writes," is a business as any other, with an underground owner who is the one who becomes rich; the visible manager (the madam), her subaltern employees (head prostitutes) and finally the unprotected proletariat (the prostitute)."[65] Hence, in Caro Patón's view it was hypocritical to blame these women for their sinful lives because it was a socioeconomic problem. "How much do they make?" he continues, "For what I know, from their net income they need to pay 50 per cent to cover the cost of room and board. The other half goes to their wardrobe and adornment (their obsession). That way they incur in debts in addition to the expense to cover the sustenance of their children."[66]

As a devout Catholic himself, Caro Patón placed in a truly Christian society the responsibility of redeeming these women. Redemption with dignity, not shame humiliation and imprisonment, was his view. Most disturbing to Patón was the freedom men had over their sexual misconduct while "[t]hey [the women] had to have medical clearance, they are humiliated with their health report, the file in the official clinics and the police record, the men don't have to give explanations to anyone." And, he continued, "Tolerance of prostitution is based on the protection of some women's virtue dishonoring a few. Tragic paradox! Would it not have been better to focus on the cultivation of men's virtue to protect women's completely?"[67] Most interesting are his proposals for a solution to the moral problem prostitution posed to modern society. According to Caro Patón, a *Catholic feminism* was the best antidote for prostitution. He lamented the objectification of women in modern society and viewed motherhood as the most important role to preserve. "Motherhood is the inalienable function of women," he remarked, "She is life's vessel. Her harmonious amphora-shaped hips . . . prove it physically."[68]

For this reason he considered women superior to men. The role of men in the reproductive process, in Caro Patón's view, was insignificant compared to the transcendentalism he sees in women's maternal function. "We must admit their [women's] superiority" he affirms, "and cannot call them the weaker sex because they fulfill a much more important role than we do."[69] The ultimate purpose of sexuality is reproduction in the vision Caro Patón proposes. He sees a clear difference between men and women in the sexual game. Men, he says, "confuse the means with the end and don't look at women as the transcendental subjects of procreation that they are but rather as sexual objects to satisfy his urges." Patón considers that the disdain modern society has for motherhood is what leads to the objectification of women as sexual objects and gives men license to act on their low desires. Therefore, women are turned into "dolls" and under this concept their worth is measured by their sexual appeal and beauty. This, he concludes, leads to a charged, lustful environment, a state of "collective obsession," and a hyper-sexualized society. "It is the sharp look; following young women, undressing them with our eyes, thinking voluptuously and so intensely as if we would want to make her feel our thoughts, a chill down her spine and obtain a look in return from her. It is the ardent flirtatious comment, the rubbing and even the brutal shove, that daily street behavior that makes honest young women to be afraid to go out by themselves."[70]

The Spanish *piropo,* a flirtatious comment (sometimes flattering, most times crass) any man could shout to women on the street, was a form of sexual harassment condoned by tradition. It was common practice for women (good and bad) to suffer fondling from perfect strangers in movie theaters, public transportation, and even on the street. This practice was carried out in plain sight with few, if any, sanctions by the Church or state. To the male-dominated hierarchy, and the men in the street, this overtly sexual attention was seen, in its twisted way, as a form of flattery. Such public male appraisal of the "livestock," as some men referred to women, was at odds with their longing for virginal purity. They were defiling those that they sought to keep most pure.

Catalan photographers captured the sexual tension played out in the streets. Some of their pictures capture the sexually charged relations between men and women in 1950s Spain. Xavier Marisach's photograph entitled "Piropo en la via Layetana" (1962) illustrates the predatory behavior of men in the street and the vulnerability of women, good and bad alike, forced to run this daily gauntlet of harassment (see fig. 4).

Caro Patón acknowledges that the modernization of the country had an impact on sexual mores and relationships. Advertising of cosmetics for women, brought by consumerism, had a significant impact on sexual relations in the 1950s. Like the Hollywood starlets they saw in the movies, women in 1950s Spain sought to enhance their natural beauty in the hope of attracting a husband. Caro Patón called this "Muñequismo" (turning themselves into "dolls"), objectification that led to the impoverishment of women's worth in society. "It is the standard eyebrows. The wavy hair . . . the cheek's blush, the doughy foundation, the bright lipstick with devilish overtones, the studied moves of an automaton . . . These are not women; they are dolls who present themselves in this guise to incite men . . . But the true *macho* does not want that."[71] Caro Patón proposed to educate both men and women to enter marriage as companions beyond sexual attraction. Women had to be educated to rise from servant to partner of her husband and men needed to be taught to respect women as companions. Caro Patón believed that because women follow men's lead it was men's responsibility to show a higher moral behavior. The best way to reach this goal was by applying a "sensible feminism." Patón does not agree with women exercising a sexual independence in the same fashion that men had done historically, rather he sees in feminist principles the door to mutual respect and the best antidote to prostitution. For him the main problem was not just prostitution but the dysfunctional sexual relations men and women lived by. On several occasions he quotes Simone de Beauvoir's *The Second Sex* to substantiate his arguments. "The woman who has in society a different role than what is 'proper of her sex' in the eyes of men is not any more a sexual object only valuable until it is possessed and thrown away. The new social role of women forces men to measure them beyond their beauty. The very occasion of working in the same environment will change the relation between the sexes leading to a healthy and happy camaraderie and making sexual desire more natural. The sexual tension increases with the extreme differences we place between men and women."[72] Caro Patón, however, sees the rejection of motherhood by feminism as a problem. Motherhood and homemaking should be respected and incorporated into the feminist agenda, in Patón's view, to really elevate women's social status. He even encourages men to wear "aprons" and collaborate in the housework, "like American men." It will

Figure 4. ***Piropo*** **by Xavier Marisachs, 1962. Courtesy Herederas Xavier Marisachs.**

be futile for the feminist to attract the mass of women if they only focus on their turning into little men, a devaluing move according to Patón. Women will find themselves with the double burden of home and work, and men, entrenched in their old chauvinistic privileges, will not collaborate. "Comprehensive feminism was born against male oppression and therefore developed with a revenge sentiment and an exaggerated thirst for equality between the sexes in all aspects. This feminism has not worried about a just equality elevating men to the virtue expected from women but rather bringing women down to the vice tolerated for men."[73] Chastity was the ideal solution to free love and prostitution. According to Patón, chastity was not only a moral solution but a hygienic safeguard against venereal diseases. In his eyes, chastity was not incompatible with feminism. Feminism, when "well administered and applied correctly," will be the best advocate of chastity for men and women. The legal changes, although important, will not produce the immediate solution to the moral problems society faces. Patón proposes a thorough change of the education to change the attitudes and the customs.

A convinced abolitionist, Caro Patón mentioned in his book, as an example, the expansion of abolitionism throughout Europe as a sign of civilization. In addition to Spain, there were three more countries in Europe in 1954 that tolerated prostitution as a lesser evil: Portugal, Italy, and Greece. The brothels had been closed in France in 1946 and ten years earlier in the United Kingdom.

In 1949, the United Nations' Geneva Convention[74] led to most Western countries signing the international agreement to fight human trafficking and sexual exploitation. Spain continued to practice a policy of tolerance that quickly became outmoded with the signing of the economic and military agreements in 1953 with the United States. The entrance of Spain in the United Nations in 1955 led inevitably to the abolition of prostitution in early 1956.

In order for abolition to work in Spain, Caro Patón proposed to listen respectfully to the voices of the prostitutes themselves, and although he acknowledges the work of the Foundation for the Protection of Women, he sees the work of Isabel Garbayo's private shelters known as "Villa Teresita" as much more productive in dealing with those women. The Foundation could not do away with the infrastructure provided by the old Magdalene houses, run by the orders of nuns, but as Dr. Caro Patón pointed out, these institutions had to lose their convent smell and become more of a home environment where these women received assistance and support. "The convent milieu, locks, iron bars, large dormitories, coarse uniforms, the eradication of all feminine beauty instinct, the forced entry, the exit under surveillance and spies; all this clashes with the deficient mind and unruly spirits of these women, whether young or old, who wasted their honesty in the brothels."[75]

Like those in France under Dr. León Brizar (known as "Le Nid" and founded in 1944 by Father Talvas) and Germany (the "Fürsergeverein Für Madchen, Frauen und Kinder") the lay shelters in Spain followed the model set by the convents. In Pamplona, Isabel Garbayo, a member of the Catholic Action, established in 1942 a shelter known as Villa Teresita run by the diocesan volunteers of Catholic Action. These middle class, pious ladies visited the brothels to rescue fallen women. Their shelter followed an open-door policy and hosted no more than fifteen women at a time. The inmates lived in a halfway house, each with their own private room and had the help of career counselors. Caro Patón felt the worst possible job for them would be domestic service because they found themselves sexually at risk again of being raped or harassed by their employers. Finding a job in the honest world was not easy for these women. Society was openly hostile and they often ended up returning to clandestine prostitution if they were not able to find a good job, find a husband or a religious order. By the 1950s this model was implemented in other Spanish cities. There were two more Villa Teresita shelters, in Valencia and Granada. The one in Granada received the name Hogar Pio XII (Pius XII Home). It was opened after the decree abolishing prostitution in 1956, exclusively to receive those women "liberated" from the brothels of the city. Caro Patón concluded his book with the following pieces of advice in a lecture to Valladolid Catholic Working Youth:

1. Look at women in general and to those you work with in particular with your soul's and reason's eyes, not with your senses.
2. Despise women's "Muñequismo" (excess of make up and artifice).
3. Be Catholic feminists, recognize in women capable human beings able to perform activities beyond those domestic ones assigned historically to their sex.
4. Combine this feminist concept with the love of virtue, with motherhood, the rearing of the children and the domestic administration of the home, because they are functions specific to women.
5. Respect women's virtue not just as a matter of courtesy and good manners, but rather because you seek your own virtue, your own chastity, and repress your passions.
6. Avoid with contempt those frivolous male friends who love women as sexual objects and try to attract them to your way of thinking.
7. Deeply feeling and practicing these pieces of advice, you will not have any problem in socializing with girls who practice them as well. Socialize with them not only at work but also during leisure time, in walks, parties, sports, avoiding the sad misogyny. With your coexistence full of grace, the healthy happiness of youth will flourished and love will be real, not as a vice but as God's blessing.

In reality it was much more difficult to change, taking more than the three months the abolitionist legislation planned for. Patón calculated between two and four years to achieve some change. It was the beginning of a long process. The changing social relations wrought by capitalism were on their way in spite of Francoism.

1956 Abolition: Buying Love/Consuming Sex

"In Spain sex has been converted into a medium of exchange for almost all kinds of commodities and services to the degree that cannot be found in any other European country."[76] This was Richard Wright's opening statement to chapter 26 of his travel log, *Pagan Spain.* Although the book was published in 1957, a year after Francoism decreed abolitionism, the American writer was most disturbed by the brutal misery he witnessed in two short visits in 1954 and 1955. "Barcelona and Sevilla" he wrote, "literally crawl with hungry women willing to grant access to their bodies for bread or its equivalent."[77] In Madrid, of the hundred thousand prostitutes acknowledged by the Church hierarchy, only sixty thousand were registered with the police or health authorities. Carmen Martín Gaite's *The Backroom* illustrates the urban segregation between good and bad women that helps us imagine a map of urban desire. "It was hard to imagine those sections of the city, slums and cheap cafes, through which these girls aimlessly wander in anonymous dishonor, the lodgings and rooms in which they holed up, yet one felt that they were much more creatures of flesh and blood that those other pairs of lovers in the boleros who swore in the moonlight to love each other forever."[78] Richard Wright tells us these women were referred to as a "wall of flesh"—the barrier men needed until they could marry their virgin fiancées. Wright reflects, "The Spanish male learns early to divide all women into two general categories: one group of women are those with husbands, children, and a home; or they are young women whose hymen rings are technically intact. These are the good women and you bow low to them and tenderly kiss their hands, murmuring compliments the while. The other group of women has been placed on earth by God, just as He placed rabbits, foxes, lions, etc., to be hunted and had."

Richard Wright did go to the brothels with André, a young man he befriended in Barcelona. André had a fiancée, but his friend Miguel would not commit himself. In their minds the difference between *good* and *bad* women was clear. "'Good' women were women like their mothers, sisters, and sweethearts: 'bad' women were the women who could be bought, or that could be slept with for nothing. Since they had to have women and could not have the 'good' ones, they frequented the 'bad' ones. And since going to bed with either a 'good' or a 'bad' woman was a sin, it was necessary to be forgiven. Both boys went to confession regularly."[79] The two young men took Richard Wright first to the Cathedral and showed him the magnificent spectacle of devotion and ritual in which the country was immersed. Brenan would comment too on the religious practices of Spaniards. For him religion in Spain was an affair of "ritual and observance." André and his friend were devoted Catholics who frequented the church and the brothels alternatively. The next important scene to share with Wright, their guest, was the brothel.

> We pushed through a rattling curtain made of long strings of black beads, flinging aside the strips and hearing them clack and settle into place behind us; we entered an oblong dive whose background was lost in smoke. An unshaven, Greekish face, with an unlighted cigarette stub in its partly open lips, eyed us coldly from behind a cash register as we moved forward through fumes of tobacco smoke that stung the throat. Strips of bamboo covered the walls; I supposed that tropical orientation was to make sailors feel that they were in the emotionally abandoned atmosphere. Some thirty women of all ages and descriptions and sizes sat at tables and at the long bar, their shiny black purses—the international trademark of their profession—blatantly in evidence. They weighted us with restless, surfeited eyes.[80]

The three men sat at a table and the women started to gravitate toward them. Wright noticed one of the girls; "not pretty, not ugly" he remarked. "She wore the golden medallion of the Virgin between her enormous breasts."[81] Her name was Pilly. She had managed to learn a few English-like formulas of communication from her experience with American sailors. "You no man from sheep [*sic*]" she asked Wright; and then blatantly invited him: "No possibility fuckie [*sic*]." Wright politely refused her solicitation. Once sex was out of the way she went straight to the heart of her business "*Pesetas para los niños,*" she begged, for her children. Another girl, called Isabel, sought the opportunity missed by Pilly. "You *mí* telephone, *sí?*" she told Wright. When he extended a pen and his notebook for her to write it down she replied "Me no write." Wright noticed the shame in her face to have to admit her illiteracy.[82] "I drove slowly toward my pension. Poor, 'bad' illiterate girls . . . I glanced at the tall, dark middle-class apartment buildings and hotels that loomed to left and right of me; they were filled with respectable Catholic families in which all the women were 'good.' The sailors, soldiers, the men who were married to 'good' women and the young sons in 'good' families became the clientele of 'bad' girls . . .[83] Photographer Joan Colom declared, "I discovered the Barrio Chino in 1958. I understood that it was my world. I was fascinated by its diversity and its social richness . . . I literally got sucked in by the human quality of these characters." From 1958 to 1961, Colom took undercover photographs of the red light district of Barcelona, the Barrio Chino or Raval. He captured the dealings of the prostitutes and their patrons.[84] Colom first exhibited this series in 1961 at the Aixela Salon in Barcelona and then the show traveled throughout Spain. In 1964 he published them in a book authored by 1989 Nobel Prize winner Camilo José Cela entitled *Izas, Rabizas y Colipoterras.* The book caused extreme controversy and angered the regime, causing Colom to abandon photography for over twenty years. His photographs represent some of the modern avant-garde style of the fifties, intertwined with the "dark" and pessimistic tradition of Spain in the Franco era. They represent the stills of the neorealist trend in the film industry in Italy and Spain at the time. Contrary to the benign image of gender relations the regime presented in the official propaganda, these photographs denounced the tragic reality of so many women under the dictatorship. Still some of the characters show defiance to the camera. They are the raw representation of survival in the face of adversity.

By decree of March 3, 1956, the regime moved officially from tolerance to the abolition of prostitution. The 1956 ruling reinforced the Foundation for the Protection of Women as the state agency in charge of the "re-education and social re-insertion of fallen women."[85]

Minister of Justice at the time, Antonio Iturmendi, issued the decree of March 3, 1956. The law made prostitution illegal. Article 1, if you read its justification, was enacted to "ensure women's dignity and the interest of social morality." The abolition of all bawdy houses and official brothels was established and had to be accomplished within three months of the publication of the law. Article 5 charged the Foundation for the Protection of Women with the responsibility of reeducating those women freed from the official brothels by creating "non penitentiary" shelters. The Foundation for the Protection of Women had received further support from the government by law of December 20, 1952, which strengthened its role as an agency to protect minors and women. According to the law, these shelters functioned as employment clearinghouses "providing jobs appropriate for women."[86] Articles 6 and 7 of the law of 1956 assigned the responsibility of fighting the spread of venereal diseases to the General Secretariat of Health, and the responsibility for the implementation of the new abolitionist legislation to the Ministries of Justice and Interior. The order of April 23, 1956 laid down the regulations to implement the law. According to this order, the government authorities had to close down the brothels and official bawdy houses, while the Foundation had the responsibility to "dignify" the women by implementing "tutelary surveillance" ("vigilancia tutelar") and even "putting them in a shelter if these women were homeless and lacked licit employment."[87] Government authorities and the Foundation were expected to cooperate with each other without meddling in the other's jurisdictions. Hence, the local branches of the Foundation for the Protection of women had to collaborate with both the police and the Civil Governors. A Foundation delegate was appointed in those cases where there was not a branch of the Foundation.

The authorities issued a detailed record of the bawdy houses and legal brothels that were slated to close in their respective jurisdictions as well as a detailed disciplinary file verifying that illicit activities were held there. Once the authorities finalized the inventory of all the illegal businesses in their areas they had to send notification to the owners for the immediate closure. Owners had a five-day period to close and provide the authorities with a list of the names, ages, and "nature" of the women working there as prostitutes.[88] The local branch of the Foundation for the Protection of Women received these lists and in turn provided a copy to their national junta. Because the entrance into a Foundation's shelter had to be voluntary, the regulations allowed for the authorities to send these women back to their home towns. Many of the women who were evacuated from the brothels did not take either of those two options, and instead went into clandestine prostitution. However, government spies followed them everywhere. Not only did their names appear on the closing lists, but they had a health report on file in the official clinics. Tutelary surveillance over women remained at the heart of the new legislation. If the government failed to monitor them, the responsibility fell to their parents or immediate relatives.

> The concept of the prostitute's polluted body had its counterpart on the pure woman—The virgin fiancée. Seduction was central to the sexual game.
>
> Seduction is in itself innocent, even a natural means to confirm love. . . . Between men and women the art of seduction is an important stage into good loving. If we were to observe eroticism we could clearly see that it is all the time around us—intensely and passionately surrounding us.[89]

Along with this "innocent seductive game" there was another illicit seduction. This seduction was immoral or criminal. While the former led to marriage the latter was the trap for women to fall into "bad life." Within the illicit seduction there were several categories. The first was rape, a crime the penal code defined as "the violent access to the woman's honor." The crime was not only a violent aggression, explained the code text, but also a crime perpetrated against a woman's free will. According to Article 429 of the penal code, there was a crime when "laying with a woman by force or intimidation . . . when she was unconscious for any cause . . . and finally when the woman is younger than twelve."[90] This crime was punished with fifteen years of prison on average and the material reparation and acknowledgment of the resulting offspring. A second form of illicit seduction was statutory rape. The crime was aggravated if there was also an abuse of power by "public authority, priest, domestic servant, tutor, teacher or guardian of the young woman."[91] The punishment on average was three months to three years of imprisonment plus economic retribution and acknowledgment of the offspring.

Acceptable seduction was out of the legal penalization. When a woman over twenty-three years old was abandoned by her boyfriend, and possibly pregnant, the law offered no protection. Therefore any consensual sexual relations outside of wedlock stained the reputation of a woman for life if the man did not marry her. It was the civil code that dealt with the problem of paternity out of wedlock. Article 129 of the Civil Code read: "The natural child may be acknowledged by the father and the mother together or by one of them only."[92] The law protected the privacy of men. According to article 132 of the civil code "when the father or mother acknowledge the paternity separately, the name of the other parent will not be disclosed," and article 141 read: "The court will not accept any lawsuit that directly or indirectly might have as an object the investigation of paternity."[93] Therefore, it was up to the father to acknowledge his paternity in a consensual extramarital affair. The single mother suffered the social condemnation, while the law protected the man's privilege to a licentious life even after marriage.

By law of December 23, 1961, the regime launched the reform of the penal code to adjust Spanish legislation to the international abolitionist agreements.[94] Chapter 7 of the Penal Code was created to cover crimes "contra la honestidad" now called "crimes pertaining to prostitution."[95] The final text of the penal code reform was published on May 28, 1963. The main elements of the reform included the deferral of penalties to certain individuals; increasing penalties to those who have authority over minors; the possibility to suspend in certain cases the custody rights; and finally, the creation of new punishments.

The responsibilities fell on the owners and managers or any other individual who knowingly participated in financing the business premises where prostitution or any other form of illegal activity was practiced. In addition, the penal code extended punishment to those individuals who provided buildings or spaces within buildings for the prostitution or corruption of others. The reform of the Spanish penal code followed the reform on November 25, 1960, in France. The French model emphasized the prosecution of procurement, broadening the definition to cover a larger number of individuals involved in the crime.

The Spanish reform also ordered the intensification of some punishments. Article 445 of the Spanish Penal Code affected those with a criminal record—tutors, teachers, or any person who could abuse their power and might have cooperated in the exploitation of prostitution. These individuals would receive imprisonment of one month and one day to six months, a fine of one thousand to five thousand pesetas, and when the crime included public indecency, they faced medium-term prison sentences of six months to six years. Those involved in the prostitution of others faced the punishment of having their business closed permanently and their license suspended. Finally, the penal code imposed the suspension of the custody rights for those individuals who practiced or benefited from prostitution or any illegal activity connected with it.[96] These norms only penalized the prostitution resulting from exploitation but were unable to prosecute the clandestine activity. Enrique Jiménez Asenjo, supreme court magistrate and ex-member of the Foundation for the Protection of Women, identified two types of prostitution; one illegal and the other immoral but not illegal per se. Spain was joining the rest of the civilized world in the fight against prostitution in the name of women's dignity. However, Christian values remained at the heart of the shift to modernization. Spanish sexual practices remained untouched for the purpose of preserving public decency. Clandestine prostitution had to be contained, isolated from respectable society. "The streets cannot be a brothel in broad day light," remarked Jiménez Asenjo. "While the furtive exchange might be ignored; any public display must be repressed."[97] There was an acknowledgment of the unavoidable permissive sexual behavior that a free trade society entailed, but at the same time the moral double standard remained in place. Jiménez Asenjo considered the Swiss legislation on matters of prostitution and public morality particularly apt to the Spanish reform of the Penal Code. In his appraisal he commented on article 206 of the Swiss legal text. "It is punishable the professional individual who in public incites a person to prostitution by signs or indecent proposals."

> A prostitute who goes out for example to the market to buy groceries, and in the mean time, takes advantage of the situation to make a proposition of her trade would not be prosecuted under article 206 but if her behavior on the street consciously and voluntarily incites carnal exchange; for example . . . dressing and standing in the way those professionals do, and she gives eye signals looking straight at men or swinging slowly her body for sale. *This conduct means she is offering herself to any man on the street* . . . [my emphasis].
>
> The essential argument here is that she is exposing her body, like the merchant exposes his merchandise, to attract clients and make a profit. It would be contrary to the nature of things to penalize a woman who is trying to conquer a particular man, when it is obvious by her interaction with the passersby that she may be possessed, leaving it up to the men to solicit her. In a certain way there is an invitation to all of them, and hence she is most dangerous in this context than if she just made a pass discreetly to one man only.[98]

Clearly women's bodies were marked as public sexual objects —either as virgins to be married or as prostitutes to be possessed. The art of controlling every move turns into a serious legal matter in this context. The prostitute's body was an open site for the aggression of male sexual needs. She was marked as the social pollutant from which society had to protect itself by mapping her movements on the street and monitoring the times when they could be visible to respectable eyes. In some cities the prostitutes only could go out during a few hours a day, from 3 pm to 11 pm; at night they had no restrictions since there was a conventional curfew for the decent woman.[99]

A good economic plan was essential to make the legal switch work. Just in Barcelona ninety-eight authorized and forty-two clandestine bawdy houses were closed. This legal shift led to great commotion in the Barrio Chino district. To keep their business afloat many of the brothels turned into meublés, hostels, or boardinghouses. Some reopened as taverns or nightclubs but most had to close down. Prostitution's physiognomy changed. Clandestine prostitution rose. Sex traffic boomed with clandestine business in the 1950s. Sham dance companies advertised castings to hire chorus girls to perform abroad. Once they signed their contract these young women realized they had entered an international prostitution ring. Richard Wright witnessed in

Seville how young women in need were victims of fraud and ready to sell their bodies and risk their lives to escape indigence. An American called S. in his narrative invites Wright to go to a nightclub to see a flamenco show. To the writer's amazement S. has no problem in admitting to using him (his blackness specifically) to trick the dancers to sign a fraudulent contract to work in the whorehouses in North Africa.

> Four girls were at our table now. The orchestra played and they wriggled their shoulders, rolled their eyes, and snapped their fingers. Most of them were in their twenties. And they kept looking expectantly at me.
> "I you go Africa," a young girl said to me.
> S. bent over with laughter, enjoying my bewilderment.
> "But I'm not an African," I told S. "Tell her that I am American."
> S. Laughed even harder, slapping his thighs.
> . . .
> "Look, I'm organizing these girls to take them to Africa next week." He explained. "They think that you are the boss. You see, you are *dark* [Wright's emphasis].
> . . . It hit me like a ton of rock. *White slavery* [Wright's emphasis].
> No. Not white slavery," he chuckled. "Olive-skinned slavery."
> I looked at the girls again. They were fresh, young, happy, pretty, healthy. . . .
> "But . . ." I tried to speak.
> "What's the matter with you?" He asked me, clapping me on the shoulder, bending double with laughter.
> "You mean they *want* to work in the *whorehouses* in Africa?" I asked. [Wright's emphasis].
> "They are *dying* to go," [Wright's emphasis] he told me. "I got the pick of thousands of women to make up my quota. That's why they were eyeing you; they thought that you were the black boss from Africa." He went off into another long laugh.
> I managed a sick smile.[100]

Far from solving the problem, abolition only exacerbated it. Wright predicted that the closing of the brothels would "scatter a vast horde of hungry women" through the country. Simple abolition was not the answer to what he saw as a social and economic problem. The political decision had little to do with the well being of this segment of the population but rather with the regime's desire to ingratiate itself into the international community. The decision came in time for the celebration in October 1956 in Frankfurt of the Twentieth International Abolitionist Conference.

The regime reconsidered, if only nominally, women's sexuality as part of the package of modernization that the new 1950s consumer economy inaugurated. In 1963 Enrique Jiménez Asenjo, magistrate of the Spanish Supreme Court and member of the Foundation for the Protection of Women executive committee, published *Abolicionismo y prostitución. Justificación y defensa del Decreto-Ley de 3 de Marzo de 1956* (Abolitionism and Prostitution. Justification and Defense of the Decree of 3 March 1956). The preamble was written by the president of the Foundation for the Protection if Women, Luis Martínez Kleiser, who explained the purpose of the Foundation and the significance of the new legislation utilizing a language packed with somatic metaphors. Kleiser pointed out that the Foundation's task was "preventing and healing, shaping and strengthening the social spirit with the medication that combats moral anemia." The "disorder" caused by prostitution was in his view "not just a tumor for the scalpel to cut off, but rather an infection that only moral antibiotics could cure."[101] "The State is the physician that determines which are the cases that need the prophylaxis, and the Foundation is the hospital where those who are contagious are isolated and cured."[102]

Redemption through penance remains at the core of this medical metaphor. In order to implement its new legislation the state issued an instructive order on April 26, 1956, to establish new institutions that helped with the "isolation" of those cases considered most urgent. The cities opening new establishments were scattered all over the country: Granada, Vigo, Cuenca, Albacete, Cartagena, and Leon. In Madrid, the establishment of Our Lady of Almudena housed pregnant adolescents and single mothers with their children. The capacity was 150 spaces for pregnant women and 350 for single mothers and their children. Martínez Kleiser mentioned the state investment of ten million pesetas (about $100,000) per year to cover the cost of over 3,000 inmates all over the nation. By 1963 the Foundation had a budget of thirty-five million pesetas a year to run its old and new institutions.[103] However, the increasing number of women that had to be "isolated" after the 1956 regulations required the additional financial support of the local authorities and the Foundation's regional offices.[104] According to the official reports, 5,050 "freed" prostitutes received the services of the Foundation in different cities: Madrid, 41; Barcelona, 618; Valencia, 400; Bilbao, 800; Seville, 232; Malaga, 300; Cadiz, 300; Zaragoza, 248; Palma de Mallorca, 200; and Las Palmas, 202. With regard to the official brothels, or "Casas de Tolerancia," the decree called for their closure. In Madrid there were three official houses closed along with 42 tolerated: in Barcelona, 98; in Valencia, 38; in Seville, 74; in Malaga, 65; in Bilbao, 60; in Zaragoza, 35; in Badajoz, 40; and in las Palmas, 37.[105] The figures show clearly the insignificant number of women who requested the protection of the Foundation. The Foundation faced the enormous task of rehabilitating an unknown but massive number of the fallen women that went into the clandestine practice of the profession. The Foundation aspired to follow the model of the Public Clinic in Paris under the direction of Dr. León Brizar where 74 percent of the women who arrived there were able to reintegrate into society. However, the experience in Spain was less than promising in the immediate closure of the brothels. The data from the Foundation showed a highly hostile attitude toward the ex-prostitutes. In Alava, the Foundation placed one of these women in a factory and the co-workers threatened the owner with a strike if she was not fired. In Albacete these women were not taken for factory work or domestic service. With regard to the public morality the Foundation acknowledged that most of these women continued working underground. Most urgent was the planning of a sound system of public health regulations to control the spread of venereal diseases.

When these women voluntarily turned themselves in to the Foundation for protection, they were divided into two categories according to their age. The group under eighteen years old were considered more innocent and malleable while the older they were, the more challenging the task confronted by the Foundation's officials and educators. However, this rule was sometimes deceiving and the Foundation resorted to psychological assessments to decide on each individual case. The process of rehabilitation followed a precise program: "Plan for the better ones: It will be based: 1st, Preliminary medical appraisal to be able to guide her in her future professional re-education; 2nd, the formation of the moral character with Catechism and pious practices; 3rd, Regulation of their will and their character with the aid of intelligent female monitors who will guide them in the compliance of regulations. These practices must be very mild to avoid the resemblance to a prison-like environment; 4th, identification of a skill to be able to make an honest living and therefore overcome the complex of inferiority; 5th, Cultivate an environment of sympathy based on mutual trust."[106] The plan for the older ones called for much harsher measures. They were characterized as "know-it-all and unruly" because they have almost "lost the joy of life." The Foundation pointed out there were many types and it was imperative to consider each case individually when designing the plan of action. In order to be successful in the rehabilitating business, the Foundation needed a master plan that included the opening of new shelters and the reform of the old ones to fit within the modern abolitionist attitude toward the problem of prostitution voiced in Frankfurt Abolitionist International Congress in October 1956.

The Foundation insisted on the urgent recycling of the education and training of their monitors and instructors in the new attitude of abolitionism. The twentieth Congress of the International Abolitionist Federation celebrated in Frankfurt 17–19 October 1956 made clear that the term "relevement" [*sic*] to recover employed in 1939 has been replaced after World War II with the term "reclassement" [*sic*] to readjust and then with reeducation, which indicates "an important shift of perspective."[107] The elements of this shift included: the voluntary entry in the reeducation institutions, which were independent from police and hygiene forces; respect for the freedom and dignity of the person who enter to received active education and support; important emphasis in artistic and cultural developments; important emphasis in the professional training offering a variety of trade options; and psychological counseling to foster healthy family and couples relationships.[108] It was impossible to accomplish this task without the support of the state, local authorities, and the public in general. In Spain the responsibility fell solely on the Foundation for the Protection of Women. The minimum requirements to receive subsidies to open a shelter, according to Foundation officials, were to cover five to twenty inmates who voluntarily came looking for shelter. These centers were managed by female personnel: a director, a social worker, and one instructor/monitor for twelve women and two monitors if there were more than twelve inmates. The facilities had to comply with the hygiene standards and were designed as a homelike atmosphere but "with a freely accepted disciplined spirit." The young women were to pass medical and psychological exams prior to entering the shelter. Those people affected by contagious diseases were not admitted until the infection had been cured.[109]

According to a summary issued in the court of first instance, number eleven, in 1962, white slavery had intensified. Richard Wright's predictions were not so far fetched after all: "Since the beginning of 1960 till February 1962 the defendant Manuel G.V.

has been working in Barcelona in collaboration with an associate in Algeria to recruit women to send to that country as if they were singers and performers but in reality they were to work in cabarets and similar places to attract clients, with the obvious risk to fall into prostitution. The defendant received a commission for this work per each contract he arranged."[110]

This was the time when the nightclubs boomed in Barrio Chino and the waitresses were in fact there to attract and make the night pleasurable for the clients. Flamenco shows, disco pubs, and all kind of nightlife populated the district well until the end of the regime and into the transition period. The fallen woman, as symbol of the decaying Spain, was experiencing the pressures of consumer culture in which penance as redemption and the purification of the nation's body turned into obsolete concepts. The religiously charged imagery gave way to a more lay and maybe dehumanized version of gender relations. Modernization was in the making. Spanish women were joining their Western counterparts in fighting for their rights.

4
Perfect Wives and Mothers

> Why did all novels have to end when people got married? I liked the whole process of falling in love, the obstacles, the tears and misunderstandings, the kisses in the moonlight, but once the wedding had taken place there didn't seem to be anything more to tell. It was as though life itself had ended.
>
> —Carmen Martín Gaite (2000), *The Backroom*

THE FORTIES WERE A TIME OF HUNGER—*HUNGER YEARS* IN MARriage too. Ration books were recalled only in 1952, and Cardinal Vicente Enrique Tarancón had published his pastoral letter "Our Daily Bread" a year earlier denouncing the misery of the larger population. "The ration consisted of a small roll of bread a day, a quarter of a litre of olive oil, and three ounces of sugar a week, with minute quantities of chick peas and rice, very irregularly distributed. Even these rations are not always honoured. And on the black market the bread are twelve pesetas the kilo—just the average daily wage."[1] Brenan describes his book *The Face of Spain* (1950) as "an account of the journey my wife and I made in the center and south of Spain" in 1949. He decided to keep a diary to answer a few fundamental questions: "What was Spain really like? What was the character of Spanish culture and civilization? How did it compare with the French and the English?"[2] Brenan reports a few early signs of economic betterment, although the main source of income for many derived from the black market or estraperlo. This corrupt modus operandi had the support of the Francoist establishment, with many officials partaking in the profits. Brenan observed the impact of the war in the bodies of the walking wounded in stark contrast with the numerous examples of American-made cars the nouveaux riches drove in the capital. "One of the sights of Madrid are the new American cars. I should say that there are more of these than in any capital in Europe. Most of them, I'm told, belong to govern-

Figure 5. Newlyweds. Author's private collection.

ment officials, but rich people can also get permission to import them if they are prepared to pay what is asked. They cost anything from £3,000 to £5,000."[3]

In 1949 the service sector started to take off. Hospitality and construction employed a large number of people. Brenan noticed with surprise how in their hotel, fourteen waiters just in the dining room, were all showing what the author calls "their waiterly rank" as revealed in a variety of white jackets and insignias displayed at different times of the day.

> The waiter makes one of the most striking and representative types of the country. With their thick eyebrows and erect, stylized posture they have the air of bullfighters' *manqués*, of *toreros* who wisely prefer the white napkin to the red cloth and the pacific dinner to the charging bull. They move with the same litheness and ballet dancer's precision and put a certain solemn operatic air into every gesture. How refreshing to see people doing the supposedly humdrum and mechanical things with artistic relish and gusto! It is something that the Englishman, accustomed to the utilitarian outlook of his countrymen, to their mixture of sloppiness and Puritan Philistinism, can hardly understand. It makes one realize the price we have had to pay for Locke's and John Stuart Mill's philosophy.[4]

Brenan points out how during the ten years following the civil war there had been an astonishing amount of building in the capital. New blocks of flats, business premises, and monumental ministries were under construction, while in the outskirts of Madrid new suburbs of five- to six-story buildings had started to be developed when he visited in 1949. The observations of maids, waiters, and construction sites led him to reflect on the fact that labor cost was extremely low in Spain.

In the midst of economic stagnation, André, one of the characters Richard Wright met in his first week in Barcelona, could not marry his beloved virgin fiancée yet. The only option for her was to wait patiently. Richard Wright saw a Spain highly polarized along gender lines. André's working-class family welcomed him for Sunday lunch. He noticed how, "as though in response to some signal," women gravitated toward each other leaving the men alone. "I noticed," he writes, "there was always an attempt to herd the men with the men and the women with the women; it was as though they wanted to protect the men from the women and the women from the men, even in public." This ritual, Wright observed, "made one conscious of sexual differences when normally such notions would have been far from one's mind."[5]

Most striking was for him to meet his host André's fiancée. Wright described her as the "living personification of sexual consciousness; one could have scraped sex off her with a knife."[6] André lamented his economic situation and inability to get married yet. When Wright asked him about his fiancée's profession the young man, astonished, replied "She is a virgin." Wright realized that

> being a virgin, evidently, was a kind of profession in itself. It seemed that she stayed home with her mother and was never allowed out except in the company of the immediate members of the family, a situation that constituted proof of her virginity. I understood now why she had been so wonderstruck by me; she had not had an opportunity to meet many men, and I was, moreover, a different sort of man: brown. . . . Her being a virgin was all in the world she knew, felt, and thought about. Hence, each man that she saw she regarded as a possible agent of defloration, an agent which, no doubt, she longed to meet and embrace. Her living the role of a virgin has steeped her personality with an aura of sex and she unconsciously attracted men to her body with more definiteness than even a professional prostitute. Her entire outlook was one of waiting to be despoiled, longing for the day when she could shed her burdensome and useless role, when she could live a free and normal life like the older women about her.[7]

Figure 6. Author's father in his waiter uniform. Melilla, 1958. Author's private collection.

Young women patiently waited to find a man who would marry them. For working-class women their virginity became part of their dowry. Honor, male honor specifically, was a precious possession imbued in the fabric of society since the Golden Age. Francoism restored the eternal Catholic family values and elevated them to national duties for men and women in order to rebuild the country.

Finding a husband was not just a survival skill but also a national responsibility; for a woman remaining single under Francoism turned into a personal tragedy and a source of public embarrassment. Marriage, in this context, rather than a social event, was a politically charged venture—the prerequisite for the lawful encounter of the sexes. Through marriage, individuals (particularly women) were recognized as national subjects within the political and personal family unit.

The regime saw to it that Catholicism was to guide the lives of men and women. The Christian prescriptions of the Catholic Church on marriage translated into laws. Religious supremacy was the major difference between Spanish women's postwar experience and that of their European counterparts. Marriage under Franco developed into a political ground where men and women encountered each other for the sole purpose of procreation.

In 1950 there were still a high number of single women as a result of the Civil War casualties and subsequent male mortality in the immediate postwar period. Concha Piquer, one of the most loved singers of the forties and fifties captured with her voice the hearts of many young Spanish girls when postwar male casualties had drained the marriage market. "Lime and lemon / You have no one to love you," Piquer sang, "Lime and lemon / you will be a spinster / what a pity, what a sorrow / you have no one to love you."[8]

The trend in the 1950s was to delay marriage due to economic hardship and to avoid reproduction. Men married in their late twenties while women maintained the average age to get married in their early twenties. Between 1955 and 1970, however, men and women got married younger as a result of the economic takeoff of the 1960s.

By the early 1970s Ireland and Spain were the countries in Europe with the highest number of single people, both ultra-Catholic nations where heterosexual mandate ruled. In Spain, the so-called *law of vagrants and criminals* (ley de vagos y maleantes) of July 15, 1954, criminalized homosexuality. Those individuals declared homosexuals upon arrest under this law were

Average Marriage Age in Spain

Year	Men	Women	% difference
1915	28,14	24,76	3,38
1920	27,98	24,97	3,01
1925	27,85	24,67	3,18
1930	27,59	24,87	2,72
1935	**28,24**	**25,16**	**3,08**
1940	29,50	26,12	3,49
1945	29,63	26,12	3,51
1950	29,09	25,97	3,12
1955	28,89	25,88	2,97
1960	28,79	25,89	2,90
1965	**28,43**	**25,26**	**3,17**
1969	27,56	24,66	2,90

Source: Fundación FOESSA, *Estudios Sociológicos sobre la situación social de España 1975* (Madrid: Editorial de Euroamérica, 1976), 33.

incarcerated in concentration camps to rehabilitate them. In the Tefía Agrarian Penitentiary Colony in the Canary Islands, homosexuals served their sentences along with political and common prisoners.[9] In 1967 the regime established a commission to draft a new law to replace the law of the vagrants and criminals with a Law of Dangerousness and Social Rehabilitation. The latter showed a shift in the consideration of homosexuals now as antisocial individuals clinically ill and subject to rehabilitation rather than just morally flawed.

The regime's official heterosexual mandate, and in particular the discourse on "True Catholic Womanhood," faced the challenge of modernization in the 1950s and 1960s. A new generation of Catholic women (and men) found ways to circumvent the official Catholic straitjacket that the regime imposed on them in the transition from autarky to consumerism. Consumerism opened the door to alternative venues to the parish or family gatherings for men and women to encounter each other socially. Monitoring public morality became increasingly harder as waves of tourists brought their mores into the country and migrant workers were exposed to European ways of life. Movie theaters showed the Hollywood-manufactured American dream and cafés offered young people a pastime spot to drink Coca-Cola and smoke Marlboros. Modernization was unavoidable. It was the result of a slow but constant transformation of Catholic values with regard to marriage, family, and child-rearing among the younger generations. By defining the female citizen as self-effacing wife and prolific mother the regime articulated a tight control of women's bodies, but the secularization of customs and the economic takeoff begged for a redefinition of gender roles. It is important to examine the political and symbolic significance of the wifely body and its maternal destiny in the transitional period of the 1950s and 1960s. Multiple factors influenced the public perception of authority and ultimately had an impact in everyday life choices and behaviors. By the mid-sixties Spanish women had access to the birth control pill just like their counterparts in the western hemisphere. Although contraception was illegal until 1978, Spanish women had been prescribed the pill, but only under the confluence of two circumstances: being married and alleging some gynecological malady, rather than to avoid pregnancy.

Therefore, the nationalization of the wife's body through mandatory motherhood remained at the center of the Francoist regime's discourse on Spanish women's national identity. Multiple discourses of Catholicism emerged in the aftermath of the Second Vatican Council that led to alternate Catholic womanhoods in dispute with the traditional Francoist version. I examine in this chapter the religious discourse that emerged in the transitional period of the 1960s and its legal translation. I then examine the religious values that informed the prescriptive literature on marriage and sexuality authored by physicians and moralists. These works represent the official discourse on the nationalization of the family as one of the strongholds of the state apparatus. "How-to" literature in the 1950s and 1960s insisted on perpetuating domesticity in the face of unavoidable modernization. Interestingly, such publications mirror the Spanish baroque tradition of conduct manuals. Close reading of the definition of the wife's body in 1500s prescriptive literature (such as de León's *La perfecta casada*), in the guidebooks, and in women's magazines published in the fifties and sixties, sheds light on the religious, political, and sexual nature of the marriage market under Francoism as the *anteroom* to the family—the family as a politically charged meeting place of the sexes in transition.

National Catholic ideology conceived the "perfect" wife's body in the image of the sixteenth and seventeenth centuries' values.[10] The regulation and control of the wife's body highlights the intersection of gender with the political and cultural realms,

Figure 7. Honeymoon. Author's private collection.

endowing with a historical continuity the gendered politics of authoritarian Spain from the baroque period to the twentieth century. Francoism did not invent women's inferiority; it simply perfected it by updating it and modernizing it in the name of God and Country.

National Catholic Discourse on Marriage Neo-Baroque Style

National Catholicism, a fusion of old Catholic and new Falangist nationalist principles, was Francoism's malleable ideological substratum in the Cold War. It lent cohesion to the corporate state apparatus' components: family, syndicate, and municipality. Men and women were enlisted to join these political bodies in the 1940s reconstruction of the fatherland, and the principles remained constant in the official discourse until the early 1970s. To guide Spaniards through the new era, a single party, Falange Española Tradicionalista de las JONS, legally replaced in 1937 the multiparty democracy embodied in the Second Republic (1931–36). Falange's Women's Section, by law of December 28, 1939, assumed the responsibility of making Spanish women patriotic homemakers. A year earlier the Labor Charter (*Fuero del Trabajo*, 1938) had explicitly pronounced the state intention to "*free* married women from factory work,"[11] settling their national duty as wives and mothers.

The regime defined women's political persona in accordance with National Catholicism. Religious discourse sanctified biological determinism. As mothers, women's relationship to the Francoist body politic was officially articulated around the policing of their bodies. In postwar Spain the moral/national duty for women was to surrender their bodies to the regime's demands, since men had already sacrificed theirs in the battlefront. As pointed out in previous chapters, in the New Spain dawning in 1939, the body became the sign of oppression and resistance as it had been in the 1500s and the Golden Age. The symbolic isomorphism between the state and the human body is better understood when examining it from a gender perspective. The nationalization of women's bodies under Francoism mimics that of the early modern period. The wife's body was the antagonist of the prostitute in Francoist legal discourse—two sides of the same coin. In order to inscribe the female body onto the Francoist body politic, the regime nationalized marriage and motherhood as the only way for women to become full citizens. The married woman's body turned into a primary site of political signification in the Francoist preservation of National Catholic family values. The Francoist state followed the directives of Pope Pius XII, who publicly reiterated that procreation was the sole purpose of Christian marriage in 1951. "In accordance with the Creator's will, matrimony, as an institution of nature, has not as a primary and intimate end the personal perfection of the married couple but rather *the procreation and upbringing of a new life.* [my emphasis] . . . One of the fundamental demands of the true moral order is the sincere acceptance of motherhood's function and duties."[12] Post–World War II demographical needs prompted the papal attention to family values. The Pope echoed his predecessor Pius XI's dictum in his *Casti Connnubii* encyclical about Christian marriage (1930). The family's political purpose was to renew the depleted postwar population. In the Spanish case, Franco's demographic aspiration meant to reach the goal of forty million people. More importantly, procreation ought to never happen out of wedlock.[13]

Since demographic recovery became a top priority after the Spanish Civil War, women's patriotic duty was to fulfill their maternal destiny. To accomplish this, the regime officially instituted the Women's Section of Falange under the leadership of Pilar Primo de Rivera to impose an iron control over Spanish women.[14] Until its dissolution in 1977, Women Section officials trained their fellow countrywomen to become *perfect* wives and mothers through the six-month mandatory Social Service to the state. Being one of the three pillars of the new state (along with the syndicate and the municipality) the family became more than a private *emotional domain.* In the hands of the Women's Section, the family turned into a political site of gender contention, and so, Falangist women's control over family matters placed them as historical agents at the center of the political arena making them personal and political.

Based on the antagonism between men and women, the Francoist articulation of a gender ideology was crucial to the national reconstruction in the postwar period as much as during the transition to consumerism. "True Catholic Womanhood" guided official directives on women throughout the period. With the transition to consumerism, a multitude of Catholic "womanhoods" questioned the regime's revival, in the 1940s, of Renaissance treatises such as Juan Luis Vives's *The Instruction of the Christian Woman* (*La instrucción de la mujer cristiana*) (1523) and Fray Luis de León's *The Perfect Wife* (*La perfecta casada*) (1583). In addition, the Vatican doctrine on marriage as prescribed by Pius XI and Pius XII encyclicals ruled sexual relations until the early fifties. And finally, the Women's Section of Falange implemented the domesticity required for the pronatalist policies of the regime to come to fruition.

Pope from 1939 to 1953, Pius XII[15] was the major architect of the definition of marriage within canon law. His explanation derived from the definitions of matrimony in Roman law, which emphasized the heterosexual union of man and woman and their partnership in all aspects of life. For Pius XII, the Council of Trent (1545–63) mandate on the indissolubility of marriage between man and woman symbolized the indissoluble bond between Christ and His Church.[16] The Vatican distributed the 1917 code of canon law to clergy throughout the world, which created a means of establishing, imposing, and sustaining a strong "top-down" power within the Catholic Church.[17] This compilation of Church laws retained many conservative concepts about family and marriage developed during the 1500s.[18]

Pius XI had added in his encyclical *Casti Connubii* (1930) the concept of the hierarchy of love within Christian marriage. This hierarchy of love meant the husband was the "head" of the institution like Christ was the head of the Church, while the woman represented the "heart." Pope Pius XII reiterated this hierarchical love and further explained the doctrine of the mystical body of Christ in his encyclical *Mystici Corporis Christi,* issued on June 29, 1943. Man and woman became "one flesh" in the image of the Union of Christ and his Church—an indissoluble union under God. (See diagram)

Mystic Body Politic
&
The Hierarchy of Love

Christ	Church
Head	Heart
Franco	Spanish Nation
Husband	Wife

In the same way there existed an indissoluble contract between Franco and his people. Like the groom, the Francoist state joined his bride, the motherland, in a union consummated by the blood spilled during the Spanish Civil War. Official propaganda devoured the "madre Patria" becoming one flesh with Francoism forming, as scholar José Antonio Maravall pointed out in 1956, a mystic body politic. Likewise, men's and women's bodies developed into indispensable members ("limbs") of the Francoist mystic body politic, men as soldiers and producers, women as political and biological reproductive mothers. The human body in general and the female body in particular occupied a primary site of political signification under Francoism. National Catholicism represents a clear example of the "mystic body" in which the members assume their places and duties in the social and political order. In this mystic body politic, gender was crucial to lend a sense of natural order to the dictatorship. Duties were clearly defined along gender and class lines and sanctified by the Catholic Church.

Marriage was the rite of passage to belong to the mystic body politic. The Spanish word "mujer" translates as both wife and woman into English. This semantic duality in Spanish illustrates the fusion of biological (male/female, man/woman) and cultural discourses (religious, legal, economic) in identity building.[19] The category "wife" under Francoism transformed women into political subjects both in religious and legal terms. The law of March 12, 1938, reestablished the 1889 civil code, which defined the legal status of women as homemakers.[20] This law faithfully adhered to the directives of Pius XI's encyclical *Casti Connubii on Christian Marriage.* It revived both the Council of Trent and Pope Leo XIII's (1878–1903) mandates on the sacred nature and indissolubility of marriage, making women subject to their husbands: "Let women be subject to their husbands as to the lord, because the husband is the head of the wife, and Christ is the head of the Church."[21] Following Vatican directives on marriage, a wife in Franco's Spain had to obey her husband and follow him wherever he went because they were "no longer two, but one flesh."[22] The law of March 12, 1938, annulled civil marriages and the law of September 23, 1939, made divorce illegal.[23] Chapter 2, Article 22 of *The Spaniards' Charter* (*Fuero de los Españoles*) issued in 1945 defined the family as a natural institution. "*The State recognizes and protects the family as the natural and fundamental institution in society,* with rights and obligations beyond any positive human law. The state will protect in particular prolific families. *Marriage will be one and indissoluble*"[24] [my emphasis].

A wife became one flesh with her husband and legally this meant she had no power to sell or buy any property, or get a job or an education without her husband's permission. But the notion of one flesh lends itself to further analysis when considering the semantics of the wife's body with regard to female and male individualities. Because they are proclaimed husband and wife and pronounced one flesh, the husband's honor is conditional on the wife's faithfulness. By establishing that male honor be located in the wife's body, the husband's respectability is vulnerable to the wife's will.[25] Under Francoism, adultery was defined in Title IX articles 449 through 452 of the Civil Code: "Adultery will be punished with imprisonment. Those who commit adultery are: any married woman who lay with a man other than her husband; he who lay with a woman knowing she is married; and a husband who maintains a mistress in the conjugal household, or publicly outside the conjugal home."[26]

Punishment was harsher for the adulterous wife than the adulterous husband. Article 428 on crimes against persons declared that the husband who found his wife with another man and killed them on site suffered *destierro* (exile), not being punished if he only injure them. By contrast, a wife's adultery represented the most serious transgression to the "no longer two but one flesh" nature of marriage. The problem arises from the crucial distinction between the bodies of the single woman (marked as virgin) and the wife. While the premarital female body may be easily read and identified by her intact hymen, the wife's body loses this physical legibility. This physical lack in the wife's body threatens not only the preservation of male honor (husband, father, brother) but most importantly the legitimacy of his offspring. Article 108 of the Civil Code regulated the legal status of those children born out of wedlock. The document defined *legitimate* children as born one hundred and eighty days after their parents' wedding and before the 300 days following the dissolution of the union or separation of the spouses. *Natural* children were, according to the legal text, those conceived before marriage and became legitimized and legally accredited only after the parents' matrimony and explicit parental recognition. Any other *illegitimate* progeny were considered a product of "sin" and so they were only entitled to minimal support from the father. Since there was no way to accurately prove paternity at the time, the entire responsibility of rearing these children fell on the mother who suffered social contempt as a *fallen woman.* Within marriage the *patria potestad* (custody) was in the hands of the father. It only transferred to the mother when he died. However, if she remarried, she lost custody unless the deceased husband had ordered otherwise in his will. The custody, then, would fall into the hands of male relatives of the children.

The state also issued a series of laws penalizing the so-called crimes against decency (*crímenes contra la honestidad*) that clearly point to the political significance of the wife's body. By law of January 24, 1941, abortion was declared illegal as well as any kind of contraceptive propaganda. Any attempt to disseminate information about "means to prevent procreation" was penalized with imprisonment and a fine between 5,000 to 50,000 pesetas (about \$50 to \$500).[27] This legislation responded to the Catholic Church commands as expressed by Pius XI's encyclical *Casti Connubii* (1930) in which the Pope condemned any kind of heterosexual encounter other than for the purpose of procreation and always within marriage. As St. Augustine notes, "Intercourse even with one's legitimate wife is unlawful and wicked where the conception of the offspring is prevented."[28] Motherhood remained women's destiny whether biological or social under autarky and consumerism. Beyond national duty in the case of Spanish women, Church fathers reminded them it was the only way for women to achieve salvation. "Even the pains which, after original sin, a mother has to suffer to give birth to her child only make her draw tighter the bond which unites them: the more the pain has cost her, so much she felt love for her child . . . Yet *women will be saved by child bearing.*"[29]

The regime presented women with the opportunity to readily achieve salvation by being prolific mothers. The state offered families financial incentives and symbolic rewards while the Women's Section, through their instruction of the Social Service, turned infant care into an almost exact science to perform with religious devotion. Prolific families received financial credit, access to housing, free school and university tuition, and reduced public transportation fares. In addition, the state introduced salary incentives for prolific working fathers. Family allowances consisted of two varieties: the family subsidy introduced in 1938 and family bonuses called *cargas familiares* implemented in 1945.[30] These wage bonuses were directed almost exclusively to the male head of the family and did not include, for example, service labor sectors such as domestic workers who were, in the majority, women. The Ministry of Labor and Social Action published the statistical figures on family protection policies. For the years 1940 to 1957, there were 19,007 applications for the so-called *Nuptial Awards* in 1941–45 of which 7,802 were awarded at a cost of 24,595,5 pesetas (about $200). In 1950 there were 32,947 applications of which 12,191 awards were granted for a total cost of 30, 477, 5 pesetas. In 1957 the Ministry did not provide the number of applications received but they published that 79,764 nuptial awards were granted at a total cost of 239,265,9 pesetas. The birth awards in 1957 were itemized by province; the total number of applications for that year was 1,965. In most provinces the number of children of those couples receiving the first and second awards was between 13 and 20 children born per family. However, the statistics also recorded the number of children alive. For example in Leon the family that received the first prize had had 20 children of whom only 16 lived. In Madrid the family that received the second prize had had 16 children and only 14 lived.[31] Family planning was not only a sin against the Catholic Church mandates but also illegal. However, there was a 20 percent decrease in fertility rate between 1950 and 1981. The number of children per woman was 2.5 to 3 between 1950 and

1964 and a sustained decline followed the more generalized use of contraceptives by 1972.[32]

Modernity posed a challenge to Christian women. In an Allocution to the Congress of the International Union of Catholic Women's Leagues held in Rome on September 11, 1947, Pius XII addressed the role of women in modern times. In his speech the Pope warned them of the dangers of modern society dominated by materialism: "We then referred especially to what might be called the secularization, the materialization, the enslavement of woman, all the attacks directed against her dignity and rights as a person and as a Christian. The dangers have become greater every day. World War II and the postwar have presented and continue to present to woman, in entire groups of nations, in practically all parts of the world, a tragic picture without precedent. . . . In the course of these awful years, women, old and young, have been forced to practice more than manly virtues and to practice them to a degree required of men only in extraordinary circumstances."[33] The Pope lamented how even among Catholics "false doctrines on the dignity of woman, on marriage and the family, on conjugal fidelity and divorce, even on life and death" prevailed. It was at this crucial juncture in history that the Pope saw these secular values had "stealthily infiltrated souls, and like gnawing worms had attacked the roots of the Christian family and of the Christian ideals of womanhood."[34] The purpose of the pontiff's speech was to offer guidance on what direction to take on this matter. First, the Pope urged Catholic women to keep a faith "proud, alert, fearless, firm and alive to truth, to the triumph of Catholic doctrine," indispensable to fighting the intellectual and political forces of atheism set to destroy Christian civilization. Second, Pius XII reminded his female audience that "Satan does not accept defeat: as in Eden, he continues to cajole woman to her downfall, playing upon her nature to seduce her." It was important to show a testimony with their own lives of their faith for Christ by swearing fidelity to the Social Program of the Church. With regard to the place and role of women in political life he distinguished several distinct aspects: "the safeguard and care of the sacred interests of woman, by means of legislation and administration that respects her rights, dignity, and social function—the participation of some women in political life for the good, the welfare, and the progress of all." Pius XII promptly emphasizes that this does not mean that all women ought to have political careers as members of public assemblies. "Most of you must," he asserts, "continue to give the *greater part of your time and of your loving attention to the care of your homes and families. We must not forget that the making of a home in which all feel at ease and happy, and the bringing up of children are very special contributions to the common welfare* [my emphasis]."[35] The elitist component in his argument is clearly stated: "Those among [you] who have more leisure and are suitably prepared, will take up the burden of public life and be, as it were, your delegated representatives." No doubt the Women's Section of Falange represented in Spain this female elite.

Pius XII was very conscious of the impact of modernity, technology, and the media in the social behavior of Catholics. Therefore, the Pope was very actively involved in spreading his doctrine on marriage and procreation through radio speeches and allocutions to different groups within the medical profession. For Pope Pacelli, "the purpose of marriage was not the child per se but rather the fulfillment of the natural matrimony act" to engender a new life.[36]

In an address in 1951 to midwives on the nature of their profession, Pius XII examined the medical and moral dilemmas motherhood presented to this group of health professionals.[37] The Pope starts by reminding midwives about the inviolability of life even when it may mean the death of the mother to save the child. "The child is '*man*,' even if he be not yet born, in the same degree and by the same title as his mother. . . . Therefore, there is no man, no human authority, no science, no 'indication' at all—whether it be medical, eugenic, social, economic, or moral—that may offer or give a valid judicial title for a *direct* deliberate disposal of an innocent human life, that is, a disposal which aims at its destruction, whether as an end in itself or as a means to achieve the end, perhaps in no way at all illicit. Thus, for example, *to save the life of the mother is a very noble act; but the direct killing of the child as a means to such an end is illicit*" [my emphasis].[38] The Pope warns the professional midwives to "be prepared to defend resolutely, and when possible, protect the helpless and hidden life of the child," and holds governments responsible for issuing laws that will protect the divine precept. The authority of the father in the reproductive process was highlighted in the Pope's 1951 address when he advised midwives to place the newborn immediately in the arms of the father. If they never bear children they must devote themselves to a life of service to others. Once married the most important goal was to accept their biological destiny—"Woman walks in the path marked by the Creator towards the goal which is her sincere acceptance of motherhood. God makes her, by the exercise of this function, partaker of His goodness, wisdom and omnipotence, in accordance to the Angel's message *Concipies in utero et paries*—you will conceive and bear forth a child."[39] Therefore the foundation of midwifery was, in the Pope's words, "to maintain, revive, and encourage the logic and love of motherhood." "You must exercise your apostolate both efficiently and efficaciously: first of all, by refusing any immoral cooperation. Second, by positively turning your delicate care to one task, that of removing those preconceived ideas, fears, or faint excuses, and so removing any obstacles which may make the acceptance of motherhood painful."[40] The Pope considered contraception and any form of sterilization immoral and illegal. Not even public authority had any right, under the pretext of any "indication" whatsoever, to permit it, and less still to prescribe it or to have it used. If there were health concerns the Pope explained how important it would be to inform couples about what he called the "heroism of abstinence." To justify his argument Pius XII brought forward the mandate of the Council of Trent, referring to a passage of St. Augustine, that teaches: "God does not command the impossible but while He commands, He warns you to do what you can and to ask for the grace for what you cannot do and He helps you so that you may be able" to accomplish grace . . . 'God does not force anyone to do what is impossible. But God compels husband and wife to practice abstinence if their union cannot be completed according to the laws of nature.' *Here is what concerns your apostolate for winning married people over to a service of motherhood, not in the sense of an utter servitude under the promptings of nature, but to the exercise of the rights and duties of married life, governed by the principles of reason and faith"* [my emphasis].[41]

Therefore the Pope established the indissolubility of marriage with procreation as its only purpose. Sexuality in this sense turned into a collateral means to redemption. In the event unplanned complications in delivery occurred, women were to be prepared to give their lives for their baby.

Modernity, Marriage, and Motherhood

Science came to add his voice to religious discourses on the matter of women's nature and their role in modern times for her family and country. The medical profession had much to say about the importance of marriage and reproduction for the good health of the fatherland. Doctors like Antonio Vallejo Nájera or Gregorio Marañón sought to find the key to a Hispanic version of eugenics.

Antonio Vallejo Nágera's racial ideas were synthesized in a short work entitled *Antes que te cases* (*Before You Get Married*), published in 1946. This work was the first title published in a popular series called "la sabiduría del hogar" (The wisdom of the home) presented to readers not as a medical collection but rather as "true conduct manuals for life." The doctor in the texts was presented as a "counselor and moralist" rather than physician. In the preface to the book Vallejo Nágera writes: "Racial decadence is the result of many things but the most important is conjugal unhappiness. A child born deformed, mad, imbecile brings unhappiness in the most prosperous and happy of homes. . . . Eugenic precepts may avoid morbid offspring . . . It is impossible a robust race without a sound preparation of youth for marriage, through Catholic morality. This little work is a minuscule contribution to the exaltation of the Fatherland."[42] Medical jargon prevails in the work that supposedly is directed to a general audience and particularly young people who are considering marriage.

Gregorio Marañón examined the issue of motherhood in his essay "Maternidad y Feminismo" ("Motherhood & Feminism").[43] First published in 1926, the version I discuss here is his second edition, published in 1951, which the author thoroughly revised to tune it up with the times. For Marañón the different activities assigned to men and women were based in their biological distinctions. He hastened to assert that this fact did not entail any kind of inferiority or superiority of one sex over the other; they were "simply different."[44] "The difference between the sexes is insurmountable. Such difference emerges from the anatomical surface of each man and woman, and it goes to the deepest, darkest roots of life, to the home of the cells."[45] Marañón explained how scientific studies at the time proved indeed that each cell in male and female organisms was distinctively different. Their most important function was the absorption and elimination of nutrients, what he called "organic metabolism."[46] This organic metabolism was, according to Marañón, the foundation of human chemistry and perfectly different in each sex. Following Geddes and Thompson's[47] study he established that men's metabolism was "katabolic," characterized by the fast transformation and high exhaustion of nutrients. By contrast women's metabolism was "anabolic," characterized by a tendency to syn-

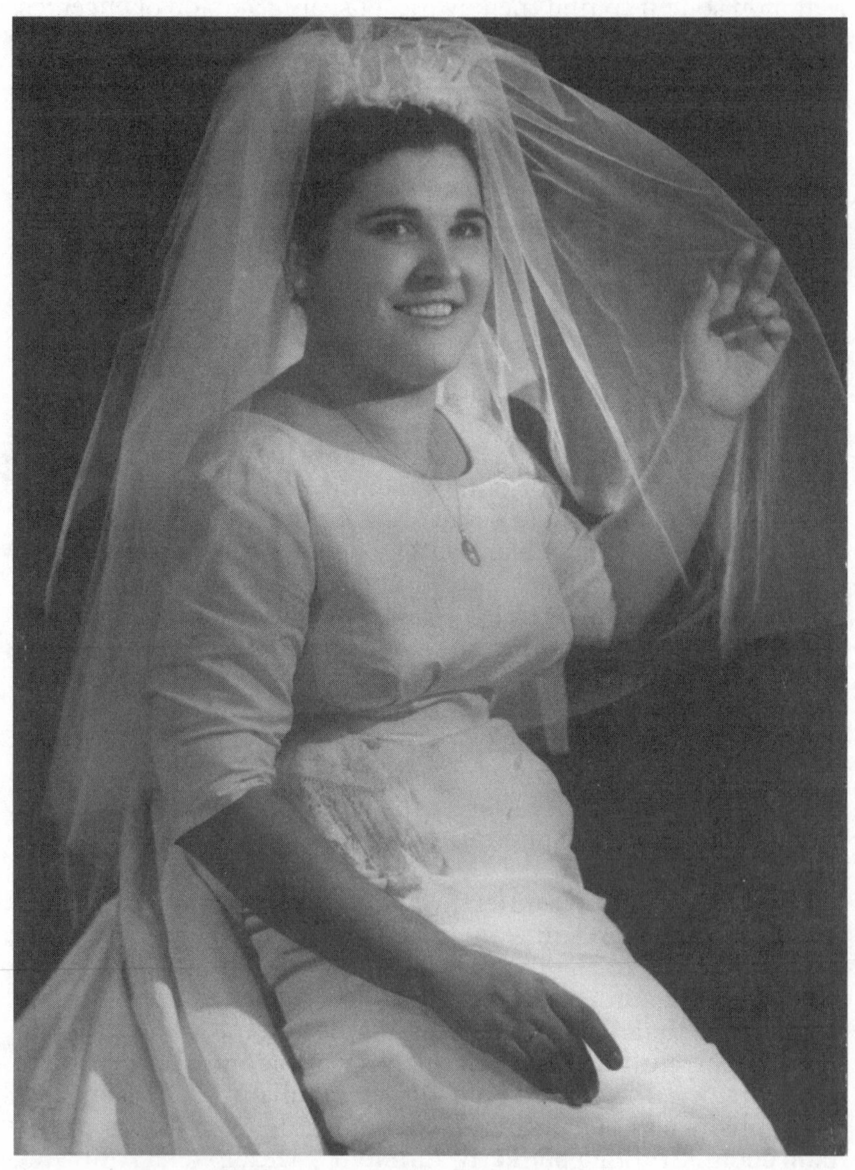

Figure 8. The bride (1961). Author's private collection.

thesize and accumulate. While men's metabolic system was hyperactive, women's was passive. Such differences started, in this premise, at the time of conception. Marañón's description is evocatively similar to that of Aristotle. "The egg is a passive cell, endowed with large reserves for nourishment. A nest equipped with abundant supplies to feed the new being. While the spermatozoid is an aggressive cell, endowed with great mobility, but lacking any kind of reserve: a guerrilla soldier, only action, carrying just a small backpack. It is there in the very deep life of the organism that such difference teaches us with physico-chemical exactness, and in the simple existence of the cell, the divergent paths established by God for each sex."[48] These considerations led Marañón to affirm that women must be mothers to the sacrifice of everything else in their life, and this he believed was a biological imperative. He recommended, however, a redefinition of motherhood that would not only alleviate but also enrich women's God-given maternal predestination. In his view the key to this new and fulfilling motherhood was education for girls to become independent from men as women and wives. "It doesn't really matter what they learn," said Marañón, "as far as it is useful to facilitate her co-existence with the husband." For Marañón the real feminism consisted in making "manly men and womanly women."[49] The maternal obligation of every woman was the responsibility of all women. Referring to the majority of Spanish women, those from the popular classes, Marañón characterized their collective maternal duty with the following metaphor: "I am talking about more than two thirds of all Spanish women; *the grand uterus where a people are created, the racial nerve of tomorrow*" [my emphasis].[50]

This statement echoes the notion of racial purging proposed by Vallejo Nágera in his work *Eugenesia de la Hispanidad* discussed above. Women's bodies became repositories of national reproduction not only figuratively but clearly in biological terms as well. The immediate postwar years' demographic policies called for the goal of forty million Spaniards. Women's biological destiny was compromised if they did not find a husband, because it was only within marriage that motherhood was possible.

Modernity unavoidably arrived with American dollars in the late 1950s. Although a changing labor market would eventually open more jobs for women, marriage continued to be Spanish women's fate in the new consumer economy as much as under the postwar autarky. The *Pact of Madrid* signed between the United States and the Francoist regime in 1953 provided the financial aid that eased the transition of the Spanish economy from autarky to consumerism.

In 1956 TVE (Television Española) began daily programming, and by the following year it was five hours per day. In 1959 Barcelona saw the inauguration of the first TV station in Catalonia. State funding and the income from commercials sustained the programming. By 1963, 92 percent of the funding came from commercials and the weekly television programming rose to 66 hours. Television sets were an important household item by the beginning of the 1960s.[51] Radio audiences were still larger than television viewers but steadily the visual medium entered Spanish homes captivating spectators who sat now in front of their sets rather than going about their daily routines while listening to radio shows.

Magazine ads and Hollywood movie stars presented a new and glamorous female image. One of the transformations wrought by consumerism was the possibility of exercising individual agency in the process of consciousness and identity shaping. In this way, Spanish women could refashion themselves inside and out. But in the process they were told to remain faithful to their domestic and motherly national destiny.

Although National Catholicism continued to glorify domesticity, modernization was inevitably forcing the regime out of isolationism. Traces of the change Spain was about to experience were present in André's parents' apartment. Richard Wright described it as bare and poverty-stricken. "One wall of the living room boasted a loud and vulgar print of the Last Supper; another wall was claimed by a huge calendar showing a laughing, pretty girl, her head flung wantonly back, her merry eyes contented and mischievous and watching you as you moved about the room—and all the while she was about to take a sip from a cold, sweating bottle of Coca-Cola."[52] This image encapsulates the transitional nature of the 1950s. Spain was caught between the old stale official Catholicism and the seductive phallic image of modern capitalism. However, motherhood remained at the center of the national women's duty—children being the country's future. Richard Wright noticed how children were the center of attention in Spain.

> No people on earth so pet and spoil their young as do the Spanish. Hence if a woman in later years sells her body to feed her hungry children, that in itself is almost a justification of what she is doing. *Para los niños* (for the children) is a slogan among Spanish prostitutes that

Figure 9. Mother and child (1964). Author's private collection.

> is almost as prevalent as *Arriba España* (Spain—Arise), the slogan of totalitarian minded Spanish men.
>
> Perhaps their making a cult of the child stems from their feeling for the Virgin and the child; I don't know. In any case, all Spanish children are, to their families as well as to outsiders, *guapos,* that is good-lookers. They are pinched, patted, tickled, indulged, stared at, waited on, kissed, fondled, worshiped, dangled, crooned over, hugged, and generally made to feel like they are the rightful center of the world.[53]

Women were expected to give their lives for their children figuratively and literally. According to the Annual Statistical Report of the Spanish Ministry of Labor and Social Action in 1957, the official figure of mothers who died during delivery was ninety-five for the period 1941 to 1957. The numbers had decreased progressively from 220 deaths in 1941–45 to 146 fatalities between 1946 and 1950.

Only from the year 1950 and after are there statistics of the total number of births in the state-owned "Casas de Maternidad" (Maternity Homes). For 1950–55 ninety-one centers assisted a total of 39,939 mothers in their facilities. The numbers increased in the next two years. In 1956, 130 centers assisted 52,222 pa-

Figure 10. First Communion. Author's private collection.

tients and in 1957, 141 centers reported 56,221 cases. The two maternity homes reporting from Barcelona served 4,450 mothers in 1957, the highest number in the peninsula, followed by the six maternity homes in Madrid where 14,430 mothers delivered their babies.[54] The marriage rate between 1945 and 1955 rose slightly from 7.06 to 7.78 per thousand. The birthrate decreased for the same years from 21,63 to 20,29 per thousand. Due to the

Natural Population Growth 1954–1964* Per 100 Inhabitants

Countries	1954	1955	1956	1957	1958	1959	1960	1961	1962	1963	1964
France	0,6	0,6	0,5	0,6	0,7	0,7	0,6	0,7	0,6	0,6	0,7
Italy	0,8	0,8	0,7	0,8	0,8	0,9	0,8	0,9	0,8	0,8	1,0
Japan	1,1	1,1	1,0	0,9	1,0	1,0	0,9	0,9	0,9	1,0	1,0
Spain	**1,2**	**1,2**	**1,1**	**1,0**	**1,1**	**1,3**	**1,2**	**1,2**	**1,2**	**1,2**	**1,3**
Portugal	1,2	1,2	1,1	1,2	1,3	1,3	1,3	1,3	1,3	1,2	1,3
Greece	1,2	1,2	1,2	1,1	1,1	1,2	1,1	1,0	1,0	0,9	0,9

*natural growth = number of births–number of deaths
Source: Fundación FOESSA, *Informe Sociológico sobre la situación social de España,* (Madrid: Editorial de Euroamérica, 1966), 38.

significant decrease in the mortality rate from 14.35 to 9.80 per thousand, the total population increased from 26,389,030 Spaniards to 28,529,263 between 1945 and 1955. The most significant improvement was the decline in infant mortality both for children under one year (2.24 per thousand in 1945; 1.10 in 1955) and children under five years old (3.13 per thousand in 1945; 1.45 per thousand in 1955).[55] Spain's natural population increase was 1.0 to 1.4 from 1954 to 1965. These figures are similar to those from France, Italy, Japan, Portugal, and Greece. While the growth is similar to that of Japan, Portugal, and Greece, France and Italy show a lower percentage in the decade 1954–64.[56]

The nationalization of motherhood was administered by the Head Office of Health Section of Childcare, Maternity and Hygiene Schools under the Ministry of the Interior. Dr. Juan Bosch Marín was Head of the Maternal and Child Foundation (Obra Maternal e Infantil) between 1940 and 1950, head of the State Services of Infant Care, and Demographic Policy Advisor between 1937 and 1972. Dr. Bosch Marín published several works about the new state natalist policies. For example, he supervised Madrid's social and medical assistance of mothers. In a report of September 1948, Dr. Bosch pointed out the negative demographic factors in Madrid to be the following:

1. Big industry and urbanization
2. Increasing number of women in the labor force
3. Rise in individual needs without the necessary rise in income
4. Increase of sexually transmitted diseases as a result of urbanization, leading to sterility and of birthrate and rise of mortality
5. Miserable housing, especially in the outskirts of big cities

6. Progress of immorality as a result of everyday promiscuity and the spread of vice[57]

Bosch Marín pointed out that vice and neo-Malthusianism dominated big cities and therefore was the "tomb of the races." For a nation to grow demographically it was necessary that each family have at least four children. "Two will replace the parents when they die," he said," one at least will die in infancy and it is the fourth child who will make the population of the country grow."[58] One of the improvements Bosch pointed out was the implementation of universal health care regardless of socioeconomic status. Conceived as a social insurance rather than a mercantile enterprise, he called the duty of the doctor that of a priest. In Bosch's own words it was important to implement prophylactic criteria to social medicine; it was "necessary to modernize charity." Maternal insurance predated the regime's General Social Security system. The Maternal and Child Foundation (Obra Maternal e Infantil) was in charge of maternal protection with 250 clinics throughout the country. These centers served one-third of the births in Spain, which in 1948 were 650,000 births from 500,000 working beneficiaries of the so-called Law Girón. Mothers were assisted both in maternal residences and at home.[59] In 1950 Dr. Bosch Marín presented a paper entitled "270,000 Deliveries: Sanitary Teachings" ("270,000 partos. Sus enseñanzas sanitarias") in the Third Congress of Spanish and Portuguese Obstetrics and Gynecology in Barcelona. This was a study report of the Social Security (established by law of June 18, 1942) assistance for a period of two years—1947 to 1949—to the wives of those public servants affiliated with the state insurance program. Of a total of 273,476 deliveries assisted, 15,965 happened in the maternal residences while 257,511 were home births.[60] The number of births that took place in clinics was still very low in Spain in the late 1940s. During 1947, midwives were in charge of normal pregnancies and deliveries with a physician intervention only when there were complications. In 1948 the organization changed the regulations, and all deliveries had to be supervised by a physician with the assistance of a midwife. However, the implementation of this new ruling became more complicated for the rural areas where a single doctor had to take care of several villages. The assistance that Bosch describes in his report did not reach the entire female population but only those who were part of the state apparatus as public servants within the machinery of the new Social Security System. Moreover, for the total

15,965 deliveries that took place in the maternal clinics, women stayed an average of 8.76 days in the clinic. Only those women of the regime's emerging urban middle class who might have domestic servants could afford to stay away from home for that period of time.

Midwives became the essential mediators between mothers and doctors. As appointed expert of the World Health Organization since 1955, Bosch authoritatively claimed that in the early 1960s the world birthrate was rising rapidly to an average, he said, of "eighty million births in a year."[61] In his address to the Thirteenth International Confederation of Midwives in 1963, Dr. Bosch highlighted the important role of these professionals, echoing Pius XII's speech twelve years earlier. After a brief historical introduction to midwifery and its Christian origins that included references to the Old and New Testaments, Bosch described the high standards of the profession in Spain. A midwife must be experienced, skillful, and moderate in her habits and behavior: "She should be healthy in complexion and shapely in body and limbs. She should not be over-imaginative, nor quarrelsome, but good-humored, cheerful, with encouraging words for the patient. She should be honest, chaste, set a good example, and give good advice, in such an important profession. She must be very discreet."[62] The doctor appealed as well to the ideal midwife Christian virtues: "She must love God, be a good Christian, so that things shall turn out well. She must not believe in spells, superstitions or omens, because they are abhorred by Holy Mother Church. She must be pious, worship the Virgin Mary, and the Saints in Glory, so that they may all come to her aid."[63] These were also the character traits demanded of a midwife in the Spanish court of the 1500s, and Bosch found great value in looking back to the baroque period to once again reiterate the Christian nature of what he called this *mothercraft.* Like sixteenth-century authors such as Juan Luis Vives and Fray Luis de León, Bosch declared that women's value resided in their physical and spiritual chastity, and therefore when a woman devoted herself to aid her counterparts to become mothers, she must be the purest of all. Later in his speech Bosch elaborated on the qualities of a good midwife for the twentieth century; very much in line with the Christian values of the 1500s, he remarked: "she must have good health, good knowledge and experience, and a sense of duty. In the latter are comprised all the obligations laid down in your code of professional morals and in the Ten Commandments, which need not be repeated here. In the list of professional duties," he continued, "I wish to point out those connected with the doctors and other midwives you work with. I have often said that the Commandment that is inculcated most strongly in your case is the eighth: 'Thou shalt not bear false witness, nor prevaricate, nor jump to hasty conclusions.'"[64] Therefore the most important role of the midwife in the modern world was to prepare women for their sublime function: motherhood.

Bosch also recognized that assistance in labor was not the sole objective for a midwife. "Once you have learned," he says, "the technique of childbirth, normal or abnormal, you are able to master its peculiarities, scientifically step by step, and after mastering it you can *make the process more domesticated.*"[65] What Bosch is referring to here is the midwife's new skills as crucial in the Francoist control and nationalization of motherhood. Obstetrics had given place to "mothercraft," rationalizing it somehow but justifying it from the Christian point of view—that of the salvation of souls.

To train midwives in their national duties the state established the Schools of Infant Care. These schools offered hundreds of premarital courses sponsored by secular or religious institutions. In conjunction with the official social service administered by the Women's Section of Falange. These Falangist women completed the state's professionalizing of a cadre of women to aid their sisters to be mothers. The rationalization of motherhood was imbued with Christian values, turning health professionals into missionaries and moralists. "While the human body is taking shape, *the soul or spirit goes through a uterine period of its life.* Philosophers and Theologists admit its existence without further doubt, *and modern psychology confirms it.*"[66] However, Spanish couples practiced contraception, and that showed in the birthrate decline, as discussed below. There had been a gradual decline in the birthrate in Spain since 1922, first year of the publication of any data about birthrates by the age of the parents, until the Civil War. The decline was fast and constant with a big fall as a result of the Civil War. Fertility rates increased after 1955 and fell again in 1965.

Vatican precepts weighed heavily on Spanish political and moral consciences; well beyond Franco's death in 1975 contraception remained illegal until 1978 and abortion a dark secret until the 1990s. According to Article 416 in the penal code of 1963 those who facilitated contraceptives or abortions were punished with imprisonment (a period of between one month and a day to six months) or a fine between 5,000 to 100,000 pesetas. The text is specific in enumerating those who would be punished.

Percentage of Polled Individuals by Education Level and Birth Control Method They Declare to Know, 1974

Birth control method known	Without any education	Primary education	Middle education	Technical and professional education	Higher education	All levels of education
None	24	14	6	8	8	12
Coitus interruptus	19	22	57	44	66	31
Rhythm method and derivatives	13	30	72	60	83	41
Condoms	36	44	71	71	82	51
Pill	37	60	79	76	80	64
No answer	27	18	9	6	4	16

Source: Fundación FOESSA, *Estudios Sociológicos sobre la situación social de España 1975* (Madrid: Editorial de Euroamérica, 1976), 47.

1. Those with or without a medical or nursing degree merely involved in providing information
2. The manufacturer or distributor who sells or those individuals outside of the medical profession who sell these products
3. Anyone who sells, offers, provides or advertises in any way these products
4. Any kind of propaganda of those products that prevent procreation as well as the public display and sale
5. Any kind of contraceptive propaganda[67]

The Catholic Church only made allowances for the practice of the Ogino-Knaus "rhythm" method. Most Spanish couples relied on the unreliable coitus interruptus since condoms were not legal either. Americanization in the late 1950s affected Spaniards' sexual modus operandi.

How to Attract and Make a Man Fall in Love

No question, motherhood represented the main and only natural destiny for Catholic women. The centrality of motherhood marked Catholic women's bodies. Motherhood being at the center of women's patriotic duty in Franco's Spain serves as an indicator of the relationship between the material/maternal body and its discursive signification: maternity.[68] The cultural meaning of motherhood under Francoism is inseparable from the maternal body upon which it inscribed itself. Such a maternal body was historically specific both in time and space to the Francoist body politic under autarky and consumerism. Moreover, it was only within wedlock that women were elevated to the altar of motherhood and their children considered legitimate rather than the offspring of sin.

To their aid came a series of publications on how to fare in the marriage market, published in the 1950s and 1960s. Lucia Graves remembers in her memoirs, *An Unknown Woman,* a booklet called *What Every Woman must know before her Wedding* that the parish priest in Palma gave her before her marriage to Ramon, her husband for the next twenty years. "My wedding day—for all the happiness—remains fixed in my mind more as a farewell to the past than a celebration of the future. . . . [B]eing given away by my father to my husband, having the skin-lines of my index finger recorded by the Spanish police—had I been renouncing my original identity? Did I become a different person? . . . I took my role of musician's wife, ironing his work shirts—though they never looked quite as white and smooth as the shirts ironed by other musicians' wives—doing all his paperwork, going along to recording studios and rehearsals, listening to his compositions."[69] The intent behind these manuals was to guide women in modern times in their pursuit of the perfect husband that would forever turn them into perfect wives. Some of these works included Antonio Guerra Gallego's *Cómo se atrae y se enamora a un hombre* (1953) and Carmen Sebastián's *Antes de casarte,* written during the Civil War and published after the conflict, along with the sequel *Después de casarte.* Due to the high demand for her first book she received the commission to write the second volume in the forties. Both works were reedited in 1965. While Guerra Gallego used a fictional lay school to train women in the art of attracting the best husband, Carmen Sebastián's works looked at the institution of marriage from the Vatican directives.

The Catholic publisher Desclee de Brouwer published a series entitled "El Angel del Hogar" (The Angel of the Home) for a French audience. This collection was translated into Spanish in the late 1950s and 1960s including René Boigelot, *El Matrimonio: El libro de la novia* (*Marriage: The Book of the Bride*) with its companion by the same author *El Matrimonio: El libro del jóven de 17 a 20 años* (*Marriage: The Book of the Young Man between 17 and 20 Years Old*). Boigelot's work on motherhood, *Maternidad: La maravillosa aventura de la célula humana desde el gérmen al recién nacido* (*Motherhood: The marvelous adventure of the human cell from seed to newborn*) also was edited several times within the series *The Angel of the Home* between 1960 and 1965 in Spain.[70]

As a result of the Second Vatican Council a plethora of publications on the sanctity of marriage were published. Some of these publications included Concilio Vaticano Segundo, *Comunidad de amor: el matrimonio cristiano según el Vaticano II* (Madrid: Parroquia Santa María Madre de la Iglesia, Colección Temas Conciliares, 1967). The archdioceses of Valencia issued a pastoral letter on courtship and established premarital training groups mandatory for those couples seeking to get married within the Church. During a five-day course couples received a series of lectures from priests and Christian married couples on the sanctity of marriage and the responsibility of the spouses to come together only for the purpose of reproduction and the Christian education of the offspring. The course included an explanation of the male and female reproductive anatomy and some advice to better conceive. "After intercourse we advise women to clean their **external** [*sic* bold] genitals, avoiding the vagina because it would go against the moral dignity of the act (to retain the semen) [*sic* parenthesis]."[71]

A doctor imparted a lecture entitled "Grandeza del cuerpo humano" ("Nobility of the human body") making it not only a moral but a hygiene priority of the Christian family to correctly relate to their sexual being. "It is important to train our children to clean their genitals every day as they clean the rest of their body." "During menstruation," continues the text, "It is necessary to clean the external genital area with tepid water—Not the inside because it could cause psychological disturbances."[72]

For the conjugal act to be licit the document poses three conditions:

Introduction of the penis in the vagina.
Ejaculation inside the vagina.
Retention of the semen.
We emphasize that the act performed in state of grace only increases that state and therefore you may receive communion immediately after.

It is not allowed:
Any natural or artificial onanism.
Washing the inside of the vagina immediately after intercourse.
Inducing abortion.
Solitary pleasure.[73]

In contrast with this explicit description of marital duties was the advice given to young brides on how to behave during courtship to secure a serious marriage proposition. In the manual *Matrimonio: El libro de la joven* (*Marriage: The Book of the Bride*) marriage is defined as "the total communion of two human beings of different sex in harmony."[74] The union between the spouses must occur at three levels: spiritual, intellectual, and physical. For many young women the "union of the bodies" is a traumatic experience, according to the *Book of the Bride,* a duty they must accept as the means to achieve their maternal destiny. The brides-to-be must reach marriage in a virgin state, and in the chapter on courtship they are warned against kissing as the door to falling into sin. "There are many ways to kiss. . . . It is possible to distinguish three types of kisses: the respectful kiss; the affectionate or loving kiss; and the passionate kiss. . . . As soon as there is any desire and pleasure experienced and feeling of possession and donation of the self it turns into something reprehensible and bad. Such is the case of the passionate kiss, long and ardent, mouth to mouth."[75]

The book of the bride echoed Fray Luis de León *La perfecta casada* (1583) teachings of self-effacing marital duties for the perfect wife. A man will not choose a "pompous, know-all" girl, because men "like to dominate and are afraid of a woman who is ahead of him."[76] Rarely a serious suitor will chose a young woman because of her beauty. "It is not necessary to be beautiful to get married" reads the text, "That young woman who is not pretty do not despair, it is enough to get married *just not to be repugnant"* [my emphasis].[77] The author advises to not abuse makeup in their pursuit of a happy marriage and laments that "some young women exaggerate their use of lipstick and powder. Those anti-aesthetic colorings they use to disguise themselves and some of older age."[78] The women chosen by serious suitors are those who never give an impression of being "self-sufficient and independent"; they are also not interested either in those girls who are "mentally unbalanced." "What a serious young man looks for in a future wife is a young woman full of ingenuousness, happiness and optimism." The young wife must exude "simplicity, charm, smiling, gentleness, sweetness, frailty, innocence, healthiness, in addition to a solid virtue which highlights discreetly her general pose."[79]

Chapter 22, "Para adquirir el arte de ser madre" (To acquire the art of being a good mother), in the book of the bride is about choosing healthy wives to become healthy mothers. Therefore, physical education becomes a means to discipline their bodies in the art of self-restraint and the practice of a gymnastic routine will strengthen their abdominal muscles to prepare them for labor.[80] The manual is highly critical of the modern poor eating habits to lose weight. "So many young women, with futile pretexts such as aesthetics, eat poorly to follow fashion trends."[81]

In order to preserve the happiness of the home and the sanctity of marriage, the manual of the bride advises her to acquire some intellectual training to be a good educator for her children but most of all to avoid becoming a wife "cuchara y olla" (a spoon and pan wife).[82] Domestic knowledge such as cooking and sewing become a given in the manual, and the modern wife now must also be educated in the humanities to make her husband proud.

Marriage remained the main entrance to the public sphere for women under consumerism. Antonio Guerra Gallego's *Cómo se atrae y se enamora a un hombre* represents a good example of a conduct manual in the transition from autarky to consumerism in the 1950s. The book, written by a male author, was directed to a female audience and divided into three sections: single women, married women, and widows. The author chooses to set the plot in a fictional school exclusively created to train women in the art of attracting men to become their husbands. The teacher's name, Iluminada (Enlightened, Illuminated), is a premonitory sign of dexterity in the art of courtship and marriage partner pursuit. Doña Iluminada is an educated lady with a degree in philosophy and letters that the author describes as "fifty-two years old, married, medium height, thin, well-proportioned and of pale complexion." The book starts with the pupils waiting in a pink waiting room presided over by an oil painting of Saint Antonio de Padua, patron saint of marriageable ladies, accredited provider of husbands. Right up front the author makes clear the universal value of marriage for all women when describing the diverse composition of the student body in terms of age and class. "The room was filled with a dense cloud of smoke from tobacco mixed with the scents of expensive perfumes and cheap cologne of some of the women. There were young ladies of beautiful faces and full of optimism, spinsters of hopeful façade, married ladies with weathered features, and happy and trusting little coquette widows. All of them made lively conversation in small groups. You could see the most humble and homely dress to the most luxurious one designed by accredited couture. All of them, however, came with faith and enthusiasm."[83] Smoking, an activity considered not a ladylike habit for women, is presented here as a natural pastime. In the mid-1950s we begin to see ads in Spanish magazines for American cigarettes (Winston, Marlboro) in which young attractive women appear smoking in sophisticated poses. Sara Montiel, the great sex symbol of the decade, made the song "Fumando espero" (Smoking I Wait) popular. In it she seductively related how she consumed her life smoking while waiting for the man she most loved. Needless to say this recreational activity as part of the new consumer economy was aimed more toward the middle-class woman than her working-class counterpart.

Doña Iluminada informs the ladies about the impressive reputation of her school and how the numbers speak for it. She mentions that the previous year they had 586 students divided as follows: 328 single, 110 married, and 148 widows. Two hundred and fifteen single women got married, 86 widows remarried, and 94 married women restored peace to their home. The "pedagogical method" used in the school is a theoretical exposition followed by a practical case to be resolved in each class period, based on the event presented to the class by a particular student.

The interaction between Doña Iluminada and her apprentices is presented in the format of an advice column. Different women pose their particular problem to the teacher who then preaches about the way to resolve the predicament. The author always describes these women so that the reader knows their age and class background: first he lets us know whether the woman is blond or brunette and the color of her eyes, and then the quality of her clothing. Almost every time the lady is blond and blue-eyed, she belongs to the upper class, carries herself with elegance (meaning always she is thin rather than heavy) and speaks in soft voice.

Each apprentice has provided physically descriptive details on the enrollment form during the application period. This is the way one of the students is addressed by Doña Iluminada:

—Miss Eduviges del Olmo Pérez.

—At your service

—Listen with attention and correct me if any of the data is wrong: twenty-two; single; tall; straight posture; prominent scapulae; brunette, fake blond, natural hair color dark; broad forehead; eyebrows arched and thin; black eyes; straight nose; big mouth with high commeasures, prominent chin, high voice; happy expression; Castilian accent; shaky pronunciation; typist; middle economic status. Never had suitors.

—I agree with everything; the age is not exact.

—It is the one you have inscribed yourself with.
—Yes ma'am, but I deducted a few years.
—I thought so-said the teacher in the midst of laughter and murmurs of speculation-How old are you really?
—Thirty-two—clarifies the interrogated one who blushed red as a poppy
—Taking ten years off is too much of an exaggeration. There is no man who believed that.
—Some, yes ma'am, would believe it . . .
—Well they would be the stupid kind.
—They are so many stupid ones!
—True—some other pupil's remark.
—Very stupid—others say.
—Silence! orders the teacher, getting up from her seat.[84]

The whole training was based on the belief that men were gullible, docile, and easily tamed by a smart and proficient lady. As one of the students shared with the rest of the class, "With determination a woman can do with a man whatever she wants."[85] "When daddy gets mad, mom softens him with words and attention to better control him, and once she has succeeded, he is a different being; everything in him is sweetness and goodwill. He is absolutely convinced that he is in control, but it is really the opposite: the one that rules is my mom."[86]

However, there are diverse opinions on how to approach the taming of the man. For married student Emerenciana Cortés Heredia, a man should be replaced when he does not "perform." According to her enrollment card she was: "Forty-seven; friendly, separated from her husband; short and heavy, pale; hair died in platinum blond; natural color of her hair is dark brown; bulky forehead; eyebrows thick and straight; gray eyes; hooked nose; small mouth; thick lips; chin of oblique inclination; uncertain gaze; mannish voice; southern accent; painful expression; funny pronunciation; profession, her sex (homemaker); economic status, precarious; she got married at eighteen." Emerenciana also admitted to have taken eight years off to be able to find a replacement for her husband. Doña Iluminada strongly disagreed with her taking years off. This is a bad thing if you are single but it is even worse if you are married. "What an atrocity!!" the teacher remarks, ". . . If your husband does not 'perform' as you put it, he must have a justified reason that you may have not realized or understand. Every woman who fulfills her wifely duties has plenty of means if reason is on her side, to achieve conjugal appeasement with her most praiseworthy behavior."[87]

All of the women, regardless of their civil status, took years off hoping to remain younger looking in the marriage market. For the teacher this attempt to appear younger is rather innocent since in the long run it can only hurt those who practice it. "There is no doubt there are young women who look older and older women who look younger. The former have lived too intensely, practicing all kind of excesses, or had a hard life, with misfortune, worries, and bitterness. The latter, on the contrary, were able to preserve themselves by fleeing from evil, shielding themselves against any disagreeable situation, and making sure to live a methodical existence, serene, tranquil, and free of any excess. . . . Any intelligent woman must not abuse the exaggerated makeup. It is dangerous; it is a double-edged sword . . . Sincerity about your age will be norm of your conduct."[88]

This rejection of makeup was also present in the conduct manuals of the 1500s such as de Leon's *La perfecta casada.* Dopico Black points out that "the greatest threat of makeup is precisely that it empowers women with the ability to remake themselves as something other than what they *truly* [my emphasis] are."[89] In the 1950s the commercialization of cosmetics became one of the most important areas of consumption for Spanish women. They saw the colorful ads of Ponds, Cutex, or Chanel, in magazines and tried to emulate movie stars. But mostly they tried to refashion themselves to increase their opportunities in the marriage market. Certainly the conduct manuals would be faithful to the saying "la suerte de la fea la guapa la desea" (the fortune of the ugly girl the pretty one hopes for), but the truth of the matter was quite different. In order to outdo the work of nature women were to be masters in the art of seduction.

A woman was always a project in pursuit of perfection. "Even the most beautiful woman," reads the manual, "does not have all the qualities for physical perfection. If we examine meticulously her head, torso, and limbs, we surely will find a flaw."[90] Being kind, benevolent, and modest was the best strategy to show her soul's beauty. A beautiful woman had to be virtuous too. But both physical and moral beauties were not enough to "conquer the strong sex." As the manual suggested, "It is necessary to act and behave according to the character of the chosen man" so that he surrenders to the one who "is not beautiful but an angel."[91] "It is important to practice in front of the mirror to correct our flaws and practice the manners and simple, sweet, and soft behavior. We must completely eliminate exaggerated gestures, loud laughter and immodest postures."[92] Doña Iluminada summarizes the school's principles on a woman's physical and moral beauty:

1. To attract the opposite sex, a beautiful woman, must be nice, benevolent and tolerant.
2. A beautiful woman with a temper might get admiration for her beauty but she will not attract any suitors.
3. A beautiful woman with no education is unnoticed by the members of the opposite sex and her own.
4. A shy beautiful woman loses a percentage of her charm.
5. Expressive, suggestive eyes spellbind more men than those that are inexpressive.
6. A charming ugly girl, sweet, and nice, well educated, understanding, is a terrible rival for those who only have their physical beauty.
7. Physical beauty without moral beauty attracts but does not make a man fall in love.
8. When a beautiful woman is vain it will be acknowledged by men through their physical eyes and will not reach their soul's eyes.
9. Between two women equally beautiful a man will choose the richest one.
10. Between two beautiful rich women he will choose the one who is most agreeable.
11. Between two that meet all of the above he will choose the best educated.
12. If they are equally educated he will choose the thinner one.
13. If they are both thin he will choose the one with brighter eyes.
14. If they have the same eyes he will choose the one who has dark, long, wavy hair.[93]

Obviously, physical appearance won over spiritual beauty, which ultimately contradicts the dictum of the school "la suerte de la fea la guapa la desea." In lieu of the physical attributes necessary in the courtship battle, the best weapon to conquer the heart of the chosen man was to master a seductive gaze. "To attract the opposite sex we must stare with penetrating kindness, trying to blink in long intervals; in other words keeping our eyes open as long as possible during the conversation. Fix your gaze in the middle of their forehead so that our thoughts are imprinted in his mind."[94]

Richard Wright noticed this hypnotizing gaze as well: "Spanish women have evolved a manner of staring at men with long, intense, bold looks."[95]

According to the manual, a woman must never contradict her suitor or tell him "he is wrong" or any other statement that might show her "mental superiority." On the contrary, Guerra Gallego asserts that the duty of a woman is to listen with devoted attention and reply with sweet words: "I am very sorry, maybe you are right."[96]

Guerra Gallego devotes an entire chapter to a discussion of body language. There will be no attraction without a careful performance of body language. The arms will move elegantly when one walks, never hanging next to the body. The head must be still and held high with dignity, but not too far back or forward. The hands are very important. They must be always clean and well cared for. Never move them violently. The body movements must be as natural as possible: soft and modest in married ladies; soft and chaste in the single woman. Women will never employ symmetrical postures. "When standing up our feet won't be at the same level but one tip ahead of the other. Our arms must fall naturally, away from the body, moving them slightly without exaggeration. Our torso must be softly straight. Our head must be high with a natural posture, alternating a slight inclination that will follow the conversation. Our facial expression will show happiness and goodness."[97]

The careful performance a woman had to master shows the bodily nature of the courtship endeavor. Love was conquered through a studied masquerade in which the two sexes remained an enigma to each other. Locked into a contract for life, some women had to endure domestic violence and infidelity, looking the other way. They had to forget about themselves and entirely live for the sake of a third party: their husband, their children, and their family of origin's reputation.

The popular song, "A la lima y al limón," in the voice of Concha Piquer spoke to the hearts of many Spanish women looking, as the saying goes, for their "media naranja" ("their half orange") or soul mate.

Family and Society in Spain: Toward a Modern Model of Family

In opposition to the extended family proper of the rural society, urbanization was creating a new model of family, more autonomous and independent. This autonomy and independence led to a family life centered in emotional and intercommunication skills of the couple and their ability to educate the offspring.[98]

Figures 11–12. Once the wedding ceremony concluded it became customary in the 1960s and 1970s to photograph the newlyweds in the back seat of the bridal car. The automobile, a symbol of status in the new consumer economy, had entered everyday imagery. Author's private collection.

Figure 13. The wedding banquet was a must in an increasingly better-off economy. In the 1960s and 1970s the multilayer wedding cake would emulate a skyscraper. Author's private collection.

Traditional patriarchal authority over the wife began to deteriorate with a more fluid division of roles and tasks and a more equitable modus operandi. The Spanish family, however, was still more traditional than modern in the early1970s in spite of clear signs of evolution to the new model. The ambiguous delimitation of gender roles was proper in a society in transition.[99] Indicators of the remains of traditionalism include the fact that the majority of polled individuals, both men and women, believed housework was the wife's duty rather than a shared responsibility with the husband.

Signs of modernization were evident in the decline in birthrate as a result of birth control practices—a behavior that responded to a more permissive mentality with regard to sexuality among the new generations. The regime was in crisis as a result of being out of phase between the economic developments and cultural changes and the prescriptive traditional family relations. A clear example was the generational conflict between parents and children with regard to parental control.[100]

The new model of family had consumption rather than production as its primary purpose. Leisure became a central aspect of economic and social relations. The television now kept families at home during the weekend.

Fomento de Estudios Sociales y Sociología Aplicada was established in 1965 with the support of Cáritas Española to identify the areas to tackle in the development plans. The FOESSA studies saw this indicator as a leisure activity that favored a depoliticization of the masses with less communal solidarity. There was a privatization of lifestyle, a withdrawal of the family from social affairs and an increase of family-centered activities. The survey refers to the U.S. family to illustrate the path Spanish families were taking. In the United States the new suburbia developed a so-called conjugal familism, a life centered on the couple and their children, creating a universe of intimacy separate from the outside world.[101] In 1965 FOESSA established a charity-teaching institution, followed the United States' model of philanthropic foundations with the purpose to advise economic and political institutions in their social duties. From its very beginning "FOESSA intended to align itself with modernity and efficacy."[102] The members of the FOESSA foundation were economists, researchers, sociologists who cooperated to build a more just society. FOESSA's first report was directed by sociologists Amando de Miguel, Manuel Gómez Reino y Carnota, and Francisco Andrés Orizo. They received a two million-pesetas grant to conduct a survey of 2,500 homes where they interviewed separately housewives and "heads of the households."[103] According to the study, the average number of children per couple was three in 1966 (as in Italy for the same period of time). However, the study indicated a clear tendency to have fewer children. Most of those women interviewed who had three children had mothers who gave birth to at least six children.[104]

Those women from the northeast (Catalonia and Balearic Islands) had an average of 3.92 while in the southeast the average number of children was 6.01. The survey also showed a clear increase in the upper middle class in the number of children per couple—4.03. While those from the lower and working class had 2.44, the peasant class and the urban working class had fewer children, data already apparent in some population studies conducted in Madrid and Barcelona in the 1940s. Of course the infant mortality among the lower classes affected the total number of children at the end.[105] The number of illegitimate children births in Spain in 1954 was 4.6 percent, and in 1964 1.8 percent. Galicia and Andalucia showed a higher percentage of illegitimacy. The figures are close to those of other countries in 1955. In the United States the number of illegitimate births was 4.5 percent; in England 4.7, in France 6.6, in Italy 3.1, and in Japan 1.7 according to the study.[106]

Modernity prompted the redefinition of the boundaries of the family unit, and especially the role of women within it. Signs of change translated into a major university crisis in 1956 that led to the replacement of Joaquín Ruiz Giménez as Minister of Education and further remodeling of the entire cabinet. The new government appointed by Franco in 1957 endorsed economic liberalization with the *Stabilization Plan* of 1959 and sponsored the revision of the civil code, announced on April 24, 1958. Although the new civil code gave Spanish women certain legal leeway, they remained subject to their husbands, fathers, or male guardians. The family continued to be the axis around which social gender relations revolved. Different minimum ages for marriage continued: fourteen years old for women and sixteen for men. Single women were not allowed to abandon the parental household before twenty-five years of age unless they got married or entered a convent. Under the new civil code of 1958 married women could be a guardian, an executrix, or a testamentary witness with their husbands' permission. In addition, the household was now declared *hogar conyugal* rather than *casa del marido.* Civil marriage was tolerated only when one of the spouses was a non-Catholic. And finally, to assure the posthumous paternity of a husband, a widow could not remarry any sooner than 301 days after he died.[107]

The birth control pill arrived in Spain in 1963.[108] But instead of being commercialized as a contraceptive and to avoid the violation of article 416 of the Penal Code, the pill was authorized as a medication to treat gynecological maladies. The pharmacies were not to sell the pill without a doctor's prescription. Nevertheless, in the first half of the 1960s Spaniards' consumption of the contraceptive pill increased rapidly regardless of the prohibition from Church and state.

The fertility growth between 1955 and 1965 is not exclusive to Spain but rather a process similar in all western Europe, a result of the economic prosperity in that decade. Therefore there are two different readings possible for the rise in the fertility rate: the growth in the marriage rate for the same years; or the positive effect of economic takeoff. The fertility rates differed according to urban or rural divide and in accordance with class. The Spanish middle class behavior was closer to the French middle class than to the Spanish working class with regard to birth control practices. There is a Malthusian indicator in the middle section of the social pyramid that clearly illustrates birth control practices among middle class educated couples in this period. Pharmaceutical companies did not find any kind of restrictions on producing and advertising contraceptives in medical journals. In 1966 the sales rose to 789,000 boxes; in 1967, 1,262,000; in 1968, 2,716,000; and by 1970 pharmaceutical companies sold 3,229,000 boxes of contraceptives in Spain.[109] The average family size declined from 4 in 1960 to 3.2 in 1975. The use of birth control also varied depending on age, place of residence, and socioeconomic status. Married women under thirty-four who lived in urban areas were more likely to use birth control.[110]

Spain Diverse Fertility Indicators (Per 1000)

Years	Gross birth rate	Global fertility rate
1955	20,44	123,26
1956	20,60	123,51
1957	21,73	129,85
1958	21,79	129,48
1959	21,65	128,18
1960	21,60	127,63
1961	21,13	123,50
1962	22,08	123,05
1963	21,32	124,24
1964	21,98	127,92
1965	21,13	122,78
1966	20,70	120,06
1967	20,81	121,20
1968	20,22	117,85
1969	20,00	116,56
1970	19,50	114,198
1971	19,55	—
1972	19,37	—
1973	19,18	—

Source: Fundación FOESSA, *Estudios Sociológicos sobre la situación social de España 1975* (Madrid: Editorial de Euroamérica, 1976), 40.

Average Number of Children According to Income and Length of Marriage

Monthly income in pesetas	Less than 5 years married	5–8 years married	9–12 years married	13–16 years married	17–20 years married	21–24 years married	More than 25 years married	Total average
Less than 10,500	1.20	2.17	3.31	2.94	2.33	2.19	2.98	2.05
10,500 to 14,499	1.03	2.11	2.50	2.91	2.80	2.21	2.72	1.89
14,500 to 20,499	0.85	2.00	2.23	2.90	2.73	3.03	3.13	1.89
20,500 to 30,499	1.11	2.18	2.67	2.91	3.00	2.56	3.35	2.09
30,500 and more	1.32	2.00	3.30	3.66	3.15	4.73	4.88	2.67
All incomes	1.00	2.09	2.54	3.00	2.86	2.75	3.24	2.01

Source: Fundación FOESSA, *Estudios Sociológicos sobre la situación social de España 1975* (Madrid: Editorial de Euroamérica, 1976); data from a 1974 survey FOESSA, 45.

Also to be considered are those women who migrated to industrialized parts of Spain or other European countries or had their husbands working abroad learned about and had access to birth control information beyond the power of the state. Between 1941 and 1964 more than one million people left Spain.[111] Interior migration was also very important: Barcelona received 681,562 immigrants in this period and Madrid 637,151, Vizcaya 115,277, and Guipuzcoa 59,314. The provinces with the higher numbers of emigrants were Jaen, 227,660; Granada, 190,513; Cordoba, 165,395; and Murcia, with 125,646. The migratory flow was from Andalusia, Extremadura, and Galicia to Barcelona, Madrid, and Basque country. In 1960 the migration movements increased both to other countries and inside Spain. In 1961 there were 175,340 migrants and in 1962 that number rose to 350,000 and in 1964 to 500,000. In 1965 the number of people migrating went down slightly to 466,755.[112] Almost two million people moved from region to region within Spain. Sixty-five percent of those emigrants moved to cities larger than their own. It is very difficult to estimate the number of people who migrated to other countries from Spain because the statistical data are scarce. Ac-

International Migration Balance

Years	General Directorship of Employment	OCDE
1959	9,906	130,000
1960	36,716	138,000
1961	117,730	131,000
1962	106,635	171,000
1963	83,013	196,000
1964	79,161	227,000
TOTAL	433,161	993,000

Source: Fundación FOESSA, *Informe Sociológico sobre la situación social de España* (Madrid: Editorial de Euroamérica, 1966), 62.

cording to the General Directorship of Employment in 1959–64 there were 433,161 people leaving the country while the Organization for Econmic Coopeartion and Development (OECD) offers a very different number: 993,000.[113]

These figures show that Spain was not far behind the western world's 1960s sexual revolution with regard to birth control. In the United States Katherine McCormick had funded Gregory Pincus in 1951 to perform research to develop the contraceptive pill, but it was not until 1959 that the FDA approved the pill under the commercial name Enovid for therapeutic purposes. By late 1959, over half a million American women were taking Enovid, officially prescribed for menstrual disorders, but users were also benefiting from the contraceptive side effect. On May 11, 1960, Searle Laboratories received FDA approval to sell Enovid as a birth control pill. Searle was the first and only pharmaceutical company to sell an oral contraceptive and it had a lucrative monopoly. In Europe, Italy and Ireland followed Spain's lead in making contraception illegal. France legalized contraception in 1967 and abortion in 1975 while in West Germany abortion was legalized in 1976.[114] The use of the contraceptive pill during the 1960s and 1970s was limited in every society to the married woman who depended on the control of a predominantly male medical profession to prescribe it. Hence, in terms of birth control, Spanish women were not significantly worse off than their counterparts under democratic regimes.

The "no answer" about these matters is tied to socioeconomic status, but the reticence is higher among the lower classes. Those with a higher social status know more about birth control meth-

Percentage of Number of Children Desired According to Income, 1974

Income in pesetas	None	One child	Two children	Three children	Four or more children	Total
Less than 10,500	9.67	6.98	19.35	21.14	42.83	100 (558)
10,500 to 14,499	6.84	7.46	25.93	20.74	39.00	100 (482)
14,500 to 20,499	3.07	8.98	32.15	22.45	35.69	100 (423)
20,500 to 30,499	4.47	5.59	28.35	24.99	36.56	100 (268)
30,500 and more	7.89	7.14	23.21	19.64	43.74	100 (112)
All incomes	5.88	7.22	24.34	20.90	41.64	100 (2,497)

Source: Fundación FOESSA, *Estudios Sociológicos sobre la situación social de España 1975* (Madrid: Editorial de Euroamérica, 1976), 47.

Stand With Regard to Birth Control Methods According to Education Level Based on 1974 FOESSA Survey in Percentages

	No formal education	Primary education	Middle education	Technical and professional education	Higher education	All levels of education
No method is reprehensible	9	15	20	15	24	16
All methods are bad	26	24	15	26	18	22
Mentions a particular one which is reprehensible	5	20	42	27	50	25
No answer	60	41	23	32	8	37
Totals	100	100	100	100	100	100
Among the polled who answered those who mentioned the pill as reprehensible	10	24	31	20	22	24

Source: Fundación FOESSA, *Estudios Sociológicos sobre la situación social de España 1975* (Madrid: Editorial de Euroamérica, 1976), 48.

ods. The latest method most utilized is the pill. Less than 50 percent of the polled people mentioned any method as morally reprehensible. At least 63 percent of the polled people found the use of the pill not reprehensible. These results, higher than expected, highlight the relatively tolerant attitude toward the limitation of pregnancies. The old methods such as the extension of breast-feeding were not the most utilized at this time. Among polled people coitus interruptus is the method least utilized among the upper classes and practiced more among the lower social strata. Among those with higher economic and social status there is more use of the pill and the rhythm method over the condom or coitus interruptus.[115]

The century's decline tendencies in the fertility rate suffered a break in 1954–65 due to the use of birth control methods rather than to the economic takeoff. Changes in the marriage rate had an important impact on the fertility growth in 1954–65. However, after 1964 the fertility rate declined again. The 1974 FOESSA survey showed increasing use of the pill among Spanish women, and this clearly predicts the decline of the birthrate in Spain as the norm for the rest of the century.

Opinions About Pre-Marital Sex, 1974

	There is nothing wrong with a couple going for a walk to a solitary place	**It is all right if couples kiss in public**	**If a couple is committed it should be allowed they make love**	**It is not too important that a man is virgin when he gets married**	**It is not too important that a woman is virgin when she gets married**
Completely agree	9.2	5.1	5.4	7.2	3.3
Agree	63.4	30.9	26.7	42.1	17.1
Disagree	21.8	50.6	44.5	36.5	49.1
Completely disagree	5.6	13.4	23.4	14.3	30.5
Total	100% (2,027)	100% (2,007)	100% (1,898)	100% (1,892)	100% (1954)[?]

Source: Fundación FOESSA, *Estudios Sociológicos sobre la situación social de España 1975* (Madrid: Editorial de Euroamérica, 1976), 391.

Opinion About the Selection of Spouse and What to do With a Daughter Getting Pregnant Out of Wedlock

	Farmers	Rural day laborers	Businessmen with employees	Businessmen without employees and independent workers	Professionals with higher education	Middle classes	Public servants	Workers	Total
% of those who think the family has the right to intervene in the selection of spouse	43.8 (73)	14.7 (34)	32.0 (25)	28.1 (171)	24.2 (62)	12.5 (32)	21.4 (299)	16.3 (300)	22.6 (996)

What to do With a Daughter Getting Pregnant Out of Wedlock

	Farmers	Rural day laborers	Businessmen with employees	Businessmen without employees and independent workers	Professionals with higher education	Middle classes	Public servants	Workers	Total
Try to have her marry at all costs	39.1	45.0	25.0	24.2	7.5	—	14.7	11.6	17.9
Try to understand her and help her	50.0	50.0	68.7	67.7	80.0	78.6	76.7	80.9	73.3
Nothing would change	10.9	—	—	7.1	10.0	21.4	6.0	6.4	7.0
Other answers (throw her out of the house or have her have the baby in hiding)	—	5.0	6.3	1.0	2.5	—	2.6	1.1	1.8
Total	100%								
	(46)	(20)	(16)	(99)	(40)	(14)	(150)	(173)	(558)

Source: Fundación FOESSA, *Estudios Sociológicos sobre la situación social de España 1975* (Madrid: Editorial de Euroamérica, 1976), 393.

Favorable attitudes toward sexuality and divorce were becoming increasingly prevalent in Spanish society of the 1960s and early 1970s.[116]

A total of 72.6 percent of the polled saw nothing wrong with a couple going to a solitary place for a walk, but kissing in public places was not so accepted (64 percent). Therefore there was a certain concern with keeping up appearances and maintaining a certain "public morality" standard. Those who accepted kissing in public also agreed with the premarital sexual relations between couples engaged to be married. However, the double standard with regard to sexual independence continued. Forty-nine percent considered it was not too important for a man to be virgin when he got married; however, only 20 percent considered this should be the case for a woman. The attitudes changed from rural to urban areas. Madrid and Barcelona showed a more liberal outlook versus those locations with under two thousand inhabitants.

The FOESSA 1974 survey concluded that the majority of the young people polled rejected the traditional morality transmitted through the family, the school, and the Church. Sexuality was for them an enriching and positive experience. Some called this a "sexual revolution" but the analysis called it an "evolution" since the changes were not yet as radical and the double standard still prevailed between the sexes.

> We need to consider that in the society we live in it is not easy for the young generations to experience their sexuality responsibly. There is a clear contradiction in the way of behaving in a capitalist society with regard to sexuality: on the one hand, sex is cynically and shamelessly utilized according to economic demands, and on the other hand sex is repressed by means of social and legal norms. This is a contradiction at the root of the bourgeois morality, always efficient in the exploitation of the individual for profit utilizing an individualistic and hypocritical morality. Sufficient proof is provided by the prevalence of sex in marketing and publicity aimed at manipulating the individual and especially the young consumer. The problem is that capitalism seems to require this constant sexual perversion in order to survive. While there is a need to make people constantly buy things they do not need for the capital benefit, it is evident sex and marketplace will remain intimately connected. The end result is that sex is objectified, dehumanized, losing any personal dimension.[117]

Young people came to believe that in the modern family there is an emphasis on the personal realization of each spouse, and therefore divorce is one consideration to solve irreconcilable differences. Women were the ones who insisted in the indissolubil-

Opinions About Divorce

	Divorce should be allowed in Spain in certain circumstances	The couple must stay married when they have small children
Completely agree	18.0	20.2
Agree	53.6	65.0
Disagree	17.7	11.8
Completely disagree	10.8	2.9
Total	100% (1965)	100% (2000)

Source: Fundación FOESSA, *Estudios Sociológicos sobre la situación social de España 1975* (Madrid: Editorial de Euroamérica, 1976), 395.

Do You Believe Marriage Must be Indissoluble?

	Men	Women	Total
Yes	39%	51%	45%
It depends	37	31	34
No	23	17	20
No answer	—	1	1
Totals	100% (661)	100% (611)	100% (1272)

Source: Fundación FOESSA, *Estudios Sociológicos sobre la situación social de España 1975* (Madrid: Editorial de Euroamérica, 1976), 396.

Opinions About Divorce According to Religious Practices and Sex

Divorce should be allowed under certain circumstances	Indifferent	Non-practicing Catholics	Occasional practicing Catholics	Regular practicing Catholics	Very Good [*sic*] Catholics
Men	89,5 (95)	84,9 (178)	74,9 (231)	70,6 (306)	50,0 (36)
Women	90,0 (40)	74,5 (110)	77,4 (231)	63,9 (585)	51,6 (96)
TOTALS	89,6 (135)	81,3 (288)	76,2 (462)	66,2 (891)	51,5 (132)

Source: Fundación FOESSA, *Estudios Sociológicos sobre la situación social de España 1975* (Madrid: Editorial de Euroamérica, 1976), 397.

ity of marriage. Of the total people polled, 45 percent were in favor of divorce and 34 percent would consider it under certain circumstances, which would make a majority of people in favor of divorce in the early 1970s. The attitude toward divorce depended as well on the socioeconomic status. The middle and upper classes were more inclined (84.4%) to allow divorce to be legal in Spain while the working class strata were in agreement with divorce under certain circumstances (65.1%).[118] The Catholic Action journal *Senda* published the following Test for Brides to measure if they truly were in love:

> Clearly a "test" does not fit perfectly everyone. However, when the test is serious and sincere the answers—absolutely sincere and personal—the result may be a clear indication of the feelings dominating us. The test we offer here today has been designed by Fray Gerald J. Schnep and Reverend Alfred F. Schnep in their work "Through Marriage Towards God."

Questionnaire:

1. Am I only interested in physical satisfaction?
2. Is sexual satisfaction the most important thing in marriage?
3. Do I try to do as much as I can to fulfill my boyfriend's happiness?
4. Am I willing to make any sacrifice to obtain something beneficial for him?
5. When he is not with me, do I desire him and wish happily to meet him again?
6. Do I feel well when I am and only when I am with him?
7. Am I happy to sacrifice myself for him?
8. Do I desire with all my heart the perfect union with my beloved one, including the perfect physical, emotional and intellectual union?
9. Am I happy when I think about sharing my life until death do us part, exclusively with this person?
10. Would I dare to lie or hide anything from him?
11. Am I sure he is the man I desire, above everything, to be the father of my children?
12. If after our wedding he suffered an accident that would disfigure or hurt him severely, would I be able to love him, completely, sincerely and with devotion?
13. Is it my supreme hope that his soul is saved and goes to heaven?
14. Do I love him with a love similar to the love I profess to God?

15. Am I sure he will never propose to me an act that would offend God?
16. Is religion the strongest foundation of love? Is it the sexual pleasure, the emotional satisfaction or the intellectual union?
17. Do I conceive of my marriage as a transit through life with my loved one and loving him in God until death do us part?

KEY TO MEASURE THE ANSWERS

The answers must be absolutely sincere
Each negative answer to 1 and 2 is worth one point
Each affirmative answer to questions 3 to 14 (both included) is worth one point
Each affirmative answer to questions 15, 16 and 17 is worth five points
Questions unanswered are worth zero

Points	**Meaning**
Twenty	A+ in true love
Between 15 and 19	A
Between 11 and 14	B
Between 8 and 10	B–
Less than 8	Must start thinking about an alternative

Three threads run through the narrative of this chapter–traditional discourse, modernized discourse, and popular culture changes. The traditional discourse on marriage and motherhood was contested by the economic changes that demanded women enter a 1960s depleted labor market in which men were migrating to other European countries, and an avalanche of tourists brought new mores in public places. The FOESSA reports showed clear changes in behavior and with those changes came the need from the official propaganda to adjust and to coin a more "modern" discourse. What the Ministry of Tourism delivered was a slogan, "Spain Is Different" that banked on the nineteenth-century French "orientalized" image of Spain. But Spanish women were not the "Carmens" that seduced European fantasy; they, as Richard Wright declared, were the agents of change.

5
Modern Women's Docile Bodies

> We, who are deeply Catholic, want to strengthen the body to better serve the spirit.
>
> —*Sección Femenina de Falange*

THE STRONG VIRILE BODY EPITOMIZED THE POWER OF RISING TOtalitarian regimes throughout Europe in the 1930s. In a highly militarized context, political, religious, and medical debates characterized women's bodies as conduits of biological and spiritual purity and national regeneration.[1] Racial hygiene focused on a highly gendered conception of the ideal body type and corporeal beauty. The emphasis of these political discourses was to create a virile state to ensure safekeeping of the nurturing motherland.

In Spain under Francoism, traditional Catholic principles on womanhood guided women's physical education: to be fit mothers for the fatherland. This chapter focuses on women's physical education in the 1950s and 1960s through the examination of the 1961 law of physical education along with the religious discourse on physical training to unveil the efforts of the regime to maintain a hold on women's domesticity in the transition from autarky to consumerism.

The law of physical education was one of several reforms of the regime to catch up with the times and withstand international scrutiny. As discussed in previous chapters, National Catholicism informed Francoist institutional adjustments that included the reform of the civil code and the enactment of the Fundamental Laws of the State in 1958; the Stabilization Plan in 1959; and the Law of Political and Professional Rights for women in 1961. A close reading of the law of physical education from a gender perspective helps us understand Francoism's reinvention of domesticity through the modernization of the country.

Modernization led to a new rationalization of the concept of female frailty and domesticity that the regime sought to maintain. The state charged the Women's Section of Falange to carry out this task.[2] The 1950s and 1960s were a period of crisis for the Women's Section. The organization struggled to maintain its hold on women's consciences and bodies through three settings: the instruction of physical education, mandatory from primary school to university level; the six-month-long Social Service, mandatory for all Spanish women who earned a high school diploma, applied for a passport, or wanted to get a driver's license; and finally, through the cultural organization *Coros y Danzas* (Choirs and Dance), a voluntary organization that allowed young women to travel around Spain and abroad as cultural emissaries of the Francoist national spirit.

Francoist Physical Education: *"Mens Santa in Corpore Santo"*

After the Civil War, physical education promised to be a concrete means not only to regenerate the New Spain but also to guarantee effective political and social control within the context of the postwar "reconstruction of the fatherland."[3] From the very beginning, Francoist physical education suffered an institutional fragmentation that the law of 1961 intended to resolve. In the 1940s Falange was charged with the task of making new Spaniards fit. Falange regulated both physical education and sports through the Youth Front and the Women's Section with a negligible state legal articulation. Falange carried out the state's mandate in different realms. The Ministry of National Education established physical education as mandatory in all levels of schooling, drawing instructors from the rank and file of the Falangist Youth Front, Women's Section, and the SEU (Falange's University Student Union). Falangist instructors were also responsible for the extracurricular activities of youth organizations controlled separately for each sex by the Women's Section since 1938 and the Youth Front since 1940. In a militarized postwar environment Franco appointed General José Moscardó (1878–1956) as head of the National Delegation of Sports and charged the ministries of the army, navy, and air force with the task of military physical instruction. The army and the Ministry of National Education were marginal in the implementation of a centralized physical education. Even when the regime established a National Junta of Physical Education by order of June 5, 1944, a true centralization never ensued.

Figures 14 and 15. Spanish Falangist women and Nazi women performing the same exercise movement. Courtesy Archivo General de la Administración, Alcalá de Henares, Spain.

An order of January 24, 1945 zealously implemented segregation of physical education by sex. This norm recognized the independence of the National Secretariat of Physical Education of the Women's Section, established since 1938. Cándida Cádenas was the head and Dr. Luis Agosti the medical advisor of this agency. In 1952 the organization reiterated its foundational purpose emphasizing the spiritual (meaning Christian spirituality) value of physical education. "Our main objective was, and still is, that our Physical Education has a spiritual base . . . Thus, this is the goal of our Physical Education: *perfecting the body, to better serve the interests of the soul that it encloses* [my emphasis]."[4]

This objective echoed the Vatican dictum on physical education. In a speech to Italian sports clubs on May 20, 1945, Pius XII had pointed out how "far from the truth were those who accused the Church of not taking into account the body or physical culture." According to the Pope, "Our body is temple of the Holy Spirit who resides in ourselves by God's will and so *we are no longer just matter* [my emphasis]." Modernity turned the faithful into bodies that mattered to the Church for effective spiritual guidance. The Pope urged the community of Christians to "glorify God through their bodies."[5] By moderately practicing sports one would achieve the Christian aspiration of a complete human education. "Sports fortify the body," Pius XII held, "turning it into a healthy, new, operational organism." But the Pope also affirmed the need of making the educational process "rigorous and disciplined, routinely grueling, *a process that tries to shape a true docile body* [my emphasis]." It was important, according to the Pope, "to get our bodies used to exhaustion, to endure pain, to create in us a habit of stern continence and self-control," all of these regarded by the Holy Father as indispensable conditions for spiritual victory. "Sport is a school of loyalty and valor, of fortitude and resoluteness, of universal fraternity; all of them material virtues, which supply the supernatural qualities for a solid foundation and prepare man to handle the hardest responsibilities without failure. If you are able, through sports activity, to build a more docile body and a more submissive spirit to your moral obligations; if in the end your example contributes to endow modern physical activity with a more dignifying relation to the human life and divine precepts, then your physical culture will acquire a supernatural value."[6] In this light the practice of physical exercise is the means to generate the docile body in the purest Foucauldian fashion.[7] Pius XII's notion of physical education as a means to spiritual perfection furthers the Foucauldian argument on disciplining the body to reach spiritual salvation. The Pope's words demonstrate the Church's genuinely modern concern of bio-power. The Vatican dictum followed the Enlightenment notion of the body as a useful object of control. Seventeenth- and eighteenth-century techniques of disciplining the body were new on the scale of control; on the object of control; and on the modality. The Enlightenment treated the body as a unique entity, reduced to a machine that had to be finely tuned: its activity, gesticulations, posture, and swiftness. Consequently, as Foucault puts it, "The only truly important ceremony is that of exercise" and the modality implies an "uninterrupted and constant coercion."[8] Religious discourse bestowed this Enlightenment notion of the body-machine with a soul. The dictum *Mens Sana in Corpore Sano* turns thus into *Mens Santa in Corpore Santo,* making thus health and holiness inseparable in religious discourse.

Pius XII addressed the International Scientific Congress of Sport and Gymnastics in 1952 to explain the religious and moral principles of physical exertion. The ultimate goal according to the Pope was to bring man closer to God. "The body is the instrument and the artist is the soul. Both of them are fused in natural unity." He emphasized how the body from the religious perspective "has a sacred character that natural sciences and art do not consider."[9] God elevated matter to the service of the spirit. The human body, elevated thus to the honor of being the host of the spirit, must be prepared to receive the dignity of being God's temple, a building consecrated to God. The body belongs to God. As a result of Original Sin there must be complete subordination of our corporeality to the glorification of God. The quotidian drama of modern man is the struggle to avoid the temptation of falling prey to the body's instincts. Pius XII reminds us of Saint Paul's letter to the Romans: "I see in my members another law opposed to my spirit—A law that enslaves me to the law of sin latent in my flesh." Pius XII warns us about the danger of certain forms of sports and exercise that "awaken [the senses] through violent strength or through sensual seduction."[10] The Church is clear: the goal of physical exertion must be to refrain, to discipline the body for the glory of God. The spirit invigorates us; our flesh is good for nothing.[11] Therefore, the aims of sports according to the Vatican are twofold: "[T]o develop and strengthen the body from the dynamic and aesthetic point of view. [And] the soul's utilization of the fit body. [The fit body] will expand the interior and exterior life of the individual, contribute to his perfection, and at last bring man closer to God."[12]

The Law of Physical Education of 1961

The Francoist law of physical education of 1961 clearly typifies the Vatican prescriptive notion of sports and exercise. Furthermore, the religious overtones reveal the Foucauldian concept of bio-power exercised through the discursive constitution of the body.[13] This legal document exemplifies the notion of docility afforded by the Enlightenment and the Catholic Church precepts on physical education and sports. Spaniards' political docility remained at the center of the dictatorship's stability and longevity in the transition from autarky to consumerism. Docility was no strange concept to Catholicism and in the hands of Falange the Catholic element acquired nationalist connotations.

National Catholicism informed the 1961 law of physical education that eased Spain's entrance into the international sports scene through the Spanish Olympic Committee. The head of the recently established National Delegation of Physical Education and Sports, José Antonio Elola-Olaso, presented to the Cortes a new law of physical education on December 20, 1961. Elola's appointment meant a departure from a military physical education to a civilian model under the supervision of Falange's youth, labor, and women's subdivisions. Falange's Youth Front and the Women's Section fulfilled three state functions: first, the masses' mobilization and control in support of the regime; second, a strong nationalist popular education; and finally, the supervision of social and labor relations.[14]

The Falangist National Movement drafted the law of which the prime goal was to accomplish "a more comprehensive instruction of Spaniards." Catholic traditional values as prescribed by papal encyclicals permeate the text along with Falangist nationalism. In his presentation to the Cortes, José Antonio Elola-Olaso described physical education as one of the ancient classical age's most "gallant" legacies, but also as the means for any Christian man to achieve spiritual fulfillment. "It might be regarded as a quixotic craze. Blessed be those quixotic ways if they take us to achieve that a number of Spaniards, large or not, have the means to get a physical health that in mutual and lasting union with the spirit will lead to the health of the soul; because to improve the body in robust and Christian principles of physical education necessarily leads to the enlightenment of the soul."[15]

Elola echoed the Vatican precepts on physical education in his statement. The attention paid to the body in the context of a modernizing industrial society was of great importance for the Vatican. As mentioned above, since Pius XI every Pope had emphasized the significance of physical education to keep safe man's soul rather than for the sake of corporal health exclusively. But the Catholic establishment could not ignore the modern approach to the body as a precise machine, as an object of medical study.

The law of 1961 defines physical education as "school of virtues and an indispensable part of man's complete instruction within the principles of the National Movement." Elola clearly stated the main goal of the law was to renew the Christian values informing the National Catholic agenda since the regime's induction: "because to improve the body in healthy and Christian principles of physical education necessarily implied enlightening the soul."[16] Precisely what was most important, in the end, he declared, was the taming of the Spaniards' souls. Their bodies represented the conduit into their spirit that had to be entirely devoted to the Francoist national project. Modernity and the advent of consumerism eroded the stability of the regime. The regime invested in the preservation of the eternal Christian values in every aspect of everyday life. The challenge was to preserve tradition in the face of unavoidable modernization. Modernity and democratization meant a redefinition of gender relations and the implementation of equal rights between the sexes. The law emphasized in its preamble the religious spirit with the following quote from Pope John XXIII: "Sports can certainly develop true and sound Christian virtues, that God's grace makes later more fruitful and stable. The spirit of discipline encourages obedience, humility, renunciation; team interaction and competition foster charity and fraternal love as well as respect and magnanimous attitude, even forgiveness. The firm laws of physical endurance elevate chastity, temperance, and forethought."[17]

The Church regarded sports as a means to discipline the body of modern man, an individual faced with constant temptations. Modern women had to be deflected from modern materialism as well. The moral double standard prevalent in Christian values meant a dual problem with women as both subjects and objects of temptation in modern society. Women's modesty and physical preparation for motherhood were at the core of any physical instruction, making competitive sports problematic. The historical participation of women in sports and the practice of physical education in general had been at best problematic. When John XXIII addressed the world at the celebration of the Olympic Games in Rome in 1960, a total of 5,346 athletes from 83 countries participated and only 610 of those were women. The Pope's address contained highly gendered overtones.

In Spain women's physical education had been historically neglected because of being closely related to military affairs since the turn of the twentieth century.[18] Women's physical education was supposed to prepare them for motherhood but never subject their bodies to strenuous exercise. Francoism charged the Women's Section with the responsibility to shape women's bodies for their maternal duty. Women's Section's medical advisor, Dr. Luis Agosti, echoed Pius XI's document *Dobbiamo Intratenerla* (1931):[19] "Our desire to educate women to equate them physically with men is in conflict with universal biology laws. This is not the result of the imposed division of labor of modern civilized life since even in the most primitive communities women are biologically weaker than men. The same thing happens, with rare exceptions in the zoological scale in which females are weaker than males. This means that the origin of physical differences between the sexes is not phenotypic but genotypic. Hence, it is ridiculous to alter them in light of the recent discoveries in biology and genetics on this matter."[20]

Agosti tried to dispel any ideas of equality between the sexes in a convoluted mix of biology, genetics, and religious values. This effort to maintain a hold on the docile bodies of Spaniards became urgent by the late 1950s and 1960s when consumerism, migration, and tourism exposed the average citizen to new models of femininity. Spanish women dared to remake themselves through a new cult of their bodies. Now magazines and Hollywood movie stars presented a new and glamorous female image. The female body became an ideological weapon against the regime's moral/sexual politics that changed the whole fabric of society and led eventually to the collapse of the Francoist ideological hold based on Catholic values. In the midst of American-friendly modernization, Spanish women's bodies turned into more than vessels of motherhood, at least in the anteroom to marriage.

Concepción Sierra y Gil de la Cuesta, national delegate of the Women's Section Physical Education, made it clear in a questionnaire from the S.E.M. (Seminario Español de Magisterio, Spanish Teachers' Association) the fundamental differences between physical education for girls and for boys:

> Sex determines the fundamental differences in physical education. Not only with regard to the exercises but also with regard to the structure of the lessons—since age is an important factor in the physical distinction.
>
> Another crucial point for the difference is *the goal or purpose of the instruction. We must see a future woman whose primordial and lofty destiny is motherhood* [my emphasis].[21]

Women's bodies were once more nationalized with the enactment of the 1961 law of physical education, reaffirming the Women's Section's absolute control over Spanish women. The National Catholic spirit of the law intended to maintain a draconian normalization and disciplining of Spaniards' bodies—bodies that were conduits to their political consciences. The Ministry of National Education issued several decrees to complement the text of the 1961 law of physical education that directly addressed women's physical training under the responsibility of the Women's Section. The degree of instructor of physical education was regulated by decree of November 10, 1960 and by order of November 28, 1961, the Julio Ruiz de Alda's diplomas were rehabilitated. This legislation afforded the Women's Section the absolute control of girls' and young women's instruction through their instructors' school, Julio Ruiz de Alda. These legal documents bolstered article 16 of the law of physical education, which read: "The preparation of female instructors for the National Institute of Physical Education will be carried out at the National School 'Julio Ruiz de Alda,' official center dependent of the Women's Section and authorized by the Ministry of National Education."[22]

Concepción Sierra y Gil de la Cuesta celebrated the sprit of the law that created the National Institute of Physical Education and the categorization under the law of the National School Julio Ruiz de Alda as the branch for women's training within the National Institute. In addition to the Julio Ruiz de Alda School in 1959, there were fourteen regional schools throughout Spain that trained women physical education instructors.[23] The legislation complemented the law of professional and political rights for women approved also in 1961. Earning a degree in Physical Education opened a variety of job opportunities for women in the educational field and public health profession. The Julio Ruiz de Alda graduates found jobs as teachers in private and public schools, instructors in the Women's Section Social Service, as physicians' aides in physical therapy settings, in labor and delivery instruction, in sports medicine, in physical education of the mentally handicapped population, and in training of women workers within the Falangist movement. Some of these instructors would continue working after they got married.[24]

Some of the public entities that supported the task of the Women's Section included the Catholic Church, through their private schools and the parish activities; the state through the Ministry of National Education; and within Falange the University Student Union SEU, Youth Front, and syndicates through the organization known as Educación y Descanso (Education and Leisure). Educación y Descanso was the Spanish version of the Italian ODN (Opera Nazionale Dopolavoro).[25] Educación y Descanso was one of the most effective organizations of the Francoist corporatist syndicate. It promoted leisure activities among the workers that included sports and physical education along with theater, folk music, dance, and choral music. In order to have access to these activities, the workers had to join the so-called *grupos de empresa* (company groups). Educación y Descanso was founded in 1940 and existed until 1977. There was a network of cultural centers affiliated with the organization that included sports facilities and holiday residences known as *parques sindicales,* or syndicate parks. Some of the activities organized under

Educación y Descanso included theater groups, cinema clubs, choirs, and dance groups. Educación y Descanso also organized trips and holidays, and the most important activity was sports competitions that led to the Juegos Deportivos Sindicales (Syndicate Sports Competitions). Some of the most important Francoist businesses under the National Institute of Industry generously funded their company groups. Some of the most important were the company clubs subsidized by ENSIDESA (Empresa Nacional Siderúrgica Sociedad Anónima). Championships and all kinds of competitions culminated in the yearly May 1 celebrations at the Madrid soccer stadium, Santiago Bernabeu. The massive gymnastic and dance exhibitionsrepresented a spectacle of power of the synchronicity of the individual producers' (as the workers were referred to) bodies with the Francoist body politic. The Women's Section was in charge of the training of the working-class women. The Women's Section followed the regime's directives, which saw Educación y Descanso's enterprise as a means of social integration: "The task of *Educación y Descanso* is to incorporate, organize and sustain sports plans among women producers. These plans must be developed under the strict supervision of the Women's Section who due to its educational mission must be always part of any activity that targets women."[26]

In order to accomplish this task the Women's Section collaborated with several entities. The Regiduría del Trabajo (Labor Secretariat) formerly known as Hermandad de la Ciudad y el Campo (City and Countryside Fraternity) was charged on behalf of Educación y Descanso to recruit women workers who wished to participate in sports. The Secretariat was also in charge of any joint venture between the syndicates and Women's Section. The teams were put together according to the classification of Educación y Descanso (ED) by trade and company. Any team had to receive the approval of the provincial chief of the ED organization and the provincial labor secretariat. It was the Women's Section physical education secretariat who estimated the skill of the teams to compete in the national championships.[27] The Women's Section physical education secretariat was in charge of designing the technical planning and providing instructors in order to prepare the women workers within the parameters of "proper" feminine fitness. Those women members of the syndicates were allowed to use the Women's Section sports facilities as well as those of Educación y Descanso. Their official uniforms and swimsuits were those approved by the Women's Section and carried the label of the National Confederation of Syndicates (C.N.S.) and the emblem of Educación y Descanso. The general sports' regulations and specific rules for each competition were designed by Educación and Descanso and the national labor secretariat. The funding of the national championships was the responsibility of Educación y Descanso.

The regime saw physical education as a means to achieve social integration in order to erase class conflict and polarization between urban and rural areas. Through the so-called *Cátedras ambulantes* (mobile teaching teams), the Women's Section reached out to both the countryside and suburbia in the large cities. In a 1966 report the Women's Section highlighted the positive effect of sports among adolescents. The instructors noticed "quick obedience, respect to the teachers, and teamwork,"[28] and the practice of sports also molded their character, helping them gain patience to execute more difficult tasks. Sports also provided a form of entertainment in the rural areas where there were "scarce movie theaters that show bad films from time to time, and there is just one television set in a tavern, a weekly dance in very inadequate facilities."[29]

The most important advance in the early 1960s, and as a result of the law of physical education of 1961, was the support of the National Delegation of Sports and Physical Education to the Women's Section instruction of Spanish women. This facilitated the task of the instructors who faced social hostility up until this point.

> With regard to women's physical education our main struggle has been to change a mentality not only indifferent but hostile due to old-fashioned ideas, erroneous outlook, and ideas exclusively theoretical. Consequently, the prevalent ideas of women's natural stillness, isolation, fear of taking any risks.
>
> On the other hand, there is the atavistic attitude of the Iberian male who did not see these or any other activities as positive. And those others, who, due to their zealous defense of women's physical education, imbued it with a certain fanaticism giving it a masculine character.[30]

This quote shows the intrinsic paradox in the Women's Section's discourse on womanhood in the transition to consumerism in the 1960s. The modernization of women's roles and gender relations was unavoidable. The predicament in this juncture was to remain "at the core" faithful to the docile femininity ideal José Antonio envisioned.

The Women's Section answered a questionnaire from the First Sports Christian Conference held in Austria in 1963. The topic was "Limits and Possibilities of Sports for Women and Young Girls." The Women's Section emphasized the importance of implementing a physical education curriculum to prepare women for motherhood: It is important to select exercises and sports that, rather than harm, foster in women:

a) Their primordial feminine function: motherhood
b) Aesthetics
c) Their duties: 1) from early games to the practice of sports it must be geared towards the future maternal function, not just biological but also psychological and moral preparation; 2) Today more than ever we need sportswomen who embody feminine beauty not only in their appearance but also in their physical execution; 3) We must always follow the principles of sports (as clearly offered by Pius XII), never interfere with the ultimate goal to please God, the family, with a life of study and labor.[31]

The Women's Section of Falange

The Women's Section tried to maintain the docile Christian mother model that consumerism threatened to topple. The transition to consumerism posed a continuous tension between the centripetal forces of change and the centrifugal pull of the regime's continuity. In imparting the political and civic instruction of girls, the Women's Section textbooks offered clear orientation about how a young woman had to treat her body. Appearance and careful containment of movements was of the essence. "Avoid swinging your hips," read one text." Naturally you have to move your legs when you walk, but avoid any swinging that is so vulgar."[32] It was very important to keep one's physical composure because this was an indication of a disciplined soul.[33] To better fit the docile female model proposed by Church and state, the domestication of gymnastics became the safest option. "A woman who has to tend domestic chores with regularity has the opportunity to exercise much more than if she were to work outside the home. Just the cleaning and polishing of the floors is most effective, and if we think of the movements needed to dust high places, cleaning windows, shaking dust off a suit, they will realize how the movements are really gymnastic exercises; even though not destined to develop body aesthetics they actually have that effect."[34]

Sport, in the Women's Section view, should not be taken as an opportunity to gain independence from family obligation or as license for indecent display. "We must not utilize sport as a pretext to dress in scandalous sportswear. We can exhibit our sporting skills, but not let these abilities become the excuse for indecent display. We must not either take sports as a means to independence from family duties, or any kind of freedom against conventional decorum."[35]

Some of the sports recommended for women included tennis, swimming, and neo-Swedish gymnastics. In an article entitled "Los deportes más propios para la mujer" published in *Blanco y Negro* on November 29, 1958, the author, Carlos Delfino, added golf, basketball, and skating to the list. According to Delfino sports were the monopoly of "the stronger sex." Latin women preferred, in his view, to seek entertainment in closed-door activities: movie theaters, dance halls, or simply staying home. However, there are a few more sports he adds to the list: fishing, diving, and climbing were a few of them.[36]

The Women's Section central secretary of physical education divided sport and physical education into two categories according to age group: under Youth were those girls under seventeen years old, and under Adults those young women over seventeen years old[37] (see table below).

			Enrolled	**Camps and Miscellaneous**
Categories	**Youth** up to 17	Schoolchildren	50,762	42,634
		Apprentices	5,121	3,586
	Adults over 17	SEU	4,695	821
		Syndicates		968
		Social Service	11,122	281
		Women's Section Clubs		7,088

The state made physical education mandatory in all school levels and the university. By decree of December 29, 1939, Women's Section instructors became the legal guardians of Spanish schoolgirls and young college women in the realm of physical fitness. Physical education supplemented mandatory home economics and political indoctrination. These subjects fell exclusively under the responsibility of Falangist women instructors trained at the Escuela Superior de Profesoras "Julio Ruiz de Alda" in Madrid from 1956 until the downfall of the organization in 1977. The prerequisites to enter the Julio Ruiz de Alda School included the following: to be sixteen years old, to obtain medical clearance for the practice of physical training, to have a high school diploma, and to pass an entrance examination.[38] The instructors studied for four nine-month academic years. The students had to attend a total of thirty-three hours of classroom instruction in order to graduate. During the second year they performed some practical training. The curriculum included biology, psycopedagogy, gymnastics, sports, hygiene, and health education. The students also received lectures on art, film, theater, and literature. These cultural activities were programmed and carried out by the students themselves. Upon graduation, students presented a research thesis and had to pass some comprehensive examinations in front of a Graduation Committee composed of representatives of the Minister of National Education, the Sports and Physical Education Delegation, the school faculty, and the Central Secretariat of the Women's Section.[39]

Under the legal reforms introduced with the 1961 law of physical education, the School Julio Ruiz de Alda offered postgraduate preparation in specific areas such as pedagogy, psychology, medicine, arts, and music. International interest led to foreign languages courses and religious and political instruction continued to be part of all the training. Although originally the school had been opened only to members of the Women's Section, in the 1960s this prerequisite was annulled. In the academic year 1961–62 there were one hundred students enrolled at the Julio Ruiz de Alda School.[40]

The Women's Section always emphasized its interest in practicing sports rather than in competing for Olympic records. However, in the 1950s the Women's Section had to moderate its rhetoric of docility with its commitment to prepare high-quality athletes.[41] In April 1952, there were Gymnastic Regional Competitions in Madrid. In sports, basketball was the game in which Women's Section athletes excelled: They defeated the Brussels team and obtained second place in the basketball championship celebrated in Bordeaux in May 1952.

The norms for instruction mailed on August 19, 1953, to the provincial delegations of the Women's Section emphasized that their fundamental goal was to promote healthy and disciplined social coexistence as well as to impart three behaviors: emulation, solidarity, and comradeship. The means to achieve these goals was the practice of sports during the mass leisure hours without disrupting work or study.[42] In a circular communication to Women's Section officials of the University of Granada, Concepción Sierra y Gil de la Cuesta, National Head of SEU, specified the goals of physical education in the summer retreats (Albergues):

1st To correct and perfect their attitude
2nd To apply themselves to achieve a *minimal aptitude*
3rd To know sports and love the practice of sport to achieve a better bodily function and the advantages that it offers[43]

In order to achieve these three goals each class was divided into three periods. The first twenty minutes were to mold the attitude by practicing arm, leg, and abdominal exercises. All of them were to be performed with "ease and showing feminine grace."[44] But the desire to compete still existed. The gymnastic performances showed rigor and along with basketball, handball turned into one of the successful games that Women's Section coaches trained. In March 1955 gymnastics and handball teams traveled to Paris as guests of the Fédération Sportive de France to participate in a friendly round of competitions. Women's Section instructors followed a curriculum based on the methods proposed by Dr. Agosti, which included gymnastics, aptitude tests, rhythm, games and sports, outdoor activities, traditional folk dances, and arts and crafts. The Women's Section applied the neo-Swedish method of gymnastics of Per Henrik Ling (1776–1839). Throughout the nineteenth century and well into the twentieth century, the Swedish method competed internationally with the German and English methods. The Swedish method had an important role in spreading and establishing fixed concepts of gender and body.[45] Because the pedagogical goal of the Ling method was to harmoniously develop the body, the Women's Section wholeheartedly adopted it. Ling conceived the body as the temple of the spirit. His method paid close attention to detail by targeting each body part individually. A severe control, surveillance, and order characterized the Ling method, creating in the process a docile body to hold harmoniously the individual's soul. In Ling's gymnastics, women's duties as mothers were highly emphasized. It was Hjalmar, Ling's son, who developed female gymnastics. Women were regarded as physically slower and weaker than men and hence the exercises were designed in quantitative terms rather than qualitative. After WWI a more militaristic manliness arose and competitive sports were regarded as more appropriate for men than gymnastics. Therefore, Ling gymnastics became more suitable for the new woman of the 1920s and 1930s and naturally the fascist femininity advanced by organizations like the Women's Section found the neo-Swedish method appealing. In the aftermath of the Spanish Civil War women had to toughen up yet remain feminine. The frailty myth was not viable in times of postwar, but at the same time the Women's Section regarded the feminist alternative as an aberration of the natural gender order of things. The Women's Section adapted neo-Swedish methods to Spanish idiosyncrasy. "Gymnastics rooted in neo-Swedish method add modern techniques of rhythm, coordination and relaxation to the purest Spanish tradition. We accomplish this objective through the movement, stimulating exercises and the music based in our cultural heritage. Our gymnastics, being absolutely modern . . . has characteristics that gives it a Spanish seal."[46]

Preserving Spanish national idiosyncrasy in the face of manifest modernization guided the Women's Section's work in the late 1950s and early 1960s. According to Dr. Carlos Gutiérrez, technical director of the National School of Physical Education and gymnastics consultant for the Women's Section in this period, the most important contribution in Spain was the introduction of popular folklore to girls and women's gymnastics. "Hence almost in an intuitive way we incorporated Spanish music to gymnastics. There is an important contribution of popular instruments, mainly percussion, instruments utilized by our people to mark the rhythm of their dances and which we now use in our gymnastics: The popular castanets, sticks, shells or simply whistling and clapping with fingers and hands."[47]

With these words as part of his allocution to the World Conference for Physical Education, Dr. Gutiérrez explains how inseparable the national spirit was from the design of a gymnastic method for women. In order to reach the mind and soul of girls and women Dr. Gutiérrez proposed the fusion of popular folklore and gymnastics. Gutiérrez presented this as a modernizing method to design female physical education that departed from making it a mere imitation of male gymnastics. "Women's physical education should not and must not be a poor imitation of men's physical education. We must, consequently, typify it and look for those qualities that we must emphasize for the psychosomatic affirmation of their femininity. We must reject entirely the wrong idea that girls become manly with the practice of exercise."[48] Popular folklore's traditional national values imbued

Figure 16. The castanets and the pose of a Spanish gymnast. AGA Sección Femenina.

the Women's Section's modernizing discourse on female physical education in the 1960s. Through the establishment in 1944 of exclusively female groups of Coros y Danzas (Choirs and Dance),[49] the Women's Section reinvented women's bodies, making them living enactments of Spanish cultural and national heritage.[50] The groups of dancers from the different regions of Spain incarnated the organic parts of the nation's body. Through their bodies' performance of these regional dances women were to maintain alive the unity of the organic nation.

Massive gymnastic concentrations provided the regime with an opportunity to turn power into spectacle. Each individual on the stadium field was part of a whole—a clear materialization of the symbiosis of the one and the many: the national body and its members. Women partook in the collective spectacle of power through Coros y Danzas. Their performances of national folklore turned women into small embodiments of the motherland.

The regime utilized the Women's Section Coros y Danzas not only in Spain but also as international cultural emissaries. By 1960, 23,378 participants competed in the dancing contests. The most important period in the history of Coros y Danzas was 1948 to 1962 under the leadership of María Josefa Hernández Sanpelayo. During this period they visited Greece, Turkey, Lebanon, Egypt, France, Belgium, Italy, GDR, and Cuba. Eva Perón's visit to Spain in 1947 led to the idea of sending a group of Coros y Danzas to Buenos Aires in the spring of 1948. The group traveled on the *Monte Albertia* ocean liner of the Aznar shipping company. Eulalia Ridruejo and María Josefa Hernández Sampelayo went as head of the 150-person expedition that included not only young women but old musicians from different regions, mostly men, to accompany the dancers. They arrived on May 11, 1948, at Mar del Plata, Argentina, where General Perón and his wife Evita, along with the Spanish delegation, welcomed them. The 1948 tour included several cities in Argentina and a short visit to Brazil. So successful was this venture that in 1949 Coros y Danzas embarked on their second tour of Latin America. This time the 125 members of the expedition visited several countries including Chile, Peru, and Colombia.

The Spanish ambassador in Chile, José María Doussinague, celebrated the visit of Coros y Danzas to this country as the regime's best international political mission: "People opposed to our politics or even worse, indifferent or contemptuous, are changed and comforted by that something that floats over the entire group, by that mysterious and strange feminine magnetism,

Figure 17. Coros y Danzas group. Courtesy Archivo General de la Administración, Alcalá de Henares, Spain.

by that Spanish notion of movement, of life, of thinking, and believing. The girls don't know and no one knows what they have brought with themselves. . . . *Spain is felt closer, more perfect, more defined and corporeal* [my emphasis]."[51] The ambassador was also very impressed with the young women dancers' response to the press and the Republican exiles in Chile. At a cocktail party offered at the embassy, a Chilean woman journalist was characterized by Doussinague as having "airs of intellectual superiority" that in his view made "poor young Spanish girls" shine by contrast with their natural innocence. The ambassador introduced them to each other highlighting the dancing over the intellectual abilities of Spanish young women. The humbling effect of these young angelical girls over the Republican exiles was also emphasized by the ambassador: "I think it is important to remember what happened to a girl from Murcia. Among a large group of people one told her 'that man over there staring at you is also from Murcia.' He was standing aside, silent, contemplating them. She walked towards him and held out her hand to him. She said hello and asked him if it is true he is from her country. He replied 'Yes I am, but I did not dare to talk to you because we are the "bad guys."' Statement spoken without affectation or irony but with all the bitterness *of a confession coming from the lips of someone after ten years of remorse* [my emphasis] . . . Naturally, she was able to say warm and tactful words as the circumstances required."[52]

The ambassador presented the redeeming value of the Coros y Danzas emissaries for the Francoist regime in exile. Only these young girls could heal the broken Spanish nation with their dances and their natural femininity, presenting themselves as the new benign generation of Spaniards who "wanted to overcome the bitterness of the Civil War" in the international scene. Dancing and singing the regional folk songs, these women fulfilled their role as cultural reproducers of the Francoist nation's spirit in the world. But as individuals their travels abroad allowed them to view themselves outside the straitjacket of marriage and motherhood and enjoy an ephemeral independence of sorts. "Those young women who evoked the authentic folklore of Spain, not that un-natural other of show business—as the daily *Siglo de Bogotá* published a few weeks later—had awakened the interests of the Chilean audience, brother from the other side of the ocean, and for the first time, pieced together the bits of a broken Spain and made the exiles in foreign lands burst into tears and applause."[53]

Now the Women's Section counted with a phenomenal instrument of international promotion and they were ready to exploit this power to the extreme. The regime utilized Coros y Danzas as a vehicle of its goodwill. It represented the regime's simplistic version of the overcoming of the Civil War differences. Those who were vanquished felt under the spell of the Coros y

Danzas girls' Spanishness, and the logical effect in the eyes of the regime's officials was to admit the evil of their past actions. The success of the first Latin American tour led to a contract with the film industry. The Women's Section signed a contract on December 20, 1950, with Estudios Chamartín for the production of a film entitled "Ronda Española"—a two-hour romantic rendition of their goodwill mission to the world showing the amicable image of the regime to international audiences. Five hundred young women and men acted in the film without pay. The Women's Section committed themselves to not allowing Coros y Danzas to appear in any other film until 1956. Under the contract, the Women's Section received 15 percent of the royalties and 200,000 pesetas from the state subsidy if the film received a rating of extraordinary merit. The film, under the direction of Ladislao Vajda, opened on November 8, 1951, in Madrid and a month later in Barcelona. It was a success for critics and audiences alike. Not all the exile communities received the groups of dancers with a friendly welcome. In Paris and Belgium they encountered open hostilities on their 1951 spring tour. When the expedition departed from Paris on the way to Brussels, agitators threw stones at the bus breaking the windows, which they then had to cover with cardboard on the trip to Belgium. The rest of the trip continued without any major incidents. The most important trip from a political point of view was to the United States. The trip began on June 3, 1953, a couple of months before the signature of the Pact of Madrid between the United States and Spain. The Women's Section dancing group signed a contract with Harry L. Sokol to tour the United States for four months. Although Falangist officials considered the tour a tremendous success, the July 20, 1953, *San Francisco Chronicle* reported protests against them. Although Coros y Danzas offered women the opportunity to be ambassadors of Spanish nationalism around the world, the regime continued to emphasize domesticity as central to Spanish womanhood.

But the opposition to the regime was clear by the mid 1950s, not only in the exile communities in America and Europe but also in Spain. The university crisis of 1956 cost the resignation of Minister of Education Joaquín Ruiz Giménez and signaled the beginning of a clear institutional transformation of the regime. Conscious of the unavoidable transformation of women's role, the Women's Section hurried to redefine its responsibility in this new phase of Francoist politics. The recently founded Women's

Section magazine *Teresa* echoed its commitment to renewal. The Nineteenth Congress of the Women's Section assembled January 7–12, 1958 at the Castle of la Mota in Medina del Campo. In her address to the assembly Pilar Primo de Rivera remarked: "There is no doubt a new political era is dawning. In this point in time the most important thing for us women is that neither the essence nor the efficacy of the Women's Section is lost for Spain. Necessary premise to reach our goals is unity."[54]

The effects of the Nineteenth Congress showed in a circular letter of June 9, 1958, signed by Pilar Primo de Rivera. In this letter she called for strengthening the responsibilities of the local delegations now in charge of planning intensive instruction and the preparation of Women's Section leadership. Physical education and home economics instructors fell under the educational competencies of the Women's Section. The organization was subsidized by the Ministry of National Education, Ministry of Interior, National Delegation of Syndicates, and the General Plan for Professional Education from the General Secretary of the Movement. The Women's Section's total operating budget for 1958 amounted to 110,054,057.57 pesetas. More than 81 million pesetas came from the Ministry of National Education, which made the Women's Section an organization eminently educational. This meant that the salaries of physical education and home economics instructors would experience an increase particularly after their diplomas were officially recognized by a report issued on March 22, 1958, by the National Education Council.[55] According to the order of January 11, 1965, physical education instructors would make 36,000 pesetas a year and teaching assistants would make 24,000 pesetas per year. In addition to this net pay, instructors would receive two annual bonuses. The university districts affected by this regulation included: Granada, Madrid, Murcia, Oviedo, Salamanca, Santiago, Valencia, Valladolid, and Zaragoza.[56]

Nineteen hundred fifty-nine was a key year. The Stabilization Plan signaled the beginning of what in the 1960s was called the "development plans" orchestrated by the new technocratic Francoist elite led by Opus Dei. For the regime, 1959 was also a very important year. Franco celebrated twenty years of uncontested dictatorship and had received the blessing of the western powers in the context of the Cold War. To celebrate the twentieth anniversary of Francoist victory the regime planned a series of massive celebrations and orchestrated a major spectacle of power. The most important was to take place at the Valley of the Fallen outside of Madrid. This was Franco's mausoleum outside Madrid, finished in March 1959 after two decades of construction. The Valley of the Fallen can be regarded as an ideologically charged "site of memory," as cultural theorist Pierre Nora proposes.[57] There, in the very same location, the regime had come together in a symbolic spectacle in the fall of 1939. The Falange exhumed the body of their founder, José Antonio Primo de Rivera, from his burial rest in Alicante and transferred the corpse to the Monastery of El Escorial in the hills above Madrid, built by Phillip II as a mausoleum, which Franco's Valley of the Fallen wanted to emulate. For ten days and nights one uninterrupted funeral pageant of five hundred kilometers unfolded in the most pure baroque style. Falangist members of different local units transported the coffin on their shoulders, halting only to change the men honored with the task. The baroque spectacle at the Escorial combined military and religious elements in a ceremony to lay José Antonio's body to rest before the high altar above the crypt where the kings of Spain lie buried. On the tomb were placed monumental wreaths sent by Hitler and Mussolini. Francoist National Catholicism brought together in baroque pageantry and public political spectacle: Spanish tradition, religion, monarchy. The anniversary of Jose Antonio's execution in Alicante on November 20, 1936, became a national festival with the Francoist victory. On the outside walls of churches throughout Spain the name "José Antonio" was painted, above those of the local men who had died "for God and for country," almost as if they were martyr saints.

As soon as the Valley of the Fallen was finished in March 1959, the remains of José Antonio were again to be relocated from El Escorial to the new Francoist mausoleum twenty years later. Pilar Primo de Rivera received the news from the caudillo and reported it to all the provincial delegates. "Other than the unpleasant task of having to exhume the remains, since we wish our dead ones to remain in peace," she alleged, "there is no doubt, his final resting place must be among those who fought and fell defending his doctrine."[58]

Just as twenty years earlier, the regime capitalized on the symbolic power of pageantry. José Antonio's body symbolized the Francoist hold of power. The grave's transfer was planned for March 30 at eleven in the morning. Falangist men transported the casket again on foot from El Escorial to the Valley of the Fallen. On April 1, 1959, twentieth anniversary of the end of the civil war, a mass rally took place with Falange representatives from every province.[59]

The Twentieth National Congress of the Women's Section assembled January 11–17, 1960, in the Valley of the Fallen.[60] The choice of this site for the Twentieth National Congress of the Women's Section is highly significant. The Women's Section was celebrating there its twenty-fifth anniversary. The Congress was inaugurated with a solemn holy Mass in the Valley of the Fallen where, to celebrate the victory, with the symbolic presence of her brother's remains in the Valley of the Fallen, Pilar inaugurated the Twentieth Congress of Women's Section (January 1960). The Women's Section displayed a massive propaganda campaign in the press, in radio, and in cinema. The state issued a commemorative stamp. Several public lectures throughout the country as well as the reedition of José Antonio's works contained at its core two slogans: emphasis on teamwork and strengthening the spirit of service and sacrifice that guided the Women's Section since its creation within Falange. The purpose of the Twentieth Congress was "not to study new directions but rather strengthened the principles of the Women's Section." Nineteen provinces presented their reports to the Assembly.[61] The report of the Central Physical Education Secretariat confirmed that in spite of the past steps forward in this area, in 1960 there still were serious difficulties to be overcome. The Women's Section remained faithful to the method introduced by Dr. Agosti. The report mentioned the success of the physical education annual contests that had gathered a total of 50,000 participants; however, the report lamented the official neglect of physical education regarded by officials of public opinion as subsidiary matter. The Women's Section felt strongly about the importance of gymnastics as a means to infuse the social fabric with harmony and discipline. The Barcelona delegate, Monserrat Tey, submitted a report that made clear the affiliation crisis the Women's Section was facing. According to Tey the Women's Section had 6,462 affiliates with the Falangist Identification Card and 2,714 without it. In the youth section there were 502 members. She felt the only recruiting pool potential was the Social Service. The conclusion certainly was that the Women's Section in Barcelona was navigating a hostile environment. The reports from other provinces tried to show enthusiasm to compensate for the apathy that surrounded them. The Twentieth Congress closed with a mixture of preoccupation and commitment to continue carrying out José Antonio's legacy for the glory of the caudillo.[62]

In order to adjust to the changes Spanish society was experiencing, the regime introduced some institutional and legal reforms that affected the status of women and led in 1961 to the enactment of the Law of Professional and Political Rights for women. The Women's Section sought the opportunity to be one of the arbiters of the new governmental initiative. By decree of July 15, 1961, the state established the National Fund for the Promotion of Equal Opportunities. This fund was one of the areas of investment that the Stabilization Plan of 1959 opened, what is known as the 1960s Development Era. Six hundred million pesetas were budgeted into the fund: One hundred and eighty million for primary education and two hundred and ninety to professional training. The Women's Section saw this as a great opportunity to increase its resources and reinsert themselves into the social service plan of the state apparatus. The funds would facilitate the completion of a series of causes already in progress since 1960: defense of the family as an institution and infant care as central to women's national duty, social work, summer camps, youth groups, university and secondary school residence halls. In addition to political and Bible-based religious instruction, the youth groups and residence halls offered sport competitions.

Pilar Primo de Rivera appointed a board of adjudicators that included lawyers such as Roberto Reyes and Manuel Fraga. The commission drafted a bill for the political, professional and labor rights of women. In the presentation of the law to the Cortes plenary session, Pilar Primo de Rivera remarked in her speech: "We believe that by protecting the work and the right to an education for women we are not being impudent. A refined and sensible woman because of her education can better teach her children and be a companion for her husband."[63]

The spirit of Christian domesticity dominated the law. It was one more legal reform in the area of social relations that started in 1958 with the reform of the civil code and the Law of the Fundamental Principles of the State. To these legal documents we need to add the law of physical education of 1961 that clearly incorporated the National Catholic values that inspired the transition from autarky to consumerism. The Women's Section continued to be at the center of the political arena. It was a member of thirty-five state agencies that allowed Falangist women officials to have a direct intervention in the policymaking of at least eight ministries. The Women's Section was also a member of several international organizations that included: The International Catholic Federation of Physical Education (FICEP), the Sport Federation of Catholic Teaching (FISEC), International Tourist Youth Center (CTG), Children's International Catholic Commission (OICI), International Federation of Youth Hostels (IGF), International Union of Folk Groups; European Organization of Economic Cooperation (OECE), and International Congress of Social Service (CISS). All of these organizations opened the doors to UNESCO and the United Nations for the Women's Section.[64]

Women's Physical Education in Crisis

Consumerism posed serious problems to the safekeeping of a docile domesticity. The effects of social change ignited by the US-Spain economic and military agreement in 1953 made urgent the reevaluation of the Women's Section's role. In January 1956 the Seventeenth Women's Section Congress met in Málaga with the exclusive objective of discussing the reorientation of the Falangist Movement in the transitional political juncture. Unity was at the center of the debate. Because the new generations were not keen to embrace Falangist principles, the organization felt deeply that they did not face a bright future. Like the regime, the Women's Section recognized religion as the agglutinating agent in the transition to consumerism. In her inaugural address to the National Congress in Málaga, Pilar Primo de Rivera declared: "We have been absolutely right about one thing. . . . religious training. Finally we are achieving what religious life must be for us something we feel deeply rather than a means of propaganda. Finally, we are shaping clear consciences whose sole motive is honest behavior before God."[65]

Following the deep self-reflection in Málaga, the Women's Section initiated its internal renewal on several fronts. First, they felt it was crucial to revise the doctrine taught in all the centers of instruction. The instruction had to better echo the polarization between communism and democracy, making sure to highlight the significance of the Arab world. Second, they realized the national movement was not monolithic but plural and therefore the affiliates had to be informed and instructed in respect to the different Falangist factions. In addition to the content, the

Women's Section acknowledged the need to do away with the uniform and the fascist salute, reserving both for specific (more private) official events. Finally, they felt it was necessary to pay close attention to historical and social events to bring the Falangist doctrine up to date.

The Women's Section acknowledged the serious lack of interest in physical education among young women at the college level. María de Miranda Huelin, national vice inspector for college physical education submitted a detailed report on December 15, 1959, about the state of affairs at the University of Sevilla. Miss Huelin paid a three-day visit early that month to the Sevilla district that left her with the worst possible impression.

> Saturday, December 5
> I start the inspection at half past three in the afternoon.
> According to the schedule submitted by the local instructor, María Josefa Barreto, on Saturdays there is practice class from eight to nine in the morning, from three thirty to four thirty and from four thirty to five thirty.
>
> I go to the college stadium. There are many young men practicing and playing basketball only they are not college students but members of the Youth Front, according to the field security guard. No female in sight. We make further inquiries. There has been no competition in the morning either.[66]

Huelin's report shows the frustration of Women's Section's officials. After several hours of waiting for the instruction to start she was informed the reason there were no classes that particular day might be because the local head of SEU was getting married that very day. After witnessing the classes and a couple of basketball games, Huelin remarks: "Here everything is improvised: the referee, the scorer, the uniforms; all in all, low class in everything; although there is a cordial environment."[67] The report concludes with several major issues to address:

1- The reality of what we witnessed does not correspond in the least with the information submitted by this district and it is very deficient.
2- I believe short three-day visits are not sufficient to determine what part of the information submitted is truthful.
3- The President of the university is dissatisfied with the men's Physical Education faculty and has not even met professor María Josefa Barreto[68]

The lack of commitment on the part of the female physical education faculty may be the result of their dissatisfaction with salary and facilities. During the academic year 1965–66 the faculty at the universities of Vigo, Sevilla, Murcia, Valladolid, and Madrid had not been paid. Several complaint letters were sent to Rafael Cháves, General Secretary of the National Junta of Physical Education.[69] Rosa Tobalina Espiga, head of Sección Femenina Physical Education in Valladolid, sent the acknowledgment of a total of 45,000 pts (about $450) for the payment of the salaries of six Women's Section SEU physical education instructors:

María López Delgado	9,000
Carmen Tejeiro Núñez	9,000
María Pilar Conejo Ruiz	9,000
Julia Mayo Castellanos	6,000
Mercedes Guerras Loras	6,000
Carmen Guerras Loras	6,000[70]

The economic context of these figures is one of crisis. Since 1962 there had been great dissatisfaction amid the economic power centers due to the slow results the 1959 Stabilization Plan delivered. The escalating discontent among the working class was the result of a salary blockade, and a rise in unemployment and cost of living. Finally, the emergent liberal opposition to the regime was also dissatisfied because the political opening-up they expected with the advent of economic liberalization did not take hold. Certainly, 1962 was an important year in political terms because it showed the main traits that prevailed until 1973: labor protests and the democratization push of the more liberal forces within the regime. Thus, 1962 is a key year in the transformation of the political nature of the regime. Gender relations were profoundly affected by the economic turn of events. The Law of Political and Professional Rights of women, approved in July 1961, began to impact those young women who managed to enter the university classrooms. The 1960s would transform the student relations within the university with the establishment in March 1962 of the so-called Free University Assemblies, with the central coordination based in Barcelona. Physical education was certainly the last priority for the student movement.

María de Miranda Huelin as inspector of physical education for the Ministry of Education ensured the continuity of sports education policies. In August 1962, Huelin traveled to Washington DC to participate in the Fourth International Congress of the Association for Women's and Girls' Physical Education. During her stay she also had the opportunity to visit the facilities of some American schools. This visit guided her recommendations to provincial delegates to better implement the new law of physical education of 1961. Two major issues were emphasized in her report: the importance of state and local public funding for sports activities and the emphasis on the health aspects that physical education promoted.

The Women's Section created the "Medina Clubs" in 1962 to stimulate competition and the promotion of track athletics as one of the priorities for Women's Section sports. The Women's Section participation in the International Games of Sport Federation of Catholic Teaching (FISEC) in Lisbon in the spring of 1962 made Huelin proud. These were no doubt positive developments, but Huelin also noted the serious crisis the Women's Section faced with regard to physical education. Neither the family, nor the business establishment, nor the schools, took physical education seriously. Huelin pointed out the "excessive materialism and the push to professionalize within sports life," something the Women's Section saw as contrary to the sacrificial code of the sportsman. In a 1973 publication of the Women's Section, the "Sportsman's Rules of Conduct" read:

1. Compete always with enthusiasm
2. If you win do not be petulant
3. If you lose do not be defiant
4. If you are a replacement be patient in waiting
5. Accept without complaining the referee's decisions
6. When you play do not lose control of your behavior
7. When the opposing team wins congratulate them
8. If your coach corrects you accept it humbly and be willing to improve
9. If you perform a good play, attribute it to the team play of your fellow sportswomen [*sic*]
10. Respect the rules not as an imposition but as guiding you in the clarity and objective of the game. It is not a matter of winning but of always looking like a winner.
11. In sports as in life the most important thing is to fight with Great Spirit and nobility in pursuit of success, but also to achieve self-control and recognition of the others' merits.[70]

This code shows the power to mold the spirit through the disciplined body and reminds us of the Vatican dictum described at the beginning of this chapter. A fit individual is a good (meaning docile) one. The qualities of the good athlete are very compatible with the virtues of the docile woman. In fact many of the commands recall those of the code of the Women's Section in 1937:

1. At dawn raise your heart to God and think of a new day for the Fatherland.
2. Be disciplined, disciplined, disciplined.
3. Do not comment on any order; obey without hesitation.
4. Never under any circumstance excuse yourself from an act of service.
5. Action is not yours; encourage others to act.
6. Let the man in your life be the best patriot.
7. Do not forget that your mission is to educate your children for the good of the nation.
8. Compensate for the anguish of your young woman's heart with the serenity that you are helping to save Spain.
9. Work with joy and without hesitation.
10. Obey and by your example teach others to obey.
11. Try always to be the wheel of the cart and let the one guiding it be in control.
12. Do not stand out; help someone else to excel.
13. Love Spain over anything else, so as to be able to inculcate in others your love.
14. Do not expect any reward for your efforts except your own satisfaction.
15. Let the Falangist bundle of sticks be rooted in a common individual yearning.
16. Whatever you do, improve yourself doing it.
17. Your strength will encourage the victory.
18. There is no glory comparable to the glory of having given everything for the Fatherland.[72]

Athletics helped maintain docility in the new modern woman. Through the practice of sports the Women's Section renewed the spirit of sacrifice and camaraderie. Winning remained marginal in a discourse in which competing for self-improvement and the glory of the fatherland were one and the same. The Women's Section participated in the Tokyo Olympics in 1964 under the slogan "What is important: participate!" not to win. Concepción Sierra y Gil de la Cuesta succeeded María de Miranda Huelin as head of Women's Section Physical Education. Sierra also joined the Spanish Olympic Committee. She did not see much improvement during her tenure.

On June 3, 1965, the Women's Section regional delegate of Physical Education in Murcia wrote a lengthy letter delineating the problems (not only in Murcia but at the national level) and proposing immediate solutions to improve the conditions of what she considered a severe crisis in the physical education of Spanish university women. A concern of most university districts was the lack of appropriate facilities. In addition to the infrastructure problems the letter highlighted the hostile attitude among students toward physical education, considered a burden rather than a serious subject. In many instances students would seek the forgery of medical certificates to avoid their physical education classes.[73] No doubt, by the mid-1960s university students were not interested in the mandatory subjects: religion, political instruction, and physical education known derogatorily as the "Three Marías." Most students saw no intellectual or personal value in these subjects and sought ways to avoid them as best as they could without damaging their GPA. In addition, these are the years that followed the big university crisis of 1956 leading to a timid democratization and loss of control on the part of the Falangist university student union, SEU. The University Regulatory Law of 1943 had established the absolute control of Falange over the university. Every student had to join the student union when they paid their tuition. But Falange lost its effective power in the academic establishment in favor of Opus Dei that took the lead in the Francoist apparatus after the mid 1950s. Consequently, it is not surprising that the students displayed a lack of interest and almost a mockery of the Falangist hierarchical structure. The truth is that women's sports and physical education had been always designed to foster the biological destiny of the female population: motherhood. A Women's Section official report remarked that the "importance of healthy mothers for the racial hygiene of the nation is more than evident."[74] Physical education had to start when they were little girls and, far from imitating male physical education, it was supposed to emphasize "femininity" and "the primordial biological function of women: motherhood."[75]

A timorous approach guided the Women's Section physical education curriculum. Certain exercises such as the somersault were considered particularly "dangerous" for young women. This concern led Ana Dangual, Granada's provincial secretary, to report a complaint to the national head of Physical Education Concepción Sierra y Gil de la Cuesta. In her letter, Dangual explained Dr. Juan Roldán's objections to the exercises taught by the Women's Section instructors in the Social Service that were extremely dangerous for young women. Of particular concern for Dr. Roldán, colonel and director of the army hospital in Granada, was the practice of the somersault. This exercise, he believed, could lead to serious "cervical dislocation."[76]

As a result of the promulgation of the Organic Law of the Movement there was a revision of the objectives and purpose of the Women's Section Secretariat of Physical Education. In the Twenty-Fifth National Congress celebrated in San Sebastian, Concepción Sierra y Gil de la Cuesta, national secretary of physical education pointed out the responsibilities of her office:

a) Coordinate the activities of the Women's Section with the National Delegation of Physical Education as well as with other sport agencies.
b) Prepare and train Physical Education female instructors.
c) Ensure the highest technical quality in the schools of physical education.
d) Prepare the questionnaires, pedagogical norms and curriculum for physical education.
e) Plan and carry out the task assigned to the Women's Section in this area.
f) Serve as a consultant to different institutions with regard to women's physical education.
g) Inspect the implementation of the physical education planning.
h) Organize competitions and other activities.

The crisis of interest led the Women's Section to seek an increase in the number of instructors to facilitate the preparation and organization of more competitions. All women between seventeen and thirty-five years of age were obliged to join the Social Service for a given period of six months. Exempted from this obligation were elder daughters of widowed parents, elder daughters of parents of more than eight siblings, nuns, married women, widows with children, women with physical handicaps or illnesses, and domestic servants.[77]

The Spanish Social Service, created by decree on October 7, 1937, promoted the participation of Spanish women in the community's social tasks. This service mirrored the military service for Spanish men. Both were mandatory. Women needed to fulfill the Social Service in order to get a school diploma, a driver's license, or a passport. The areas of instruction covered included health in the rural and urban environments, children's and mothers' health, feeding habits, sports, home and domestic tasks, social work, and social welfare. The objective was to educate women on various levels: community, family, home, school, university, workplace, and emigration situations.[78]

The six months of service were divided into two periods. The training period of three months was accomplished at the 605 training schools established by the Women's Section across the country. The organization reported an average of seventy-thousand women per year trained in these centers.[79] During these three months, the participating pupils received the following instruction: home economics, nutritional education, health and sanitary education, infant care, first aid, maritime and mountain-rescue techniques, physical education, family and social training, religion, history, handiwork, dressmaking and sewing, laundry and ironing, cooking, knitting, embroidery.[80]

The second period of three months consisted of a practicum of personal assistance work, providing for the carrying out of tasks or functions of interest to the community, performed at institutions and establishments devoted to social assistance work, of governmental, semi-governmental, or private nature. Among these institutions were: homes, children's dining halls, clinics and hospitals, maternity and children's centers, social assistance services, nurseries and orphanages, cancer prevention clinics, rehabilitation facilities for the handicapped, housing centers, campaigns against illiteracy, slums and "twilight areas," workshops and offices, and science laboratories for university students.[81] According to the Women's Section, the objectives and results of the Social Service fulfilled a double function. First of all, it provided an increased awareness among the Spanish population of their responsibility to the community; and second, it made those women involved in the service come in contact with many sanitary and social problems of the lower classes. The effectiveness of the Service is still unclear because the statistical figures are the ones provided by the organization itself.

A Women's Section Commission established in 1968 after the Twenty-Foruth Congress determined the urgent need to reform the Social Service. The commission established five points to undertake in the reform:

1. The performance of the Social Service was inseparable from theoretical and practical training.
2. The performance must be qualitative, taking into account the condition of the women serving.
3. The instruction must be oriented to domestic, family, professional and social-political training.
4. Participation in a task for the common good is a right and a benefit no woman should be excluded from; therefore the criteria for exemption must be revised.
5. Subsudies are not justified at all.[82]

The Social Service was one of the first tasks of Falange the regime did away with. In vain, the Women's Section tried to maintain and justify the maintenance of the Social Service. In 1968 the organization conducted a survey to determine the most urgent areas of intervention and immediate reform. In the 1970 Congress in San Sebastian the delegates agreed to establish a Social Service Department and the Women's Section Governing Board drafted nine points to guide a governmental order or decree that would carry out the reform they envisioned. The nine points were:

1. The Social Service is a right of the Spanish woman as active member of society and also her duty since she must serve the society in which she lives.
2. Such contribution is, to be exact, a total preparation of women for their incorporation into society.
3. The Social Service is geared toward women's preparation for their family, socio-political and professional responsibilities.
4. We understand as proviso the generous and free contribution of women to the social activities of national interest
5. Therefore, the providers of services must be highly qualified
6. The fulfillment of their provision of services will be supervised and guided by the appropriate personnel.
7. Due to the early incorporation of women in public life as a result of the new educational reform it is advisable to modify the age of service providers to a range of between 17 and 30 years of age, and even a few might be able to fulfill the service when they are as young as 15 years old.
8. On the other hand, the evolution of social instruction allows for a reduction of the Social Service to three months with a concurrent theoretical and practical training.
9. Society and the state share the responsibility to carry out this task.[83]

On December 15, 1969, José Antonio Samaranch, national delegate of physical education and sports presented to the National Council of the Movement a report on the current status of physical education and sports in Spain.[84] Samaranch took office in January 1967 after the administration of José Antonio Elola, who had followed after General Moscardó, first head of the department. Under Elola the government issued the law of physical education of December 23, 1961.

Samaranch's report summarizes the reforms introduced within the legal framework of the 1961 bill. During his two-year tenure, the National Council conducted an inspection of every province to assess the needs and design the necessary course of action. The conclusions according to Samaranch highlighted a "great awakening" about sports among young people and demonstrated how sport activities had slowly become part of the "free time" occupation for most Spaniards "thanks to the rise in the standard of living."[85] On the other hand the sport infrastructure was still very deficient, especially the lack of appropriate facilities, technical personnel, and sport associations.

In order to foster an interest in physical education and sports among Spanish people Samaranch instigated two mechanisms: first, to launch a publicity campaign with the slogan "we are counting on you" (*Contamos contigo*) and the publication beginning in February 1968 of a sports magazine called *Deporte 2000* to educate readers on the different sports and the benefits of physical exercise. Second, the state had to invest considerable economic resources to accomplish the extension of physical education and sports culture. Some of the actions taken by Samaranch's agency included: biennial arts and sports fairs; a public competition on sport architecture, an international seminar on sports facilities that gathered architects, academics, and sports officials from several European countries; telephone service for sport information that has proven valuable in serving the customer who wants to know the sport news immediately; sports cinema, particularly NO-DO's "Sports Images," a newsreel that received the first prize in the Newsreel World Contest celebrated in London.

All these actions were the result of careful planning orchestrated under the General Plan for Physical Education and Sport. The four-year plan (1969–72) covered three areas of intervention: organization, activities, and facilities.

BUDGET EVOLUTION 1967–1969[86]

Years	**Expense in millions of pesetas**	**Organization %**	**Activities %**	**Facilities %**
1967	1.043.621.259,74	3.40	58.84	37.74
1968	1.324.778.619,92	3.51	54.87	41.60
1969	1.795.708.317,00	3.06	52.68	44.25

It was in the organization sector where the investment decreased from 3.40 percent to 3.06. According to Samaranch, personnel did not receive any salary raises due to the "devotion and commitment of those who made the rank and file."[87] This might explain the salary crisis and complaints the Women's Section instructors mentioned above. The National Delegation of Physical Education and Sports was charged with the coordination of the plan utilizing several organizations and state agencies to better implement it. To provide sport facilities and material to the public elementary, middle, secondary, and professional schools the delegation counted on the assistance of the Ministry of Education. Private schools received from the National Junta of Physical Education forty-three million pesetas, 20 percent of the total economic state national investment for sports facilities. Most of these private schools were run by Catholic orders. The Ministry of Information and Tourism, through the General Board of Radio and Television, programmed sports shows and games to inform the incipient television audience. Sports were also a means to attract a different kind of tourist that would boost the Spanish economy. Samaranch's delegation also enlisted the assistance of the National Service of Land and Rural regulation to create local sport organizations. The National Statistics Institute played an important role as well in the process to turn the average Spanish citizen into a modern sport aficionado. This task was to be accomplished through a national sport interest survey and the design of a guide of sport facilities across the country. Finally, the delegation joined forces with the army with the establishment of a Coordinating Committee High General Staff.[88]

The state budgeted one billion pesetas to fund the four-year General Plan of Physical Education assigned within the Second Social and Economic Development Plan. The delegation counted the funds from the sport pools, which represented 22 percent of its gross income.[89] The law passing the Second Social and Economic Development Plan in 1969 made an explicit reference to the importance of sports and physical education as an economic priority in the modernization of the country.

The role of the press is extraordinary in the late Francoism although the circulation of daily, weekly, and monthly publications was still far behind other European countries.[90] In 1971–72 only six magazines published over 200,000 issues.[91] Of those six, only four were weekly: *Hola* (456,041 issues per week), *Semana* (310,136 issues per week), and *Lecturas* (293,097 issues per week) all targeted women and were what was known as "prensa del corazón," what nowadays are the tabloids. The forth weekly was *Teleprograma,* a television guide with a circulation of 600,836. The book catalogue *Circulo de lectores* published 1,000,000 issues every three months. These figures show the high distribution of women's and sports magazines that consumerism wrought in the 1960s. Those other weekly publications of general or political information had a much smaller circulation: *Destino* (41,980 per week), *Triunfo* (45,934 per week), and *Cuadernos para el diálogo* (33,675 per week).[92]

Women's magazines grew extraordinarily in 1971–72 over the other types of publications: *Hola, Lecturas, Semana, Garbo, Ama, Telva,* and *Miss* published more than 2,000,000 issues. Important to highlight is the significance of religious periodicals such as *La familia Cristiana* with a circulation of 127,832, or *Mundo Cristiano* with 116,250.[93] The sports weekly *AS Color* had a circulation of 133, 717 and the accident and crime report weekly *El caso* published 166,220.[94]

The 1950s and 1960s brought fundamental changes to gender relations under Francoism. Physical education turned into the means of the regime to maintain domesticity among Spanish women. National Catholicism informed the text of the 1961 law of physical education. This law revitalized the Vatican dictum of the disciplined body as conduit to the soul's salvation. The Women's Section of Falange continued to carry out the task of indoctrinating women for the glory of the fatherland. They were charged with the responsibility of imparting physical education among women in three contexts: the school system, the Social Service, and the organization Coros y Danzas. The latter was the star of the regime. The young women who participated traveled abroad as goodwill ambassadors and incarnations of the motherland.

Physical education became the means of disciplining and controlling bodies and souls in the transition to consumerism and modernization. Physical education under the control of the Women's Section showed a strong case of women's complicity with the system, while it also provided visibility and public participation to women, who were otherwise relegated to the domestic realm. This contradiction was also prevalent in other media such as cinema and advertising and inherent to female allegorizations of the body politic.

Women's Section Physical Education National Courses

Place	Year	Length
Santander	March 1939	3 months
Ciudad Lineal (Madrid)	July 1941	3 months
Ciudad Lineal (Madrid)	May 1942	3 months
Ciudad Lineal (Madrid)	December 1942	1 months
Ciudad Lineal (Madrid)	October 1943	3 months
Ciudad Lineal (Madrid)	January 1944	3 months
Deva (Guipuzcoa)	July 1944	3 months
Santander	July 1945	3 months
Ciudad Lineal (Madrid)	March 1949	4 months
El Pardo (Madrid)	January 1952–53	9 months
El Pardo (Madrid)	1954	Closed for Remodeling
El Pardo (Madrid)	October 1954–55	2 years
Escuela Julio Ruiz de Alda (Madrid)	October 1956	2 years
Escuela Julio Ruiz de Alda (Madrid)	October 1957–66	3 years

Source: Sección Cultura Women's Section Papers AGA.

Women's Section Competitions Growth

Gymnastics		
I Championship 1939	47 teams	664 participants
Year 1959	113 teams	1,923 participants
Last Championship 1961–62	2,235 teams	22,442 participants
Volleyball		
I Championship 1949	59 teams	472 participants
Year 1959	336 teams	2,688 participants
Last Championship 1962	996 teams	8,226 participants
Handball		
I Championship 1952	210 teams	1,917 participants
Year 1959	219 teams	1,782 participants
Last Championship 1962	588 teams	7,061 participants
Basketball		
I Championship 1939	18 teams	144 participants
Year 1959	40 teams	360 participants
Last Championship 1962	1,526 teams	18,312 participants

Source: My own elaboration based on Women's Section Papers AGA.

6
Strangers in the Dark

Ramiro pushes himself against her. He kisses her in her mouth. Ramiro's knee feels like a wedge. Tula sunk her chin into her chest. And when Ramiro, with both hands, pulls her head, Tula pushes him and runs away.

She goes into the bathroom and locks the door. She stumbles with the sink. Ramiro bangs the door:

Tula closes the window. Then she falls on her knees on the floor. And she starts sobbing.

—*La Tía Tula (1964)* film by Miguel Picazo[1]

YOUNG COUPLES LEARNED ABOUT LOVEMAKING AT THE MOVIES, IN the dark. Sexual fantasizing and clumsy petting was an evasion from reality that the authorities penalized. The National Catholic agenda shaped both religious and political consciousness and fused moral and political misconduct in a draconian censorship system.

This chapter focuses on the Spanish film industry in the 1950s and 1960s. The Cold War rapprochement to the United States with the Pact of Madrid in 1953 eased consumerism in the 1960s while international anti-Communist politics led to a timid cultural aperturismo (opening) in Spain. In turn, these processes led to a redefinition of the regime's rationale geared to safeguard its foundations. Cinema represented the best medium to reach international approval.

Particularly important was the so-called *New Spanish Cinema* launched by José María García Escudero, General Director of Cinematography within the Ministry of Information and Tourism in 1951–52 and again in the early 1960s. Although *New Spanish Cinema* codified precise censorship regulations, it may also be considered the cultural prelude to post-Franco transition to democracy.

Figure 18. Movie still from *La Tía Tula* (1964) film by Miguel Picazo. Courtesy Filmoteca Nacional Madrid, Spain.

Censorship became the regime's crusade in peacetime and women's bodies its conduit. Women's cinematic bodies turned into symbols of political contention. Official censorship portioned and labeled women's cinematic (and real) bodies in sinful or virtuous parts, dissected to preserve Christian order and political immovability. The transition from autarky to consumerism facilitated a shift in film production and spectatorship. In post-Civil War Spain, moviegoing functioned as an escapist experience in which viewers had an opportunity to forget their daily misery. In the winter, movie theaters were improvised in rural areas in churches or warehouses where the crowd would sit eating roasted chestnuts to escape the rigor of the weather. And during the torrid summer nights in southern Spain, open-air cinemas became one of the scarce outlets for forgetting. In the dark, under Andalusia's stars, audiences experienced in their own flesh the dreamlike life of another constellation of stars, those created in Hollywood. Moviegoers felt a sharp contrast between their reality and the lavish excesses on the screen. Foreign and domestic celebrities like Sophia Loren, Elizabeth Taylor, Sara Montiel, and Aurora Bautista were a few of those stars that Spanish men fantasized about and women admired.

Francoist cinema cultivated a misogynist otherness. The 1940s cinematography represents deeply polarized and one-dimensional gender roles that enshrined the inquisitorial Puritanism of "true Catholic womanhood."[2] The virgin and mother duality was played against that of the fallen and sick woman. To illustrate this tension, I examine the cinematic personae of two Spanish actresses: Sara Montiel and Aurora Bautista. Both of them started their careers in the 1940s and became stars in the next two decades.

Cuts Both Ways: Censorship Reinvented

The 1940s meant a strong Nazi presence in the Spanish cultural industry. German interests were in control of commercial societies (Hisma, Sofindus), newspapers (*Informaciones* in Madrid), radio stations (Valladolid Radio), film distributors (Alianza Cinematografía Española), and exhibition theaters (the Muñoz Seca Cinema in Madrid).[3] *Primer Plano,* a Falangist cinema journal, published at the time some columns praising Nazi and Fascist cinema industries and their censorship apparatuses, while American cinema was presented as decadent.[4] Pro-Nazi Ramón Serrano Suñer, brother-in-law of the caudillo, had sponsored in 1938 as Minister of Interior the Press Law of April 22 and the order of November 2, concerning cinematography. The preamble of the order reads: "Being unquestionable the great influence that cinematography has in the dissemination of thought and in the education of the masses it is a must that the state exercises surveillance in every realm to avoid the risk of deviance from its mission."[5]

The order created two entities under the Ministry of Interior's control: The Committee for Cinematographic Censorship, responsible for reviewing private productions, and the High Junta for Cinematographic Censorship, to examine newsreels and documentaries as well as the appeals against the committee's decisions. These two offices were staffed with representatives of the Secretariats of National Defense, National Propaganda and Education, and members of the Catholic Church hierarchy, the latter being the majority in both units. To fulfill the indoctrination of the masses, the Francoist regime created NODO (Noticiarios y Documentales Cinematográficos) on November 17, 1942, by a legal disposition issued by the Vice Secretary of Popular Education.[6] NODO was a government newsreel that theaters were obliged to show preceding every feature film.[7]

Franco was so fascinated with cinema and its power over the masses that he ventured, under the pen name Jaime de Andrade, a script for a semiautobiographical film: *Raza* (1941).[8] The film is a one-dimensional rendition of "cainismo": two brothers confront each other in the battlefront, one an army officer, the other a republican MP. The mother's character (embodiment of the motherland) is pained by her sons' hatred for each other. The army officer played by handsome Alfredo Mayo, Franco's screen alter ego, embodied the Christian soldier savior of the nation.

Hypernationalism and ultra-Catholicism guided the Francoist crusade against the moral depravation opened by the lay governments of the Second Republic. Catholic morality helped the regime in restoring order in the immediate postwar period. The Francoist state articulated its censorship philosophy five months into the Civil War by order of December 23, 1936. "It is declared illegal," Article 1 read, "the production, marketing, and distribution of all kinds of pornographic pamphlets, prints and engravings, or any kind of socialist, communist, libertarian and in general unsettling literature."[9] Sexual transgressions were in this way persecuted under National Catholicism as severely as political misconduct.[10] The censor's scissors cut all the kisses as well as different women's body parts—legs especially. In an *expediente* from the National Commission for the Cinematographic Censorship of Falange, the list of cuts for *Moon over Burma* (1940) starring glamorous American actress Dorothy Lamour included the following:

Roll 1. Kiss
Roll 2. Shot of legs in the dance hall, before the close-up of the customers sitting at a table.
Roll 4. End of the scene of the bathroom from the first shot.
Roll 7. Kiss[11]

Kissing was the prelude to lust. But not just any kiss. A popular song would explain how special a kiss in the mouth was to assure eternal love.

The Spanish woman,
When she kisses,
She kisses truthfully
Because none of them is interested
In kissing just for fun.
You may kiss my hand,
You may give me a brotherly kiss
That way you may kiss me as much as you want
But a kiss of love
I don't give it just to anyone[12]

A man and woman's lip contact sealed their carnal closeness and moved their relationship to a more intimate level. In foreign dubbed films kissing made the relationship closer, moving from the formal "usted" treatment to the more intimate "tú."[13]

Even when films had the official stamp of approval, there were occasional complaints from local authorities in the provinces. This was the case of the film *Blood and Sand* (1941) starring Tyrone Power and Rita Hayworth.[14] Based on the novel of the same title by Vicente Blasco Ibáñez, the plot had all the elements that Francoist establishment in the 1940s exploited. It tells the story of Juan Gallardo, a village boy born into poverty who grows up to become a great bullfighter. Juan is married to beautiful and virtuous Carmen, but after he achieves fame and fortune, he falls in love with Doña Sol, a wealthy, seductive widow. They embark on a torrid affair that ends when he dies on the arena while fighting in the bullring. The provincial delegate of the Ministry of National Education in the northern city of Lugo did not like the version of the film he saw at the theater on December 20, 1949, and hurried to make a long-distance phone call to the general director of Cinematography and Theater in Madrid. The call was followed with a letter of December 21, 1949, explaining the "multiple anomalies" and discrepancies between the film and the list of scenes that should have been censored as noted on the back of the rolls. The cuts had not been made. "In roll 8, the exhibition of the matador's nudity until he starts reading the letter was not cut out" and "in roll 10, the short shots of Doña Sol, in which her breast show through her blouse, were not cut" either.[15]

Not only did the cuts affect the images but also the dialogues, which were modified in the dubbing process. Jean Cocteau's *Beauty and the Beast* (1946) was classified as tolerated for viewers under sixteen years old. The general director of Cinematography and Theater in an official telegram directed his homonymous delegate in Sevilla to "modify the sentence 'hairy husbands with horns.'"[16] Cultural ultranationalism led to the enactment of two ministerial orders in 1938 and 1941 banning any civil registration of foreign names for any purpose, private or public. In this context film dubbing became mandatory in Spain and was always done by Spanish actors. This measure led to the artistic damage to the foreign films since censorship reached the texts themselves, rewriting lines to better fit the ideological Francoist agenda; ultimately, Spanish cinematographic industry was severely harmed by Hollywood productions. Well known is the case of the dubbing of *Mogambo* (1955). The Spanish censorship establishment changed the story to avoid the sin of adultery. Set in Africa, this John Ford movie tells the story of a married couple (Grace Kelly and Donald Sinden) who follow a professional safari guide (Clark Gable) in a research expedition. The plot also includes a music hall beauty (Ava Gardner) who is in love with Gable. However, Grace Kelly's and Clark Gable's characters have an affair that never is serious enough to break her marriage. Spanish censors changed the relationship of Grace Kelly and Sinden to be brother and sister. In this way those scenes where the characters shared their conjugal tent seemed ambiguously incestuous, something the Spanish establishment let go to avoid the sin of adultery.[17]

Franco strengthened the domestic mechanisms of social control with particular emphasis on cinematographic censorship after WWII. The Ministry of National Education established the Junta Superior de Cinematografía (Cinematography Secretariat) by order of June 28, 1946, to classify cinematographic material with a protectionist economic criterion.

The Vice Secretariat of Popular Education of FET y de las JONS dictated the regulations to protect Spanish films on June 15, 1944. The main goal was to elevate the national industry to "promote Spanish culture and disseminate *our racial truths* [*sic*]"[18] The document acknowledged the existence of some foreign films that without any Spanish intervention reflected the moral, social, and political values of the New State.[19] Those films classified by the National Delegation of Propaganda as of "national interest" would enjoy preferential treatment in all respects, including contracts with movie theaters within the country. Only Spanish movies produced in Spain could opt for the category of "national interest" and in very rare occasions, foreign productions that contained explicit praise of Spanish National Catholic values. Films of national interest content had to "explicitly sing the praises of racial values or teachings of our moral and political principles."[20] Their accreditation as such issued from the vice secretary of Popular Education with the advice of the National Delegation of Propaganda and prior approval from the Section of Cinematography and Theater and the National Committee of Cinematographic Propaganda. Accreditations could not be appealed. Economic pressures were the best censor. Spanish films could hardly compete with foreign productions. In order to get official funding the Spanish film industry exploited an already flourishing genre of national historical melodramas. The industry's protectionist policy under this rule fueled a black market to get licensed and to sell the films. By 1949 the Secretariat of Cinematography and Theater was under the Ministry of National Education. An order of October 29, 1949, issued under José Ibañez Martín, General Director of Cinematography and Theater, sent a circular letter to the Chief Commissary of Entertainment Brigade in Madrid clarifying the government ruling on the classification of movies for minors:

> This Ministry orders the following:
> 1- Those movies already reviewed and cleared in the future by the Junta Superior de Orientación Cinematográfica as "tolerated" will be so for those individuals under fourteen years old.
> 2- From now on, it is rigorously mandatory that all cinemas make explicit in their publicity, posters, boards, programs and in all sorts of propaganda the relevant classification assigned by the Junta Superior de Orientación Cinematográfica whether being "tolerated" or "authorized"[21]

Ibañez Martín's wrote this detailed letter in response to a memorandum from the Junta Superior de Orientación Cinematográfica of January 7, 1949, that highlighted how Madrid newspapers did not specify clearly whether the films advertised were "tolerated for minors" or "authorized for adults."[22] According to the accounting records for the year 1949, the Ministry of National Education spent 24,063 pesetas as payment to the fourteen members of Junta Superior de Orientación Cinematográfica. Each received 100 pesetas per film for services rendered from January 1 to 20, 1949.[23] The extra income these men received for twenty days of service was considerable for the 1940s, a period known as the hunger years.

By order of March 8, 1950, the regime established the National Classifying Entertainment Office under the leadership of the Catholic Church.[24] By July 1952 a joint order from the Ministries of Commerce and Information and Tourism established a new directive for the next ten years. The order of July 16, 1952, instituted a gradation for those films already declared of "national interest" as: 1st A; 1st B; 2nd A; 2nd B; and 3rd. According to these categories producers eligible for financial support received funding according to a pre-established categorization. Those films classified under the rubric of "national interest" received fifty percent subsidy; forty percent of the total cost for those of 1st A classification; 35 percent for 1st B; 30 percent for 2nd A; and 25 percent for 2nd B. Those films classified as 3rd category did not received any funds at all.[25] These directives followed the Catholic Church dictum. Sexual license was not to be tolerated any longer, and relations between the sexes had to remain confined to marriage and procreation for the good of the fatherland and in accordance to Catholic Church dictum in encyclicals such as: *Vigilanti Cura,* June 29, 1936, by Pius XI, echoed in *Miranda Prorsus* on the Communications Field: Motion Pictures, Radio, Television, promulgated on September 8, 1957, by Pius XII. "Public authorities are bound, beyond all doubt, to observe carefully these new means of communication. They should look on this matter not from a political point of view alone, but from that of public morals, whose sure foundation rests in the natural law."[26] Pius XII, in 1957 quoted Pius XI's words twenty years earlier in *Vigilanti Cura* "[T]ables or lists should be compiled and published in a definitive arrangement, in which films distributed will be listed, as frequently as possible, so as to come to the attention of all."[27]

The regulations established by the Francoist regime followed the Catholic Church directives. Enrique Songel Mullor who represented the Valencia studio CIFESA (Compañía Industrial Film Español SA) in Madrid sought the official approval to show three religious films during Holy Week. The films had been cleared by the censorship authorities but Songel explained: "There are serious difficulties to exhibit these films in commercial venues, since theater owners push them out of the schedule in favor of more recent arrivals." The only solution Songel Mullor foresaw was to get an official order from the authorities to force theater owners to show them during Holy Week. Two days later he received the general director of the Junta Superior de Orientación Cinematográfica's answer: "With regard to your petition of 2 March seeking authorization to exhibit in Holy Week a few religious films distributed by your studio: I inform you that hitherto the superior order on the matter continue to be the same ruling for the last few years and consequently, during Holy Thursday and Friday it is not allowed the exhibition of any other films but those that depicted the Passion and Death of Jesús."[28] Religion remained at the center of social life in the 1950s. The regime's religious foundations had to accommodate the new economic demands from the film industry. Consumerism and the spread of leisure activities posed some problems in a market economy and the formula was to maintain the movie theaters open but allow only religious films to be exhibited.

The 1960s economic takeoff, however, signaled the beginning of the regime's cultural aperturismo (opening) to the international community, a community that was not exclusively Catholic. To present a most modern image of Francoist Spain, cinematographic censors utilized women's cinematic bodies as the token in the new economy of desire inaugurated with American dollars. Far from doing away with censorship, the regime issued more precise regulations in 1963 ending the existing random policy. The new regulations provided room for the production of two versions of every film made in Spain: one censored for national consumption, the other uncut for international markets. It was through censors' mutilation of women's cinematic bodies that the regime made the distinction between those two versions of every film. Censors' cuts responded not only to their mandate to preserve Spanish women's virginal innocence but also to protect the National Catholic integrity of the nation's body.

The New Spanish Cinema

In 1955 the film industry addressed the regime's intolerance head-on during the "Salamanca Conversations." The most important new directors of the Spanish cinema like Juan Antonio Bardem, Luis García Berlanga, Basilio Martín Patino, and Ricardo Muñoz Suay gathered to discuss the future of Spanish film. Juan Antonio Bardem presented the meeting conclusions with the following statement.

Spanish cinema is:
1. Politically futile
2. Socially false
3. Intellectually worthless
4. Aesthetically valueless
5. Industrially paralytic[29]

The *New Spanish Cinema* formula was the official response to the sentiment of the First National Film Congress held in Salamanca in 1955. A Catholic faction participated in the congress, in which the central figure was García Escudero who belonged to the reformist elements within the regime. Arias Salgado, minister of Information and Tourism had appointed Escudero undersecretary of Cinema in 1951. García Escudero, a Catholic with a "modern" approach to censorship declared: "I have written about the danger of confusing Catholic censorship with bourgeois censorship. In other words, confusing Catholic censorship with a censorship concerned exclusively with a censorship of naked legs."[30] Escudero was not only concerned with the visible but also with the invisible seductive power of cinematography. He proposed a more "intelligent" way of going about Christian preservation; he proposed "forbidding" as a more viable censorship rather than "mutilating" celluloid bodies. "Because if we are not precise on this matter," Escudero added, "it might happen that just because there are no legs in sight," the censor might neglect a close scrutiny of the plot and hence condone other moral problems such as adultery "and this, in the long run, will do more damage than a dozen naked calves" he concluded.[31] During his time in office García Escudero publicly defended the film *Surcos* that caused serious discontent among the more authoritarian elements of the regime because of the criticism of class divisions. *Surcos,* a film of Falangist director José Antonio Nieves Conde, told the drama of a rural family of immigrants to Madrid. The rural exodus to industrial cities had caused serious class conflict. The Church hierarchy declared this film to be "extremely dangerous." There were scenes from the slums where prostitutes and delinquent characters scandalized censors, especially some bed scenes and the last frame in which the oldest daughter jumps off the train to return to Madrid. The regime, however, was not ready for this kind of "aperturismo" and Escudero was sacked only six months later and replaced in February 1952 by Joaquín Argamasilla de la Cerda y Elio.

Since the Pact of Madrid (1953) between the Francoist regime and the United States opened Spain to Hollywood, American studios saw Spain as a cheap location in Europe for its super productions. Numerous North American films were produced under the pretense of coproduction between the two countries. Spain contributed to these coproductions its sun and cheap labor. The first super production filmed in Spain was *Alexander the Great* (1955). The deal was so good that Samuel Bronston negotiated several films in Hollywood and ended in 1959 establishing Samuel Bronston Productions Inc. This was a company operating in Spain exclusively with North American capital and personnel. Several blockbusters resulted from this arrangement such as Nicholas Ray's *King of Kings* (1961) and Anthony Mann's *El Cid* (1961). Bronston in turn produced Francoist propaganda documentaries, most notoriously Andrew Marton's *El valle de la paz* featuring the monument of the Valley of the Fallen where Franco would be buried in 1975.[32]

The appointment of Manuel Fraga Iribarne as head of the newly established Ministry of Information and Tourism (1962–69) inaugurated a period cultural "aperturismo." He replaced ultraconservative Rafael Arias Salgado in this office. Fraga was an intransigent authoritarian professor of political science at the Universidad Complutense de Madrid. As part of a cabinet dominated by army and Opus Dei members, his professorial conservatism made Fraga the liberalizing element in charge of offering a freer image of Spain. No doubt, the Ministry of Information and Tourism responded to the regime's need to display a more democratic image to the world. Censorship, however, far from being removed, had to be reinvented with the arrival of tourism and the regime's international rehabilitation as a member of the UN and UNESCO in 1955. Fraga chose José María García Escudero as general director of Cinema. García Escudero made censorship directives more concrete in 1963. He also reorganized the Research Institute of Cinematographic Experiences (Instituto de Investigaciones y Experiencias Cinematográficas), where a new generation of progressive filmmakers like José Luis García Berlanga and Antonio Bardem had studied. Under Escudero the institute turned into the Official School of Cinematography (Escuela Oficial de Cinematografía). In order to internationalize the Spanish film industry, Escudero increased government funding and introduced changes on the official categorization of films. The 1940s category of "national interest" gave way to the government's sudden support of aesthetic concerns under the rubric of films of "special interest."[33] It was Escudero himself who coined the label *New Spanish Cinema.* The regime thought this "new way" of making films most effective to show a more "liberal" image abroad. Reinventing censorship proved no easy task. The Francoist censorship became even tighter. On February 16, 1963 the first Spanish Censorship Code regulating cinematography appeared.[34] Many of the films produced during this period applied innovative plots that combined Hollywood-like lavish material culture with sober Italian neorealist imagery.[35] The new code represented the end of the legal vacuum and to a certain extent responded to the demands voiced in the Congress of Salamanca. Regardless, the new code retained fundamental National Catholic principles and furthered the inequality between Spanish and foreign films. According to order of February 9, 1963, the Norms for Film Censorship forbade:

1. validation of suicide
2. validation of mercy killing
3. validation of revenge and dueling
4. validation of divorce as an institution, of adultery, of illicit sexual relations, of prostitution, and of anything harmful to the institution of matrimony or the family
5. validation of abortion and contraception.[36]

Particularly important in the text was the preservation of Catholic dogma and public morality. Therefore it forbade "the presentation of sexual perversion as central to the plot or even in a secondary story," unless there was a clear exemplary moral consequence derived from the plot. According to the Order, "the intimacy of conjugal love must be respected, and all offensive images and scenes" were prohibited.[37] Anything remotely contrary to the following was forbidden:

1. the Catholic Church, her dogma, morals and cult.
2. the fundamental principles of the state, national dignity and the internal and external security of the country.
3. the person of the Head of the State.[38]

The expansion of the *New Spanish Cinema* was furthered with the order of the Ministry of Tourism and Information "for the development of the cinema," a measure that fit within the framework of the 1964 *Plan for Economic Development.* The new legislation changed the status of official subsidies no longer granted by the Board of Classification but given automatically. Every Spanish film received 15 percent of the gross box office takings. The aim was to produce a self-sufficient cinema by way of a rigorous control of the box office earnings and passing on part of the earnings to the producer. The new category of "special interest" replaced and modernized that other of "national interest." Of "special interest" were those projects "which offer[ed] sufficient guarantees of quality, contain relevant moral social, educational or political values."[39] At the same time the order facilitated the incorporation of the graduates from the Official School of Cinematography into professional life. These movies received a subsidy of one million pesetas in advance.

By order of August 19, 1964, new regulations applied to the production film companies, which were intended to protect the Spanish industry. The regulations intended also to rationalize the films' commercialization by adjusting the Spanish system to international markets. However, the industry mechanism did not change significantly. The state continued to protect a nationalist cinema based on the autarky's principles and which was barely competitive.[40]

Spanish films were financed in different ways: by professional contributions provided by the production companies (studios, laboratories, and skilled personnel) who were paid once the film was finished; by state advance payment for distribution; by bank loans from the National Entertainment Syndicate or the Bank for Industrial Credit; and finally by selling the film in the international markets. Most of the films were the result of the hard work of skill professionals who agreed to be paid after the film was done. The state continued a protectionist policy on the cinema industry. According to the Ministry of Information and Tourism there were 118 production companies between 1952 and 1972. Most of the coproductions were between Italy and Spain.

The cinema industry was very important in the national economy since it represented 53.6 percent of the total value for the entertainment services including radio and television.[41] In the five-year period 1965–69 television viewing showed a slight increase over movie going; however, in the 1960s cinema remained a mass leisure activity in Spain.

This period of timid liberalization faced a serious crisis in 1969 with the financial scandal of MATESA textile industry. On August 10, 1969, the government admitted that credits in the millions granted to the textile firm for the export of machinery had in fact been used for private investment abroad. The scandal intensified Spain's economic crisis on the eve of the international oil crisis of the 1970s and cost Fraga his post as minister. Fraga had shown some leaning toward making public the involvement

Value (In Millions of Pesetas) of Entertainment Services 1965–1969

		Cinematography		
Years	**Total**	**Production**	**Distribution and exhibition**	**Other including radio and TV**
1965	17,511,2	1,074,5	9,441,2	6,995,5
1966	20,333,2	1,268,6	10,970,3	8,094,3
1967	22,416,9	1,213,2	11,720,7	9,483,0
1968	23,390,6	1,054,8	11,904,5	10,431,3
1969	25,030,4	1,185,0	12,226,5	11,618,9

Source: Fundación FOESSA, *Estudios Sociológicos sobre la situación social de España 1975* (Madrid: Editorial de Euroamérica, 1976), 1064.

of three Opus Dei cabinet members in the business. Franco replaced Fraga with the ultraconservative Alfredo Sánchez Bella who held the ministry from 1969 to 1973. Sánchez Bella restored strict censorship, and government subventions to filmmakers were severely cut.

The Ministry of Information and Tourism implemented in 1964 the control of the box office. This data allow us to appreci-

National Cinema Industry Between 1966–1971

Conceptualization	1966	1967	1968	1969	1970	1971
Feature films premier in Madrid (Total)	321	327	396	402	396	365
German	5	7	10	6	5	2
Spanish	49	51	48	67	49	40
USA	95	98	97	91	90	82
UK	34	38	34	40	39	37
French	13	12	19	27	34	26
Italian	11	8	31	28	28	40
Mexican	8	6	6	9	11	5
From other countries	10	15	28	21	23	22
Spanish coproductions	52	51	67	61	66	60
Foreign coproductions	44	51	56	55	51	51

Box Office 1966–1971

Conceptualization	1966	1967	1968	1969	1970	1971
Registered theaters	9,523	9466	8,689	8,324	8,363	8,282
Functioning theaters	8,193	8,059	7,761	7,234	6,911	5,939
Films exhited	5,309	3,663	3,755	3,930	4,007	3,581
Spanish	1,303	1,345	1,405	1,501	1,519	1,383
Foreign	2,206	2,318	2,350	2,429	2,488	2,198
Viewers (millions)	403	393	377	365	331	146
Of Spanish films	101	119	123	118	110	47
Of Foreign films	302	274	254	247	221	99
Box Office in milllions	5,753	6,147	6,239	6,410	6,590	3,673
Spanish films	1,290	1,668	1,849	1,795	1,960	1,066
Foreign films	4,463	4,479	4,390	4,615	4,630	2,607

Source: Both tables Fundación FOESSA, *Estudios Sociológicos sobre la situación social de España 1975* (Madrid: Editorial de Euroamérica, 1976), 1075 [my own elaboration].

ate the audience size only for the 1960s on, since there was not such information recorded previously.

Some of the most important Spanish female filmmakers and actresses became directors within the *New Spanish Cinema* period.[42] These women followed in the footsteps of Rosario Pi, the first Spanish woman film director in the 1930s. Ana Mariscal (1923–95) actress,[43] director, and scriptwriter, founded a production company with her husband in the 1950s called Bosco Films and tried directing. Some of her films include *Segundo López* (1952), *La Quiniela* (1959), and *El paseillo* (1968). Josefina Molina was the first woman to earn a degree in directing from the National School of Cinema in 1969. Born in Cordova in 1936, her career developed in Spanish Television (TVE) in the next four decades. Molina specialized in the production of drama plays and television series. In 1982 she directed *Teresa de Jesús,* a miniseries that has turned into a classic. She also directed documentaries such as *Cárcel de mujeres* (1964). Her cinematographic directorial debut was *Vera, un cuento cruel* (1973). María Suárez Lafuente explores the way in which Molina examines the impact of traditional education on Spanish women in two films: *Evening Performance* (1981) and *Most Natural* (1990). These films show the difficult transition Spanish women had to undergo, going from a society dominated by National Catholic education to contemporary democratic Spain. Ultimately Josefina Molina is concerned with the process women underwent in the transition to democracy to view themselves as independent citizens.[44]

The best-known female film director of the period is Pilar Miró (1940–97). She studied law and journalism at the Universidad Complutense in Madrid. She graduated with a degree in scriptwriting and editing from the National School of Cinema where she was a faculty member as well. Like Josefina Molina, she started in TVE. In 1960 she was hired as assistant producer and in 1963 she produced a magazine show entitled *Revista de mujer.* Miró is considered one of the first self-proclaimed Spanish feminist filmmakers. Often her work is semiautobiographical, dealing with power relations and social injustice.[45] Her first film in the big screen was *La petición* (*The Engagement Party*) in 1976. This film was censored due to its violent sexual content. The film was originally banned because of the sexually activity of the female protagonist: a woman who seduces a man in order to help her dispose of her previous lover's corpse, and who then kills her new lover in order to marry a third man—this one from a better social class. *La petición*'s main character is Ana (played by actress Ana Belén), based on *Thérèse Raquín,* a novel by Emile Zola that scandalized the French audiences of his times. Pilar Miró's adaptation unleashed a scandal a century later. The film wandered around in the administration halls in search of final authorization for several months and only was released after considerable pressure from filmmakers in Spain and abroad.[46]

La petición was shown first at the Teheran Film Festival in November 1976 and a year later in Belgrade Film Festival where over two hundred-fifty thousand viewers attended screenings in multiple venues.[47] In an interview with *El País,* Pilar Miró explained:

> I tried to reflect about early education. As children, we have put up with that and suffered an extremely conventional upbringing. Paradoxically, everything we desired to do was forbidden. In other words, I have tried to analyze how it is so completely futile to pretend that an individual accepts an imposed morality that [he/she] does not assumes as real and rational.
>
> What made this idea so attractive to me was the opportunity to show a myriad of things which "ought not to be done"; that a young lady might be completely amoral. Furthermore, the fact that the protagonist is a woman, in a country as sexist as it is Spain, I think radicalizes even more the situation.[48]

In 1979 Pilar Miró wrote the script and directed her second film, *El crímen de Cuenca,* again facing censorship. This film, sequestered by military authorities for seventeen months, was released in 1981 for Spanish audiences with a tremendous success at the box office. After several years of suffering from a heart condition, Pilar Miró died of a heart attack on October 19, 1997.[49] She was fifty-seven years old, never married, and left a seventeen-year-old son. It was her son who encouraged author Diego Galán to write her biography, entitled *Pilar Miró: Nadie me enseñó a vivir* (2006).

Sara Montiel and Aurora Bautista's Cinematic Bodies

The advent of consumerism and the economic takeoff changed the cinematic experience as well, making it more than an emotional or psychological experience. The body, magnified on the big screen, plunged audiences into a sensual experience. According to literary critic Steven Shaviro, "Film theory should be less a theory of fantasy (psychoanalytic or otherwise) than a theory of the effects and transformations of bodies."[50] In the movie theater we physically experience whatever event is displayed before our eyes on the screen in what Shaviro calls "similarity disorder."

Given the mutual dependency of body and cinematography, Steven Shaviro's "similarity disorder" theory helps us rethink the cinematic experience of the *New Spanish Cinema* from a gender perspective.[51] "Libido is like money," he says, "and the laws of its transformation are of the utmost importance."[52] The gendered body in this context becomes the means of social, political, and economic transformation, through its (inward and outward) regulation and control. Cinema, like sex, is a kind of nonrepresentational contact, thrusting us into the mysterious life of the body, into the visualization of desire. In the dark movie theater we are confronted face to face with desire that we can neither incorporate nor expel. The cinematic apparatus and the body, far from being opposites, are actually inseparably linked by desire. We cry or laugh in communion with the images displayed.[53]

Furthermore, because the relationship between body and cinematographic practice is male centered, the female body is the conventional incarnation of desire, hence the predominant display of the female over the male body in film. This in turn leads censors to the more prevalent dissection and distortion of the cinematic female body. Therefore, censorship under Christian beliefs becomes so concerned with the cinematic experience and the mutilation of female bodies.

Francoist cinema's social and economic organization, its modes of production as well as its censorship, technology, and state-controlled propaganda, continued to work only in relation to the effect on audiences in the transition to consumerism.[54] The relationship between spectator and film is conceivable only on the basis of the regulation, manipulation, and exchange of desire in the Francoist transition from self-effacing autarky to exuberant consumerism.

Important questions pertaining to the economy of desire come to mind: How was the Francoist editing of female body parts lived by women in their real bodies? How did men relate to those female parts cut out of sight? Parts usually violently desired and appropriated against women's will. All these questions must always be confronted from a historical context since the cultural construction of bodies is historically determined.

As the transition to democracy followed Franco's death, the display of the naked female body overtook the screen in Spanish films. "Destape" meant female nudity on display and "destape" meant in political discourse "uncovering." Female nudity became the object of heated debate about political liberalization. The commodification of the female flesh became the sign by which to measure the degree of political freedom. In the process, the female body became associated with female identity—an object of exchange in political discourse. Women's political persona, their citizenship and partaking in the democratic process, was fashioned around the symbolic marking of their bodies. Although those women that chose to expose their bodies did exercise an act of defiance and sexual affirmation that broke with National Catholic puritan agenda, their representation was appropriated and subverted in a misogynist exchange of words that brought into sharp focus the sexism prevalent both in the Spanish left as much as in the right.

Director Juan de Orduña shaped Sara Montiel and Aurora Bautista's screen images in *Locura de Amor* (1948) where they play opposite roles. This CIFESA's production was translated into English as *The Mad Queen.* Sara Montiel and Aurora Bautista embody in the film the symbolic binary virgin/whore. Montiel played a Moorish princess in hiding who becomes the king's lover while Aurora Bautista stars as Queen Joan the Mad. Both actresses' careers took off after this film was released in Spain and internationally. Montiel became the sex symbol of Francoist Spain in the 1950s while Aurora Bautista moved on to become an extraordinary stage actress. Banking on her astonishing beauty Sara Montiel appeared in some Hollywood films. Her acting talent was not comparable to that of Aurora Bautista. When asked about her beauty Bautista expresses amusement and says, "My mother used to tell me 'child you have a rare beauty.'"[55]

> I had a little insecurity. I used to say "I'm not as beautiful as . . ." because really, Sara was so beautiful when she was young. Sara Montiel was gorgeous. And also Carmen Sevilla has been a very pretty girl. And so, there were many young actresses from my period that were very beautiful. And I used to say "what a pity, I am not so pretty." [Laughter] But I really had no trouble. Because I always had suitors there . . . waiting for me [little laughter] I have been lucky. Because . . . I have been a normal person. Maybe, I have been attractive. A friend of mine used to say that when a beautiful woman entered a place people would say "oh what a beautiful woman!" but when you show up they all say "Damn [*sic*] who is that woman!! [Laughter]."[56]

Certainly projecting an image of a "normal" person had an impact on the audiences who identify with Aurora Bautista. Meanwhile, Montiel's appearance has taken over her private life. She, even now in her eighties, continues to wear heavy make-up, and still performs her role of femme fatale manufactured under Francoism. In post-Franco Spain, however, Sara's character has been imitated affectionately by cross-dressers in a twenty-first-century gendered twist.

Sara's Smoke Signals

Sara Montiel loves cigars. Ernest Hemingway taught her to smoke cigars in 1952 when she visited Havana. Almost eighty years old, she frequents the Spanish celebrity spotlight parties smoking a huge Cuban cigar, which she delicately holds between her index and middle fingers—her extremely long nails perfectly manicured, sharp, shocking. For Sara Montiel a cigar is not just a cigar. "Is the cigar you smoke after a meal erotic?" she was asked in an interview in 1988. "There is something sexual about it, because I like to savor it," she replied.[57] Sara had made smoking a sexual statement in the late fifties with a song: *Fumando Espero.* "Smoking is a swell sensual pleasure. Smoking I await the man I love the most," the lyrics go, "And, while I smoke I don't waste away my life. Since the floating smoke usually numbs me."[58]

After several failed attempts, I was able to speak on the phone from my home in New Mexico with Sara Montiel in Madrid in May 2000. I was traveling to Spain that summer and was seeking an interview with her. I only discovered it was Sara Montiel herself speaking on the other end of the line halfway through our conversation. The woman on the other end of the line had been suspicious and introduced herself as Ms. Montiel's secretary. Once she realized my intentions were legitimate and I was not harassing her like the many journalists she fights daily, she politely declined my request. She said her memoirs were to be published in the next few months.

Sara Montiel. Vivir es un placer was published in November 2000. The book cover shows the aged sex symbol applying golden lipstick. Her heavily made-up eyes stare at the viewer with a studied flirtatious look. Sara Montiel's persona still revolves, after sixty years in show business, around her physical beauty and her seductive sex appeal. Sara's cinematic body has taken over her life off the big screen, turning into a Möbius strip continuum. The public presentation of her memoirs to the Spanish press was held in her home in Madrid, a spectacular penthouse filled with paintings, photographs, and objects that tell about a full life. Four weeks after its release the book had reached its fourth printing. She had recorded her life experiences over the years in fifteen two-hour tapes, which according to the star did not follow any particular chronological order. Sara chose writer Pedro Villora to transcribe the material and give it some structure to turn it into the final printed version.

She was born in 1928 in the village of Campo de Criptana, Ciudad Real, María Antonia Alejandra Abad Fernández. Her father was a farmhand and her mother a hairdresser who went to the houses of her clients. Sara was the youngest of a large and very poor family. Functionally illiterate, she did not learn to read and write properly until she was sixteen, when she met her first lover, dramatist Miguel Mihura. "With him," she remembers, "I started to scribble on a piece of paper; I filled up pages of ma, me, mi, mo, mu. He used to read the scripts for me and I learned them by heart."[59] Mihura was forty-three years old and according to Sara he adored her while she was afraid to fall in love.

Sara Montiel's memoirs are weighted with stories of her multiple love affairs. Most of the men in her life were significantly older than her, intellectuals or artists from whom she says she sought knowledge and protection. "I wanted some shelter because I had lost my father very young. My father for me was a prince. Young men my age seemed to me just pipsqueaks." She explains how "without realizing it I always was drawn to painters, writers, and intellectuals."[60] Some of her lovers included in addition to dramatist Miguel Mihura, poet León Felipe, actor Gary Cooper, American director Anthony Mann, whom she married, Joe Kanter, and Giancarlo Viola. She devotes chapter 12 in her memoirs to what Montiel declares was "the love of her life": her affair with 1959 winner of the Nobel Prize in medicine, Spanish scientist Severo Ochoa. Their relationship lasted from 1951 to 1955 with secret encounters in New York and other United States cities where the scientist lived at the time.[61] "I was 22 years old, and listened to my mother's advice and chose my career rather than marriage to Severo. What was I to do? Have tea with scientists' wives?"[62]

Sara Montiel has been married four times. Her first husband was Anthony Mann. Then she was married for fourteen years (1964–78) to Vicente Ramírez García-Olalla, an economist and businessman from Bilbao. The couple stopped living together two years after the wedding. It was then that Sara started her relationship with impresario Pepe Tous, her lover for several years.

They finally got married in 1979 and adopted two children. Sara Montiel suffered eleven miscarriages, the last one when she was fifty-one years old. Pepe Tous and she adopted a Brazilian girl, Thais, in 1979 and a boy in 1983 they named Zeus.[63] Pepe Tous died in 1992. Sara Montiel's last marriage took place in 2002 to thirty-three-year-old Cuban Tony Hernández. This marriage only lasted nine months.

Her extraordinary beauty opened the door to the entertainment industry for her. When asked if it is difficult to age, knowing she is so beautiful she replies:

> It is not normal how I look for my age. I see women in her 60s that look like my grandmothers, in their bodies, in their skin, in their faces and their minds. My open mind helps me live my life.
>
> I don't believe in age, I believe in life. We are nothing. Our physical looks are worth nothing, it's gone and the spirit remains . . . I am indignant about my beauty: what hindrance I have damn it!—with my physical beauty. Because the critics always mentioned how gorgeous I was but never any comment on my acting. I am a good actress.[64]

When she was fifteen she won a beauty contest held by CIFESA that secured her an exclusive contract with that film studio in 1944. For the next four years she appeared in fourteen films,[65] including *Locura de Amor* that opened the international market and took her to Mexico where she appeared in thirteen films[66] between 1950 and 1954. Then she went to Hollywood where she played a leading role in V*eracruz* (1954) starring Gary Cooper and Burt Lancaster. Later she signed a contract with Warner Bros. and appeared in *Serenade* (1955) with Mario Lanza, Joan Fontaine, and Vincent Price. Not only did Sara Montiel find success but she also found her first husband in Hollywood—the director of *Serenade* Anthony Mann. Their marriage lasted seven years.

Nineteen hundred fifty-seven was the most successful year in Sara Montiel's career. After starring in *The Run of the Arrow* with Rod Steiger, Brian Keith, and Charles Bronson, she returned to Spain to work on her breakthrough *El último cuplé,* a musical production that became a box office success in Spain and catapulted her into the film industry of western Europe and Latin America. Her career in Hollywood-like her marriage to Mann, did not last. They had a long-distance relationship between the United States and Spain due to their professional obligations.[67] Some critics see *El último cuplé* as the film that deterred Montiel from her new career in Hollywood, but looking back on it today she has no regrets about her decision: "Look, Columbia

[Pictures] offered me a contract in 1953 and I did not accept it because it was a seven-year contract that prevented me from getting married, traveling, or doing anything at all. The studio owned you in body and soul. I was 23 years old and did not take it. That is my lost stellar moment because of my independence. Besides, in those times you know, being black, Mexican, or Spanish meant to wear the dagger in the garter and always repeating the same part. They changed my name to Sarita in the United States, a name that I do not like at all, and they gave it to me because Sara was a black name, and they wanted to avoid misunderstandings, which I would have had no problem at all."[68] *El último cuplé* was the film that locked her in the role as "the other woman," the sex symbol of Francoist Spain.[69] Almost ten years after playing the role of *the other* in *Locura de Amor,* the same director Juan de Orduña sought her to perform the leading role in *El último cuplé,* María Luján a *cupletista,* a cabaret singer. The story is told in flashback mode—a confession of sorts of now retired and forgotten Luján to the first impresario that hired her, now her friend. Once a famous singer, she had a heartbreaking love life. Montiel embodied the good tramp. She was the other woman for whom any man would abandon his wife or fiancée. She was *the other* who struggled to become *the pure* and redeemed fallen woman. That was the main difference with our celluloid fallen woman par excellence, Sara, Sarita Montiel. If she had been German the role would have been performed by Marlene Dietrich, if French by Simone Signoret, if British by Sarah Miles, all of whom would refuse any kind of penance. But in Francoist Spain the other woman, the fallen woman on the big screen that Montiel embodied, was exemplary and always showed the audiences that there was redemption and like Marguerite Gautier she would "die trying," that is smoking.[70]

El último cuplé was the beginning of a series of films that established Montiel's cinematographic career in Spain. These films were extremely successful box office events that showcased Sara Montiel and revitalized the old-fashioned Spanish variety song known as *cuplé.* In 1958 Sara Montiel made *La violetera* by Luis Cesar Amadori, an Italo-Argentine director and scriptwriter who made a successful career in Spain. In 1959 *Carmen la de Ronda* by Tulio Demicheli; in 1960 *Mi Último Tango* and in 1961 *Pecado de Amor* both by Luis Cesar Amadori. In 1962 she made *Noches de Casablanca* by Henri Decoin; *La Bella Lola* by Alfonso Balcázar; and *La Reina del Chantecler* followed by *Samba*—both by Rafael Gil; in 1964, *La Dama de Beirut* by Ladislao Vajda in 1965;

La mujer perdida by Tulio Demicheli in 1966; *Tuset Street* by Luis Marquina in 1968; and *Esa Mujer* in 1969 by Mario Camus. In the latter film she played a nun, Soledad de Jesús, who after being raped while in missionary service had a baby girl who was stillborn. Soledad abandoned the order and eventually became a cabaret singer. In the 1970s Sara Montiel made *Varietes* (1971) by none other than Juan Antonio Bardem, and under the direction of Pedro Lazaga she made her last film entitled *Cinco Almohadas para una noche* (1973). The artistic career of Sara Montiel continued in the 1980s with her appearing on television shows and on the stage mainly as a singer. Sara's seductive voice entered Spanish homes. Her films had been repeatedly shown on television to three generations of Spaniards.

Sara received a special tribute to her career in 1982 in the Paris Fall Festival organized by Frederic Mitterrand at the Casa de España in the French capital. "How can we talk" he explained, "about Spanish cinema without mentioning Sara? It would be like talking about German cinema without mentioning Marlene Dietrich."[71] The French minister of Culture, Jack Lang, designer Pierre Cardin, and leading figures of French cinema attended the event. The audience interrupted Sara's thank you speech: "you are so beautiful; we want to see you, Sara. Look how my mother cries Sara; she spent long nights watching your films until she was thrown out of the theater."[72] To these expressions of devotion she replied: "I am yours, and you are mine. This is a Christmas present. What happens is that *I have four breasts instead of two breasts* [my emphasis]."[73] And in a midnight dinner with the press at Bofinger restaurant she explained her role in the Francoist cinema: "I made movies in the time period that I lived in, like Mr. Joan Miró painted in his times. During the Francoist era, *we artists* [women] *had not tits or belly-buttons,* and I had crooked legs. Cesáreo González did as he pleased, because he was Franco's right eye."[74]

She speaks of her breasts as maternal as much as sexual parts of her body and her self as the nurturance needed by the masses. Psychologically starved with frustrated sexual desires men fantasized and women admired Sara's fallen character. Sara Montiel's seductive cinematic body was ultimately imbued with a maternal nature during the 1950s and 1960s. Her cinematic body will only reveal explicitly its sexual temperament during the political transition. Since the end of the regime and the explosion of nudity and eroticism in the film industry, Sara Montiel has refused to make any more films. However, she appeared naked in the political magazine *Interviú* in 1980. The actress made clear she did not agree to the publication of the pictures: "These guys from the yellow press, with all due respect to their saintly mothers, are son of a bitch. And the photographer, José María Castelví, nursed from my breasts as a professional, he has eaten at my table, he offered me his admiration. But now he behaved dirty taking these pictures by trickery from afar."[75]

Although clearly put out by the publication of the photographs, Sara Montiel quickly clarified she was not upset due to a false sense of decency. "I am not a prude," she declares, "All my life I have walked naked. For twenty years I have shown my naked tits [*sic*]. One knows she is beautiful and does not mind showing it—but in private with closed ones." Because in the film *Varietés* I had no problem in accepting the suggestion of this great director Bardem to ride a gentleman, naked, while behind me horses galloped. And I appeared thus, having a roll in bed, without a problem."[76] The editor of the magazine declared they did not know anything about the matter and emphasized this was a deal between the actress and the photographer. Sara Montiel denied having been paid for the photographs and refused to file a lawsuit. "I would be pleased to file a lawsuit but we always lose here, because in this country there is not a strict law to protect the privacy of a star."[77]

As we will discuss in the epilogue, the female body became the symbolic representation of the fragile democratic body politic—a naked woman. Sara's maternal breasts were again nurturing democracy. The actress had declared openly in a 1963 interview with writer Manuel Vázquez Montalbán that she was a socialist[78] so her nudity is doubly significant in the immediate post-Francoist cultural scene. It was the commodification of her cinematic body that allowed her to be able to express her political views without consequences. "It was a miracle we didn't go to jail, because my producer Cesáreo González did not want to lose the money of five films already signed. They covered it up."[79] Her sex appeal made her useful to the regime. She declares: "One day Franco called me and told me I had to go to Italy with Antonio Garrigues y José Mario Armero, to persuade Alberti to come back to Spain. Once we got to Rome, I called Alberti, he told me to go immediately to his house. He made me sit in a sofa. 'Don't you move' He spoke with those gentlemen and they did not get anything out of him. 'Because you are Spain and Spain is you.'"[80]

She was not the only one who took off her clothes in front of the camera; many actresses chose to do so and did not apologize for it. Sara Montiel today openly speaks about sex: "The normal thing to do is sex; if you don't do it you are not normal. To make love when you are in love is the most natural and marvelous thing. One thing is sex and another is love." Montiel says she did not have lovers but she actually loved outside of marriage. "Women must be whores out of kindness, in other words: give themselves to men out of kindness, never reject the one who loves you, because it is a harm you never forgive yourself for.[81] Famous writer and socialite Francisco Umbral (1935–2007) made Sara Montiel a regular subject of his journalistic chronicles of Madrid's celebrity scene. In an article entitled "Antoñísima" he described his encounter with her: "María Antonia Abad, Antoñísima, is wearing transparent gauze over her *naked and Spanish breasts* [my emphasis]: 'These have never been in the operating room, unlike the ones of so many others, Paco, but you are making me feel inadequate with your staring so much at them. . . . stop it with the transparent gauze . . . you filthy.'"[82]

Aurora Bautista: Mad Desire

In a brief column for *El País* entitled "God," Francisco Umbral declared, "God lives in Aurora Bautista."[83] Aurora Bautista, today a celebrated actress, started playing historical heroines for the Franco regime cinema and later became the most important and versatile actress in the history of Spanish theater and possibly film. In a personal interview with her in May 2000 she remembered her childhood and the hardship of the Spanish Civil War. Her father, Santiago Bautista, worked for his future brother-in-law, a very successful furrier with a prosperous business in the Calle del Carmen in Madrid. That was where her parents met when Aurora's mother, Sagrario Zumel, stopped by the store while shopping in Madrid to get her bridal trousseau. They fell in love and she broke her engagement to marry Aurora's father. They lived in Madrid where their first son was born. Aurora Bautista's grandmother asked for the second child to be born in Valladolid. So her mother went to Villanueva de los Infantes, Valladolid, where Aurora Bautista was born on October 15, 1925. The Civil War changed their lives completely due to her father's liberal ideas. "After the war my father had political problems and he was arrested. He was three years in prison. . . . lots of problems. . . . they rescued him, helped him and he was able to get out [of prison] in three years. But all that time for us, logically, was miserable. I stayed with some relatives and my brother went elsewhere. When we finally were able to reunite, they made my father move to Barcelona. He had to leave Madrid. Then we were living in Barcelona for a while . . . quite a while. They were there ten years and I five."[84] Aurora Bautista attended the Instituto del Teatro in Barcelona where she discovered her lifelong passion for acting. This Barcelona institution provided very inexpensive instruction and this was the reason the Bautista family could afford sending their daughter to drama school to satisfy the young girl's thirst for knowledge. She attended classes every evening from 7 to 9 PM with a course of study that included history of theater, painting, music, and declamation. After three years of training, students received a diploma and were ready to enter the world of entertainment.

When Aurora was in her last year of instruction, Cayetano Luca de Tena visited the institute from Madrid and listened to her reciting García Lorca. Luca de Tena was director of the National Theater Company, and was so impressed with her performance that he decided to offer her a contract with the National Company after her graduation.[85] She traveled to Madrid with her father and when they read the contract decided not to accept the salary of 75 pesetas per day. Instead she boldly asked for 225 pesetas and returned to Barcelona. Although her peers at the Instituto del Teatro told her she should have accepted and she was sure she was not going back to Madrid, Cayetano Luca de Tena offered her the job and the salary she had asked for.[86] Aurora Bautista made her acting debut in William Shakespeare's *A Midsummer Night's Dream.* "The debut was beautiful. I had a very good reception and reviews . . . lots of applause. The audience was fascinated with me. So that season I played different roles in different plays. Among them a play by Schiller called the *Conjuración de Fiesco* [*The Fiesco or Genoese Conspiracy*] which was also set approximately in the sixteenth century, the wardrobe and . . . everything."[87] It was 1948. At that time the major Valencia film studio CIFESA was looking for the protagonist of *Locura de amor* [*The Mad Queen*], the story of Queen Juana of Castile, known as Joan the Mad, daughter of Isabella and Ferdinand and mother of future emperor Charles V. Cayetano Luca de Tena brought Aurora Bautista to CIFESA's attention. Bautista remembers her first encounter with the film director Juan de Orduña

> So he saw me, and he liked me a lot. He liked me a lot in the sense of my work because this gentleman was homosexual and he was not attracted to me in that way [laughter] So he saw me and he asked me

"So do you like cinema?" And I said "Well as a spectator I love it," and he said "No I want you to be a movie star. I want you to be the protagonist of a film," and I said, "Well I don't know if I will be good, because I have never done it. I don't know the camera, I don't know anything." He said, "I will teach you. Do you want to do a test?" "Well all right I will do it" "Then choose," he gave me the script, "choose the scene you like better and I will make you perform it in front of the camera." So we were there from seven in the evening until one in the morning making the scene several times. And then I told him [laughter] "look I'm not sure if I am doing this right but I want to go home because I am exhausted." I did persuade him and he liked my performance very much so he proposed my name to the studio. . . .[88]

Orduña was so convinced, that in order to get CIFESA to take a risk with this newcomer he offered to finance the film for the first fifteen days. "During those fifteen days I will see if this girl is able or if she is not." Bautista remembers him saying. "'If she is no good we will give her a present and send her home.' And really [laughter] I think I did very well because every thing they asked me to do I just performed beautifully. So that's how the events took place. We made a very good film. The opening . . . Oh it was fantastic! People loved it. It was a whole year in the theaters. The reviews were fabulous. And that's how I started to work in this profession."[89]

Film scholar Román Gubern considers *Locura de amor* to be a necrophiliac film that reveals the tortured conception of sexual relations under Francoism.[90] Aurora Bautista embodies the queen madly in love with her womanizer husband Felipe el Hermoso who falls in love with a Moorish princess in hiding, portrayed by a young Sara Montiel. She became the sex symbol in the 1950s Spanish big screen while Aurora Bautista went on to become a grand stage actress.[91] In *Locura de amor* the queen orders the corpse of her husband Felipe to be embalmed. She follows him during their journey through Spain to Granada for his burial.[92] The queen makes the guards watch the corpse to prevent women coming close to him. The necrophilia present in the film emphasizes the negation of sexual desire for good pious women that the regime wished to forge—wives were to remain faithful to their husbands even after their death. Aurora Bautista reflects on the repressive sexual mores of the period:

That problem was not addressed at home. I don't know why. We were so preoccupied with survival. So preoccupied with other things. . . . I have, you know, avoided it completely from my life until I was

> much older. Until I had to face my personal problem . . . right? I had not resolved it; I had not resolved it because I really was living outside of time. Because, I think that a woman between 16 and 18 becomes an adult and she has knowledge of sexual issues and all that, and I had no education in this area. It was much later when I . . . almost in a way [small laughter] out of time right? I started to be concerned with that problem . . . and I had young men who approached me and . . . Then of course there was more res . . . no, no, not respect, because respect there is now too but there was no easy access of a young man to a young woman. There were a series of obstacles. . . . And for us, girls did not consider correct that they [men] could trespass certain affections right? with a girl. Anyway, everything was a little strained right? No, it was not normal . . . Maybe the people that had suffered so many vicissitudes as I endured. . . . Because I . . . I suffered hunger for example, I have had need of clothing I had as a young girl . . . because I saw how other people were able to do it more . . . and I did not have access to all that . . . So I was preoccupied with . . . well I was a normal being and I liked guys very much telling me little things and so on . . . but sex did not even cross my mind. . . . I don't know if it is that I have been a little slow in that area right? or life placed me in a different path right? I had to fight for my survival, for my education, for my family . . . I had other problems that any other normal human being must have right? Therefore the sexual matter did not exist.[93]

Aurora Bautista got married late in her life. She was already thirty-six when she married Mexican physician Dr. Hernán Cristerna, a gastroenterologist, whom she tells me, "was the man of her life." The marriage did not last because they lived apart, he in Mexico and she in Spain, neither wanting to abandon their professions. But she was also disappointed as a result of her husband having an extramarital affair. "And we end up being very unhappy because when you are young you do not put up with being belittled, right? And I did not tolerate it and said no. I did not want to live like that. Over there [Mexico] they are used to that and there are people who live with two women. And women put up with that . . . I cannot tolerate such thing. We are not used to such thing right? [laughter]"[94]

They had a son, born in Spain, that Aurora raised on her own. The baby was baptized in Spain with the duchess of Alba and Dr. López Ibor as his godparents. Aurora Bautista remained married from afar. The separation lasted twenty years with yearly visits of Dr. Cristerna to his wife and son in Madrid. "Three years after I came back to Spain he showed up asking me to forgive him and to go back to Mexico. I told him I would never go back to

Mexico [little laughter]. In Spain anything he wanted but Mexico never. So he kept coming back almost ten years. Every year . . . to see us, and ask us to go back. I would say no. He never helped me economically. I always had to face life by myself. Because he said he would help . . . eh it was almost like a punishment you know? He would agree to help if I went back with him but if I stayed here he would not give me a cent. And he never gave me a cent. But I fought hard and gave my son a good start in life. I managed as best I could and then I met Luis."[95]

During their separation she was known publicly in show business as the "white widow"—always faithful and in love with her estranged husband. Finally, she filed for divorce in 1986.[96] Three years later she got married in Gibraltar to Cuban exiled engineer Luis de Luis. "I need a companion," she tells me, "and my husband is very cultured . . . I don't know he is my kind of person. He is a great companion."[97]

Aurora Bautista is an extremely independent woman who always had to fend for herself and to provide for others. Certainly the main concern was survival and everything else was secondary in the early stages of her career. The Bautista family suffered tremendous economic hardship as a result of Francoist reprisal against Aurora's father. She felt economically responsible for their well-being as soon as she signed her first cinematographic contract. Aurora Bautista received 40,000 pesetas for *Locura de amor* and signed a three-year exclusive contract with CIFESA that paid her 500,000 pesetas per film. Three movies followed: *Pequeñeces* (1949), *Agustina de Aragón* (1950),[98] and *Condenados* (1951). In these films she played historical heroine roles.

It was her role as Agustina de Aragón that led to her meeting Franco in person. Bautista did not want to attend and claimed she was sick with a fever. Encouraged by her father's advice to never decline an audience with a head of state, she went to El Pardo with Juan de Orduña and CIFESA's owner, Vicente Casanova, and his wife. Bautista's recollection of that evening's audience with the Francos is that she just did it out of obligation.

> He [Franco] wanted to be my escort all the time. He told me he loved cinema and he had a script or not . . . not a script. . . . rather he wanted *Marina* to be filmed. *Marina* as you know is a Spanish opera with a beautiful music . . . and he said he would love for this work to be filmed. They served an afternoon tea. And then, they showed the film.
>
> Then without me saying anything, "I made you an autograph" [she speaks with a diminutive voice imitating Franco's] "so you may keep

> it" and . . . I said "Thank you very much" [laughter]. I didn't ask him for it. But he gave me the autograph, no photo just his signature. It was a spontaneous act on his part . . . to give me his signature. That's how the audience went [little laughter].[99]

The production of another historical film, *Teresa de Jesús,* suffered strict censorship and was only possible to make ten years later in 1961 under the *New Spanish Cinema* regulations. "For the first time," she declared in an interview to the newspaper *Informaciones* in 1983, "I faced the artistic censorship in Spain. The representation of Teresa de Jesús as a normal young woman, who thought of marriage and was good at using the sword with her brothers, or the fact that she dreamt to go to the Indies rather than being predetermined, was unacceptable. We went to the Vatican with the script, the Pope authorized it, but they did not accept it here. We are more papists than the Pope."[100] Not all the characters played in the big screen by Bautista were asexual. The first cinemascope film produced in Spain was called *La Gata* (1956) and Aurora Bautista remembers how sexually charged this film was. She plays the part of a young woman who was raised in the fields of rural Andalusia; Jorge Mistral played the young beau in this film in which they experienced an intense and passionate affair. "There are some moments that you *can feel the heat.*" Interestingly a foreign version of this film was manipulated and two other actors posed naked in place of Bautista and Mistral.[101]

In several interviews with the press in the 1980s she lamented: "I only made four historical films and everybody remembers me for those."[102] Aurora Bautista is well known for her leftist politics. On June 5, 1976, the civil governor of Granada authorized a public event to celebrate the 73rd anniversary of Federico García Lorca's birth in the village of Fuente Vaqueros. Aurora Bautista was one of the artists and intellectuals that gathered for this occasion for which the authorities allowed only thirty minutes. Under banners that read "Socialism and Freedom" and Andalusian flags, more that 15,000 people cried the name of Federico, executed in August 1936, victim of the military uprising. The crowd dissolved promptly when the thirty minutes were up.[103] On June 5, 2006, the same event was reenacted and Aurora Bautista, now in her 80s, was there again reciting Lorca's poetry and proclaiming her faith in democracy and freedom.

In 1978 Aurora Bautista produced and acted in a play by controversial author Fernando Arrabal entitled *Oye Patria mi aflic-*

ción (*Hear Motherland My Sorrow*) with excellent reviews. This play is a grotesque comedy that incorporates the eternal national symbols of Spain.[104] In Aurora Bautista's career it represented a radical departure from the initial roles she played for CIFESA. For a critic the production was "an avalanche of visual and sonorous stimuli seeking the personal response of the spectator."[105] "And Aurora Bautista—An actress who comes out of a semi-silence, marginalization—places herself at the very center of the ring to occupy at once the first row of our grey [*sic*] . . . generating a continuous action engagement with a physical, oral, a bodily ability that fuses talent and technique."[106]

Bautista received several awards for this work: in January 1979 the prestigious theater Mayte Award, and in February of the same year the Theater Awards from Audience and Critics for her interpretation in the play. Financially, however, this venture cost her dearly. The play was never presented outside of Madrid.

Some of the theatrical productions she appeared in included: *Requiem for a woman* by Faulkner and Camus; *The Ad* by Natalia Ginzburg; *Yerma* by García Lorca; *The Youth of Celestina* by Martín Recuerda.

La Tía Tula's Economy of Desire

Miguel Picazo's film *La Tía Tula (*1964*)* illustrates the central role of desire in cinematic experience in Spain's transitional 1950s and 1960s. Aurora Bautista plays Tula in this adaptation of Miguel de Unamuno's novel by the same title published in 1921.[107] The film is a masterful rendition of the core theme in the novel: motherhood as female destiny. The story of a spinster turned surrogate mother of her deceased sister's children. Picazo, however, brings up to date, in his own words, the story inspired by a case of "tulismo" he learned about in his own town, Guadalajara.

Several elements make *La Tía Tula* an important film for the understanding of women's cinematic bodies and the economy of desire in 1960s Francoist Spain. First, this is a film produced in the context of the *New Spanish Cinema.* Film critics and scholars agree that this is a turning point in Spanish cinema, the seed of modern Spanish film. Although it received at the time the categorization of "special interest," it did not escape the draconian censorship of the new code of 1963. Second, Picazo's choice for the leading actress Aurora Bautista was received with skepticism but proved to be right. Bautista, known as the Jennifer Jones of

Figure 19. Movie still from *La Tía Tula* (1964) film by Miguel Picazo. Courtesy Filmoteca Nacional Madrid, Spain.

CIFESA, gained great fame with her hyperbolic interpretation of Queen Joan the Mad in *Locura de Amor* (1948) and had become the Francoist screen embodiment of female historical figures in the 1940s such as Agustina de Aragón, Queen Isabella, and Teresa de Jesús. Third, the focus of the film on surrogate motherhood turns into a somber exploration of sexual desire, gender relations, and female self-effacing tyranny profoundly rooted in provincial Spain and continuing still in the mid-sixties—exploration even more relevant in the context of transition from autarkic to consumerist Spain that makes this film utterly modern. Picazo's 1964 version of Tula preserves the eternal values of True Catholic Womanhood that Unamuno had infused her with in 1921. What makes this new Tula modern is precisely her self-definition and self-determination to impose her will against her earthly desire. The denial of her body makes her a tyrant and puts her in control of her destiny.

The most important film in Aurora Bautista's career was this adaptation of Miguel de Unamuno's novel *La Tía Tula* (1921). The film was designated "special interest" and received the maximum subsidy. It enjoyed a commercial success in Spain and received several international awards. At the San Sebastian Film Festival in 1964, Picazo received the award for best director and best Hispanic film. The same year in Prades, France, it received the prize for best foreign film, and it won the critics' prize in New

York in 1965. Aurora Bautista received from the government Sindicato del Espectáculo, the best actress award, not only for her role as Tula but for her entire career, particularly her historic roles that the regime endorsed.

Picazo was able to bring to the audience the real talent behind Bautista's acting in this 1960s cinematographic version of Tula, a spinster who takes into her home her deceased sister's widower and two children. Picazo's *La Tía Tula* is a masterpiece that could not escape, however, the censor's scissors. Some of the cut scenes included one in which a religious group of women discussed the importance of virginity and chastity, and another in which the widower visits the grave of his wife in the cemetery where a sign reads "Do not enter: ladies and señoritas without stockings or couples who do not keep moral decorum."[108] Female sexuality was only permissible within marriage and only for the purpose of procreation. Tula embodies the symbols of the virgin and mother enshrined by the regime. "It is true. And . . . and never . . . never as something [sexuality] separate from motherhood. It is true, it's true. And I think that that has been something that Miguel Picazo wanted to stress didn't he? That is a bad education of Spanish women . . . And as a result there have been many unhappy women. . . . as it was the case of aunt Tula right? Who in the end does not know love."[109] Motherhood devoid of any sexuality as the supreme aspiration of a good woman is a genuine element of the National Catholic rhetoric masterfully displayed in this film in which Tula's negation of her body is enacted by her living by proxy the sexual and maternal experience of her deceased sister Rosa. Although Tula completely embraces the role of mother of her niece and nephew she rejects all physical contact with her brother-in-law Ramiro with whom she only relates in a maternal way. In fact Ramiro's character is constantly infantilized. In different scenes Tula takes care of Ramiro; nursing him back to health when he is sick or disciplining him at the dinner table. The sexual tension fills the screen. Tula rejects his marriage proposal. In turn Ramiro becomes increasingly frustrated and attempts to rape her but she successfully escapes. "Remember that scene in *La Tía Tula* at night when I get up to get a glass of water and he follows me. And then he goes into the young girl [Tula's cousin Juanita] and makes love to her and gets her pregnant. Well that is it; it feels that you can breathe the heat. It was wonderfully achieved by the director."[110]

As a result of the pregnancy Ramiro has to marry Juanita and take the children leaving Tula alone. The film is a clear denunciation of the dysfunctional sexual relations perpetuated under Francoism.

> In Spain there is, I think repression about the sexual education of women. And in *La Tía Tula* Miguel Picazo wanted to show that women in Spain were not educated sexually and neither were men. Neither men, because men could have helped women but. . . . they wanted her to be like that. . . . like a wild animal, a beast, instead of being another human being in a world where both have to understand each other, and make each other happy . . . and enjoy what nature has given us. Sex is a nice thing . . . and . . . and very beautiful and very poetic, and fantastic, right? It is a gift that human beings have to reproduce but also to enjoy ourselves very much, right? And enjoy our body. And so I think all this is not taught in the beautiful way that it really is. Never, ever have we been taught in this manner. Always it is something. . . . sinful . . . that we are not supposed to know about . . . that we cannot even name.[111]

The fear of sex was not new under Francoism. Picazo adapted Unamuno's novel to the reality of Spain in the 1960s. The director transforms the abstract character of Tula in Unamuno's novel into a quotidian and concrete woman in provincial Spain in the 1960s. In this way the audience recognizes themselves and feels close to her and her entourage. As he puts it, his intention was "to make the problem real" and give the spectator the opportunity "to reflect on the consequences of Tula and Ramiro's behavior."[112] Miguel Picazo laments today the mutilation of the film: "Everything that was cut was essential and regrettably irretrievable because the negatives were destroyed."[113] In total the censors cut four minutes and forty-seven seconds, which according to Picazo meant that 40–50 percent of the impact of the film was lost.[114] But Picazo's film highlights the contradiction between modernity and tradition that the regime was experiencing in the 1960s. The Women's Section dictum of the times called for the ostensibly modern but persistently old-fashioned woman for a regime in transition to consumerism and new ways of relations between the sexes. The Women's Section, in an attempt to prepare women to enter a depleted labor market, sponsored the Law of Political and Professional Rights for Women in 1961. Four million Spaniards, mostly men, had immigrated to different parts of Europe. The development, inaugurated with the Stabilization Plan in 1959, required a redefinition of what the regime expected from women, yet it continued to espouse Catholic traditional values.

In Picazo's film Tula's sexless motherhood exposed audiences to the suffocating and absurd demands placed on women: be a mother yet pure. The characters in the film, not only Tula but Ramiro as well, are trapped in their bodies that almost act in defiance of their will, outmoded anachronistic bodies in 1964. The choice of Aurora Bautista for the role of Tula could not have been better, precisely because of her beginnings as Joan the Mad and other historical heroines enshrined by the regime. Audiences witnessed and experienced in the dark how tortured and stale the Francoist femininity was. Martyrdom, suffering, self-denial was the only destiny for the good woman in the old and new times.

Self-denial of sexual desires and containment is displayed by Picazo's mastery of cinematic creativity. Tula is trapped in her body—diligently performing its new role of mother and surrogate wife: There are several close-ups of her hands busy sewing, ironing, or cleaning. Her hands are also sexualized in a scene where Ramiro kisses them, after which she proceeds to wash them in disgust.[115] If not through Tula's experience, we learn how to become a pious woman through Tulita, the little girl that Tula adores. Tulita spends two hours every day in silence. She times herself using an alarm clock and when it goes off she screams "I can talk now."

In addition to close-ups, Picazo also uses cinematic techniques to create emotion and to proscribe desire. He accomplishes this by suturing different frames together again and again, as well as using the soundtrack. A narrator's voice or tense music introduce emotions into the plot that the audience clearly recognizes as located off screen. These cinematic techniques emphasize sexual repression. One scene in which Tula, alone in her room, reads a letter from Ramiro to her sister exemplifies the repressed desire. The audience sees an utterly disturbed Tula and listens to the voice of Ramiro reciting the content of the letter: "Rosa, don't be mad. I love you like I have not loved anyone; and it is for that reason, for love, that I could not contain myself. I hope you will forgive me and I promise you not to try it again. I will go to visit you tonight and will talk about the wedding, of our wedding. We must get married at once. I need it, I love you. In the mean time, I kiss your hands, your arms, your eyes, the nape of your neck, your lips. Yours, Ramiro."[116]

The words of Ramiro map the sites of his carnal affection on Rosa's body. Tula's clandestine reading of the letter and Ramiro's voice naming each body part he intends to kiss parcel the spinster desire on her own flesh. Tula's body is never seen in any sexualized way. One scene cut off by the censors showed Tula in lacy black underwear.

The viewer never sees Tula's body, but it may be imagined. In this way, as Sally Faulkner points out, Tula's body "becomes a potent aspect of unseen off-screen space." The censor's cut actually enhances, in Faulkner's words "the association of off-screen space with repressed desire, which is central to *La Tía Tula*."[117] There is a cut-off scene that is described in the script as follows: "She left the shutters ajar leaving the room in semidarkness. She stays in her slip. She looks at her reflection in the closet. She picks up from the dresser the bar of deodorant. She rubs it under her arms. She slips into her skirt from head down . . . She is still when she is about to lift her skirt. Listens and then she pulls up her black stockings that sharply contrast against her white flesh."[118]

In Steven Shaviro's words, "The ambivalent cinematic body is not an object of representation but a zone of affective intensity, an anchoring point for the articulation of passions and desires, a site of continual political struggle. The cinematic apparatus is a new mode of embodiment. It is a technology for containing and controlling bodies, but also for affirming, perpetuating, and multiplying them by grasping them in the terrible, uncanny immediacy of their images."[119] The erasure of women's cinematic bodies in the domestic versions of the 1960s highlighted their overexposure for international consumption. Spanish women's cinematic experience as spectators was one of psychological mutilation, their invisible bodies turned into taboo terrain that they had to defend against the fondling of strangers in the dark movie theater. A prudish sexuality and self-effacing aspirations were the immediate results. There are a few conclusions and further questions we can derive from the reading of women's cinematic bodies in the *Tardofranquismo* that might shed some light on the way gender relations were redefined in the transition to democracy.

Only those women like Tula and her circle of friends who belonged to the petty bourgeoisie could afford to be self-righteous and turn down a marriage proposal. Picazo's Tula was self-sufficient. She is the one who opened her home to her sister's widower and the two children. It is her territory—her house, her terms. She even refuses the advice from the priest to get married to Ramiro. "No, father, I won't get married," she stubbornly repeats over and over. "Do you have any fear . . . any qualms of physiological nature?" asks the priest during Tula's confession talking to her through the lattice of the confessional. "You see my child, there are many women who, before getting married are afraid to be intimate with a man. . . . You understand me? I warn you that if that is so with you, you are not the first one. These are common things that nature takes care of with time."[120] But Tula has become even more righteous than the priest. "Father I am not anyone's remedy." When the priest warns her of the sin of pride, Tula replies indignantly: "No father, do not think so. It is rather self-respect,"[121] and without waiting for absolution she leaves the confessional.

La Tía Tula offers us the opportunity to look at the economy of desire in the latter period of Francoism. A look at women's cinematic bodies helps us understand the commodification of sex in modern societies. Sexuality is a good tool to measure women's independence; sexual self-sufficiency is problematic when women exercise it—problematic morally and economically. Contrary to Tula, Juanita had no other choice but to get married to Ramiro as a consequence of his raping and impregnating her. Marriage and motherhood were the only options for women of the popular classes. For the majority of Spanish women, chastity was not only a moral but also an economic asset. We cannot forget that prostitution was tolerated until 1956. Prostitution was a necessary evil from the Catholic point of view. A necessary evil, as explained in chapter 3, controlled by the state and orchestrated through the Patronato de Protección de la Mujer to protect the chastity of the virtue of the fiancées of the fallen women's clients. The sexual economy will determine the opportunities women of different classes have in order to survive financially.

Aurora Bautista received the "Miguel Picazo" award on March 10, 2006, for her role in *La Tía Tula.* In her acceptance speech to the Diputación Provincial de Jaén conferring the award she remarked, "*La Tía Tla* is the best film I have made in my life."

The reading of women's cinematic bodies in Tardofranquismo might shed some light on the way gender relations were redefined in the transition to democracy.

Marsha Kinder points out how the *New Spanish Cinema* of the 1960s highlights the contrast between "the neorealist Italian cinema and Hollywood escape to excessive pleasures." Spanish filmmakers recaptured the artistic license that played the tension between crude reality and frivolous overindulgence. This artistic ability had been present in the works of Golden Age writers like Cervantes, Lope de Vega, Calderón de la Barca, and

Quevedo. This "baroque-like" contrast between realistic depiction and false idealization became particularly vivid in Francoist Spain in the transition from autarky to consumerism. Sara Montiel as María Luján in *El último cuplé* and Aurora Bautista's Tula embodied on the screen this neo-baroque quality that will imbue the most recent Spanish cinema. I use here the definition of neo-baroque proponed by Alejandro Valeri: "Neo-baroque is associated with post-modernity due to its ability to establish continuity with the past by appropriating the baroque aesthetics."[122] Neo-baroque receives the category of aesthetic movement that could even replace the postmodern concept in the Spanish speaking context. We assist to the loss of integrity and unity to give way to instability and multidimensionality in the transitional period of the 1950s and 1960s undergone by Francoism. The constant malleability the regime self-inflicted in the last two decades of existence will prepare the terrain for the transitional period to democracy in the immediate post-Francoist era. The transition to democracy was a period characterized for mass culture under a strict though eventually futile, official control.[123] From the excessiveness of postwar historical melodramas that exemplified the most traditional kitsch the cinema of the 1960s inaugurates the kitsch of the consumer society. While the erotic site in autarkic cinema resided not on the skin but on the garments worn by female stars from the 1940s to the 1960s, there was no other way to excite eroticism and seduction but to unveil the female body after the dictator was gone.

Conclusion: Carmen No Longer

There was something strange and wild about her beauty. Her face astonished you, at first sight, but nobody could forget it. Her eyes, especially, had an expression of mingled sensuality and fierceness, which I had never seen in any other human glance.

Prosper Mérimée, *Carmen*, 1845

TWO MAJOR CONCLUSIONS MAY BE DRAWN FROM THIS STUDY: FIRST, that baroque and Francoism were ideologically, politically, and religiously close. Second, the study of the gender dynamics in the transitional period of the 1950s and 1960s allows us to shed some light on the discussion of Spain's modernization.

Spain's "special" relationship with the rest of Europe was not new.[1] It had entered modernity as a lesser brother.[2] While the rest of Europe was rebuilding, Spain was isolated and surviving with autarkist formulas. Although the regime longed to be part of the European continent, at the same time the foundations of the Movement remained alive though hidden behind the manufactured "organic democracy" enacted in the Organic Law of the State in 1967. Nine years earlier, the 1958 Principles of the State had been presented as the National Catholic constitutional document framing such organic democratization. In the context of the Cold War, Spain was at the same time trying to dance with the West without being seduced. Francoism reinvented itself utilizing trends emanating from the broader centuries-long Western culture in which Spain has been both "orientalized' and seductive."[3]—an orientalization that Francoism reinvented during the Cold War with the regime's international rehabilitation.

Spain, in the European imagination, has been a dark and mysterious neighbor, in part because of its location on the margins of the continent and its historical ties to the Muslim and North African community—what has been referred to as "Pagan Spain." This seductive mysteriousness is embodied in the figure of Car-

Figure 20. © Ricard Terré, *Holy Week,* Barcelona 1957. Courtesy of Ricard Terré.

men. Frenchman Prosper Mérimée in his novella *Carmen,* which became widely popularized by his fellow countryman Georges Bizet's operatic version in 1875, prolonged the female stereotype into twentieth century European/Western psyche. Mérimée's description of Carmen captures the irresistible sexual power of the Spanish Gypsy woman whose charms will beguile the helpless male leading character: "Her skin, though perfectly smooth, was almost of a copper hue. Her eyes were set obliquely in her head, but they were magnificent and large. Her lips, a little full, but beautifully shaped, revealed a set of teeth as white as newly skinned almonds. Her hair—a trifle coarse, perhaps—was black, with blue lights on it like a raven's wing, long and glossy. Not to weary my readers with too prolix a description, I will merely add, that to every blemish she united some advantage, which was perhaps all the more evident by contrast."[4]

Mérimée's Carmen embodied the Spain that attracted European travel writers. Like Carmen, the Gypsy tobacco factory worker, Spain was different, the *Other,* desirable yet not to be imitated. Spain was, like, Carmen irrational (dominated by superstition and obsolete Catholicism) and wildly passionate, mysterious, and childish.

The seduction of Modern Spain in my reading is based precisely in its malleable *otherness* rooted in a rich history of cultural and religious hybridism. The location of Spain in the margins of European consciousness helps to further its seductiveness for outsiders. While the Spanish intellectuals have struggled to define *el ser de España* (Spain essence) from the left and the right.

The Catholic values and "technologies of power" developed during the Counter-Reformation period were reinvented and deployed by the regime with the elaboration of the concept of "organic democracy. Therefore, I identify a neo-baroque quality to the nature of the Francoist regime. The concept of organic democracy, as explained in chapter 1, was bound up in National Catholic discourse with two elements: the concept of *la madre patria* in the modern sense of nationalism fused with the Catholic dogma of the *mystic body politic* rooted in the sixteenth and seventeenth century.

The Neo-baroque Nature of Francoism

In this book, I have examined the somatic metaphors present in the political and religious discourse of National Catholicism. In order to write women's historical experience under Francoism I have utilized feminist theories of the body. The discourse analysis in chapters 3 and 4 shows the centrality of corporeal gendered metaphors in the Francoist regime's rhetorical framework to regulate prostitution until 1956 and prescribe marriage and motherhood with national awards for prolific families. The regime's bio-power technologies were rooted in the idea of "organic" democracy. Organic democracy, sustained by the regime's notion of *La madre patria,* paradoxically conveys a hermaphrodite-like essence of the nation's concept. *Mater* and *pater* fused in the unfolding of time. Within this organic, biological metaphor of the nation, women's bodies played a central role in the political imagination, and the control of those bodies was key to the biopower the regime tried to establish in domestic policies. While the regime pursued the control of women's bodies through various legal, social, political, and cultural technologies of power, the book also makes the case for a shift in discourse, from the early to the later dictatorship, in which elements of "modernity" were injected into the Francoist gender discourse as a way of adapting or responding to the economic and social transformations that economic liberalization unleashed in the 1950s. Exploring sexuality under Francoism unveils the sharp light and shadows of eroticism at the end of the regime with the so-called *ola de destape.*

Spain represents a key piece in the conflict to understand how Europeanism turned into a metaphor for modernity, whiteness, and Christian values.[5] Religion had a lot to do with it. The cultural monolith established in 1492 by Isabella of Castile and Ferdinand of Aragon avowed Catholicism as the guiding force behind Spanish national identity. Such cultural monolith was re-enacted in the Civil War (1936–39) to be restored and propped up after 1939 under Francisco Franco's dictatorship. Certainly, this prolonged understanding of Spanish identity led scholars inside and out of the country to see Spain as a European anomaly or a subaltern appendix at best.[6]

This study sheds light on what I would call the "Spanish model of modernization"—crucial in the transitional period from autarky to consumerism of the 1950s and 1960s in which gender relations evolved to adjust to foreign models of modernity, namely Americanization as it appeared in cinema and magazines.

The Other Within: Modernization Francoist Style

The Franco's regime tried to use the concept of Spain's "specialness" to isolate the country from the rest of western Europe, and to invent a culture by selectively drawing on the past—neobaroque, Golden Age, religious orthodoxy, and orientalism all stitched together. What emerged was a doctrine that was as "inorganic" as it could be, a bizarre, often contradictory official body politic that was often in conflict with itself. The attempt to remake Spanish women in the piety of the past was especially tortured, as I have shown. Prostitution, for example, was legal for much of the early part of the regime, even though prostitutes were seen as a threat to the true Catholic woman. The modern female icon from film and ads, though manufactured by the image makers of the West, was organic, allowed to grow out of the new freedoms of the secular, democratic West. The female tourists emerging from Spain's pristine beaches in the 1960s in their scandalous bikinis were like Venuses rising from the half-shell of modernity. Franco's homemade cultural construction of womanhood could not compete against this imported embodiment of feminine bio-power.

The 1960s economic plans favored Spain's transition to consumerism opening the door to an avalanche of tourists.[7] The result was an increasing tension between the regime's attempt to control and discipline women's bodies in the service of its National Catholic ideals, and the changes that threatened and weakened that control. In order to remain untouched yet modern in the eyes of the Western powers the newly appointed minister of Information and Tourism, Manuel Fraga Iribarne, coined the slogan "Spain is different" to better attract visitors with the promise of an exotic seductive Spain in 1962. At the same time Spain was "inviting" in the West it was also enacting strict censorship codes in the belief that it could inoculate its own population from foreign freedoms. Inevitably, with the dollars and the recognition from abroad, came new ideas and new mores.

Paradoxically, the purpose of the Spanish brand of "orientalism" was to utilize this oppositional discourse based on *otherness within* to Europeanize Spain. In this sense the national identity developed by Spanish intellectuals fits Homi Bhabha's notion of mimicry understood as; "a strategy of colonial power/knowledge emblematic of a desire for an approved, revised Other"[8] The Spanish version of Europeaness becomes thus problematized because it is based on the notion that it is almost the same but not quite European; an "in-between" space essential to bridge the gap between the west north of the Pyrenees and South of Gibraltar.

This conclusion illustrates the explicit connection between political transition and images of women's bodies in the common metaphor of "destape," which signified both political opening and naked women. In closing one may argue that it will be promising to study, how the counterimages of seductive womanhood that appeared in the popular culture from the 1960s to the end of the dictatorship undermined the regime's gender discourse and prepared the way for the transition of the 1970s.

Epilogue: Viva La Pepa!: Body Politic and the Transition to Democracy

I do not need to liberate myself of anything. *I am absolute liberty.*[1]
—Susana Estrada, *Humedo Sexo,* 1978

ALTHOUGH 1975 SIGNALED THE BEGINNING OF A POLITICS OF CONSENSUS and compromise, gender relations, and in particular women's sexuality remain to this day a volatile issue. Women's bodies represent the symbolic site of the political and social tension that Spain endured in the three years that lapsed between the death of the dictator and the proclamation of a new democratic constitution in December 1978. A political *via crucis* ensued after the embalmed body of the caudillo was buried in the Valle de los Caidos, the monumental mausoleum that republican prisoners of the Spanish Civil War erected for the glorification of the regime.

In contrast to the solemn and stale style of the old Francoist guard, an explosion of eroticism inundated the media what was called "destape"—literally meaning to uncover. Journalists proclaimed "destape" to be the key word in the wake of Franco's death. The political meaning attached to this term implied the liberalization of the country's political and social affairs. Films such as Fellini's *Satiricón,* censored under the dictatorship, were shown in theaters and the literary work of forbidden authors like Ernest Hemingway and George Orwell were published.

In addition, a rapid urbanization and the modernization of the social customs followed the economic boom and the tourists who arrived to Spain by the millions. Spaniards had crossed the Pyrenees to watch films like Bertolucci's *Last Tango in Paris* and

Figure 21. Enrique Tierno Galván, Mayor of Madrid, and Susana Estrada, queen of striptease, 1978. Courtesy *El País Internacional* (2007). The photograph was published in 1978 by the daily *Pueblo.* It captures the ceremony of this journal's awards to popular celebrities of the times. In this image Susana Estrada is receiving her award as most popular actress of the year from Mayor Tierno Galván. She received the award showing her right breast just as Delacroix depicted Liberty guiding people in his 1831 painting.

had endured and resigned themselves to a chaste public sexual existence disturbed by foreign tourists on our beaches in anti-Spanish bikinis and tight Speedos.

As the 1970s were inaugurated, Franco realized he needed to have loose ends "tied" off to perpetuate Francoism after his death. The international community was able to clearly see the mockery of democracy behind the "liberalization" afforded by the state apparatus. Demonstrations against the regime in the major universities were promptly repressed and Franco issued in Burgos the death penalty for six ETA activists accused of sabotage and homicide. The Burgos trials turned into the symbol of the anti-Francoist struggle. Three hundred intellectuals locked themselves in the monastery of Montserrat in Catalonia; even the Spanish Episcopal Council of the Catholic Church added their voices in solidarity with those on death row, demanding their amnesty. Under pressure Franco signed the pardon.

Close to eighty, Franco realized that he could suddenly die and needed to prevent a political void. In June 1971, Franco announced that in the event that he fall ill or be away from the country, His Highness Prince Juan Carlos must assume the duties, automatically and de facto, of the head of the state. The caudillo tried his best to close the liberal cracks in the system, worried that his successors would not be able, like him, to maintain the delicate equilibrium between liberalization and authoritarianism. Debilitated by Parkinson's disease, with half of his body paralyzed and a shaky hand, the old dictator addressed the Spanish population in the usual televised Christmas address and informed them he had planned well and was leaving everything "very well tied."

When Franco fell ill in mid October 1975 most of his ex-followers and servants aligned themselves in post-Francoist factions blaming each other for the flaws of the regime while cleaning up their personal public image. As Franco's health and body deteriorated rapidly, the medical bulletins turned into the regime's vital signs. On November 4, the morning press releases from Madrid revealed Franco's worsening. "The symptoms of congestive cardiac arrest are mild and the ventricular extra-systoles have disappeared. It continues the blackened hemorrhagic defecation. Hydropsy has increased and a collateral abdominal circulation has developed. A mycosis in the mouth was rapidly controlled. Nonetheless, the pulse was normal and the blood pressure too."[2] Statements like this using seemingly aseptic medical terms revealed the grave state of political affairs. Franco's body's breakdown was also the breakdown of Francoism. The list of ailments that fell upon the diminutive old dictator is long: flu, cardiac crisis, intestinal hemorrhaging, and peritonitis, all in addition to his preexisting Parkinson's disease that had afflicted him for years. His Catholicism carried him through until the end, as if National Catholicism had served as the ideological cloak that carried Franco's power into the 1970s. At all times in his final struggle with death, the caudillo kept close the relic of the uncorrupted hand of Saint Teresa of Avila and in his agony he was covered with the holy cloak of the Virgin del Pilar patroness of the feared Civil Guard and *Hispanidad*.[3]

Franco's body was the object of "therapeutic fierceness" in the desperate attempt to prolong his life and power.[4] He spent his last days in a state of hibernation, artificially fed and drained. Likewise, at this point the regime itself could only survive Franco by applying artificial political catheters and probes. On November 20, 1975, a cold rainy day, Prime Minister Carlos Arias Navarro announced in a television and radio bulletin, "Spaniards, Franco is dead!" After five weeks of agony Francoism came to a close.

Marisol: Viva La Pepa!

Women's bodies represent the symbolic site of the political and social tension that Spain endured in the three years that lapsed between the death of the dictator and the proclamation of a new democratic constitution in December 1978. A number of actresses would pose naked in front of the camera in film or the print media. The bodies of these "public" women became the allegorical incarnations of the nation in the given political juncture. Democratic Spain was symbolically incarnated in the naked vulnerable body of a woman. Marisol, one of the most famous child actors of the period, a blond, blue-eyed angelic girl from Malaga, became that democratic promise incarnated.

Born of humble origins on February 4, 1948, Josefa (Pepa) Flores González showed her talents as a singer and dancer from a very early age. She joined the Sección Femenina Coros y Danzas and in 1959 traveled to Madrid with the group to perform on television. It was then that producer Manuel Goyanes discovered and made her into the Spanish Shirley Temple. Goyanes signed a ten-year exclusive contract and moved the girl into his home and her mother into a pensión down the street in Madrid. The Goyanes family had six children and supposedly Marisol was to become one more of the family. *Un rayo de luz,* her cinematographic debut opened in Spain on September 9, 1960. The film was an international success in that year's Venice Film Festival where the little actress won the best child actress award, while in Spain the National Syndicate of Entertainment (Sindicato Nacional del Espectáculo) nominated her as best actress as well.

Marisol's film career was affected by her growing up in the Goyanes' upper-class household—her adolescence uprooted. She received a rigorous education from private tutors including English, interpretation, dance and voice lessons, swimming, and horse riding. Between 1960 and 1969 she made twelve musical comedies. The scripts always featured family conflict that the angelic character Marisol would help resolve, adolescent love, and childish mishaps. In 1961 Marisol went on a promotional tour for her second movie *An Angel has Arrived* (*Ha llegado un angel*) to Latin America, Portugal, Angola, and South Africa, and in the summer she went to the United States to perform on Ed Sullivan's television show for which she was paid $4,000. Later she remembered how she was under surveillance at all times. They controlled her phone calls, let her have no access to her money and was only given 100 pesetas (today's equivalent to $1) a week until she turned nineteen years old. The promotional apparatus that Goyanes built around the young icon had no precedent in the history of Spanish entertainment. A magazine devoted exclusively to the actress appeared under the title *Los amigos de Marisol* (*Marisol's Friends*); *Fher,* a commercial publisher, produced hundreds of albums, comics, paper dolls, and children's books, as well as a collectable biography in twenty issues told by Marisol herself under the title *Simpatía* (*Congeniality*). There were also dolls and records with her songs. The star received more than 1,000 letters a day that the producer's office would punctually answer. There was a team of writers that kept on file the names, addresses, and birthday information of the fans.

Between 1960 and 1969 Marisol grew into her alter ego, Pepa Flores. The manufacturing of Marisol the star affected her physical appearance and her diction. She was forced, unsuccessfully, to erase her southern accent. In 1964 she underwent plastic surgery to make her nose straighter. The anxiety any adolescent goes through was magnified by the pressures of stardom and gave her a stomach ulcer. Finally, in 1969 she entered reluctantly an arranged marriage with Carlos Goyanes, son of her producer. The unhappy union only lasted three years and after her attempt to commit suicide the couple separated. Out of this tragedy Pepa Flores emerged, a complete opposite individual. In 1973 she started a relationship with Spain's National Flamenco Dance icon Antonio Gades. They got married in 1982 in Cuba with Fidel Castro as their witness. Pepa Flores proclaimed herself a staunch Communist. Gades was the love of her life. They had three children, all girls: María, Tamara, and Celia. The union lasted until 1986. Pepa Flores moved to Málaga and has been suffering from what the media calls the "Garbo Syndrome." She refuses to be part of the entertainment industry, to give interviews or being photographed at all.

Marisol was never a folk star like the ones the regime manufactured in the 1950s. She embodied the new modern, petty bourgeois star manufactured to match the needs of the consumer economy that the 1960s development plans wrought. It was the age of radio talk shows and television, inaugurated in 1956 in Paseo de la Habana in Madrid. Marisol became successfully the Shirley Temple, the Spanish Twiggy turned Brigitte Bardot as she aged. She acquired political significance with the phenomenon of the transition period of "destape." Many actresses would pose naked in front of the camera in the late 1970s and early 1980s. They became the allegorical incarnations of the nation in such political juncture—a vulnerable naked woman, a vulnerable democratic Spain. Marisol's ultimate rebellion was to pose naked for the newly born journal *Interviu.*

These nude images were published in 1976 in *Interviu.* Marisol the angelical child actress of the Franco period. The Spanish Shirley Temple appeared naked on the cover of the magazine and the report inside was entitled "The Beautiful Path to Democracy. Marisol." The photos are supplemented by the opinions of different celebrities about Marisol as actress and as a woman but there is no interview of the actress herself. María Luisa Seco, a fellow actress, declared: "I have always found her to be a wonderful woman. I have only seen her in her films when she was a child, and I was so impressed. Now she is a beautiful woman. The image she projects is that of a woman who lives her life and does as she pleases; in a word: *a free woman,* who lives wherever and however she wants. She indulges whenever she wants to and with whomever she pleases, which it is absolutely perfect. On the other hand, she is a good actress, with an incredible body and on top of that she signs very well. She is a stupendous star."[5]

Juan Luis Cebrián, director of the major new newspaper *El País,* offered his opinion also. Although he opened his statement by declaring himself to be "definitely *Marisolista*" (pro-Marisol), he went on to point out:

> I remember with horror those films with a girl of golden braids and high-pitched voice; films, in truth, I did not watch in their entirety but only the trailers; then when the girl grew up the situation changed and I moved to her team due to mere aesthetic sensitivity. I want to say that I do not like how Marisol sings, I think she is a mediocre actress, even when Bardem directs her, and certainly there is between her and me no rational or intellectual identification. However, *Marisol has been one of the few object-women that we have been able to display at the European level. Here [in Spain] object-women always are fat and short and they wait for their husbands at home to go to the neighborhood's movie theater. Marisol, at least, is a valuable object*[6] [my emphasis].

In 2001 *Interviu* celebrated its twenty-fifth anniversary. Always at the center of the controversy in the post-Francoist transition until his death in 2007, author and media character Francisco Umbral wrote an article for the anniversary of this publication entitled "Los cuerpos y los siglos" ("The Bodies and the

Centuries"). Marisol along with other actresses that posed nude in front of the camera were remembered with a nostalgic tone:

> Then it materialized in front of us mortals the forgotten Pepa Flores, with her Marisol outfit, in her naked Marisol, and her golden bangs rescued us from our multiple jobs; and those breasts a bit excessive gave us back our faith in summers, and those little girl hands made us the boyfriends of all the adolescent girls of the decade, and those bratty nymph glutei where the word was made flesh and reigned among us. And those clear eyes, intense, sad, of the color of a green moon when we had never seen a green moon. [Those eyes] paralyzed the national life, paralyzed democracy in a crosswalk, and we believed again in general strikes, in free love unions, in socialism, in mayors dying in bulk, and in a Model Transition which only Pablo Catellano disliked, while the rest of us found our place under the little girl's double suns.[7]

The political remembrance of the end of Francoism is described along the triumph of the flesh, of male desires. "Those slim, long legs that God endowed women with," writes Umbral, "We are telling you about the 70s. . . . happy, transitional 70s. The *Caudillos* were falling like old plum trees, Spain was full of princes, and Falange found a new intellectual in Emilio Romero. . . . And democracy was like a fun fair poster, fixed every night on every corner, to appear always torn the next morning."[8] The nudity of the female body is the solace (mainly for men) of forty years of repressed sexuality for everybody. Democracy was measured by the amount of female flesh displayed. Democracy was on display, naked, like a woman. Nudity was presented as an act of rebellion on the part of women against the prudish Francoist past and the prerogative of heterosexual men, self-proclaimed free thinkers. Like his forefathers who drafted the 1812 Constitution known as "La Pepa," in 1978 democracy was incarnated in another Pepa—Pepa Flores.

Appendix: Statistical Data

Correlation Between National Income and National Fleet of Vehicles 1953 to 1963

Years	National income in thousands of million pesetas 1963	Thousands of automobiles
1953	228	257
1954	257	316
1955	260	367
1956	273	450
1957	290	539
1958	302	702
1959	311	849
1960	309	1,005
1961	331	1,224
1962	353	1,463
1963	377	1,707

Source: Fundación FOESSA, *Informe Sociológico sobre la situación social de España* (Madrid: Editorial de Euroamérica, 1966), 78.

Number of Private Vehicles Per 1000 Inhabitants in Different European Countries

Countries	1948	1955	1958	1961	1963
Belgium	21	54	70	91	—
Italy	5	18	28	49	76
Spain	3	5	6	11	17
Grecia	1	—	4	6	—
Portugal	6	11	15	19	—

Source: Fundación FOESSA, *Informe Sociológico sobre la situación social de España* (Madrid: Editorial de Euroamérica, 1966) 79.

Per Capita Income and Percentages of Agriculture, 1962

Countries	Per capita income in thousand pesetas	Agriculture income in percentages for national income
United States	145	4
Canada	90	6
Western Germany	74	6
England	71	4
Italy	37	17
Japan	27	15
Spain	**22**	**25**
Portugal	16	26
Greece	22	30

Source: Fundación FOESSA, *Informe Sociológico sobre la situación social de España* (Madrid: Editorial de Euroamérica, 1966), 84.

Spain's Nacional Income Per Economic Sector and Provinces, 1962

Provinces	Individual income in agriculture in pesetas	Individual income in industry in pesetas	Individual income in services in pesetas	Individual income total in pesetas
Alava	55,527	65,528	78,557	66,488
Albacete	39,954	40,054	58,860	44,293
Alicante	45,658	44,686	75,046	53,338
Almería	26,485	37,013	52,648	34,725
Avila	26,966	43,208	54,623	34,129
Badajoz	38,232	44,114	61,535	43,900
Baleares	36,611	42,652	77,362	53,168
Barcelona	**75,559**	**70,032**	**93,664**	**79,198**
Burgos	33,461	57,934	64,225	46,432
Cáceres	30,618	35,172	59,580	36,722
Cádiz	31,086	56,348	68,146	51,814
Castellón	37,945	43,111	67,396	45,991
Ciudad Real	37,676	46,571	57,389	43,996
Córdoba	29,321	52,355	63,855	42,252
Coruña	20,436	50,222	61,896	36,169
Cuenca	47,488	40,578	57,522	47,971
Gerona	50,608	62,375	70,272	61,371

Provinces	Individual income in agriculture in pesetas	Individual income in industry in pesetas	Individual income in services in pesetas	Individual income total in pesetas
Granada	27,536	42,908	57,522	38,260
Guadalajara	34,775	51,703	57,348	42,466
Guipúzcoa	44,039	75,640	85,282	75,045
Huelva	33,146	58,641	52,511	46,979
Huesca	55,290	66,089	59,387	59,596
Jaén	38,676	48,666	59,225	44,946
León	25,317	58,152	60,919	41,933
Lérida	54,879	64,548	68,163	61,066
Logroño	52,020	47,722	68,221	54,730
Lugo	28,588	46,992	50,772	34,914
Madrid	**45,906**	**64,286**	**93,968**	**79,984**
Málaga	27,133	46,148	59,283	41,648
Murcia	33,531	51,086	67,147	49,740
Navarra	57,694	54,360	73,476	40,525
Orense	15,721	48,685	51,224	29,608
Oviedo	26,153	77,089	73,046	57,195
Palencia	34,354	50,722	56,599	44,241
Palmas	39,475	53,900	75,170	52,814
Pontevedra	17,412	48,035	60,124	34,978
Salamanca	34,971	61,594	67,097	47,283
Santa Cruz de Tenerife	28,009	82,314	77,688	52,274
Santander	30,278	78,408	75,285	59,330
Segovia	50,530	41,887	60,990	51,129
Sevilla	40,073	54,171	75,698	55,052
Soria	41,096	43,433	55,705	45,312
Tarragona	45,809	57,937	75,064	56,622
Teruel	31,931	49,009	55,527	40,144
Toledo	37,562	39,038	60,731	42,331
Valencia	39,667	57,896	78,289	57,223
Valladolid	46,391	76,430	68,199	61,846
Vizcaya	35,173	83,798	89,681	78,742
Zamora	29,978	56,974	59,424	40,250
Zaragoza	40,894	63,456	74,643	59,092
TOTAL	**40,024**	**61,035**	**76,329**	**55,606**

Source: Fundación FOESSA, *Informe Sociológico sobre la situación social de España* (Madrid: Editorial de Euroamérica, 1966), 81.

Notes

Introduction

1. Lakoff, George and Johnson, Mark, *Metaphors We Live By* (Chicago: University of Chicago Press, 1980), 25.

2. Ibid., 34.

3. Efforts to stabilize the gender order often occur in moments of political and social or economic upheaval, something that was true in the 17th century as well as in the 20th. For the early modern period see Mary Elizabeth Perry, *The Handless Maiden: Moriscos and the Politics of Religion in Early Modern Spain (Jews, Christians, and Muslims from the Ancient to the Modern World)* (Princeton, NJ: Princeton University Press 2007); *Gender and Disorder in Early Modern Seville* (Princeton, NJ: Princeton University Press, 1990); Mary Elizabeth Perry and Anne Cruz, eds., *Culture and Control in Counter-Reformation Spain,* vol. 2, Hispanic Issues (University of Minnesota Press, 1992). For the twentieth century see Mary Louise Roberts, *France Civilization without Sexes: Reconstructing Gender in Postwar France, 1917–1927,* Women in Culture and Society Series (Chicago: University of Chicago Press, 1994).

4. Aurora G. Morcillo. *True Catholic Womanhood: Gender Ideology in Franco's Spain* (Dekalb: Northern Illinois University Press, 2000). Reviews have been published in: *The Journal of Modern History* 73, no. 3 (Sept 2001): 695; *Church History,* 7, no. 2 (June 2002): 426; *Gender & History* 14, no. 2 (August 2002): 350; *The Catholic Historical Review,* 89, no. 2 (April 2003): 320.

5. María del Carmen, see Muñoz Ruiz. "La representación de la imágen de las mujeres en el franquismo a través de la prensa feminina, 1955–1970," in *Representación, construcción e interpretación de la imágen visual de las mujeres,* ed. P. Amador Carretero and Ruiz Franco (Madrid: Instituto de Cultura y Tecnología "Miguel de Unamuno"/AEIHM, 2003): 405–21; Gloria Nielfa Cristóbal, *Mujeres y hombres en la España Franquista. Sociedad, economía, política, cultura,* Instituto de Investigaciones Feministas, Universidad Complutense de Madrid, 2003; Carme Molinero. *La captación de las masas. Política social y propaganda en el régimen franquista* (Madrid: Cátedra, 2005).

6. Leslie A. Adelson, *Making Bodies, Making History: Feminism and German Identity* (Lincoln: University of Nebraska Press, 1993), 1.

7. See Kathleen Canning, "The Body as Method? Reflections on the Place of the Body in Gender History," *Gender & History* 11, no. 3 (November 1999): 499–513.

8. Aurora G. Morcillo, *True Catholic Womanhood.*

9. Charles Fantazzi, ed. *Juan Luis Vives: The Instruction of a Christian Woman: A Sixteenth-Century Manual* (Chicago: The University of Chicago Press, 2000), 3. In contrast to the virginal model prescribed by Vives, seventeenth-century writer María de Zayas y Sotomayor narrated the sexual experiences of her female characters as a way of reclaiming the female body's power over male dominance. *Novelas amorosas y ejemplares,* (*The Enchantments of Love,* 1637) followed by another volume entitled *Desengaños amorosos* (*The Disenchantments of Love,* 1647).

10. "On Virginity" in *Juan Luis Vives. The Instruction of a Christian Woman,* ed. Charles Fantazzi, 80. Juan Luis Vives (1492–1540) was born in Valencia in a well-to-do Jewish converso merchant family. He never admitted his Jewish upbringing in his writings even though his father and mother were victims of the Inquisition's violence. His mother died of the plague in 1508 and his father was executed in 1524. Her case was made all the more bizarre when twenty years later her remains were exhumed and burned at the stake after being posthumously tried as a heretic. These events illustrate the highly corporeal nature of religious practice in the early modern period. See Carolyn Walker-Bynum, *Fragmentation and Redemption: Essays on Gender and the Human body in Medieval Religion* (New York: Zone Books, 1992). It might also explain Vives's emphasis on the somatic roots of spiritual purity and his determination to detach himself from any doubt about his Christian beliefs. He studied and worked in England along with humanists such as Thomas Linacre, John Fisher, William Latimer, and Thomas More. Although Vives had an opportunity to return to Spain, he would not accept the chair of Latin philology at the University of Alcalá, to replace Antonio de Nebrija, for fear of the Inquisition.

11. "On Virginity" in *Juan Luis Vives. The Instruction of a Christian Woman,* ed. Charles Fantazzi, 85.

12. In the early modern period and especially during the Counter-Reformation, the body became the instrument to achieve salvation. Not only had young women to abstain from foods that incited their lust but had to also avoid any stimulus of their senses "that excites our internal organs, such as unguents, perfumes, conversations and the sight of men." Cleanliness was of utmost importance. A young woman must be neat and spotless. The cleanliness of the body is nothing but the reflection of the cleanliness of the soul. A young lady must never be idle. Vives explains, "One of the principle remedies against love is that Cupid's arrow does not catch us idle and unoccupied." "How the Young Woman Will Treat her Body" in *Juan Luis Vives. The Instruction of a Christian Woman,.* ed. Charles Fantazzi, 92

13. Augustin Redondo, ed., *Le corps comme Métaphore dans L'Espagne des XVIe et XVIIe siècles. Du corps métaphorique aux métaphores corporelles* (Paris: Presses de la Sorbonne Nouvelle Publications de la Sorbonne, 1992).

14. Political and personal virtue was projected onto bodies, particularly female bodies. The same questions of identity building that preoccupied scholars and artists in 1500s Spain, haunted those intellectuals of the turn of the twentieth century as we will see below. Pornography was one of the most common vehicles of satirizing political regimes in medieval and early modern Spain. For example, early in the fifteenth century the Trastámara dynasty was crucial in the shaping of an orthodox Catholic Spanish identity predating the better known imposition of such orthodoxy by Isabella and Ferdinand at the end of the 1400s. Through the study of medieval literary texts scholars high-

light how political chaos is resolved with the advent of an authoritarian ruler who imposes his masculine supremacy to restore order while women are presented as the source of all pandemonium. For the purpose of this study it is interesting to look at the anonymous piece "Carajicomedia." Produced at a time of utter political angst, the embodiment of all evil is Queen Isabella the Catholic. Spain becomes a "hypocritical pornotopia," literally a place of prostitutes" some eight of them named Isabel as the queen herself. Certainly, these images testify to the historical sexualization of the body politic especially when the head of the state happened to be female. Any given political crisis necessarily ends up being explained as a result of the promiscuity of the female ruler whose body turns into the visible indicator of political instability. Linde M. Brocato, "'Tened por Espejo su fin.' Mapping Gender and Sex in 15th and 16th century Spain," in *Queer Iberia. Sexualities, Cultures, and Crossings from the Middle Ages to the Renaissance,* ed. Josiah Blackmore and Gregory S. Hutcheson, (Durham, NC: Duke University Press, 1999).

15. See Jerónimo Merola, *República original sacada del cuerpo humano. Compuesta por Hieronimo Merola doctor en Philosofia y medicina, Catalan y natural de la ciudad de Balaguer* (Barcelona, 1587).

16. Part of chapter 3 material has been published in my article "Walls of Flesh. Spanish Postwar Reconstruction and Public Morality." *Bulletin of Spanish Studies,* 84, no. 6, (2007): 737–58.

17. See Alejandro Varderi, *Severo Sarduy y Pedro Almodóvar. Del Barroco al Kitsch en la narrativa y el cine postmodernos* (Madrid: Editorial Pliegos, 1996), 81.

18. Kinder, *Blood Cinema. The Reconstruction of National Identity in Spain.* Berkeley: University of California Press, 1993.

Chapter 1. Francoist Power

1. "Es el Ejército la Columna vertebral de la nación. Es lo que une, sostiene y mantiene la rigidez de todo el conjunto. Por su médula corren las esencias vitales de los valores sagrados de la Patria. No es la cabeza que dirige y discurre, ni los otros miembros que orgánicamente lo constituyen, sino la columna que la une y sostiene; rota ésta, el cuerpo se convertiría en un guiñapo." Franco's speech at the Alcazar of Toledo on November 5, 1951, celebrating the 50th anniversary of his promotion within infantry corps. Quoted in "Franco 40 años de historia de España," in *La Actualidad española* (Madrid, 1975), 145.

2. "[E]l mar convertido en lago, unido tú a la orilla como el feto al útero sangriento de la madre, el cordón umbilical entre los dos como una larga y ondulante serpentine." Juan Goytisolo, *Reivindicación del conde Don Julián* (Barcelona: Seix Barral, 1970), 13.

3. The works of several intellectuals had a great influence in Vallejo Nágera's political outlook. See Angel Ganivet, *Idearium español y el porvenir de España* (1896) or Ramiro de Maeztu, *Defensa de la Hispanidad* (1934) for examples of works reedited in the 1940s and 1950s, as well as the Orteguian vision of Spanish "invertebration."

4. Antonio Vallejo Nágera, *Eugenesia de la Hispanidad y regeneración de la raza.*(Burgos: Editorial Española, 1937), 7.

5. Ibid., 8.

6. Stanley G. Payne, *The Franco Regime, 1936–1975* (University of Wisconsin Press, 1987), 324.

7. Sheelagh Ellwood, *Spanish Fascism in the Franco Era: Falange Española de las JONS, 1936–1976* (Basingstoke: Macmillan, 1987), 113.

8. Quoted in Payne, *The Franco Regime,* 448.

9. "Leyes Fundamentales: Jefatura del Estado" *B.O.E.* (Madrid, 1958), 4511.

10. Ibid., 4511.

11. Ibid., 4512.

12. Juan J. Linz, "An Authoritarian regime: Spain," in *Politics and Society in Twentieth Century Spain* edited by Stanley G. Payne (New York: New Viewpoints, 1976).

13. Carmen Martín Gaite, *Usos amorosos de la postguerra española* (Madrid: Anagrama, 1987), 69. See also Rafael Abella, *La vida cotidiana,* Rafael Torres, *La vida amorosa en tiempos de Franco* (Madrid: Ediciones Temas de Hoy, 1996); and Richard Wright, *Pagan Spain* (New York: Harper & Brothers, 1957). On the code of courtship and sexuality in the American context during the 1950s see: Brett Harvey, *The Fifties. A Women's Oral History* (New York: Harper and Collins, 1993); Elaine Tyler May, *Homeward Bound: American Families in the Cold War Era* (New York: Basic Books, 1988); Eugenia Kaledin, *Mothers and More: American Women in the 1950s* (Boston: Twayne Publishers, 1984); John D'Emilio and Estelle B. Freedman, *Intimate Matters: A History of Sexuality in America* (New York: Harper & Row, 1988).

14. Order of February 9, 1955, "Cuestionarios de Formación del Espíritu Nacional," *B.O.E.*, 4627.

15. Order of February 9, 1955, "Cuestionarios de Formación del Espíritu Nacional, educación física y escuelas del hogar, que han de cursar las alumnas de bachillerato," *B.O.E.* 28 July 1955, 4625–26.

16. Noël Valis, *The Culture of Cursilería: Bad Taste, Kitsch, and Class in Modern Spain* (Duke University Press), 7.

17. Valis, *The Culture of Cursilería,* 6.

18. [T]enemos la íntima convicción de que aquel fascismo trasnochado y ridículo que se nos imponía en nuestra infancia con recitados, lecturas y una buena dosis de palmetazos mientras nos suplementaban la escasa dieta con leche en polvo y queso de los americanos, tiene que ver mucho con las mentalidades y actitudes que hoy componen el mosaico macro y microfísica de los poderes y formas de vida hispanos que siguen haciéndonos la puñeta y, de paso, considerablemente diferentes a los ojos del mundo." Gregorio Cámara Villar, prologue in Sopeña Monsalve, Andrés, *El florido Pensil: Memoria de la Escuela Nacionalcatólica.* (Barcelona: Grijalbo, 1994), 15. Quoted in Noël Valis, *The Culture of Cursilería,* 278.

19. International Commission of Jurist, *Spain and The Rule of Law* (1962), 3.

20. Ibid., 4.

21. George Mosse, *The Crisis of German Ideology: Intellectual Origins of the Third Reich* (Howard Fertig; reprint edition, 1999), 312.

22. Richard Wright, *Pagan Spain,* 229–30.

23. Brenan, *The Face of Spain,* 60.

24. Jorge Novella Suárez, "Tierno Galván y el Barroco," *Sistema. Revista de Ciencias Sociales,* no. 121, Madrid, July 1994, 5–27. See also Raul Morodo, "Tierno Galván y otros precursores políticos, *El País,* Madrid, 1987; Elías Díaz,

Pensamiento español en la era de Franco 1939–1975, 2nd ed. (Madrid: Tecnos, 1992), 75.

25. Raul Morodo, "La politización de la opinión pública. El fin de la criptopolítica en España y la polémica sobre la monarquía y la república," in *Iberia New York,* October 15, 1966, 3 quoted in Elías Díaz, *Pensamiento español en la era de Franco,* no. 34, 77.

26. José Antonio Maravall published an article entitled "La idea de cuerpo místico en España antes de Erasmo" in *Estudios del pensamiento español* (Madrid: Ediciones de Cultura Hispánica, 1973): 193–213. This article was first published in the *Boletín de la Cátedra de Derecho Político,* Universidad de Salamanca, núm. 10–12, mayo–octubre, 1956. Maravall explicitly points out the relevance of the somatic metaphor at the end of the 1950s when he writes the article. In the year 1956, a major university crisis led to the replacement of Joaquín Ruiz Giménez as minister of education and further remodeling of the entire cabinet.

27. José Antonio Maravall, *La cultura Del Barroco. Análisis de una estructura histórica* (Barcelona: editorial Ariel, S.A., 1975).

28. Ibid., 132 (my translation).

29. Francisco Franco, "Speech of reply by H.E. the Head of the State to his Eminence the Cardinal Archbishop of Seville, Dr. Bueno Monreal, at the official opening of the Minor Seminary of Our Lady of Belen," in *Church and State in Spain: Speeches During a Journey to Andalusia* (Madrid: Published by OID, 1961), 29–35.

30. John Courtney Murray, *Religious Liberty: Catholic Struggles with Pluralism,* edited by J. Leon Hooper, S.J. (Louisville, KY: Westminster/John Knox Press, 1993) in http://www.georgetown.edu/centers/woodstock/murray/rel-liberty/rl-chap1a.htm

31. The relation of the faithful to the public political affairs is also discussed by the Pope: "The body of the faithful;" according to Leo XIII, "go to Mass on Sunday formally as the faithful, not as the citizenry. The citizenry formally as such offers its due tribute to worship on what are called 'state occasions,' occasions in which organized society gathers, at least in the persons of its representatives." Murray, *Religious Liberty.*

32. Ibid.

33. *Carta Colectiva de los obispos españoles a los de todo el mundo con motivo de la Guerra de España* (Pamplona: Gráficas Bescansa, 1937).

34. "Levantando nuestro corazón al Señor, agradecemos sinceramente a V.E., deseada victoria católica España. Hacemos votos para que este queridísimo país, alcanzada la paz, emprenda con nuevo vigor sus antiguas y cristianas tradiciones, que tan grande le hicieron. Largos sentimientos efusivamente enviamos a Vuestra Excelencia y a todo el noble pueblo español nuestra apostólica bendición." Quoted in María Carmen García-Nieto and Javier M. Donezar, *La España de Franco 1939–1973* (Madrid: Guadiana, 1975), 57; original in Pius XII *ABC* (Madrid: April 2, 1939).

35. In retaliation for the political persecution of the church in Communist Eastern Europe, Pius XII excommunicated the political leaders of Yugoslavia, Hungary, Czechoslovakia, Romania, and Poland. In 1958, the last year of his pontificate, Pius XII issued the encyclical *Ad Apostolorum Principis* on Communism and the Church in China.

36. John Courtney Murray, *Religious Liberty.*

37. Pius XI, "Casti Connubii: Carta Encíclica de su Santidad Pio XI sobre la dignidad del matrimonio," in *El papa habla a los padres de familia* (Madrid: Confederación católica de padres de familia, 1941), 25 (my emphasis).

38. *Mystici Corporis Christi: On the Mystical Body,* June 29, 1943.

39. Ibid.

40. *Mater Et Magistra,* Encyclical Of Pope John XXIII On Christianity And Social Progress, May 15, 1961, http://www.vatican.va/holy_father/john_xxiii/encyclicals/documents.

41. Since 1947 the *Hermandades Obreras de Acción Católica (HOAC Catholic Action Workers Fraternities)* had been the only alternative from the vertical syndicate of Falenge and the first outlet for workers' anti-regime organization as the Second Vatican Council progressed.

42. *Mater Et Magistra,* http://www.vatican.va/holy_father/john_xxiii/encyclicals/documents

43. Norman B. Cooper, *Catholicism and the Franco Regime* (London: Sage Publications, 1975), 28. See also Frances Lannon, *Privilege, Persecution, and Prophecy: The Catholic Church in Spain 1875–1975* (Oxford: Clarendon Press, 1987), chapter 9, "Towards Modernity," 224–58; Audrey Brassloff, *Religion and Politics in Spain: The Spanish Church in Transition* (London: Macmillan Press, 1998), chapter 1, "The Church and the Second Vatican Council," 6–24; William Calahan, *The Catholic Church in Spain, 1875–1998.*

44. Frances Lannon. "Towards Modernity," 224–58; Audrey Brassloff, "The Church and the Second Vatican Council," 6–24.

45. See Joaquín Costa, *Política quirúrgica* (Madrid: Biblioteca "Costa," 1914); Joaquín Costa, *Crísis política de España* (Barcelona: Producciones Editoriales, 1980); Joaquín Costa, *Historia política social: Patria* (Madrid: Aguilar, 1961).

46. Joaquín Costa, *Historia política social: Patria* (Madrid: Aguilar, 1961), 12.

47. José Ortega y Gasset, *Invertebrate Spain* (New York: W. W. Norton & Company, 1937), 62.

48. Ibid., 63.

49. Ibid., 64.

50. See Douglas W. Foard, *The Revolt of the Aesthetes. Ernesto Giménez Caballero and the Origins of Spanish Fascism* (New York: Peter Lang, 1989), 30.

51. José Ortega y Gasset, *España invertebrada* (Madrid: Revista de Occidente, 1959), 153.

52. Douglas W. Foard, *The Revolt of the Aesthetes,* 31.

53. Ibid., 112.

54. Ibid.

55. Ibid., 113.

56. Elana Gomel, "Hard and Wet: Luce Irigaray and the Fascist Body," *Textual Practice* 12, no. 2, 1998, 205. See also Moira Gatens's discussion of the artificial man in "Corporeal Representation in/and the Body Politic" in Katie Conboy, Nadia Medina, and Sarah Stanbury, eds., *Writing on the Body. Female Embodiment and Feminist Theory* (New York: Columbia University Press, 1997), 80–89.

57. See Douglas W. Foard, *The Revolt of the Aesthetes,* 218.

58. "The entire nineteenth century was spent devising machineries of good government. One might just as well seek to discover a machine for thinking or

for loving. No machine has ever managed to produce anything authentic, eternal and exacting such as government; it has always been necessary in the long run to turn to what has, from the beginning of time, been the only apparatus capable of governing men, namely man himself. That is to say: the leader; the hero." José Antonio "Man is the System," in *José Antonio Primo de Rivera. Selected Writings,* ed. Hugh Thomas (London: Jonathan Cape Ltd., 1972), 70.

59. The anti-Semitic European persecutions culminated with the Holocaust and Nazi characterization of the Jew as one whose blood is contaminated and therefore must be exterminated to protect the health of the German nation's body.

60. See also *Política racial del Nuevo Estado* (San Sebastián: Biblioteca España Nueva, 1938); *Divagaciones Intrascendentes* (Valladolid, 1938) or *La locura y la guerra* (Madrid: 1939).

61. Antonio Vallejo Nágera, *Eugenesia de la Hispanidad y regeneración de la raza* (Burgos, Editorial Española, 1937) 7.

62. "Tanto los médicos como los moralistas , sociólogos y políticos. . . . y otros pensadores aplicaron cantáridas que apenas produjeron escozor en la paquidérmica epidermis del cuerpo racial." Nágera, *Eugenesia de la Hispanidad,* 8.

63. "Lástima sería que la generosa sangre vertida en el altar de la Patria no fecundase el venero de virtudes raciales y que en el terreno tan costosamente regado brotasen la maleza y la cizaña. A fin de evitarlo deben reunirse los jóvenes formando grupos de selectos, precisamente de caballeros de la Hispanidad." Nágera, *Eugenesia de la Hispanidad,* 6.

64. "[A]ntes de planear los medios y objetivos de una política nacional eugenésica, deben sacarse conclusions exactas acerca de lo que sabemos de la leyes de la herencia, han de estudiarse las condiciones demográficas del país y tenerse también presentes las ideas culturales que influyen consciente, e inconscientemente sobre el pueblo." Nágera, *Eugenesia de la Hispanidad,* 81.

65. Vallejo Nágera defined the Personality, genotype, Para-type and phenotype as it follows:

> Personality: Set of hereditary dispositions that characterized the individual idiosyncrasy developed and enriched by experience.
>
> Genotype: Refers to the somatic inheritance and includes all the properties found in the gonads that transmit to our descendents.
>
> Para-type: Refers to the totality of the environmental factors that act upon any being during his life.
>
> Phenotype: Is the result of the interaction between the genotype and the Para type. And it is what we first perceive or see when he/she is under observation. Vallejo Nágera, *Eugenesia de la Hispanidad,* 84. See also by Nágera, *Niños y jóvenes anormales* (Madrid: Sociedad de Educación Atenas, S.A., 1941) and *Biotipología* (Barcelona: Editorias Modesto Usón, 1947).

66. "Colígese de las precedentes nociones el camino que debemos seguir en la higiene racial: seleccionar y mejorar los genotipos, e impedir que degeneren los fenotipos." Vallejo Nágera, *Eugenesia de la Hispanidad,* 86.

67. "Regístrase actualmente en todas las naciones un estado colectivo de desequilibrio mental . . . Han desaparecido de la conciencia colectiva las con-

stelaciones Dios, Patria y Familia que tanto influyen sobre la sensibilidad del pueblo. Las ideas religiosas se han desarraigado de las masas sin reemplazarlas por algo que pueda elevar la moral humana Se han pulverizado los conceptos de jerarquía y disciplina social. *Todo el armazón afectivo de la civilización está quebrantado y carcomido.* "Nágera, *Eugenesia de la Hispanidad,* 106 (my emphasis).

68. *Cainismo* refers to the biblical conflict between Cain and Abel.

69. "Creemos, con Splenger, que lo que importa es la raza fuerte que integra el pueblo o nación. Raza fuerte en cuerpo y en espíritu, como tantas veces hemos repetido. Al hablar nosotros de raza nos referimos a la raza hispana, al genotipo ibérico, que en el momento cronológico presente ha experimentado las más variadas mezclas a causa del contacto y relación con otros pueblos. Desde nuestro punto de vista racista [*sic*], nos interesan más los valores espirituales de la raza, que nos permitieron civilizar tierras inmensas influir intelectualmente sobre el mundo. De aquí que nuestro concepto de la raza se confunda con el de la Hispanidad." Nágera, *Eugenesia de la Hispanidad,* 108.

70. The anarchist movement in Catalonia was associated with the extension of neo-Malthusianism. Sexual freedom and social revolution were part of the discourse in the 1930s. See Mary Nash, "El neomaltusianismo anarquista y los conocimientos populares sobre control de natalidad en España," in *Presencia y Protagonismo. Aspectos de la historia de la mujer,* ed. Mary Nash (Barcelona: Ediciones Serbal, 1984), 307–40.

71. Nágera, *Política racial del Nuevo Estado,* 40–41.

72. Ibid., 5–6.

73. Ibid., 46.

74. Ibid., 52.

75. Ibid., 53.

76. Nágera's emphasis, Nágera, *Política racial del Nuevo Estado,* 55.

77. Nágera, *Política racial del Nuevo Estado,* 96–97.

78. Ibid., 32.

79. Nágera, *Eugenesia de la Hispanidad y regeneración de la raza,* 98.

80. "En contestación a su escrito de 10 del actual proponiendo creación de un Gabinete de Investigaciones Psicológicas cuya finalidad principal será investigar las raíces biopsíquicas del marxismo, manifiesto que, de conformidad con su mencionada propuesta, autorizo la creación del mismo,—Los gastos que origine la instación serán sufragados de los generales de esa Inspección, y personal que preste su servicio en el mismo será el médico que voluntaria y gratuitamente se ofrezca para ello, lo que prodrían ser mobilizados si se considera necesario.—Lo que traslado a Vd. Para su conocimiento y efectos, debiendo proponerse los médicos que deben ser militarizados, al efecto de que cuanto antes empiece a funcionar dicho Gabinete." Postal telegram 1,565 August 23, 1938 quoted in Ricard Vinyes Ribas, "Construyendo a Caín. Diagnosis y terapia del disidente: Las investigaciones psiquiátricas militares de Antonio Vallejo Nágera con presas y presos políticos," in *Ayer* 44 (2001): 227–50 (228).

81. Vinyes Ribas, "Construyendo a Caín." p. 229.

82. "Necesitamos emprender denodada lucha higiénica contra los gérmenes morbosos que carcomen la raza hispana para conducirla a la más abyecta de las degeneraciones. No se trata de volver alos valores humanos del siglo XV y XVI pura y simplemente. Trátase de reincorporarlos a la conducta del pueblo, a los fines de sanear moralmente el medio ambiente." Nágera, *Eugenesia de la Hispanidad,* 109–10.

83. Instituto Nacional de Estadística, *Anuario Estadístico de España,* (Madrid: INE, 1960), 475.

84. *Anuario Estadistico de España,* 1960. Quoted in Jordi Gracia García and Miguel Angel Ruiz Carnicer, *La España de Franco (1939–1975) Cultura y vida cotidiana.* (Madrid: Editorial Síntesis, 2001), 206–7.

85. Instituto Nacional de Estadística, *Anuario Estadístico de España,* "Morbilidad," 1964, 669–70.

86. Jordi Gracia García and Miguel Angel Ruiz Carnicer, *La España de Franco (1939–1975),* 207.

87. Miguel Juárez and Demetrio Casado, eds., *V Informe sobre la situación social en España. Sociedad para todos en el año 2000* (Madrid: Cáritas Española, 1994), 6–7.

88. Miguel Juárez and Demetrio Casado, eds., *V Informe sobre la situación social en España,* 6.

89. FOESSA published four major sociological reports: 1966, 1970, 1976, and 1980–83.

90. Brenan, *The Face of Spain,* 76.

91. Fundación FOESSA, *Informe Sociológico sobre la situación social de España* (Madrid: Editorial de Euroamérica, 1966), 74.

92. Ibid., 76.

93. Ibid., 77.

94. Ibid.

95. Fundación FOESSA, *Estudios Sociológicos sobre la situación social de España 1975* (Madrid: Editorial de Euroamérica, 1976), XX.

96. Ibid.

97. Ibid., XXI.

98. Ibid.

99. Ibid.

100. Ibid., XXII.

101. Preston, *Franco: A Biography* (London: Routledge, 1994), 323.

Chapter 2. Women's True Nature

1. Federico García Lorca, *The House of Bernarda Alba: A Drama about Women in the Villages of Spain* adapted to English by Emily Mann (New York: Dramatist's Play Service) 1999, 10.

2. Aurora G. Morcillo, *True Catholic Womanhood.*

3. The nationalization of women's bodies became part of the Falangist Women's Section in charge of physical education as a means to prepare Spanish women physically for their motherly duties. We will discuss the law of physical education in chapter 5.

4. Loci communes or commonplaces about women's nature were dictums privileged in different disciplines during the sixteenth and seventeenth centuries based on notions rooted in Aristotelian beliefs and Scholasticism that were fundamentally misogynistic. These opinions were frequently quoted by scholars of different disciplines. See Ian Maclean, *The Renaissance Notion of Woman: A Study in the Fortunes of Scholasticism and Medical Science in European Intellectual Life.* Cambridge Monographs on the History of Medicine (Cambridge: Cambridge University Press, 1995) 4.

5. Scholars of the early modern period like Mary Elizabeth Perry and Georgina Dopico Black have illustrated that the monarchy's efforts to stabilize the gender order often occurred in moments of political and social or economic upheaval. This is certainly the case for the Francoist regime in the immediate postwar first and then with the advent of consumerism. See Mary Elizabeth Perry, *Gender and Disorder in Early Modern Seville* (Princeton, NJ: Princeton University Press, 1990) and *The Handless Maiden: Moriscos and the Politics of Religion in Early Modern Spain (Jews, Christians, and Muslims from the Ancient to the Modern World)* (Princeton, NJ: Princeton University Press, 2006); Georgina Dopico Black, *Perfect Wives, Other Women: Adultery and Inquisition in Early Modern Spain* (Durham, NC: Duke University Press, 2001). These efforts to stabilize gender relations were also demonstrated in Mary Louise Robert's writing about post World War I France in her book *Civilization without Sexes: Reconstructing Gender in Postwar France, 1917–1927,* Women in Culture and Society Series, (Chicago: University of Chicago Press, 1994).

6. Gregory S. Hutcheson and Josiah Blackmore, eds., *Queer Iberia. Sexualities, Cultures, and Crossings from the Middle Ages to the Renaissance* (Durham, NC: Duke University Press, 1999), 1.

7. This imposition culminated with the control of dissent through the establishment of the Spanish Inquisition, and the expulsion and forced conversion of Muslims and Jews.

8. Castro was a strong supporter of the Spanish Republic when it was established in 1931, serving as its ambassador to Germany and also in its Council of Public Instruction and its Division of Cultural Relations. He left Spain when Franco rose to power in 1937 and, after teaching at the Universities of Wisconsin and Texas, accepted a call to Princeton in 1940. Castro was regarded as one of the world's most distinguished Hispanists. His magnum opus, *Spain in Her History* (1948), was considered a notable innovation in modern Spanish historiography. Written in Spanish, this work was later translated into English, Italian, German, French, and Japanese. He also earned international recognition as a teacher, serving as visiting professor at universities in Argentina, Chile, Mexico, Cuba, Puerto Rico, Germany, and throughout the United States.

9. For example, it would be through the schools of translation of Toledo that Europe became familiar with Aristotle's work by way of Averroes in the twelfth century.

10. Gregory S. Hutcheson and Josiah Blackmore, eds. *Queer Iberia,* 3.

11. The new educational system aspired to forge true Catholic womanhood by appealing to Spanish historical tradition. First, the regime sought to revive a sixteenth-century devotion to saintly figures—such as Santa Teresa de Jesús or the Virgin del Pilar—and hoped to repopularize Renaissance treatises on the character and proper education of women by Fray Luis de León and Luis Vives. Second, the Francoist official discourse on women rested on the traditional doctrine of the Catholic Church as prescribed in Pius XI's encyclicals *Divini Illius Magistri* (1929) and *Casti connubii* (1930). Finally, the Female Section was entrusted with the task of preserving Catholic values among Spanish women. See chapter 2 in Morcillo, *True Catholic Womanhood.*

12. On María de Zayas see: Margaret Rich Greer, *María de Zayas Tells Baroque Tales of Love and the Cruelty of Men* (University Park: Pennsylvania State University Press, 2000); Marina S. Brownlee, *The Cultural Labyrinth of*

María de Zayas (Philadelphia: University of Pennsylvania Press, 2000); and Lisa Volendorf, *Reclaiming the Body: María de Zayas's Early Modern Feminism* (Chapel Hill: University of North Carolina Press, 2001).

13. Charles Fantazzi, ed., *Juan Luis Vives: The Instruction of a Christian Woman: A Sixteenth-Century Manual,* (Chicago: The University of Chicago Press, 2000), 3.

14. See Carolyn Walker-Bynum, *Fragmentation and Redemption. Essays on Gender and the Human Body in Medieval Religion* (New York: Zone Books, 1992).

15. "On Virginity," in *Juan Luis Vives. The Instruction of a Christian Woman,* ed. Charles Fantazzi, 80.

16. Ibid.

17. Ibid., 85.

18. "How the Young Woman Will Treat Her Body," in *Juan Luis Vives. The Instruction of a Christian Woman,* ed. Charles Fantazzi, 87.

19. Ibid.

20. "How the Young Woman Will Treat Her Body" in *Juan Luis Vives. The Instruction of a Christian Woman.* ed. Charles Fantazzi, 89. See also, Carolyn Walker-Bynum, *Holy Feast, Holy Fast.*

21. "How the Young Woman Will Treat Her Body" in *Juan Luis Vives: The Instruction of a Christian Woman.* ed. Charles Fantazzi, 90.

22. Ibid., 92.

23. Ibid., 93.

24. "On Adornment" in *Juan Luis Vives. The Instruction of a Christian Woman,* ed. Charles Fantazzi, 95.

25. Ibid., 96. When referring to the adornments of the married woman Vives proclaims: "This like everything else, should depend on the wishes and character of the husband" ibid., 236.

26. "On Seeking a Spouse" in *Juan Luis Vives. The Instruction of a Christian Woman,* ed. Charles Fantazzi, 161.

27. Michael Solomon, *The Literature of Misogyny in Medieval Spain. The Arcipreste de Talavera and the Spill.* (Cambridge: Cambridge University Press, 1997). See also Ian Maclean, *The Renaissance Notion of Woman;* Margaret W. Ferguson, Maureen Quilligan, and Nancy J. Vickers, eds., *Re-writing the Renaissance. Discourses of Sexual Difference in Early Modern Europe* (The University of Chicago Press, 1986); Claudio Da Soller, "The Beautiful Woman in Medieval Iberia: Rhetoric, Cosmetics, and Evolution" (PhD diss., University of Missouri-Columbia, July 2005).

28. Maria de Zayas, *Desengaños amorosos,* Alicia Yllera, ed. (Madrid: Cátedra, 1993), 222.

29. Ibid., 48.

30. Ibid., 266.

31. Marina S. Brownlee, *The Cultural Labyrinth of María de Zayas* (Philadelphia: University of Pennsylvania Press, 2000), 12–13.

32. In 1929 Ludwig Pfandl says, "Can there be anything more gross and obscene, more no aesthetic and repulsive, than a woman who writes lascivious, dirty, sadistic and morally corrupt stories?" quoted in Marina S. Brownlee, *The Cultural Labyrinth of María de Zayas,* 19. Brownlee also points out the popularity at the time of the martyrologies and tabloid literature. "This fascination with goriness as an expression of the baroque ethos so evident in the plastic arts as well as on the stage." 19.

33. Marina S. Brownlee, *The Cultural Labyrinth of María de Zayas,* 19.

34. In 1583 Fray Luis de León published the *Perfect Married Lady* and Luis Vives wrote for Mary Tudor *The Instruction of the Christian Woman* in 1523.

35. Victoria Sau, Benito Feijóo, *Defensa de la Mujer* (Barcelona: Icaria, 1997) ed., 18. See also on the Enlightenment Rebecca Haidt, *Embodying Enlightenment. Knowing the Body in Eighteenth-Century Spanish Literature and Culture* (St. Martin's Press, 1998).

36. Benito Feijóo, *Defensa de la Mujer,* 19.

37. Ibid., 20.

38. Ibid.

39. Ibid., 22.

40. Luis Vives, *The Instruction of the Christian Woman* (1523). To guide the education of Mary, daughter of Catherine of Aragon and Henry VIII of England, this book was translated into different languages and became the basic guide to the instruction of Christian ladies in Europe, whose education was to be designed to protect their chastity. Fray Luis de León, in *La Perfecta Casada* (1583), instructed newlyweds in the sanctity of marriage and the value of chastity within it. See also Aurora Morcillo, *True Catholic Womanhood.*

41. Benito Feijóo, *Defensa de la Mujer,* 24.

42. Ibid., 40.

43. José Alvarez Junco, *Mater Dolorosa. La idea de España en el siglo XIX* (Madrid: Taurus, 2001). See also Carlos Serrano, *El nacimiento de Carmen. Símbolos, mitos y nación* (Madrid: Taurus, 1999) and Carlos Serrano, ed., *Nations en quêde passé. La peninsula ibérique (XIXe–XXe)* (Paris: Université de Paris-Sorbonne, 2000); and Lou Charnon-Deutsch, *Fictions of the Feminine in the Nineteenth Century Spanish Press* (University Park: Pensylvannia State University Press, 2000).

44. In fact this conflict is known as the Peninsular War in Anglo-Saxon historiography.

45. Benedict Anderson, *Imagined Communities* (London: Verso, 1983). The definition of nation that Anderson proposes in his book is "It is an imagined political community—and imagined as both inherently limited and sovereign," 6. Certainly the idea of an imagined political community is utilized by Alvarez Junco in his analysis of the creation of the idea of Spain in the imagination of Spaniards, a group of people that won't be able to know each other personally but who considered themselves part of the same community.

46. The "science" of phrenology for example, proposed that the structure of the skull, especially the jaw formation and facial angles, revealed the position of various races on the evolutionary scale, and a debate raged on whether there had been one creation for all mankind (monogenism) or several (polygenism).

47. Cesare Lombroso and G. Ferrero, *La femme criminelle et la prostituée* (París, 1896) Foucault's analysis of modernity calls attention to the epistemological shift in scientific discourses with the development of the pathological versus the normal.

48. In their 1973 essay "The Female Animal: Medical and Ideological Views of Woman and her Role in Nineteenth-Century America" Carroll Smith-Rosenberg and Charles Rosenberg demonstrated the connection between social change and social stress in nineteenth-century America. Carroll Smith-Rosenberg and Charles Rosenberg, "The Female Animal: Medical and Ideological Views of Woman and Her Role in Nineteenth-Century America," *The Journal of American History* 60, no. 2 (Sept., 1973): 332–56. This article was translated into Span-

ish and published in Mary Nash, ed., *Presencia y Protagonismo. Aspectos de la historia de la mujer* (Barcelona: Ediciones del Serbal, 1984), 342–73.

49. Geraldine Scanlon, *La polémica feminista en la España contemporánea (1868–1974)* (Madrid: Siglo XXI, 1976), 163.

50. Carmen the Burgos Seguí, *La inferioridad mental de la mujer,* quoted in Scanlon, *La polémica feminista en la España,* 166.

51. A. Jimeno, *La mujer,* quoted in Scanlon, *La polémica feminista en la España,* 166.

52. The works of: Urbano González Serrano, *Estudios psicológicos* (Madrid, 1892) and N. Mariscal y García, *Ensayo de una higiene de la inteligencia* (Madrid, 1898) are two examples of this mentality.

53. Quoted in Scanlon, *La polémica feminista en la España,* 174–75.

54. "Nótese por lo común la mujer, de mas baja estatura que el hombre, no tiene ni su vigor físico ni su poder intellectual. Las formas de la mujer son mas redondeadas y más trabajadas (. . .) Las Mujeres no tienen barba, lo cual les da una especie de juvenil hechizo; su voz llena de armonía y de encantamiento, su paso acompasado, sus movimientos lánguidos y llenos de gracia; todo ha sido en ella hecho para seducir, para complacer, para consolar, *pero no para mandar*" (my translation and emphasis). J. M. Otero, "Breves consideraciones fisiológicas diferenciales entre la mujer y el hombre" in *Siglo Médico,* (Madrid 13, 1866, 821), quoted in Jesús Castellanos, Isabel Jiménez Lucena, and María José Ruiz Somavilla, "La ciencia médica en el siglo XIX como instrumento de reafirmación ideological: la defensa de la desigualdad de la mujer a través de la patología femenina,." in *La Mujer en Andalucia. Primer Encuentro Interdisciplinar de Estudios de la mujer* (Granada: Colección Feminae, Universidad de Granada, 1988), 883.

55. "La especie de acción que el utero ejerce u opera en la constitución de la mujer es por lo menos tan esencial, como la que opera el sistema nervioso al que parece ligado." J. M. Otero, " Es la mujer un ser aparte de la humanidad? *Siglo Médico* (Madrid, 14 1867, 131), quoted in Jesús Castellanos, Isabel Jiménez Lucena, and María José Ruiz Somavilla, "La ciencia médica en el siglo XIX," 882.

56. Cocepción Arenal, *La mujer del porvenir,* http://www.cervantesvirtual.com/servlet/SirveObras/01372731966804617200802/p0000001.htm#I_4_

57. Feminist scholars Concha Fagoaga and Paloma Saavedra reedited Campoamor's work in 1981 to commemorate the historical achievement for women accomplished by Clara Campoamor who died in exile in 1972.

58. Margarita Nelken, "Divagaciones emancipadoras y primaverales," *La moda elegante,* mayo, 1923, 130. Quoted in Elizabeth Munson, "Walking on the Periphery: Gender and the Discourse of Modernization" *Journal of Social History* 36, no. 1 (2002): 63–75.

59. Munson, "Walking on the Periphery, 70.

60. José Ortega y Gasset, *Estudios sobre el amor* (Madrid: Revista de Occidente, 1966), 17.

61. Ibid., 25.

62. Ibid.

63. Ibid., 29.

64. Ibid., 39–40.

65. Roberto Nóvoa Santos, "La posición biológica de la mujer," in *La mujer, nuestro sexto sentido y otros esbozos* (Madrid: Biblioteca Nueva, 1929), 15.

66. Gregorio Marañón, *Ensayos sobre la vida sexual* (Madrid: Espasa Calpe, 1951). This collection of essays first published in 1926 was a second "very thoroughly revised edition"—as the cover reads. Marañón's writings on sexuality included four essays: "Sexo, trabajo y deporte"; "Maternidad y feminismo"; "Educación sexual y diferenciación sexual"; "Amor, conveniencia y eugenesia."

67. Gregorio Marañón, *Ensayos sobre la vida sexual,* 144.

68. Gregorio Marañón, "Literatura Sexual," in *Obras Completas* (Madrid: Espasa Calpe, 1968), 32.

69. Gregorio Marañón "Breve ensayo sobre la intersexualidad en la clínica" (1927) in *Obras Completas,* 48.

70. Gregorio Marañón "Medicina nueva, moral nueva" (1927), 63.

71. Order of February 9, 1955, "Cuestionarios de Formación del Espíritu Nacional, educación física y escuelas del hogar, que han de cursar las alumnas de bachillerato," *B.O.E.* July 28, 1955, 4625–26.

72. See Morcillo, *True Catholic Womanhood,* 66–70.

73. Carmen Martín Gaite, *The Backroom* (San Francisco: City Lights Books, 2000), 152. The Spanish version *El cuarto de Atrás* was first published in 1978.

74. Ibid., 154–56.

75. Lucia Graves, *A Woman Unknown. Voices from a Spanish Life.* (Washington D.C.: Counterpoint, 2000), 97.

76. Order of February 9, 1955, "Cuestionarios de Formación del Espíritu Nacional," *B.O.E.,* 4627.

77. Lucía Graves, *A Woman Unknown,* 73.

78. Ibid., 66.

79. Ibid., 74.

80. Order of February 9, 1955, 4627.

81. Order of February 9, 1955, 4624–25.

82. Order of February 9, 1955, 4627.

83. Martín Gaite, *The Backroom,* 89.

84. Lucía Graves, *A Woman Unknown,* 148. Robert Graves moved permanently to Majorca in 1946 with his family. Lucia Graves was only three years old. He had lived previously in Spain like Gerald Brenan but both British writers left Spain during the Spanish Civil War to return in the 1940s and settle indefinitely, one in Majorca and the other in Andalusia. Graves wrote in 1953 that he decided on Majorca by recommendation of Gertrude Stein. See Robert Graves, *Majorca Observed* (London: Cassel & Company Ltd., 1965), 8.

85. Richard Wright, *Pagan Spain,* 70.

86. Ibid., 227–28.

87. Ibid., 229–30.

88. Bart McDowell and Albert Moldvay, "The Changing Face of Spain," *National Geographic* 127, no. 3 (March 1965): 297.

89. On the old constraints the Church placed on morality by controlling women's bodies and dress code see Frances Lannon, "Los cuerpos de las mujeres y el cuerpo político: Autoridades e identidades en conflicto en España durante las décadas de 1920 y 1930," *Historia Social,* no. 35, (1999): 65–80.

90. Lucia Graves, *A Woman Unknown,* 151.

91. Ibid., 156.

92. Ibid., 157.

93. "Los grandes problemas de España. Declaraciones de Franco a don Manuel Aznar. 1 enero 1939," in *La España de Franco 1939–1973. Bases docu-*

mentales de la España contemporánea vol. XI (Madrid: Guadiana publicaciones, 1975), María Carmen García-Nieto and Javier M. Donezar, 50–51.

94. Aurora G. Morcillo, *True Catholic Womanhood.*

95. Moira Gatens, "Toward a Feminist Philosophy of the Body," in *Imaginary Bodies. Ethics, Power, and Corporeality* (Rutledge: New York, 1996), 49.

96. Michel Foucault, "Security, Territory and Population," in *Michel Foucault. Ethics, Subjectivity, and Truth,* edited Paul Rabinow, *Essential Works of Foucault, 1954–1984, vol. I* (New York: New Press, 1994), 67–68.

97. Richard Wright, *Pagan Spain,* 220–22.

Chapter 3. Fallen Women

Some of the information in this chapter has been published. See Aurora G. Morcillo, "Walls of Flesh. Spanish Postwar Reconstruction and Public Morality," *Bulletin of Spanish Studies* 84, no. 6 (2007): 737–758.

1. Paco Villar, *Historia y Leyenda del Barrio Chino. 1900–1992 Crónica y documentos de los bajos fondos de Barcelona* (Barcelona: Edicons La Campana, 1996), 203.

2. See Manuel Vázquez Montalbán, *Crónica Sentimental de España* (Barcelona: Grijalbo, 1998); Martín de la Plaza, *Conchita Piquer* (Madrid: Alianza Editorial, 2001).

3. *Ojos verdes* (*Green Eyes*), for example, tells of the daily routines of those women who practiced prostitution in the legal public houses.

OJOS VERDES / Green Eyes
Apoyá en er *quisio* de la *mansebía* / *Reclined on the windowsill of the bawdyhouse*
miraba *ensenderse* la noche de mayo; / I looked how a night in May would light up
pasaban los hombres y yo sonreía / men passed by and I smiled
hasta que a mi puerta paraste el caballo. / until you stopped your horse at my doorstep
"Serrana, ¿me das candela?" / Lovely, Do you have a light?
Y yo te dije: "Gaché, / And I told you "Chap"
ven y tómala en mis labios / come and get it from my lips
que yo fuego te daré" / That I will give you fire."
Dejaste *er* caballo / You left the horse
y lumbre te di, / and fire I gave you
y fueron dos verdes luceros de mayo / and two green May stars were
tus ojos *pa* mí. / your eyes for me

4. ***TATUAJE / TATTOO***

Él vino en un barco de nombre extranjero, / He came in a ship with a foreign name,
lo encontré en el puerto un anochecer / I met him in the harbor at dusk
cuando el blanco faro sobre los veleros / when the white beacon over the sailboats
su beso de plata dejaba caer. / a silver kiss let it fall

Era hermoso y rubio como la cerveza; / He was handsome and blonde like beer
el pecho tatuado con un corazón. / His chest tattooed with a heart
En su voz amarga había la tristeza, / In his bitter voice there was the sadness
doliente y cansada, del acordeón. / pain and exhaustion of the accordion
Y entre dos copas de aguardiente / And with two glasses of anisette
sobre el manchado mostrador / on a dirty counter
él fue contándome entre dientes / he told me through his teeth
la vieja historia de su amor: / the old story of his love

In the study *La mala vida in Madrid* (1901) Bernaldo Quirós and Llamas de Aguilaniedo studied the extended practice of tattooing among the lower classes. There were two reasons behind the practice according to Bernaldo and Llamas: first, ornamental and second, the remembrance of personal experiences, mainly love and/or vengeance that only could be marked on the body. Of a total of 645 criminals studied 52 were tattooed.

"Out of these 52 subjects, 23 have one tattoo, 14 have two, 10 have three, 3 have four and finally one have a total of five tattoos in different parts of their bodies. Hence there are 103 tattoos distributed as follows: In the right arm 9; in the left arm 28; in the right forearm 24; in the left forearm 27; in the right wrist 1; in the left wrist 2; in the left middle finger 1; in the chest 3; in the right thigh 5; in the left thigh 1; in the penis one." The authors explained the higher number of tattoos on left limbs due to self-tattooing. Only six tattoos in the study were blue and red the rest of them were monochromatic in blue. The themes represented in the tattoos included 26 love related images mostly a heart, a woman figure either dressed or naked, and in three instances what the authors declared to be obscene images. There were thirteen tattoos that represented religious fervor, a cross or a representation of the Virgin; seven were caricatures, either religious or political: a bishop, a soldier. According to the authors, the "normal" practice in an advanced rather than a primitive society is to place the ornamental or commemorative marks on the clothes people wear rather than on their skin. "Memories are kept in our mind or put down onto a memoir book or a diary. But in the underworld the symbols of adornment or commemoration are marks on the flesh, that highlights one's own value to himself and others. Tattooing was also a practice extended among lovers who " to prove their love for each other would tattoo each other's initials on their flesh, spilling of blood included, to make their feelings sublime in the eyes of the other. *La mala vida en Madrid,* 86–88.

5. Georgina Dopico Black takes an interesting look at the intersection in early modern Spain of three public female bodies: the saint's, the prostitute's, and the actress's. An explanation of this work is valuable here because Dopico Black's categorization is replicated during the Francoist and immediate post-Franco eras. It was a religious woman, Magdalena de San Gerónimo, probably a nun or a Magdalen herself, who worked extensively with prostitutes in the late 1500s. In 1588 Magdalena de San Gerónimo administered the Casa Pía de Arrepentidas de Santa María Magdalena in Valladolid (Pious House for Repentant Women of Mary Magdalene), a halfway house for repentant prostitutes. She established a Patronato (Foundation) in 1605. In her will she bequeathed her most precious possession, a "relic collection," and secured royal privileges and financial security for this shelter. Magdalena de San Gerónimo acquired her

relics collection during her travels to France and the Low Countries. The collection included the bodies of two of the eleven thousand virgins who accompanied Saint Ursula to martyrdom in the city of Köln, (Germany) and the heads of at least another twenty. Magdalena worked not only in establishing shelters to reform prostitutes and women's prisons but also tended to the poor and soldiers who suffered from syphilis. These sinners like her rescued prostitutes were offered the opportunity to redeem themselves through penance and contrition.

Phillip II asked her to run the Galera de Santa Isabel, a prison for women in Madrid. In 1608 she wrote *Razón y forma de la galera y casa real que el Rey, Nuestro Señor, manda hacer en estos reinos para castigo de las mujeres vagantes, y ladronas, alcahuetas, hechiceras, y otras semejantes.* In this work she requested royal support to establish a prison for "bad women." This proposal is extremely significant because it developed a gender specific penitentiary system well before institutions for private punishment expanded throughout Europe. With this venture Magdalena de San Geronimo inaugurated the move from public corporal punishment to incarceration. In the first chapter of her memorial she discussed "de la importancia y necesidad de esta Galera" (about the importance and need of this galley) delineating the different kinds of "bad women" that existed. According to Magdalena they were to blame for the fast "deteriorating health of Spain." The second and third chapters explain in detail how to build, furnish, and administer the prison for women. Recommendations include diet and daily activities so the women would not be idle. The sacrament of penance became a crucial dogma in the Council of Trent era. The fourth and fifth chapters in Magdalena de San Gerónimo's proposal explain the benefits this endeavor would bring to the country: "saving the nation, saving money, saving bodies, and saving souls." The judges and law enforcement entities had to be ready to root out the "infection that is spreading, unchecked, throughout the nation." Magdalena de San Gerónimo's request for a galley to heal the social body from the infection spread by prostitutes represents an early example of modern technologies of control imposed on the political anatomy. Her consideration of prostitution as a public health and political issue rather than simply a moral religious one was also modern. Both of these shifts toward modernity dawning in the seventeenth century were recaptured and revitalized under Francoism. Georgina Dopico Black, "Public Bodies, private parts: The Virgins and Magdalens of Magdalena de San Gerónimo," *Journal of Spanish Cultural Studies* 2, no. 1 (2001): 81–96.

6. According to the Foundation for the Protection of Women, the number of suicides in Spain rose from 1,787 in 1934 to 3,091 in 1941, while crimes for murder and assault declined from 18,952 to 15,186. There were however significantly more crimes for theft going from 50,232 in 1934 to 67,977 in 1941, a clear indicator of the extreme misery of postwar conditions. Junta Nacional Secretaría Técnica, *Informe sobre la moralidad pública en España* (Madrid: Patronato de Proteccion de la Mujer, 1943), 56.

7. "Memoria elevada al Gobierno Nacional en la solemne apertura de Tribunales el día 15 de septiembre de 1942, por el Fiscal del Tribunal Supremo, Blas Pérez González." Quoted in *Informe sobre la moralidad pública,* 57–58.

8. Ibid.

9. Gerald Brenan, *The Face of Spain* (Harmonsworth, Middlesex: Penguin Books, 1950), 81.

10. Ibid.

11. Ibid., 71.

12. Ibid., 28.

13. *Informe sobre la moralidad pública,* 13.

14. Saint Augustine, *De Ordine, libro 2, capítulo 4,núm. 11–12,* quoted in Junta Nacional Secretaría Técnica, *Informe sobre la moralidad pública en España* (Madrid: Patronato de Proteccion de la Mujer, 1943), 215. Some Seville Ordinances dating from the fourteenth century decreed the brothel to be the proper place for those women who "did not want to be good and chaste and want to sell their bodies." During the Counter-Reformation brothels became subject to tighter public supervision. As Mary Elizabeth Perry points out: "Moralists as well as pragmatists appeared to believe that social order in Counter-Reformation Spain required women enclosed under male supervision. Perry, "Magdalens and Jezebels," 139.

15. Mary Elizabeth Perry and Anne Cruz, eds., *Culture and Control in Counter-Reformation Spain* (University of Minnesota Press, 1992), ix–xxiii.

16. Mary Elizabeth Perry, "Magdalens and Jezebels in Counter-Reformation Spain," in *Culture and Control in Counter-Reformation Spain,* ed. Mary Elizabeth Perry and Anne Cruz, 124.

17. Magdalene houses were founded in the 1300s and flourished during the Counter-Reformation also. These prisonlike shelters for repentant prostitutes spread throughout Spain and were found in Malaga, Valencia, and Zaragoza. They started as convents and eventually attracted not only penitent whores but young women with religious vocation.

18. Dopico Black proposes in her article an interesting analysis of the intersection of three bodies in Magdalena de San Gerónimo's story: the prostitute's body, the virgin's body, and the actress's body. Magdalena traded in relics using the body parts of virgins' relics in exchange for official protection of her Repentants' House. At the same time the state will collect a tax imposed in the comedy houses where the actress's body is exposed, a body that incarnates the synthesis of the whore and the virgin on the stage. In the same way we might analyze the intersection of three bodies under Francoist Spain. The virginal wife's body protected by the openness of the prostitute's body and the actress body turning into the the trademark of the transition to democracy when a wave of eroticism invaded the entertainment industry and the press.

The subtext linking these three female typologies is the myth of the Magdalene. "Not unlike the actresses who portrayed her, Magdalene joins the narratives of prostitute and virgin, of saint and sinner—*beata peccatrix*—both of which are scripted upon her body, a body destined to become among the most valuable relics of the Roman Catholic Church. More important, perhaps, in terms of her role within early modern religiosity, Magdalen's penance constituted a flagrant act of self-refashioning, as did the virtual repetition of that act by the tens of thausands of *arrepentidas.*" Georgina Dopico Black, "Public Bodies, Private Parts," 88.

19. The scientific and clinical assessment of prostitution was the object of much debate and study throughout the nineteenth century. In the early 1800s two kinds of institutions that sought to contain prostitution coexisted in Spain: the penal Magdalene houses established by religious orders in the sixteenth century and modern hospitals or clinics to fight venereal disease. Discipline was very severe in the Magdalene houses. Former prostitutes followed a harsh regimen of work and prayer to cleanse their souls of sins.

20. In 1844 Mariano Cubí's *Sistema de Frenología* (*Phrenology System*) introduced in Spain the then revolutionary studies on phrenology developed in France by Gall and Spurzheim. According to Cubí's theory, "genesic desire" resided in the skull of prostitutes, and was the base to explain their behavior. In the last third of the 1800s the new Italian school of criminal anthropology and the theories of Cesare Lombroso had a great impact in Spain as well. Lombroso's ideas about prostitution appeared in several publications: "Moral Imbecility in the Female Thief and Prostitute" (1881) and, in collaboration with Ferrero, *The Criminal Woman, the Prostitute and the Normal Woman* (1893). According to Lombroso "prostitution is the equivalent of criminality for women, in other words, it is the specific way in which degeneration manifests itself in women. Lombroso pointed out what he called atavistic anomalies in the prostitute's body, comparing them with African women such as those known at the time as Hottentots. Early menstruation, low fertility and low mortality rates were defined by Lombroso as atavistic anomalies present in the prostitute's physiological profile. Prostitutes were subjected to several anthropometric studies published in the 1880s in the Italian scientific journal *Archivio di psichiatria, antropoligia criminale e scienze penali.* Spanish scientists followed in the steps of the Italian school and conducted studies about prostitution that included statistical data as well as anthropometric profiles. Manuel Carboneres studied prostitution in Valencia in his book *Picaronas y alcahuetes* (1876); Prudencio Sereñana y Partagás studied Barcelona in *La prostitución en la ciudad de Barcelona* (1882); Romualdo González Fragoso examined the issue in the urban areas in his work *La prostitución en las grandes ciudades* (1887). Madrid was the object of multiple studies: Gil Mestre studied delinquency in *Los malhechores de Madrid* (1889); Rafael Eslava investigated prostitution in his book *La prostitución en Madrid. Apuntes para un estudio sociológico* (1900) and nine years later Antonio Navarro Fernández published *La prostitución en la villa de Madrid.* Aurora Rivière Gómez, *"Caídas, Miserables, Degeneradas." Estudios sobre la Prostitución en el siglo XIX* (Madrid: Dirección General de la Mujer, 1994), 15. In 1876 Lombroso published *L'uomo delinquente,* putting forward the theory of the "born criminal" as an individual that could be identified through physiognomic measurements.

21. Official propaganda stated that the purpose of the military uprising in 1936 had been to regenerate and purify the motherland's sick body. As Michael Richards has pointed out, the immediate postwar years meant a social and political quarantine orchestrated from the state's repressive apparatus. Michael Richards, *Un tiempo de silencio. La Guerra civil y la cultura de la represión en la España de Franco, 1936–1945* (Barcelona: Crítica, 1998). David Rousse coined the term in the late 1940s with his work *L'Univers Concentrionaire.* See also Ricard Vinyes, "El universo penitenciario durante el franquismo" in *Una imensa prisión. Los campos de concentración y las prisiones durante la Guerra civil y el franquismo,* ed. C. Molinero, M. Sala, and J. Sobrequés, (Barcelona: Crítica Contrastes, 2003), 155–75, and Angela Cenarro, "La institucionalización del universo penitenciario franquista" in *Una imensa prisión,* ed. C. Molinero, M. Sala and J. Sobrequés, 133–54.

22. Ricard Vinyes, "El universo penitenciario durante el franquismo," in *Una imensa prisión. Los campos de concentración y las prisiones durante la Guerra civil y el franquismo,* ed. C. Molinero, M. Sala and J. Sobrequés eds. (Barcelona: Crítica Contrastes, 2003), 155–75.

23. *Informe sobre la moralidad pública,* 13.

24. Gerald Brenan, *The Face of Spain* (Harmondsworth, Middlesex: Penguin Travel Library, 1965), 24.

25. Ibid.

26. Ibid., 27.

27. Ibid.

28. Ibid., 29.

29. Ibid., 20.

30. Ibid., 19.

31. The Foundation's organization of women's detention centers followed the model of the Royal Foundation for the Repression of the White Slavery establish in 1902. The Spanish government established by decree of July 11, 1902, the *Patronato Real para la Represión de la Trata de Blancas* (The Royal Foundation for the Repression of White Women Trafficking) and renewed the tolerance and regimentation of prostitution in the country. The Royal Foundation was a markedly religious, paternalistic, and aristocratic state institution. A new state apparatus of repression and control emerged in the early twentieth century to fight international sexual slave trade. The Second Republic tried to resolve sex trade by declaring prostitution illegal in 1935. But the repressive police apparatus of regulation was restored with the Francoist victory in the civil war 1936–39 and further strengthened with the establishment of the *Patronato de Protección de la Mujer* (Foundation for the Protection of Women) that replaced in 1941 the Royal Foundation for the Repression of White Women Trafficking.

32. Nineteenth-century Magdalene houses spread rapidly in Catholic countries, especially Ireland and Spain. Several orders of nuns were founded whose only purpose was to redeem prostitutes and fallen women in general. The Sisters Adoratrices, Slaves of the Sacred Sacrament, and of Charity were founded with papal approval in Madrid on February 3, 1856, by María Micaela of the Holy Sacrament with the specific purpose of rehabilitating fallen adolescent girls and women and to guard those in grave risk of falling into sin.

The order of the Sisters Oblates of the Holy Redeemer was established on June 1, 1864, in Ciempozuelos, Madrid. Their sole purpose was to shelter prostitutes, women who wanted to abandon the sex work world but due to social, economic, and political circumstances in late nineteenth-century Spain could not do it on their own. The founders were Benedictine Father José Mª Benito Serra, bishop of Daulia who worked in Madrid and discovered the hardship of prostitution in the hospital of San Juan de Dios, and Antonia Mª De Oviedo Y Schönthal, who had been the governess of queen Mª Cristina de Borbón's daughters. By 1870 Pope Leo XIII defined the order as a "Congregation for redemption." In 1943 the Oblatas conducted most of the redemption of the fallen women including those the Foundation sent their way. There were four sites in Madrid: Alacuas, Carabanchel, Ciempozuelos, and Victoria.

The Congregation of Our Lady of Charity and the Good Shepherd was founded by María Eufracia Pelletier on July 31, 1829, in Anger, France. It became a most important order for the reeducation and rehabilitation of fallen women in Spain and other European countries. This order focused on the religious and moral aspects of prostitution, but it also recognized prostitution as a critical public health concern. The prostitute's sick body incarnated at once sinful human nature and self-effacing sacrifice: for the prostitute sacrificed her health to protect the pure woman's chastity. The prostitute's body was periodically examined by a state physician to clear her to remain as pure women's shield from men's promiscuity. There was little to no discussion regarding the infected male body, although the infected male joined "good" and "bad" women in a symbiotic bond for survival. Our Lady of Refuge Shelter was a transitional center where "fallen women" stayed until they were sent to their final destination, which was decided in accordance with the severity of their "sins." Because of its transitional and classificatory nature this center served as one of the sites for the Foundation guardian women to do their practical internships.

33. *Informe sobre la moralidad pública,* 21.

34. Ibid., 25.

35. France is not much different than Spain in terms of contraception and abortion legislation: 1975 for the legalization of abortion in France, and 1967 for contraception.

36. *Informe sobre la moralidad pública,* 34.

37. Ibid., 36.

38. Ibid., 41.

39. Ibid., 51.

40. Gerald Brenan, *The Face of Spain,* 102–3.

41. Ibid., 101.

42. *Informe sobre la moralidad pública,* 62.

43. Ibid.

44. Ibid., 64.

45. The meublés were establishments conceived for prostitution. Their external appearance and big signs made it perfectly clear. There was a registration counter guarded by a couple of men in waiter uniforms, a rare detail nonexistent in normal hotels. The rooms in the luxury ones had mirrors in the ceilings and changing lights. The streets of China Town in Barcelona were packed with meublés and little pensiones and hotels. The owners of these businesses had to comply with police regulations between 1945 and 1953:

1) Forbid the entrance to any woman that looked under 23 years of age
2) Forbid two men and one lady in only one room or two rooms on the same floor
3) The same as above for two ladies and one man
4) Record every person that spent the night in the hotel

See Paco Villar, *Historia y Leyenda del Barrio Chino. 1900–1992,* 188–89.

46. *Informe sobre la moralidad pública,* 61.

47. Paco Villar, *Historia y Leyenda del Barrio Chino. 1900–1992,* 176.

48. Summary 14/1945 court of first instance, num. 9. Paco Villar, H*istoria y Leyenda del Barrio Chino. 1900–1992,* 183.

49. Summary 421/1945 Court of First Instance, num. 4 de Barcelona in Paco Villar, *Historia y Leyenda del Barrio Chino. 1900–1992,* 179.

50. Paco Villar, *Historia y Leyenda del Barrio Chino. 1900–1992,* 181.

51. *Informe sobre la moralidad pública,* 153.

52. Ibid., 184.

53. Ibid., 183.

54. Ibid., 173.

55. Ibid., 182.

56. Ibid., 175.

57. Ibid., 180.

58. Ibid., 67.

59. Ibid., 68.

60. Nineteenth-century Spanish legislation followed the 1791 French penal code model. Only by the mid-1850s was there an emphasis on the need of regulating prostitution because of public hygiene concerns. By a ruling of 1865 the Spanish government established an office of Special Hygiene or Prostitution divided in three branches: an administrative office, a surveillance body, and another body of physicians or hygienists appointed directly by the governor of each province. The most important piece in the new regulation was an official registry of those women who worked as prostitutes, the mandatory periodical medical examination of those registered, and the issuing of health books where state doctors recorded twice a week the personal and medical information of those women registered. When these women suffered a serious infection they were sent to a prison-hospital, most unlikely to restore their health, and then sent back to work. This regulation, however, was less than efficient because it failed to regulate the many women who practiced prostitution clandestinely.

61. By contrast a very important movement to abolish prostitution spread throughout Europe, originating in Great Britain with Josephine Butler as the spokesperson and founder in 1875 of the International Abolitionist Federation. Butler's campaign reached Spain two years later and was manifested in a debate mostly among men, in which the medical arguments prevailed over the moral and legal ones.

62. Tomás Caro Patón, *La mujer caída. Memorias y reflexiones de un médico de la lucha Antivenérea* (Madrid: M. Montal, editor, 1959).

63. Ibid., 27.

64. Ibid., 31.

65. Ibid., 46.

66. Ibid.

67. Ibid., 50.

68. Ibid., 111.

69. Ibid., 113.

70. Ibid., 114.

71. Ibid., 115.

72. Ibid., 126.

73. Ibid., 138.

74. The Geneva Convention declared abolition as the norm to follow with regard to sexual trafficking and prostitution. In this meeting the United Nations countries attending urged the rest of the world to sign **article 23** ratifying abolition. Some of the other articles include

> **article 16.** The parties present in this convention agree to implement through their social services private or public the appropriate measures public or private to prevent prostitution and ensure the education and redemption of the victims of prostitution.
>
> **Article 1.** The parties present in this convention agree to punish any individual who to satisfy the passions of others:
>
> a) Tricks, leads, or corrupts another person to perform prostitution even when that person is a consenting adult.
>
> b) Prostitutes another person even if that person is a consenting adult.

Article 2. We agree as well in punishing any person who

a) Owns, manages finances or contributes to finance a brothel.

b) Acquires or rents a space knowing the aim is prostitution of a third party

Article 3. As much as each country's legislation allows it, any attempt to break articles 1 and 2 are equally punishable. Quoted in Caro Patón, *La mujer caída,* 89.

75. Enrique Jiménez Asenjo, *Abolicionismo y prostitución. Justificación y defensa del Decreto-Ley de 3 de marzo de 1956* (Madrid: Instituto Editorial Reus, 1963), 303.
76. Richard Wright, *Pagan Spain,* 177.
77. Ibid.
78. Carmen Martín Gaite, *The Backroom* (San Francisco: City Lights Books, 2000), 153.
79. Richard Wright, *Pagan Spain,* 14.
80. Ibid., 24.
81. Ibid.
82. Ibid.
83. Ibid.. 26.
84. Laurence Miller Gallery exhibited for the first time in the United States. Barcelona photographer Joan Colom's photographs from March 9 through April 29, 2006. Seventeen of Colom's vintage black–and-white prints were featured. Working in a style similar to his contemporary Robert Frank, Colom captured the inhabitants of the Raval or Barrio Chino as they solicited one another, and joked among themselves. The Raval prostitutes photographed exude a powerful sense of sexuality and a subtle self-assuredness that make the pictures mysterious and intriguing.
85. Jiménez Asenjo, *Abolicionismo y prostitución* 16.
86. Ibid., 321.
87. Ibid., 322.
88. Ibid., 323.
89. Ibid., 170.
90. Ibid., 171.
91. Ibid., 172.
92. Ibid., 174.
93. Ibid.
94. See José Enrique Sobremonte Martínez, *Prostitución y Código Penal* (Valencia: Universidad de Valencia, 1983).
95. Jiménez Asenjo, *Abolicionismo y prostitución,* 240.
96. Ibid., 242–44.
97. Ibid., 248.
98. Ibid., 250.
99. Caro Patón, *La mujer caída,* 73.
100. Richard Wright, *Pagan Spain,* 215–17.
101. Luis Martínez Kleiser, "Prólogo" in *Abolicionismo y prostitución. Justificación y defense del Decreto-Ley de 3 de Marzo de 1956,* ed. Enrique Jiménez Asenjo, (Madrid: Instituto Editorial Reus, 1963), 13.
102. Ibid., 16.
103. Jiménez Asenjo, *Abolicionismo y prostitución,* 221.
104. Martínez Kleiser, "Prólogo," 17.
105. Jiménez Asenjo, *Abolicionismo y prostitución,* 218.

106. Ibid., 301.
107. Ibid., 303.
108. Ibid., 312–13.
109. Ibid., 315.
110. Paco Villar, *Historia y Leyenda del Barrio Chino. 1900–1992,* 207.

Chapter 4. Wives and Mothers

1. Gerald Brenan, *The Face of Spain* (Harmondsworth: Penguin Books, 1950), 63.
2. Ibid., 9.
3. Ibid., 23–24.
4. Ibid., 21.
5. Richard Wright, *Pagan Spain* (University: University of Mississippi Press, 2002), 98. Richard Wright first published Pagan Spain in 1957 by John Hawkins and Associates Inc., New York.
6. Ibid., 99.
7. Ibid., 100.
8. *A La Lima Y Al Limón* lyrics are as it follows:

La vecinita de enfrente no, no,/	The little neighbor across the street
no tiene los ojos grandes./	Does not have big eyes
Ni tiene el talle de espiga, no, no, /	Does not have wasp waist
ni son sus labios de sangre./	Does not have blood-colored lips
Nadie se acerca a su reja, /	Nobody comes to her gate
nadie llama en sus cristales./	Nobody knocks on her window
Que sólo el viento de noche/	Only the wind at night
es quien le ronda la calle./	Comes to pay her a visit
Y los niños cantan a la rueda, rueda./	Children sing this song when they play
Esta triste copla que el viento le lleva./	This sad song that the wind carries away
A la Lima y al Limón,/	Lime and lemon
tu no tienes quien te quiera./	Nobody loves you
A la Lima y al Limón,/	Lime and lemon
te vas a quedar soltera./	you will remain single
Que penita y que dolor./	How sad what a sorrow
Que penita y que dolor,/	how sad what a sorrow
la vecinita de enfrente	
soltera se quedó./	our little neighbor will be single
Solterita se quedó./	single she will remain
A la Lima y al Limón./	Lime and lemon
La vecinita de enfrente no, no,/	Our little neighbor across the street
nunca pierde la esperanza./	Never loses hope
Y espera de noche y día, si, si,/	And she hopes night and day for
aquel amor que no pasa./	That love that never comes
Se han casado sus amigas,/	All her friends have gotten married
se han casado sus hermanas./	Her sisters as well

Y ella compuesta y sin novio/	And she is a lady in waiting without a suitor
se ha quedado en la ventana./	She is waiting at her window
Y los niños cantan a la rueda, rueda./	Children sing while they play
El mismo estribillo que el viento le lleva./	The same chorus that the wind carries away
A la Lima y al Limón,/	Lime and lemon
tu no tienes quien te quiera./	Nobody loves you
A la Lima y al Limón,/	Lime and lemon
te vas a quedar soltera./	You'll remain single
Que penita y que dolor./	How sad what a sorrow
Que penita y que dolor,/	how sad what a sorrow
la vecinita de enfrente soltera se quedó./	Our little neighbor will be single
Solterita se quedó./	Single she will remain
A la Lima y al Limón./	Lime and lemon
La vecinita de enfrente si, si,/	Our little neighbor
a los treinta se ha casado,/	She got married at thirty
con un señor de cincuenta, si, si,/	She got married to a fifty-year-old gentleman
que dicen que es magistrado./	Who is a magistrate
Lo luce por los paseos,/	She shows him off along the main street
lo luce por los teatros./	in the theaters
Y va siempre por la calle/	And always goes on the street
cogidita de su brazo./	Holding his arm
Y con ironía siempre tararea,/	And with irony she always hums
el mismo estribillo de la rueda, rueda./	the same chorus of the children's game
A la Lima y al Limón,/	Lime and Lemon
que ya tengo quien me quiera/	I have now someone who loves me
A la Lima y al Limón,/	Lime and lemon
que no me quedé soltera./	I did not stay single
Ya mi pena se acabó./	And I am sad no more
Ya mi pena se acabó,/	And I am sad no more
que un hombre llamó a mi puerta y le dí mi corazón,/	A man knocked on my door and I gave him my heart
y conmigo se casó./	and he married me
A la Lima y al Limón./	Lime and lemon

9. Fernando Olmeda, *El látigo y la pluma. Homosexuales en la España de Franco* (Madrid: Oyeron, 2004), 99–104. See also *LD.* Alberto Mira, *De Sodoma a Chueca. Una historia cultural de la homosexualidad en España en el siglo XX* (Barcelona, Egalés, 2004); Nicolás Pérez Cánovas, *Homosexualidad, homosexuales y uniones homosexuales en el Derecho español.* (Granada: Comares, 1996); Xosé Buxán, (con) *Ciencia de un deseo singular. Estudios gays y lesbianas en el Estado español.* (Barcelona: Laertes, 1997); *Patrick Paul Garlinger, Confessions of the Letter Closet: Epistolary Fiction and Queer Desire in Mod-*

ern Spain (Minneapolis: University of Minnesota Press, 2005); Nathan Baiez Aparicio, *Vagos, maleantes y homosexuals. La repression a los homosexuals durante el franquismo* (Barcelona: Malhivern, 2007).

10. Georgina Dopico Black *Perfect Wives, Other Women: Adultery and Inquisition in Early Modern Spain* (Durham, NC: Duke University Press, 2001).

11. *Fuero del Trabajo,* March 9, 1938, quoted in Lidia Falcón, *Mujer sociedad* (Barcelona: Editorial Fontanella, 1973), 293. The *Fuero del Trabajo* followed the spirit of the fascist *Carta di Lavoro* issued in 1927.

12. Pius XII, *Address to Midwives.*

13. In contrast to the Nazis who did not mind and even encouraged breeding out of wedlock.

14. The Women's Section of Falange survived the dictatorship. It would be dissolved in 1977, only two years after Franco's death.

15. Born Eugenio Pacelli on March 2, 1876, Pius XII came from a significant Vatican line of ancestors who served successive Popes as legal advisors. After ordination to the priesthood in 1899, Pacelli studied canon law, a family tradition and became a Vatican diplomat and administrator for a number of years. Pacelli's great-great-great uncle, Monsignor Prospero Caterini had sponsored Pacelli's grandfather, Marcantonio Pacelli, to study canon law in 1819. By 1834 Marcantonio was involved in the investigation of marriage annulments as an advocate in the Vatican Tribunal of the Sacred Rota under Pope Gregory XVI. Under Pius IX, Marcantonio rose to become the Pope's legal and political advisor.

16. The influence of Roman legal science in the development of canon law is very clear. The *Corpus Iuris Civilis* transmitted two definitions of marriage: the first one, "Wedlock is the union of a male and a female and the partnership of the whole of life, the sharing of human and divine law," by Modestinus included in the *Digest [23,2,1]*; the second, "Marriage is a union of man and woman involving an undivided habit of life," included in the *Institutes of Justinian [1,9,1].* See Charles J. Scicluna, *The Essential Definition of Marriage According to the 1917 and 1983 Codes of Canon Law: An Exegetical and Comparative Study* (New York: University Press of America, 1995), 21–46.

17. Monsignor Pietro Gasparri, a renowned canon lawyer, and Pacelli were responsible for the completion of the Code Roman Catholic canon law of 1917. Because a cohesive Church was crucial to the advancement of Rome's political agenda, a centralized control of the pontiffs was key. Pius XI in the 1920s rapidly invoked this authority. In 1924 he dissolved the marriage between a Protestant and a Jew. The Protestant had converted to Catholicism and desired to marry a Catholic. At least two other such cases were granted by Pius XI. Pius XII, himself one of the architects of the code, dissolved six marriages that were legalized when neither party was a Roman Catholic. In one case both were Moslems at the time of their marriage.

18. One glaring example was canon 747, which stated that if there was a danger of interuterine death of a baby, the fetus should be baptized before birth. The code also contained as an appendix with documents by Popes Paul III (1534–1549), Pius V (1566–1572), and Gregory XIII (1572–1585) at the height of the Counter-Reformation. These documents authorized pontiffs to dissolve marriages contracted between individuals, when neither of them were Roman Catholics at the time of their union.

19. Dopico Black, *Perfect Wives,* 5.

20. Fuero del Trabajo. 9 de Marzo de 1938, quoted in Lidia Falcón, *Mujer y sociedad* (Barcelona: Editorial Fontanella, 1973), second edition, 293. This document was inspired by the *Carta di Lavoro* issued in Italy by the fascist in 1927.

21. *Casti Connubii, Encyclical Of Pope Pius XI On Christian Marriage,* http://www.vatican.va/holy_father/pius_xi/encyclicals/documents/hf_p-xi_enc_31121930_casti-connubii_en.html, 2–6.

22. Ibid., 5.

23. From the very beginning Pius XI vindicates in this text the "divine institution of matrimony, its sacramental dignity and its perpetual stability" and by matrimony "the souls of the contracting parties are joined and knit together more directly and more intimately than are their bodies." Through this holy union a "domestic society" is created by the bond of love. The Pope was not referring to any kind of love but what Augustine called "the order of love" that established the hierarchical power relation between husband and wife. *Casti Connubii. Encyclical Of Pope Pius XI On Christian Marriage,* http://www.vatican.va/holy_father/pius_xi/encyclicals/documents/hf_p-xi_enc_31121930_casti-connubii_en.html, 7.

24. Fuero de los Españoles. 17 Julio 1945, in María Carmen García Nieto and Javier M. Donezar, *La España de Franco 1939–1973. Bases documentales de la España contemporánea* (Madrid: Guadiana, 1975), 196.

25. Dopico Black, points out this predicament in analyzing early modern Spanish honor plays in *Perfect Wives,* 16.

26. Dopico Black, *Perfect Wives,* 308.

27. Lidia Falcón, *Mujer y Sociedad,* 306.

28. *Casti Connubii. Encyclical Of Pope Pius XI On Christian Marriage,* 11.

29. Pius XII, *Address to Midwives on the Nature of Their Profession.*

30. Mary Nash, "Pronatalism and Motherhood in Franco Spain," in *Maternity and Gender Policies. Women and the Rise of the European Welfare States 1880s to 1950s,* ed. Gisela Bock and Pat Thane (London: Routledge, 1991), 160–78.

31. Instituto Nacional de Estadística, *Anuario Estadístico de España. Cuadro Sinóptico de las principales actividades de la vida española año 1941–1955* (Madrid: INE, 1957), 588–89.

32. Jose Linhard, "Family Planning in Spain," *International Family Planning Perspectives* 9, no. 1 (Mar. 1983): 9–15 (9).

33. Pius XII, *Allocution to the Congress of the International Union of Catholic Women's Leagues,* Rome, Italy, September 11, 1947, 2.

34. Ibid.

35. Ibid.

36. Allocution to the "Societate Internationale Hematologiae" 12.09.1958, quoted in Charles J. Scicluna, *The Essential Definition of Marriage According to the 1917 and 1983 Codes of Canon Law.*

37. Pius XII, *Address to Midwives on the Nature of Their Profession* (Vatican, October 29, 1951).

38. Ibid., 2.

39. Ibid., 5.

40. Ibid.

41. Ibid., 8.

42. Antonio Vallejo Nágera, *La Sabiduría del hogar. Antes que te cases* (Madrid: Editorial Plus Ultra, 1946).

43. Gregorio Marañón, *Ensayos sobre la vida sexual,* 67.

44. Ibid.
45. Ibid., 68.
46. Ibid.
47. Marañón citation in footnote 19 is: Geddes and Thompson, *The Evolution of Sex* (1901).
48. Gregorio Marañón, *Ensayos sobre la vida sexual,* 69.
49. Ibid., 73.
50. Ibid., 81.
51. FOESSA, Estudios sociológicos sobre la situación social de España, 1975 (Madrid: Euroamérica, 1976), 1055.
52. Richard Wright, *Pagan Spain,* 101.
53. Ibid., 180.
54. Instituto Nacional de Estadística, *Anuario Estadístico de España,* 606–7.
55. All these figures are from Instituto Nacional de Estadística, *Anuario Estadístico de España,* XXXII–XXXV.
56. Fundación FOESSA, *Informe Sociológico sobre la situación social de España* (Madrid: Editorial de Euroamérica, 1966), 38.
57. Juan Bosch Marín, "Asistencia Medico-Social en Madrid" Conferencia pronunciada en el Ateneo de Madrid en el Cursillo en honor del Excmo. Sr. Obispo de Madrid-Alcalá D. Leopoldo Eijo y Garay, en sus bodas de plata con la diócesis madrileña. (Madrid: Ministerio de la Gobernación, Publicaciones "al servicio de España y del niño español" Septiembre, 1948), 7.
58. Ibid., 10.
59. Ibid., 26.
60. Juan Bosch Marín, Juan Pedro de la Cámara, and Venancio Saenz de Tejada, "270,000 partos. Sus enseñanzas sanitarias. Observaciones sobre la asistencia tocológica prestada en el seguro obligatorio de enfermedad durante los años 1947 a 1949." Ministerio de la Gobernación Dirección General de Sanidad. Sección de puericultura, Maternología e higiene escolar. Madrid Publicaciones "Al servicio de España y del niño español" no. 152, Octubre 1950.
61. Juan Bosch Marín, "Function of the Midwife in the World Today." Madrid: Gráficas González, opening speech to the 13th Congress of the International Confederation of Midwives (1963), 25.
62. Ibid., 29.
63. Ibid.
64. Ibid., 32–33.
65. Ibid., 30.
66. Ibid., 31.
67. Oscar Caballero, *El sexo del Franquismo,* 23.
68. Judith Butler points out how the materiality of the body, as much as gender, is an effect of power: "'Sex' is, thus, not simply what one has, or a static description of what one is: it will be one of the norms by which the 'one' becomes viable at all, that which qualifies a body for life within the domain of cultural intelligibility." Judith Butler, *Bodies That Matter. On the Discursive Limits of "Sex"* (New York: Routledge, 1993), 2.
69. Lucia Graves, *A Woman Unknown. Voices from a Spanish life* (Washington, DC: Counterpoint, 1999), 170–72.
70. René Boigelot, *El Matrimonio: El libro de la novia,* 10th ed. (Madrid: Desclee de Brouwer, El Angel del Hogar, 1964); René Boigelot, *El Matrimonio: El libro del jóven de 17 a 20 años* (Madrid: Desclée de Brouwer, El Angel del Hogar, 1960); René Boigelot, *Maternidad: La maravillosa aventura de la célula hu-*

mana desde el germen al recién nacido (Madrid: Desclée de Brouwer, El Angel del Hogar, 1960, 1962, 1965).

71. José Songel, *Temario de Cursillos prematrimoniales* (Valencia: Editorial C.P.E., 1964), 76.
72. Ibid., 75.
73. Ibid., 70.
74. René Boigelot, *El Matrimonio: El libro de la novia,* 19.
75. Ibid., 135.
76. Ibid., 113.
77. Ibid., 112.
78. Ibid.
79. Ibid., 114.
80. Ibid., 79.
81. Ibid., 68.
82. Ibid., 71.
83. Antonio Guerra Gallego, *Cómo se atrae,* 11.
84. Ibid., 19.
85. Ibid., 16.
86. Ibid., 17.
87. Ibid., 22.
88. Ibid., 24–25.
89. Dopico Black, *Perfect Wives,* 15.
90. Guerra Gallego, *Cómo se atrae,* 28.
91. Ibid., 30–31.
92. Ibid., 32.
93. Ibid., 43–44.
94. Ibid., 53.
95. Richard Wright, *Pagan Spain,* 180.
96. Guerra Gallego, *Cómo se atrae,* 57.
97. Ibid., 61.
98. Fundación FOESSA, *Estudios Sociológicos sobre la situación social de España 1975* (Madrid: Editorial de Euroamérica, 1976), 399–400.
99. Ibid., 400.
100. Ibid., 401–402.
101. The author refers to Bell, "Familism and Suburbanization: One Test of the Social Choice Hypothesis," in *The Family and Change,* ed. J.N. Edwards (New York: A.A. Knopf, 1969), 101–11), Fundación FOESSA, *Estudios Sociológicos sobre la situación social de España 1975* (Madrid: Editorial de Euroamérica, 1976), 404.
102. Fundación FOESSA, *Informe Sociológico sobre la situación social de España* (Madrid: Editorial de Euroamérica, 1966), 7 For more on the origins and purpose of FOESSA see chapter 1.
103. Ibid., 8.
104. Ibid., 45.
105. Ibid., 47.
106. Ibid., 48.
107. Aurora G. Morcillo, *True Catholic Womanhood,* 66–70.
108. L. Alonso Tejada, *La represión sexual en la España de Franco* (Barcelona: Caralt, 1977), 178. See also Amando de Miguel, *Sexo, mujer y natalidad en España* (Madrid: Edicusa, 1975); Oscar Caballero, *El sexo del Franquismo* (Madrid: Editorial Cambio 16, 1977).

109. Alonso Tejada, *La represión sexual en la España de Franco,* 180.
110. Adrian Shubert, *A Social History of Modern Spain* (London: Routledge, 1991), 213.
111. Fundación FOESSA, *Informe Sociológico sobre la situación social de España* (Madrid: Editorial de Euroamérica, 1966), 57.
112. Ibid., 59.
113. Ibid., 61.
114. Richard Vinen, *A History in Fragments: Europe in the Twentieth Century* (Da Capo Press, 2001), 371.
115. : Fundación FOESSA, *Estudios Sociológicos sobre la situación social de España 1975* (Madrid: Editorial de Euroamérica, 1976), 48.
116. Ibid., 390.
117. Ibid., 395.
118. Ibid., 397.

Chapter 5. Docile Bodies

Some of the information in this chapter has been published as an article. See Aurora Morcillo, "Uno, Dos,Tres, Cuatro. Women Modern Docile Bodies," in *Journal Sport in Society,* ed. Andrew McFarland and Boria Majumdar (*Sport in Society,* 11, no. 6 (November 2008): 673–84.

1. See Ana Aguado *La modernizatión de España. Cultura y vida cotidiana* (Madrid: Coleción Síntesis, 2002), 147. See also Victoria de Grazia, *The Culture of Consent: Mass Organization of Leisure in Fascist Italy* (New York: Cambridge University Press, 1981); Gigliola Gori, *Italian Fascism and the Female Body: Submissive Women and Strong Mothers* (*Sport in the Global Society*) (New York: Routledge, 2004); J. A. Mangan ed., *Superman Supreme: Fascist Body as Political Icon—Global Fascism* (*Cass Studies—Sport in the Global Society.*) (New York: Routledge, 2000); Uli Linke, *German Bodies: Race and Representation After Hitler* (New York: Routledge, 1999), Patricia Vertinsky, *Disciplining Bodies in the Gymnasium: Memory, Monument, Modernism* (*Sport in the Global Society,* 55) (New York: Routledge, 2003).

2. The regime issued several orders and decrees from the very beginning to ensure the Women's Section control over the female population. These legal documents included:

> **Laws:** *Ley de la jefatura del Estado,* December 28, 1939, which declared Women's Section of Falange as the exclusive official organization to mold Spanish women's consciousness; *Ley de la jefatura del Estado,* December 6, 1940, entrusting the Youth Front the indoctrination of Spanish Youth in general and by order of January 24, 1945, the Women's Section take the responsibility of the female youth.
>
> **Orders:** A series of orders were enacted by the state to complement the laws mentioned above: orders of October 16, 1941, December 10, 1942, and November 26, 1946. By **Decree** of November 9, 1940, the regime declared physical education mandatory in all technical higher learning entities. With regard to physical education, the regime approved a series of decrees and orders to complement the law of physical education of 1961 that included: Decree of November 10, 1960, regulating the diploma of physical education instructors; order November 28, 1961, for rehabilitation of the diplomas of the school of instructors of physical education; and or-

der November 28, 1961, for publishing the Curriculum for the School of Physical Education.

3. José Luis Pastor Pradillo, *Definición y desarrollo del espacio profesional de la educación física en España (1961–1990)* (Madrid: Servicio de Publicaciones Universidad de Alcalá, 2000), 39.

4. FET del Las JONS (1952) *La Sección Femenina historia y organización.* Quoted in María Luisa Zagalaz Sánchez La educación Física Femenina en España (Jaen: Universidad de Jaín, 1998), 77.

5. Pius XII "Alocución a las formaciones deportivas de Italia—20 Mayo de 1945" Sección Femenina's Secretary of Physical Education Typescript, Archivo General de la Administración, Alcalá de Henares (hereafter AGA), 1.

6. Ibid., 4. "Si lograis, gracias a la actividad deportiva, conseguir que el cuerpo sea más dócil, más sumiso el espíritu y a vuestras obligaciones morales; si en fin, vuestro ejemplo contribuye a dar a la actividad deportiva moderna una forma, más en relación con la dignidad humana y los preceptos divinos, entonces vuestra cultura física adquiere un valor sobrenatural."

7. Foucault's explanation of "docile bodies" in his work *Discipline and Punish* takes us to the great book *Man—the Machine* (1748) by Julien Offrey de La Mettrie (1709–51). La Mettrie argued in *L'Histoire naturelle de l'âme* (1745) that the Epicurean notion that the only pleasures are those of the senses, an idea further developed in *L'homme machine* (*Man a Machine,* 1748). As Foucault points out: "La Mettrie's *L'Homme machine* is both a materialist reduction of the soul and a general theory of dressage, at the center of which reigns the notion of "docility" which joins the analyzable body to the malleable body." Foucault highlights that this work is written in two registers. On the one hand, the anatomic-metaphysical and on the other hand on a techno-political register. The former approach discerned by physicians with a preface by Descartes and the latter presenting the reader with a set of regulations and calculated methods as applied by the army, the school system, the hospital, and so on, with the only purpose of correcting the body's operational abilities. Michel Foucault, "Docile Bodies," in *The Foucault Reader,* ed. Paul Rabinow (New York, Pantheon Books, 1984), 180.

8. Foucault, "Docile Bodies" in *The Foucault Reader,* ed. Paul Rabinow 181.

9. Pius XII, "Deporte y Gimnasia. Principios Religiosos y Morales." Sección cultura. Archivo General de la Administración, Sección Femenina's Papers. Alcala de Henares, 1952 typescript, 4.

10. Pius XII, "Deporte y Gimnasia," 5.

11. Ibid., 6.

12. Ibid., 2.

13. That same year the Law for Political and Professional Rights of Women was approved.

14. See Estrella Casero, *La España que bailó con Franco. Coros y Danzas de la Sección Femenina* (Madrid: Editorial ENE Nuevas Estructuras, SL, 2000).

15. "Se dirá que estos son quijotismos trasnochados. Benditos quijotismos si ellos nos deparan la ocasión de que una porción, más o menos elevada . . . tengan medios y posibilidades para conseguir la salud corporal que en la unidad y mutua permanente influencia del cuerpo y del espíritu será salud del alma; porque educar el cuerpo en sanos y cristianos principios de la educación física y el deporte implica necesariamente educar el alma." Delegación Nacional de Educación Física y Deportes, "Discurso de Excmo. Sr. Don José Antonio Elola-

Olaso, Delegado Nacional de educación Física y Deportes ante el Pleno de las Cortes españolas" (Madrid: Estades, 1962), 19.

16. Delegación Nacional de Educación Física y Deportes, "Discurso de Excmo. Sr. Don José Antonio Elola-Olaso, 19.

17. "En el deporte pueden, en efecto encontrar desarrollo las verdaderas y sólidas virtudes cristianas, que la gracia de Dios hace más tarde estables y fructuosas; en el espíritu de disciplina se aprenden y se practican la obediencia, la humildad, la renuncia; en las relaciones de equipo y competición, la caridad y el amor de fraternidad, el respeto recíproco, la magnanimidad, a veces incluso el perdón; en las firmes leyes del rendimiento físico, la castidad, la modestia, la templanza, la prudencia." John XXIII words with the occasion of the Olympic Games celebrated in Rome in 1960. *Ley de Educación Física,* 1961, preamble.

18. The creation of the Escuela Central de Educación Física in the early 1920s responded to a militaristic concept of physical fitness and therefore was antithetical to classic notions feminine frailty.

19. "We think, said the Pope, "competitive athletics demands some qualities completely opposite to feminine constitution—Muscular strength, speed control, considerable resistance to fatigue." Pius XI, "Dobbiamo Intratenerla," Archivo General de la Administración, (AGA) Sección Femenina's Papers. Alcala de Henares, 1931, 2.

20. Pius XI. "*Dobbiamo Intratenerla.*" 2.

21. Delegación Nacional de la Sección Femenina de FET y de las JONS, "Contestaciones sobre las preguntas hechas por Lino de Pablo (del Instituto Municipal de Educación del Ayuntamiento de Madrid) para el semanario del SEM." Typescript October 21, 1961, 2 Archivo General de la Administración, Sección Cultura Sección Femenina's Papers caja/leg. 32.

22. "Escuela nacional de Profesoras de E. Física" Typescript 4. Sección Femenina's Papers, Archivo General de la Administración, Sección Cultura, Caja/leg. 32.

23. Organización de la Educación Física Femenina en España—Charla dada en el curso de medicina deportiva. September 2, 1959. Typescript 1–12 Sección Femenina's Papers, Sección Cultura, Archivo General de la Administración.

24. "Profesoras de educación física femenina" Typescript 1–4. Sección Femenina's Papers, Archivo General de la Administración, Sección Cultura, Caja/leg. 32, 3.

25. See Victoria de Grazia, *The Cultura of Consent: Mass Organization of Leisure in Fascist Italy* (New York: Cambridge University Press, 1981).

26. "Planes deportivos para productoras," Madrid 20 September 1958 Typescript 1–3 Sección Femenina's Papers, AGA, Sección Cultura, Caja/leg. 32, 1.

27. Ibid., 2.

28. "La educación física y Deportiva, via de integración social (los grupos sociales). Typescript 1–4. Women's Section Papers Sección Cultura AGA caja 31, 2.

29. Ibid., 3.

30. "Profesoras de educación física femenina" Typescript, 3.

31. Estudio sobre el tema: "Límites y posibilidades del deporte en las mujeres," Madrid, September 25, 1963. Typescript 1–3. Women's Section Papers Sección Cultura AGA, 1.

32. Casero, *La España que bailó con Franco,* 60.

33. Ibid.

34. See figure 3, "Gimnasia Casera."

35. Sección Femenina, Economía doméstica para Bachillerato, Comercio y Magisterio, 1958.
36. Carlos Delfino, "Los deportes más propios para la mujer," in *Blanco y Negro* November 29, 1958, no. 2,430.
37. Organización de la regiduría Central de educación Física en sus actividades deportivas. Typescript 1–4 Sección Femenina's Papers, AGA, Sección Cultura, Caja/leg. 32, 1.
38. "Escuela nacional de Profesoras de E. Física," typescript, 1.
39. Ibid., 2.
40. Ibid., 3.
41. Spain participated for the first time in the Olympic Games in 1900. The Spanish Olympic Committee was established in 1912 in Barcelona. The first medalist was D. Pedro Pidal y Bernaldo de Quirós, Marqués de Villaviciosa, member of the Asturias nobility who competed in the 1900 París Olympic Games in skeetshooting and won the second place.
42. Luis Suárez Fernández, *Crónica de la Sección Femenina* (Madrid: Asociación Nueva Andadura, 1993), 287.
43. Concepción Sierra y Gil de la Cuesta, Plan de albergues del SEU. Educación física. Madrid, Junio 3, 1959. Circular Letter Archivo Histórico Provincial de Granada, leg. 5434 7 (7).
44. Concepción Sierra y Gil de la Cuesta, Plan de albergues del SEU.
45. Jens Ljunggren, "The Masculine Road Through Modernity: Ling Gymnastics and Male Socialization in Nineteenth Century Sweden" in *Making European Masculinities. Sport, Europe, Gender,* ed. J. A. Mangan (London: Frank Cass, 2000), 86–111.
46. Sección Femenina, "Método, Planes y objetivos de la Educación, 6.
47. "Comunicación del Trabajo de Carlos Gutiérrez para el Congreso Mundial de Educación Física," typescript The Women's Section papers AGA.
48. "Educación Física Femenina. Enseñanza Primaria." Dr. Carlos Gutiérrez, Asesor de Gimnasia de la Sección Femenina, n.d. Typescript Women's Section Papers Sección Cultura AGA.
49. The Women's Section created the Secretariat of Culture in 1938, which was in charge of training music instructors and collecting traditional folklore. At the time dance instruction was under their Secretariat of Physical Education. Coros y Danzas per se was united in 1944. Casero, *La España que bailó con Franco,* 39–48.
50. See Estrella Casero, *La España que bailó con Franco.*
51. Luis Suárez Fernández, *Crónica de la Sección Femenina* (Madrid: Asociación Nueva Andadura, 1993), 222.
52. Ibid., 223.
53. Ibid., 227.
54. Ibid., 322.
55. Ibid., 328.
56. *Orden de 11 de enero de 1965 por la que se efectúan nombramientos de profersoras de Educación Física en los distritos universitarios que se indican.* Typescript 1–3. Women's Section Papers Sección Cultura AGA, 1.
57. Pierre Nora, *Realms of Memory* (New York: Columbia University Press, 1996). See also Paloma Aguilar, *Memory and Amnesia: The Role of the Spanish Civil War in the Transition to Democracy* (Berghahn Books, 2002); C. Molinero, M. Sala, and J. Sobrequés, eds. *Una inmensa prisión. Los campos de concentración y las prisiones durante la Guerra civil y el franquismo.* (Barce-

lona: Crítica, 2003) especially Nicolás Sánchez-Albornoz, "Cuelgamuros: presos políticos para un mausoleo." 3–19.

58. Luis Suárez Fernández, *Crónica de la Sección,* 332.

59. The tombstone that covered José Antonio in El Escorial was placed in the Castle of la Mota Women's Section Headquarters where remains today.

60. Construction of the monument took two decades. The architects were Pedro Muguruza and Diego Méndez, although Franco constantly intervened and strongly influenced the design of the project. The work of construction itself was undertaken by the forced labor of 20,000 Republican prisoners, fourteen of whom were killed and many more injured; it was intended that through such work prisoners would have the opportunity to "redeem themselves."

61. The delegations were: Madrid, Barcelona, Valencia, Zaragoza, Alava, Sevilla, Málaga, Alicante Asturias,, Badajoz, Tenerife, Pontevedra, Guipúzcoa, Orense, Logroño, Toledo, Zamora, Soria y Huesca. Circular letter November 1959 quoted in Luis Suárez Fernández, *Crónica de la Sección,* 335.

62. Luis Suárez Fernández, *Crónica de la Sección,* 338.

63. Ibid., 347.

64. Ibid., 356.

65. Ibid., 297.

66. María de Miranda de Huelin, "Informe que presenta la Subinspectora Nacional de Educación Física Universitaria, Doña María de Miranda de Huelin, acerca de la inspección realizada a la Universidad de Sevilla los días 5, 6, y 7 de diciembre de 1959" Madrid, 15 Diciembre 1959. 7 pages type-script Women's Section Papers Sección Cultura AGA, 1.

67. Ibid., 4.

68. Ibid., 7.

69. Correspondence Women's Section Papers Sección Cultura AGA.

70. Rosa Tobalina Espiga, Regidora Provincial de Administración de la Sección Femenina de Valladolid. 27–2-1965 Women's Section Papers Sección Cultura AGA.

71. Departamento Nacional de Participación. Sección de Educación Física y Actividades Deportivas *XXVAniversario. Juegos escolares nacionales. 1949–1973.* (Madrid: Delegaciones Nacionales de Educación Física y Deportes, Sección Femenina y la Juventud, 1973), 10.

72. Morcillo, *True Catholic Womanhood,* p. 26.

73. Delegada provincial de Sección Femenina de FET y de las JONS, Murcia. 3–6–1965 Women's Section Papers Sección Cultura AGA.

74. "Parte feminina de la política de la juventud y el deporte" typescript, 5 pp, no date. Women's Section Papers Sección Cultura AGA, 1–2.

75. Ibid., 3.

76. Women's Section correspondence, Typescripted letter from Ana Dangual, February 10, 1961. Women's Section Papers Sección Cultura AGA.

77. The Spanish Social Service, 9.

78. "The Spanish Social Service for Women: Its Objectives and Results," in Sección Femenina de FET y de las JONS, *Servicio Social de la Mujer,* Madrid, 1965, 8.

79. Ibid., 10.

80. Ibid.

81. Ibid., 11.

82. Suárez Fernández, *Crónica de la Sección Femenina,* 413.

83. Ibid., 414.
84. Juan Antonio Samaranch. "Informe presentado al Consejo Nacional del Movimiento sobre la situación actual de la educación física y el deporte español," 15 de diciembre 1969, Ediciones del Movimiento, 1969.
85. Ibid., 15.
86. Ibid., 23.
87. Ibid.
88. Ibid., 20–21.
89. Ibid., 21.
90. France, for example had more than 10 magazines with a circulation of 1,000,000 issues. Fundación *Foessa, Estudios Sociológicos sobre la situación social de España, 1975* (Madrid: Editorial Euroamérica, 1976), 1069. See also Maria del Carmen Muñoz Ruiz, "Las revistas para mujeres durante el franquismo: difusión de modelos de comportamiento femenino," in *Mujeres y hombres en la España franquista: Sociedad, economía, política, cultura,* ed. Gloria Nielfa Cristóbal (Instituto de Investigaciones Feministas, Universidad Complutense de Madrid, 2003), 95–116.
91. Fundación *Foessa, Estudios sociológicos sobre la situación social de España, 1975* 1069.
92. Ibid., 1069.
93. Ibid., 1069.
94. Ibid.

Chapter 6. Strangers in the Dark

1. Miguel Picazo Dios et al., *La Tía Tula. Guión cinematográfico* (Jaén: Diputación Provincial de Jaén, 2005), 169.
2. See María Asunción Gómez, "La representación cinematográfica en el cine español de los años 40 y 50: Del cine bélico and neorrealismo" in *Bulletin of Spanish Studies* 79 (2002): 575–89. And by the same author *Del escenario a la pantalla. La adaptación cinematográfica del teatro español* (Chapel Hill: University of North Carolina Press, 2000); Aurora Morcillo, *True Catholic Womanhood: Gender Ideology in Franco's Spain* (Dekalb: Northern Illinois University Press, 2000).
3. Gubern, *Un cine para el cadalso,* (Barcelona: Editorial Eros, 1975), 27.
4. Moral policing became commonplace outside of Spain as well in the 1930s and 1940s. World War II set in motion a strong censorship in Europe and the United States. Hollywood had to comply with the rigid Hays Code. See: Gregory D. Black, *Hollywood Censored. Morality codes, Catholics and the Movies* 1994; http://www.cinemilenio.com/articulos1.htm; Guillermo Zermeño Padilla, "Cine, censura y moralidad en México. En torno al nacionalismo cultural católico, 1929–1960" Departamento de Historia. Universidad Iberoamericana, HISTORIA Y GRAFÍA Enero - Junio de 1997 http://www.hemerodigital.unam.mx/ANUIES/ibero/historia/historia8/sec_7.html.

In 1930 the Association of Motion Picture Producers, Inc., the West Coast Producers, as well as distributors adopted the Motion Picture Production Code known as Hays Code. The original version of the code was drafted by a Jesuit, Father Daniel Lord following the order of William Hays's office to elaborate a set of rules to regulate "morally" those films produced in the United States. In order to apply the code properly Hays established the Production Code Administration under a Catholic lawyer, Joseph I. Breen, in 1934. The so-called Legions for the Preservation of Decency and Good Costumes established in 1934 helped the PCA implement its moral values. Breen's office revised and "purged" every script and image to reach the public. Only those with the approval stamp of the PCA were shown in commercial venues.

5. Gubern, *Un cine para el cadalso,* 21.

6. Rafael R. Tranche y Vicente Sánchez-Biosca, *NODO. El tiempo y la memoria* (Madrid: Cátedra/Filmoteca Española, 2002).

7. The order of August 22, 1975, ended the compulsory showing of NODO, but cinemas continued to show the newsreel until the mid 1980s.

8. Jaime de Andrade (Seudónimo de Francisco Franco), *Raza. Anecdotario para el guión de una película,* (Madrid: Fundación Nacional "Francisco Franco," 1981).

9. "Se declaran ilícitas la producción, el comercio y la circulación de periódicos, folletos y toda clase de impresos y grabados pornográficos, o de literatura socialista, comunista, libertaria y en general, *disolventes* [*sic*]." In the early twentieth century, western governments utilized film as a means to shape national consensus. In order to be effective, censorship became a must. The anonymity of the dark theater prompted authorities' concern for possible license to delinquency. By 1921 Madrid cinemas were officially divided into three areas: one for ladies attending by themselves; another one for gentlemen only; and a third one for couples. The latter had to be illuminated by a red light. Román Gubern, *Un cine para el cadalso* 9–10.

10. It is interesting to point out here how the media presented the phenomenon of "destape," inaugurated in Spanish cinema after the death of the caudillo, as a sign of political liberalization and a means to reach democracy.

11. FET y de las JONS, Vicesecretaría de Educación Popular. Delegación Nacional de Propaganda.Typescript certificate, 7 June 1944. Cultura, Censura cinematográfica, Legajo 1871. Archivo General de la Administración, Alcalá de Henares.

12. These were the lyrics of a very popular song, "La española cuando besa," played on the radio and performed by Concha Piquer and other folk singers of the period.

13. All foreign movies were by law dubbed. Even the names of the characters were converted into Spanish: Charles was Carlos and Mary, María. In turn the dubbing of these films meant further censorship. Sometimes the story was rewritten to fit Francoist Catholic moral values. See Gubern, *Un cine para el cadalso.*

14. Based on the Spanish 1909 novel *Blood and Sand* (Sangre y arena) by Vicente Blasco Ibáñez., Blood and Sand was first produced by Paramount Pictures in 1922, a silent film directed by Fred Niblo and starring Rudolph Valentino, Lila Lee and Nita Naldi. The Spanish remake was directed by Javier Elorrieta in 1989 and starred Chris Rydell, Sharon Stone and Ana Torrent.

15. Typescript letter, Lugo 21 December 1949. Cultura, Censura cinematográfica, Legajo 1870. AGA, Alcalá de Henares.

16. Telegrama official 27 September 1949 Cultura, Censura cinematográfica, Legajo 1871. AGA, Alcalá de Henares.

17. Jesús García Rodrigo and Fran Rodríguez Martínez, *El cine que nos dejó ver Franco* (Junta de Comunidades de Castilla la Mancha, 2005), 94. See also the research group out of the Universidad de León and Universidad del País Vasco

called TRACE. Established in 1997, it focuses on translation and censorship in Spain of scripts in English, and recently in French and German, during the Franco period. http://trace.unileon.es

18. Vicesecretaria de educación de FET y de las JONS. Jefatura Superior de Servicios. Normas de Protección de peliculas españolas. Madrid, 15 June 1944 Archivo General de la Administración, Alcalá de Henares, Spain Section Cultura /1871.

19. Ibid.

20. Ibid.

21. Circular letter by José Ibañez Martín, general director of Cinematography and Theater, Madrid October 29, 1949. AGA, Alcalá de Henares, Spain Section Cultura, 1869.

22. Correspondence Madrid 7 January, 1949. AGA/ Cultura 1869.

23. Ministerio de Educación Nacional, "Relación de dietas devengadas durante los días 1 al 20 de enero 1949 por los miembros de la Junta Superior de Orientación Cinematográfica. Cultura," Censura Cinematográfica Lega 1869. AGA, Alcalá de Henares.

24. Gubern, *Un cine para el cadalso,* 59. The rules for classification were: 1= authorized for everyone including children, 2= authorized for youth, 3= authorized for adults, 3= authorized for adults but with reservations, 4= very dangerous.

25. Gubern, *Un cine para el cadalso,* 68–69.

26. Pius XII, *Miranda Prorsus* (*On the Communications Field: Motion Pictures, Radio, Television*), encyclical promulgated on September 8, 1957.

27. Pius XI, *Vigilanti cura,* quoted in Pius XII, *Miranda Prorsus.*

28. Typescript , Official correspondence Junta Superior de Orientación Cinematográfica, Cultura, Censura cinematográfica, Legajo 1871. Archivo General de la Administración, Alcalá de Henares.

29. Molina-Foix, *New Cinema in Spain,* 13.

30. Gubern, *Un cine para el cadalso,* 65.

31. Ibid.

32. Molina-Foix, *New Cinema in Spain,* 12.

33. Marsha Kinder, *Blood Cinema. The Reconstruction of National Identity in Spain.* (Berkeley: University of California Press, 1993), 4.

34. Augusto Torres, *Las películas de mi vida* (Madrid: Espasa, 2002), 86.

35. Some of the award-winning works include Berlanga's *El verdugo* (*The Executioner,* 1964), Miguel Picazo's *La Tía Tula* (*Aunt Tula,* 1964), Basilio Martín Patino's *Nueve cartas a Berta* (*Nine Letters to Berta,* 1965), Carlos Saura's *La caza* (*The Hunt,* 1965) and *Peppermint Frappé* (1967), Luis Buñuel's *Tristana* (1970), and Jaime de Armiñán's *Mi querida señorita* (*My Dearest Lady,* 1971).

36. Vicente Molina-Foix, *New Cinema in Spain* (London: British Film Institute, 1977), 48.

37. Ibid.

38. Ibid., 49.

39. Ibid., 18.

40. Fundación FOESSA, *Estudios Sociológicos sobre la situación social de España 1975* (Madrid: Editorial de Euroamérica, 1976), 1061–62.

41. Ibid., 1064.

42. See Susan Martín-Márquez, *Feminist Discourse and Spanish Cinema: Sight Unseen* (Oxford: Oxford University Press, 1999), María Asunción Gomez, *Del esenario a la pantalla: la adaptación cinematográfica del teatro español*)

Chapel Hill: University of North Carolina At Chapel Hill, Dept. of Romance Languages, 2000); Steven Marsh and Parvati Nair eds. *Gender and Spanish Cinema* (Oxford: Berg, 2004).

43. Ana Mariscal was a famous actress during the 1940s. She played a role in the film *Raza* (1941) along with Alfredo Mayo as the beau in Franco's script.

44. María Suárez Lafuente, "Women in Pieces: The Filmic Re/Constructions of Josefina Molina," *European Journal of Women's Studies* 10, no. 4, (2003): 395–407.

45. Gwendolyn Audrey Foster, *Women Film Directors: An International Bio-Critical Dictionary* (Westport, CT: Greenwood Press, 1995), 263–64.

46. Angel S. Harguindey, "Problemas administrativos en la primera película de Pilar Miró," *El País,* Cultura, September 4, 1976.

47. Antonio Lara "Más 250.000 espectadores ven cada película" CINEFESTIVAL DE BELGRADO *El Pais* Cultura, October 2, 1977.

48. Angel S. Harguindey, "La petición", de Pilar Miró, al Festival de Teherán," El País Cultura–December, 2, 1976. The Teheran Film Festival was a category "A" in the same rank with Cannes or San Sebastián.

49. "Pilar Miró muere de un infarto a los 57 años" *El País,* October 20, 1997.

50. Steven Shaviro, *The Cinematic Body.* Theory out of Bounds, vol. 2, (Minneapolis: University of Minnesota Press, 1993), 255–66.

51. Ibid., 264.

52. Ibid., 67.

53. Ibid., 263.

54. Signs of the timid "aperturismo" came 1957 with the establishment of the national Delegation of Associations under Manuel Fraga Iribarne, in charge at the time of the general secretary of the Movement. This new agency facilitated the legalization of some civil groups and associations. Law 191 of December 1964 and the decree 1440 of May 20 the same year allowed the legalization of diverse associations including some women's groups. Since the first Stabilization Plan in 1959 there were several others that followed. Economic planning undertaken by the regime responded to the mandate of the International Monetary Fund and led to several devaluations of the Spanish peseta that ignited social unrest with several strikes. Some of the women's associations were Seminario de Estudios Sociológicos de la Mujer (SESM), founded in 1960 by María Laffitte Condesa de Campo Alange, in existence until 1986; Movimiento Democrático de Mujeres (MDM), which included members of the Communist Party, PSOE, and some Christian organizations. In 1974 it adopted the name Movimiento Democrático de Mujeres/Movimiento de Liberación de la Mujer and worked toward the elaboration of legislation to legalize divorce and abortion, gay rights, contraception and political amnesty. To these associations we need to add Asociación de Amas de Casa (1969), Asociación de Mujeres Separadas (1972), Asociacion de Mujeres Juristas (1971), Asociación Democrática de la Mujer spearheaded by the PTE (Partido del Trabajo de España, 1976), Seminario Colectivo Feminista y Colectivo Feminista de Madrid (1975), Colectivo Jurídico Feminista (1975), Frente de Liberación de la Mujer (FLM, 1976), Unión para la Liberación de la Mujer (1977), and Asociación Universitaria para el Estudio de los problemas de la Mujer at the Universidad Complutense de Madrid (1975). See Mary Salas, Merche Comabella et al. *Españolas en la Transición. De excluidas a Protagonistas (1973–1982)* (Madrid: Biblioteca Nueva, 1999), 25–125.

55. Aurora Bautista interviewed by author.

56. Ibid.

57. Feliciano Fidalgo, "Purísima Sara," *El País* July 10, 1988.

58. Lyrics of "Fumando Espero," one of the sensual songs that made Sara Montiel famous as an actress-singer for her performance in Juan de Orduña's *El último cuplé* (1957).

59. Interview, *El Mundo,* December 2000, http://www.el-mundo.es/magazine/m61/textos/sara1.html.

60. Ibid.

61. Miguel A. Villena, "La violetera y el Nobel" *El País,* Ultima, November 28, 2000.

62. Ibid.

63. Zeus's adoption was the subject of a press scandal when the Catholic newspaper *Ya* published that Zeus had been purchased to his biological mother, Gisela Martínez, who worked in a nightclub in Alicante. The lawsuit filed in 1985 by Montiel and her husband, led to a judicial resolution that ordered *Ya* and the two journalists involved in the publication to pay 40 million pesetas to Sara Montiel and Pepe Tous. B. de la Cuadra "La Editorial Católica, condenada a pagar 40 millones a Sara Montiel," *El País,* February 1, 1986.

64. Interview, *El Mundo,* December 2000, http://www.el-mundo.es/magazine/m61/textos/sara1.html

65. *Te Quiero Para Mí* (Spain, 1944), Director: Ladislao Vajda; *Empezó En Boda* (Spain, 1944), Director: Rafaello Mattarazzo; *Bambú* (Spain, 1945), Director: José Luis Sáez de Heredia; *Se Le Fué El Novio* (Spain, 1945), Director: Julio Salvador; *El Misterioso Viajero Del Clipper* (Spain, 1946), Director: Gonzalo Delgrás; *Por El Gran Premio*" (Spain, 1946), Director: Pierre Caron; *Vidas Confusas* (Spain, 1947), Director: Jerónimo Mihura; *Confidencia* (Spain, 1947), Director: Jerónimo Mihura; *Mariona Rebull* (Spain, 1947), Director: José Luis Sáenz de Heredia; *Alhucemas* (Spain, 1948), Director: Enrique Llovet; *Don Quijote De La Mancha* (Spain, 1948), Director: Rafael Gil; *Locura De Amor* (Spain, 1948), Director: Juan de Orduña, aka *The Mad Queen* (in the USA); *La Mies Es Mucha* (Spain, 1949), Director: José Luis Sáenz de Heredia; *Pequeñeces* (Spain, 1950), Director: Juan de Orduña; *El Capitán Veneno* (Spain, 1950), Director: Luis Marquina; *That Man From Tangiers* (US and Spain 1950), Director: Robert Elwyn.

66. *Furia Roja* (US and Mexico, 1950), Director: Steve Sekely; *Necesito Dinero* (Mexico, 1951), Director: Miguel Zacarías; *Carcel De Mujeres* (Mexico, 1951), Director: Miguel M. Delgado; *Ahí Viene Martin Corona* (Mexico, 1951), Director: Miguel Zacarías; *El Enamorado* (Mexico, 1951), Director: Miguel Zacarías; *Ella, Lucifer Y Yo* (Mexico, 1952), Director: Miguel Morayta; *Yo Soy Gallo Dondequiera* (Mexico, 1952), Director: Roberto Rodriguez; *Piel Canela* (Mexico and Cuba 1953), Director: Juan J. Ortega; *¿Por Qué Ya No Me Quieres?* (Mexico, 1953), Director: Chano Urueta; *Se Solicitan Modelos* (Mexico, 1954), Director: Chano Urueta; *Frente Al Pecado De Ayer* (Mexico and Cuba 1954), Director: Juan J. Ortega; *Yo No Creo En Los Hombres*(Mexico and Cuba 1954), Director: Juan J. Ortega; and *Donde El Circulo Termina* (Mexico, 1955), Director: Alfredo B. Crevenna.

67. In her memoirs she tells an embarrassing story that took place during one of Mann's visits to Spain at a banquet to celebrate July 18 that Franco offered in the Palace of La Granja outside Madrid. Anthony Mann got ill. "Maybe it was the heat or perhaps something he ate," Montiel says, "Tony felt queasy. It was

horrible because he made it in his pants. I stayed with him in a corner while Franco passed by. The smell was awful . . . then Franco called me on the side but he did not want to meet Tony." Upon request of the actress, Tony was rescued by a physician, no other than Cristobal Martínez Bordiu, Marquis de Villaverde, son-in-law of the dictator. Sara Montiel, *Memorias. Vivir es un placer* (Barcelona: Plaza y Janés, 2000), 221.

68. Rosa Montero, "Diva y Tierna. Sara Montiel y la estabilidad de los 55 años" *El País,* Cultura, August 28, 1983.

69. See Kathleen M. Vernnon, "Theatricality, Melodrama, and Stardom in *el último cuplé,*" in *Gender and Spanish Cinema,* ed. Steven Marsh and Parvati Nair (Oxford: Berg, 2004).

70. M.A.B. "Sara Montiel, La 'otra' del cine español," *El País,* Crítica, August 8, 1983.

71. Feliciano Fidalgo, "Sara Montiel: "Yo hice cine en mi época, como Miró hizo pintura en la suya. Homenaje a la actriz española en el Festival de París," *El País* Cultura, December 14, 1982.

72. Ibid.

73. Ibid.

74. Ibid.

75. Juan Miguel, "Me las sacaron a traición," *El País,* Cultura, September 19, 1980.

76. Ullán, "Sara Montiel: 'Las fotos en que estoy desnuda.'"

77. Ibid.

78. Interview, *El Mundo,* December 2000, http://www.el-mundo.es/magazine/m61/textos/sara1.html, 4.

79. Ibid., 5.

80. Francisco Umbral, "Sara Montiel" Entrevista Mis queridos Monstruos," *El País,* Opinión, June 4, 1984, 3.

81. Interview, *El Mundo,* December 2000, http://www.el-mundo.es/magazine/m61/textos/sara1.html, 3.

82. Francisco Umbral, "Antoñísima," *El País,* Sociedad, September 17, 1980.

83. Francisco Umbral, "Tribuna: La Elipse de Francisco Umbral," *El País,* January 3, 1987.

84. Aurora Bautista, tape-recorded interview by author, Madrid, May 31, 2000.

85. Aurora Bautista interviewed by author .

86. Gente Importante: Aurora Bautista. De Doña Juana a la Tía Tula de Unamuno-Picazo, nd.

87. Aurora Bautista, interviewed by author. Ibid.

88. Ibid.

89. Ibid.

90. A remake of *Locura de Amor* was released in 2001 under the direction of Vicente Aranda and entitled *Juana la Loca.* For a comparison of the two films see Celia Martín Pérez, "Madness, Queenship, and Womanhood in Orduña's *Locura de Amor (1948)* and Aranda's *Juana la Loca* (2001) in Steven Marsh and Parvati Nair, eds., *Gender and Spanish Cinema* (Oxford: Berg, 2004), 71–87.

91. Sara Montiel, born María Antonia Abad Fernández in 1928, traveled to Hollywood and married Anthony Mann.

92. In the same way the body of José Antonio was translated from Alicante to the Valley of the Fallen, the monumental mausoleum was built for Franco

by prisoners of the civil war. The Valley of the Fallen is the burial site of Franco himself. José Antonio's journey after death to Madrid shows the central role of the body in the symbolic spectacle of power.

93. Aurora Bautista, interview by author.

94. Ibid.

95. Ibid.

96. *Semana,* Madrid May 25, 1989, and *Hola,* Barcelona, July 1, 1986.

97. Aurora Bautista, interview by author, 2000.

98. The budget for *Agustina de Aragón* was nine million pesetas and there were 600 extras. See Jo Labanyi "Constume, Identity, and Spectator Pleasure in Historical Films of the Early Franco Period," *Gender and Spanish Cinema,* ed. in Steven Marsh and Parvati Nair (Oxford: Berg, 2004), 36.

99. Aurora Bautista, interview by author.

100. *Informaciones,* Madrid April 13, 1983.

101. "Aurora Bautista" *Interviú.*

102. *Ya,* Madrid, Friday Noviembre 29, 1985.

103. Antonio R. Vargas, "Homenaje a García Lorca. Fiesta de la Libertad Andaluza" *Interviú,* June 1976.

104. Fernando Arrabal was born in Melilla, Africa, in 1932. His father was an army officer that suffered the Francoist reprisal and disappeared in 1941. Arrabal resides in France and has published twelve novels, six collections of poems, nearly seventy plays, sixteen essays and epistles (among which is the famous Letter to General Franco), and numerous books. He has directed seven full-length films.

105. Enrique Llovet, "Admirable Arrabal, admirable Bautista," *El País,* Cultura, Madrid, May 31, 1978.

106. Ibid.

107. In the novel Gertrudis (Tula) takes care of the five children her sister leaves behind after she dies in childbirth labor. Instead of marrying Ramiro, her widower brother-in-law, she will also take care of the children he will have with his second wife, Manuela. After Ramiro y Manuela die, Tula takes care of the children. Surrogate motherhood is her only purpose in life.

108. Raquel Hernández, "Editado en Jaén guión original de la censurada version de 'La tía Tula'" *El País,* April 15, 2005.

109. Aurora Bautista, interview by author.

110. Ibid.

111. Ibid.

112. Sally Faulkner, "A Cinema of Contradictions: Picazo's *La Tía Tula* (1964) and The Nuevo Cine Español," *The Modern Language Review* 99, no. 3 (2004): 651–64 (656).

113. Hernández, *El País,* April 15, 2005.

114. Sally Faulkner, "A Cinema of Contradictions: Picazo's *La Tía Tula,*" 655.

115. Ibid., 658.

116. Miguel Picazo Dios et al., *La Tía Tula. Guión,* 143.

117. Sally Faulkner, "A Cinema of Contradictions: Picazo's *La Tía Tula,*" 658.

118. Miguel Picazo Dios et al. *La Tía Tula. Guión,* 148–49.

119. Shaviro, *The Cinematic Body,* 256.

120. Miguel Picazo Dios, et al. *La Tía Tula. Guión,* 171.

121. Miguel Picazo Dios, et al. *La Tía Tula. Guión,* 172–173.

122. See Alejandro Varderi, *Severo Sarduy y Pedro Almodovar. Del Barroco al Kitsch en la narrativa y el cine postmodernos* (Madrid: Editorial Pliegos, 1996), 81.

123. Kinder, *Blood Cinema*, 8–9.

Conclusion

1. The study of Spain's location within the European imaginary promises to shed some light on the question of Europeanism/Westerness. As Gerard Delanty proposes, "What is to be questioned is the idea of a European identity as a totalizing project." Gerard Delanty, *Inventing Europe. Idea, Identity, Reality* (New York: St. Martin's Press, 1995).

2. Some of the ideas in this conclusion are further developed in my article, "The Orient Within. Women's Self-empowering Acts under Francoism" in *Women as Agents of Change in the Middle East and North Africa*, ed. Fatima Sadiqi, Forthcoming, (New York: Routledge, 2010).

3. José Alvarez Junco and Adrian Shubert, eds., *Spanish History since 1808* (New York: Arnold, 2000), 1.

4. Prosper Mérimée, *Carmen* (1845), translated by Lady Mary Loyd, January, 2001 [Etext #2465] The Project Gutenberg Etext of Carmen, by Prosper Mérimée. [My emphasis].

5. Enrique Dussel points out that it was in the fifteenth century with the colonial expansion of Portugal and Spain that we can talk of a first step toward modernity. Europe established itself as the "center" of the world—as the embodiment of universal values and truths. Enrique Dussel, "Europe, Modernity, and Eurocentrism," *Nepantla: Views from South*, 1 no. 3 (Durham, NC: Duke University Press, 2000), 470.

6. The Enlightenment further developed the notion of "Eurocentrism." Europe is defined by Hegel as the beginning and end of history, emphasizing the diverse "Europes" as well. Southern Europe, in his interpretation described as "the land of the South of the Pyrenees," lacked a nucleus while the true modernizing drive lies in the northern European nations. There are even two Norths: the east (Poland and Russia), which in Enlightenment eyes became relatively negligible because of its relation with Asia; and the northwestern part, which becomes the motor of modernity. Hegel, *The Philosophy of History* was based primarily on lectures presented by Hegel in the winter of 1830–31.

7. See Sasha Pack, *Tourism and Dictatorship: Europe's Peaceful Invasion of Franco's Spain* (Houndsville: Palgrave Macmillan, 2006).

8. Peter Child and Patrick Williams, *An Introduction to Post-Colonial Theory* (London: Prentice Hall, 1997), 129.

Epilogue

1. No necesito liberarme de nada. *Soy la libertad absoluta* [my emphasis]." Carlos de las Heras, *Susana Estrada, Humedo Sexo* (Madrid: El Autor, 1978).

2. Ted Córdova-Claure, *España: El destape. 13 notas reportajes de Ted Córdova-Claure* (Caracas: El Cid Editor, 1977), 14.

3. Ibid., 16.

4. For a detailed explanation of Franco's clinical ordeal see *Cambio 16,* October 26, 1975, *Cuadernos de Vanguardia* (special dossier) no. 1, 1976.

5. "El bello camino hacia la democracia. Marisol." *Interviú,* Año 1, no. 16, September 2–8, 1976.

6. Ibid.

7. Francisco Umbral, "Los cuerpos y los siglos," *Interviú. Especial 25 Aniversario* (May 15, 2001): 72.

8. Ibid.

Select Bibliography

Newspaers and Magazines

Hola
Cuadernos para el Diálogo
Fotogramas
El País
Senda
Semana
Interviu

Primary Sources

Alonso Tejada, L. *La represión sexual en la España de Franco.* Barcelona: Caralt, 1977.

Barrios, Manuel. *Cronicas del destape.* Barcelona: Planeta, 1979.

Boigelot, René. *El Matrimonio: El libro de la novia.* 10th edition. Madrid: Desclée de Brouwer, El Angel del Hogar, 1964.

———. *El Matrimonio: El libro del jóven de 17 a 20 años.* Madrid: Desclée de Brouwer, El Angel del Hogar, 1960.

———. *Maternidad: La maravillosa aventura de la célula humana desde el germen al recién nacido.* Madrid: Desclée de Brouwer, El Angel del Hogar, 1960, 1962, 1965.

Bosch Marín, Juan. "Asistencia Medico-Social en Madrid" Conferencia pronunciada en el Ateneo de Madrid en el Cursillo en honor del Excmo. Sr. Obispo de Madrid-Alcalá D. Leopoldo Eijo y Garay, en sus bodas de plata con la diócesis madrileña. Madrid: Ministerio de la Gobernación, Publicaciones "al servicio de España y del niño español" Septiembre, 1948.

Bosch Marín, Juan, Juan Pedro de la Cámara, and Venancio Saenz de Tejada. "270,000 partos. Sus enseñanzas sanitarias. Observaciones sobre la asistencia tocológica prestada en el seguro obligatorio de enfermedad durante los años 1947 a 1949." Ministerio de la Gobernación Dirección General de Sanidad. Sección de puericultura, Maternología e hygiene escolar. Madrid Publicaciones "Al servicio de España y del niño español" no. 152. Octubre 1950.

Bosch Marín, Juan. *Catecismo de Puericultura.* Madrid: Editorial Nebrija, 1979.

Bosch Marín, Juan. "Function of the Midwife in the World Today." Opening speech to the 13th Congress of the International Confederation of Midwives. Madrid: Gráficas González, 1963.

Brenan, Gerald. *The Face of Spain.* New York: Penguin, 1949.

Caballero, Oscar. *El sexo del Franquismo.* Madrid: Editorial Cambio 16, 1977.

Caro Patón, Tomás. *La mujer caída. Memorias y reflexiones de un médico de la lucha Antivenérea.* Madrid: M. Montal, editor, 1959.

Cooper, Norman B. *Catholicism and the Franco Regime.* London: Sage Publications, 1975.

Córdova-Claure, Ted. *España: El destape. 13 notas reportajes de Ted Córdova-Claure.* Caracas: El Cid Editor, 1977.

Costa, Joaquín. *Historia política social: Patria.* Madrid: Aguilar, 1961.

Departamento Nacional de Participación. Sección de Educación Física y Actividades Deportivas. *XXV Aniversario. Juegos escolares nacionales. 1949–1973.* Madrid: Delegaciones Nacionales de Educación Física y Deportes, Sección Femenina y la Juventud, 1973.

Fundación FOESSA. *Estudios Sociológicos sobre la situación social de España 1975.* Madrid: Editorial de Euroamérica, 1976.

———. *Informe Sociológico sobre la situación social de España.* Madrid: Editorial de Euroamérica, 1966.

García, Nieto, María Carmen, and Javier M. Donezar. *La España de Franco 1939–1973. Bases documentales de la España contemporánea.* Madrid: Guadiana, 1975.

Goytisolo, Juan. R*eivindicación del Conde Don Julián.* Barcelona: Seix Barral, 1970.

Gubern, Román. *Un cine para el cadalso.* Barcelona: Editorial Euros, 1975.

Guerra Gallego, Antonio. *Cómo se atrae y se enamora a un hombre.* 1953.

Heras, Carlos de las. *Susana Estrada, Humedo Sexo.* Madrid: El Autor, 1978.

Instituto Nacional de Estadística. *Anuario Estadístico de España.*1964.

Instituto Nacional de Estadística. *Anuario Estadístico de España. Cuadro Sinóptico de las principales actividades de la vida española año 1941–1955.* Madrid: INE, 1957.

Jiménez Asenjo, Enrique. *Abolicionismo y prostitución. Justificación y defense del Decreto-Ley de 3 de Marzo de 1956.* Madrid: Instituto Editorial Reus, 1963.

Junta Nacional Secretaría Técnica. *Informe sobre la moralidad pública en España.* Madrid: Patronato de Proteccion de la Mujer, 1943.

Marañón, Gregorio. "Literatura Sexual." In *Obras Completas.* Madrid: Espasa Calpe, 1968.

———. *Ensayos sobre la vida sexual.* Madrid: Espasa Calpe, 1951.

Maravall, José Antonio. "La Corriente doctrinal del Tacitismo político en España." *Cuadernos Hispanoamericanos* no. 238–40 (1969): 645–67.

———. "La idea del cuerpo místico en España antes de Erasmo." *Boletín de la Cátedra de Derecho de la Universidad de Salamanca,* no. 10–12, (mayo–octubre 1956): Reprinted in *Estudios de Historia del Pensariento Español* (Madrid: Ediciones Cutura Hispanica, 1973).

———. *La cultura del Barroco. Análisis de una estructura histórica.* Barcelona: Ariel, 1986.

Martínez Pujana, Ana. *La mujer es un ser humano.* (Basque Country Spain: Irun, Editorial Ethos, 1967.

Miguel, Amando de. *Sexo, mujer y natalidad en España.* Madrid: Edicusa, 1975.

Molina-Foix, Vicente. *New Cinema in Spain.* London: British Film Institute, 1977.

Morodo, Raul."La politización de la opinión pública. El fin de la criptopolítica en España y la polémica sobre la monarquía y la república." In *Iberia* New York, 15 October 1966.

Nóvoa Santos, Roberto. *La mujer, nuestro sexto sentido y otros esbozos.* Madrid: Biblioteca Nueva, 1929.

Ortega y Gasset, José. *España invertebrada.* Madrid: Revista de Occidente, 1959.

———. *Estudios sobre el amor.* Madrid: Revista de Occidente, 1966.

Pius XI. *Casti Connubii. Encyclical Of Pope Pius XI On Christian Marriage.* http://www.vatican.va/holy_father/pius_xi/encyclicals/documents/hf_p-xi_enc_31121930_casti-connubii_en.html.

Pius XII. *Address to Midwives on the Nature of Their Profession.* Vatican, October 29, 1951.

———. *Allocution to the Congress of the International Union of Catholic Women's Leagues.* Rome, Italy, September 11, 1947.

———. "Deporte y Gimnasia. Principios Religiosos y Morales." Sección Cultura. Archivo General de la Administración, Sección Femenina's Papers. Alcala de Henares, 1952.

———. *Miranda Prorsus. On the Communications Field: Motion Pictures, Radio, Television.* Encyclical promulgated on 8 September 1957.

Samaranch, Juan Antonio. "Informe presentado al Consejo Nacional del Movimiento sobre la situación actual de la educación física y el deporte español." December 15, 1969, Ediciones del Movimiento, 1969.

San Sebastián, Carmen. *Después de casarte! . . .* Madrid: Studiun Ediciones, 1965.

Sanmarti Boncompte, Francisco. *Tácitoen España.* Barcelona: CSIC, 1951.

Scanlon, Geraldine. *La polémica feminista en la España contemporánea (1868–1974).* Madrid: Siglo XXI, 1976.

Sección Femenina."The Spanish Social Service for women: Its objectives and results." In Sección Femenina de FET y de las JONS, *Servicio Social de la Mujer,* Madrid, 1965.

Songel, José. *Temario de Cursillos prematrimoniales.* Valencia: Editorial C.P.E., 1964.

Sorel, Andrés. *Discurso de la política y el sexo.* Madrid: Zero Zyx, 1978.

Tierno Galván, Enrique. *El tacitismo en las doctrinas políticas del Siglo de Oro español.* Murcia: Universidad de Murcia, 1949.

Umbral, Francisco. *Las Europeas.* Barcelona: Editorial Andorra, 1970.

———. *Las ninfas.* Barcelona: Ediciones Destino, 1976.

Vallejo Nágera, Antonio. *Eugenesia de la Hispanidad y regeneración de la raza.* Burgos, Editorial Española, 1937.

———. *Política racial del Nuevo Estado.* San Sebastián: Biblioteca España Nueva, 1938.

———. *La Sabiduría del hogar. Antes que te cases.* Madrid: Editorial Plus Ultra, 1946.

Wright, Richard. *Pagan Spain.* Jackson: University of Mississippi Press, 1957 edition 2002.

Secondary Sources

Abella, Rafael. *La vida cotidiana bajo el regimen de Franco.* Madrid: Temas de Hoy, 1996.

Adelson, Leslie A. *Making Bodies, Making History. Feminism and German Identity.* Lincoln: University of Nebraska Press, 1993.

Aguilar, Paloma. *Memory and Amnesia: The Role of the Spanish Civil War in the Transition to Democracy.* Oxford: Berghahn Books, 2002.

Alcalde, Carmen. *Mujeres en el Franquismo: Exiliadas, nacionalistas y opositoras.* Barcelona: Flor de Viento Ediciones, 1996.

Alonso, L. E., and F. Conde. *Historia del consume en España: Una aproximación a sus orígenes y primer desarrollo.* Madrid: Debate, 1994.

Alvarez Junco, José. *Mater Dolorosa. La idea de España en el siglo XIX.* Madrid: Taurus, 2001.

Anderson, Benedict. *Imagined Communities: Reflections on the Origin and Spread of Nationalism.* New York: Verso, 2006.

Arendt, Hannah. *Eichmann in Jerusalem. A Report on the Banality of Evil.* New York: Penguin Books, 1994.

———. *The Origins of Totalitarianism. (Introduction by Samantha Power)* New York: Schocken Books, 2004.

Barrachina, Marie-Aline. *Propagande et Culture dans l'Espagne franquiste 1936–1945).* Grenoble: Ellug, 1998.

Berbel Sánchez, Sara, and María Teresa Pi-Sunyer Peyrí. *El cuerpo silenciado. Una aproximación a la identidad femenina.* Barcelona: Viena Ediciones, 2001.

Bhabha, Homi K. *The Location of Culture.* London: Routledge, 2004.

Baiez Aparicio, Nathan. *Vagos, maleantes y homosexuals. La represión a los homosexuals durante el franquismo.* Barcelona: Malhivern, 2007.

Blackmore, Josiah, and Gregory S. Hutcheson, eds. *Queer Iberia. Sexualities, Cultures, and Crossings from the Middle Ages to the Renaissance.* Durham, NC: Duke University Press, 1999.

Baudrillard, Jean. *Seduction.* Palgrave Macmillan,1991.

———. *Simulacra and Simulation. The Body, In Theory: Histories of Cultural Materialism.* Ann Arbor: University of Michigan Press, 1995.

Bowen, Wayne H. *Spain during World War II.* Columbia, MO: University of Missouri Press, 2006.

Boyd P. Carolyn. *Historia Patria.* Princeton, NJ: Princeton University Press, 1997.

Brassloff, Audrey. *Religion and Politics in Spain. The Spanish Church in Transition.* London: Macmillan Press, 1998.

Brenan, Gerald. *The Face of Spain.* 3rd ed. (Harmondsworth, Middlesex: Penguin Travel Library, 1965).

Butler, Judith. *Bodies That Matter. On the Discursive Limits of "Sex."* New York: Routledge, 1993.

Buxán, Xosé. *Conciencia de un deseo singular. Estudios gays y lesbianas en el Estado español.* Barcelona: Laertes, 1997.

Calahan, William. *The Catholic Church in Spain, 1875–1998.* Washington, D.C.: The Catholic University of America Press, 2000.

Canning, Kathleen. "The Body as Method? Reflections on the Place of the Body in Gender History." *Gender & History* 11, no. 3 (November 1999), 499–513.

Canning, Kathleen, and Sonya Rose. *Gender, Citizenships and Subjectivities Gender and History Special Issues.* Oxford: Wiley-Blackwell, 2002.

Carrette, Jeremy R., ed. *Religion and Culture. Michel Foucault.* New York: Routledge, 1999.

Casero, Estrella. *La España que bailó con Franco. Coros y Danzas de la Sección Femenina.* Madrid: Editorial ENE Nuevas Estructuras, SL, 2000.

Castejón Bolea, Ramón. *Moral sexual y enfermedad: La medicina española frente al peligro venéreo.* Granada: Universidad de Granada, 2001.

Cazorla Sánchez, Antonio. *Las políticas de la Victoria.* Madrid: Marcial Pons, 2000.

———. *Fear & Progress. Ordinary Lives in Franco's Spain 1939–75.* Malden, MA: Wiley-Blackwell, 2009.

Cela, Camilo José. *Journey to the Alcarria. Travels Through the Spanish Countryside* New York: A Morgan Entrekin Book, 1964.

Charnon-Deutsch, Lou. *Fictions of the Feminine in the Nineteenth Century Spanish Press.* University Park: Pensylvannia State University Press, 2000.

Child, Peter, and Patrick Williams. *An Introduction to Post-Colonial Theory* London: Prentice Hall, 1997.

Conboy, Katie, Nadia Medina, and Sarah Stanbury, eds. *Writing on the Body. Female Embodiment and Feminist Theory.* New York: Columbia University Press, 1997.

Corrin, Jay P. *Catholic Intellectuals and the Challenge of Democracy.* Notre Dame, IN: University of Notre Dame Press, c2002.

Cott, Nancy F. *Public Vows: A History of Marriage and the Nation.* Cambridge, MA: Harvard University Press, 2002.

Cruz, Anne, and Mary Elizabeth Perry, eds. *Culture and Control in Counter-Reformation Spain.* Minneapolis: University of Minnesota Press, 1992.

Da Soller, Claudio. "The Beautiful Woman in Medieval Iberia: Rhetoric, Cosmetics, and Evolution" PhD. diss., University of Missouri-Columbia, July 2005.

De Certeau, Michel. *The Practice of Everyday Life.* Berkeley: University of California Press, 1988.

Defourneaux, Marceline. *Daily Life in Spain in the Golden Age.* Palo Alto: Stanford University Press, 1979.

Delanty, Gerard. *Inventing Europe. Idea, Identity, Reality* New York: St. Martin's Press, 1995.

Desfor Edles, Laura. *Symbol and Ritual in the New Spain. The Transition to Democracy after Franco.* London: Cambridge University Press, 1998.

Di Febo, Giuliana. *Ritos de Guerra y de Victoria en la España franquista.* Bilbao: Desclée Brouwer, 2002.

Díaz, Elías. *Pensamiento español en la era de Franco 1939–1975.* 2nd ed. Madrid: Tecnos, 1992.

Domínguez Juan, M. M. *Representación de la mujer en las revistas femininas.* Madrid: Universidad Complutense de Madrid, 1998.

Domínguez Prats, Pilar. *Voces del Exilio. Mujeres españolas en México, 1939–1950.* Madrid: CAM, 1994.

Dopico Black , Georgina. *Perfect Wives, Other Women. Adultery and Inquisition in Early Modern Spain.* Durham, NC: Duke University Press, 2001.

Dussel, Enrique. "Europe, Modernity, and Eurocentrism" in *Nepantla: Views from South* 1.3 (Durham, NC: Duke University Press, 2000).

Enders, Victoria Loree, and Pamela Beth Radcliff. *Constructing Spanish Womanhood: Female Identity in Modern Spain.* Albany: SUNY Press, 1999.

Esenwein, George. *Spanish Civil War: A Modern Tragedy.* New York: Routledge Sources in History, 2005.

Eslava Galán, Juan. *Coitus Interruptus: La repression sexual y sus heroicos alivios en la España franquista.* Barcelona: Planeta, 1997.

Falasca-Zamponi, Simonetta. *Fascist Spectacle: The Aesthetics of Power in Mussolini's Italy Studies on the History of Society and Culture.* Berkeley: University of California Press, 2000.

Faulkner, Sally. *A Cinema of Contradiction: Spanish Film in the 1960s.* Edinburgh: Edinburgh University Press, 2006.

———. "A Cinema of Contradictions: Picazo's *La Tía Tula* 1964 and The Nuevo Cine Español." *The Modern Language Review* 99, no. 3 (2004): 651–64.

Ferguson, Margaret W., Maureen Quilligan, and Nancy J. Vickers, eds. *Re-writing the Renaissance. Discourses of Sexual Difference in Early Modern Europe.* Chicago: The University of Chicago Press, 1986.

Foard, Douglas W. *The Revolt of the Aesthetes. Ernesto Giménez Caballero and the Origins of Spanish Fascism.* New York: Peter Lang, 1989.

Foucault, Michel. *The Birth of the Clinic. An Archaeology of Medical Perception.* New York: Vintage Books, 1994.

———. *Historia de la sexualidad.* Madrid: Siglo XXI, 1980.

———. *Discipline & Punish: The Birth of the Prison.* New York: Vintage Books, 1995.

Fuente, Inmaculada de la. *Mujeres de la Postguerra. De Carmen Laforet a Rosa Chacel: Historia de una generación.* Barcelona: Planeta, 2002.

Gallego, María Teresa, *Mujer, Falange y Franquismo.* Madrid: Taurus, 1983.

García Rodrigo, Jesús, and Fran Rodríguez Martínez. *El cine que nos dejó ver Franco.* Castilla la Manche: Junta de Comunidades de Castilla la Mancha, 2005.

Garlinger, Patrick Paul. *Confessions of the Letter Closet. Epistolary Fiction and Queer Desire in Modern Spain.* Minneapolis: University of Minnesota Press, 2005.

Gatens, Moira. *Imaginary Bodies. Ethics, Power, and Corporeality.* New York: Rutledge, 1996.

Gies, David T., ed. *Modern Spanish Culture.* New York: Cambridge University Press, 2000.

Gómez, María Asunción. *Del escenario a la pantalla: la adaptación cinematográfica del teatro español.* Chapel Hill: University of North Carolina At Chapel Hill, Dept. of Romance Languages, 2000.

———. "La representación cinematográfica en el cine español de los años 40 y 50: Del cine bélico and neorrealismo." *Bulletin of Spanish Studies* 79 (2002): 575–89.

González-Anleo, Juan [et al.] *La Iglesia en España, 1950–2000.* Madrid: PPC, 1999.

Gori, Gigliola. *Italian Fascism and the Female Body: Submissive Women and Strong Mothers Sport in the Global Society.* New York: Routledge, 2004.

Gracia García, Jordi, and Miguel Angel Ruiz Carnicer. *La España de Franco 1939–1975 Cultura y vida cotidiana.* Madrid: Editorial Síntesis, 2001.

Graham, Helen, and Jo Labanyi. *Spanish Cultural Studies: An Introduction: The Struggle for Modernity.* Oxford: Oxford University Press, 1996.

Graves, Lucia, *A Woman Unknown. Voices From a Spanish Life.* Washington, DC: Counterpoint, 2000.

Graves, Robert, *Majorca Observed.* London: Cassel, 1965.

Grazia, Victoria de. *The Culture of Consent. Mass Organization of Leisure in Fascist Italy.* London: Cambridge University Press, 2002.

———. *Irresistible Empire: Americas Advance through Twentieth-Century Europe.* Cambridge, MA: Harvard University Press, 2006.

Green, Anna, *Cultural History.* London: Palgrave, 2008.

Greer, Margaret Rich. *María de Zayas Tells Baroque Tales of Love and Cruelty of Men.* University Park: Pennsylvania State University Press, 2000.

Grosz, Elizabeth. *Volatile Bodies: Toward a Corporeal Feminism.* Bloomington: Indiana University Press, 1994.

Haidt, Rebecca. *Embodying Enlightenment. Knowing the Body in Eighteenth-Century Spanish Literature and Culture.* New York: St. Martin's Press, 1998.

Hartmann, Ilse. *Sport and Women: Social Issues in International Perspective.* London: International Society for Comparative Physical Education & Sport Routledge, 2002.

Hernández Sandoica, Elena, Miguel Angel Ruiz Carnicer, and Marc Baldó Lacomba. *Estudiantes contra Franco (1939–1975). Oposición política y movilización juvenil.* Madrid: La esfera de los libros, 2007.

Holguin, Sandie. *Creating Spaniards: Culture and National Identity in Republican Spain.* Madison: University of Wisconsin Press, 2002.

Irigaray, Luce. *This Sex Which Is Not One.* Ithaca, NY: Cornell University Press, 1985.

Jensen, Geoffrey. *Irrational Triumph. Cultural Dispair, Military Nationalism, and the Ideological Origins of Franco's Spain.* Reno: University of Nevada Press, 2002.

Juárez, Miguel, and Demetrio Casado, eds. *V Informe sobre la situación social en España. Sociedad para todos en el año 2000.* Madrid: Cáritas Española, 1994.

Juliá, Santos, ed. *Memoria de la Guerra y del Franquismo.* Madrid: Taurus, 2006.

Junco, Gema. "Violence and the New Spanish Woman." MA thesis, Florida International University, Miami, June 2004.

Kaplan, Temma. *Taking Back the Streets: Women, Youth, and Direct Democracy.* Berkeley: University of California Press, 2004.

Kinder, Marsha. *Blood Cinema. The Reconstruction of National Identity in Spain.* Berkeley: University of California Press, 1993.

———, ed. *Refiguring Spain: Cinema/Media/Representation.* Durham, NC: Duke University Press, 1997.

Labanyi, Jo. *Constructing Identity in Twentieth-Century Spain: Theoretical Debates and Cultural Practice.* Oxford: Oxford University Press, 2002.

———. "Costume, Identity, and Spectator Pleasure in Historical Films of the Early Franco Period." In *Gender and Spanish Cinema,* edited by Steven Marsh and Parvati Nair. Oxford: Berg, 2004.

Lakoff, George, and Mark Johnson. *Metaphors We Live By.* Chicago: University of Chicago Press, 1980.

Lannon, Frances. "Los cuerpos de las mujeres y el cuerpo político: Autoridades e identidades en conflicto en España durante las décadas de 1920 y 1930." *Historia Social,* no. 35 (1999): 65–80.

———. *Privilege, Persecution, and Prophecy. The Catholic Church in Spain 1875–1975.* Oxford: Clarendon Press, 1987.

Laqueur, Thomas. *Making Sex: Body and Gender from the Greeks to Freud.* Cambridge, MA: Harvard University Press, 1992.

Lee Bartky, Sandra. *Femininity and Domination. Studies in the Phenomenology of Oppression.* New York: Routledge, 1990.

Linhard, Jose. "Family Planning in Spain." *International Family Planning Perspectives* 9, no. 1 (Mar. 1983).

Linke, Uli. *German Bodies: Race and Representation After Hitler.* New York: Routledge, 1999.

López Sánchez, Rosario. *Mujer española, una sombra de destino en lo universal: Trayectoria histórica de Seccón Femenina de Falange 1934–1977.* Colección Maior. Murcia: Universidad de Murcia 1990.

Luzzatto, Sergio. *The Body of Il Duce: Mussolini's Corpse and the Fortunes of Italy.* New York: Metropolitan Books, 2005.

Maclean, Ian. *The Renaissance Notion of Woman. A Study of the Fortunes of Scholasticism and Medical Science in European Intellectual Life.* Cambridge Monographs on the History of Medicine, (Cambridge: Cambridge University Press, 1995).

Mangan J. A., ed. *Making European Masculinities. Sport, Europe, Gender.* London: Frank Cass, 2000.

Mann, Michael. *Fascists.* New York: Cambridge University Press, 2004.

Maravall, Jose Antonio. *La Cultura Del Barroco.* Madrid: Editorial Ariel, 1980.

Martín Gaite, Carmen. *The Backroom.* San Francisco: City Lights Books, 2000.

———. *Usos amorosos de la postguerra española.* Madrid: Anagrama, 1987.

Martín-Márquez, Susan. *Feminist Discourse and Spanish Cinema. Sight Unseen.* Oxford: Oxford University Press, 1999.

Mazzio, Carla, and David Hillman. *The Body in Parts: Fantasies of Corporeality in Early Modern Europe.* New York: Routledge, 1997.

McDonough, Peter, Samuel H. Barnes, and Antonio López Pina, eds. *The Cultural Dynamics of Democratization in Spain.* Ithaca, NY: Cornell University Press, 1998.

Merleau-Ponty, Maurice. *Phenomenology of Perception.* New York: Routledge, 2004.

Mira, L. D. Alberto. *De Sodoma a Chueca. Una historia cultural de la homosexualidad en España en el siglo XX.* Barcelona: Egalés, 2004.

Molinero, Carme. *La captación de las masas. Política social y propaganda en el régimen franquista.* Madrid: Cátedra, 2005.

Molinero, Carme, M. Sala, and J. Sobrequés, eds. *Una imensa prisión. Los campos de concentración y las prisiones durante la Guerra civil y el franquismo.* Barcelona: Crítica Contrastes, 2003.

Montiel, Sara. *Memorias. Vivir es un placer.* Barcelona: Plaza y Janés, 2000.

Moradiellos, Enrique. *La España de Franco (1939–1975). Política y Sociedad.* Madrid: Editorial Síntesis, 2000.

Morcillo, Aurora G. *True Catholic Womanhood. Gender Ideology in Franco's Spain.* Dekalb: Northern Illinois University Press, 2000.

———. "Uno, Dos, Tres, Cuatro: Modern Women Docile Bodies." In *Sport in Society,* special issue *Sport, Mass Consumerism, and the Body in Modern Spain,* edited by Andrew McFarland, no. 6, (2008): .

———. "Walls of Flesh. Spanish Postwar Reconstruction and Public Morality." *Bulletin of Spanish Studies,* 84, no. 6, (2007): 737–58.

Morodo, Raul. "Tierno Galván y otros precursores políticos," *El País,* Madrid, 1987.

Mosse, George. *The Crisis of German Ideology. Intellectual Origins of the Third Reich.* (Howard Fertig; Reprint edition, 1999; London: Weidenfeld and Nicolson, origiinal, 1970).

Munson, Elizabeth. "Walking on the Periphery: Gender and the Discourse of Modernization." *Journal of Social History* 36 no. 1 (2002): 63–75.

Muñoz Ruiz, María del Carmen. " La representación de la imágen delas mujeres en el franquismo a través de la prensa femnina, 1955–1970." In *Representación, construcción e interpretación de la imágen visual de las mujeres,* edited by P. Amador Carretero, and Ruiz Franco Madrid: Instituto de Cultura y Tecnología"Miguel de Unamuno"/AEIHM, 2003. 405–21.

Nash, Mary. *Defying Male Civilization. Women in the Spanish Civil War.* Indian Hills, CO: Arden Press. 1995.

———. "Pronatalism and Motherhood in Franco Spain." In *Maternity and Gender Policies. Women and the Rise of the European Welfare States 1880s to 1950s,* edited by Gisela Bock and Pat Thane. London: Routledge, 1991.

———, ed. *Presencia y Protagonismo. Aspectos de la historia de la mujer.* Barcelona: Ediciones del Serbal, 1984.

Nielfa Cristóbal, Gloria. *Mujeres y hombres en la España Franquista. Sociedad, economía, política, cultura.* Madrid: Instituto de Investigaciones Feministas, Universidad Complutense de Madrid, 2003.

Nora, Pierre. *Realms of Memory.* New York: Columbia University Press, 1996.

Novella Suarez, Jorge. "Tierno Galván y el Barroco" *Sistema. Revista de Ciencias Sociales,* no. 121, Madrid July 1994.

Núñez Laiseca, Mónica. *Arte y política en la España del desarrollo (1962–1968).* Madrid: Consejo Superior de Investigaciones Ceintíficas, 2006.

Núñez, Mirta. *Mujeres Caídas.* Madrid: Oberon, 2003.

Ofer, Inbal. "Am I That Body? Sección Femenina De La FET And The Struggle For The Institution Of Physical Education And Competitive Sports For Women In Franco's Spain" *Journal of Social History* 39, no. 4, 897–1011.

Offen, Karen. *European Feminisms, 1700–1950: A Political History.* Palo Alto: Stanford University Press, 2000.

Olmeda, Fernando. *El látigo y la pluma.Homosexuales en la España de Franco.* Madrid: Oyeron, 2004.

Pack, Sasha D. *Tourism and Dictatorship: Europe's Peaceful Invasion of Franco's Spain.* New York: Palgrave Macmillan, 2006.

Passmore, Kevin, ed. *Women, Gender Fascism in Europe, 1919–45.* New Brunswick, NJ: Rutgers University Press, 2003.

Pavlovic,Tatjana. *Despotic Bodies and Transgressive Bodies: Spanish Culture from Francisco Franco to Jesus Franco.* Albany: SUNY Press, 2002.

Paxton, Robert. *The Anatomy of Fascism.* New York: Vintage Books, 2005.

Payne, Stanley G. *Fascism in Spain, 1923–1977.* Madison: University of Wisconsin Press, 2000.

———. *The Franco Regime, 1936–1975.* Madison: University of Wisconsin Press, 1987.

———. *Spanish Catholicism: An Historical Overview.* Madison: The University of Wisconsin Press, 1984.

———. *The Spanish Civil War. The Soviet Union, and Communism.* New Haven, CT: Yale University Press, 2004.

Pérez Cánovas, Nicolás. *Homosexualidad, homosexuales y uniones homosexuales en el Derecho español.* Granada: Comares, 1996.

Pérez Díaz, Victor. *The Return of Civil Society in Spain.* Cambridge, MA: Harvard University Press, 1993.

Pérez-Sánchez, Gema. *Queer Transitions in Contemporary Spanish Culture: From Franco to La Movida.* Albany: SUNY Press, 2007.

Perry, Mary Elizabeth. *The Handless Maiden: Moriscos and the Politics of Religion in Early Modern Spain (Jews, Christians, and Muslims from the Ancient to the Modern World).* Princeton, NJ: Princeton University Press, 2005.

Picazo Dios, Miguel et al. *La Tía Tula. Guión cinematográfico.* Jaén: Diputación Provincial de Jaén, 2005.

Plaza, Martín de la. *Conchita Piquer.* Madrid: Alianza Editorial, 2001.

Poster, Mark. *Cultural History. Disciplinary Readings and Challenges.* New York: Columbia University Press, 1997.

Preston, Paul. *Franco. A Biography.* New York: Routledge, 1994.

———. *Juan Carlos: Steering Spain from Dictatorship to Democracy.* 1st American Ed edition, New York: W. W. Norton & Company, 2004.

Putnam, Robert D. *Democracies in Flux: The Evolution of Social Capital in Contemporary Society.* Oxford: Oxford University Press, 2004.

Rabinow, Paul. *The Foucault Reader.* New York: Pantheon Books, 1984.

Radcliff, Pamela. "Imagining Female Citizenship in the 'New Spain': Gendering the Democratic Transition, 1975–1978." *Gender & History* 13, no. 3, (November 2001), 498–523.

Rámos, Dolores, et al. *La modernización de España. Cultura y vida cotidiana.* Madrid: Coleción Síntesis, 2002.

Redondo, Augustin, ed. *Le corps comme Métaphore dans L'Espagne des XVIe et XVIIe siècles. Du corps métaphorique aux metaphors corporelles.* Paris: Presses de la Sorbonne Nouvelle Publications de la Sobornne, 1992.

Reich, Jacqueline, and Piero Garofalo, eds. *Re-Viewing Fascism. Italian Cinema, 1922–1943.* Bloomington: Indiana University Press, 2002.

Richards, Michael. *Un tiempo de silencio. La Guerra civil y la cultura de la represión en la España de Franco, 1936–1945.* Barcelona: Crítica, 1998.

Richards, Michael, and Chris Ealham. *The Splintering of Spain: Cultural History and the Spanish Civil War, 1936–1939.* Cambridge: Cambridge University Press, 2005.

Richmond, Kathleen. *Las mujeres en el fascismo espanol / Women in the Spanish fascism: La Seccion Femenina De La Falange, 1934–1959.* Madrid: Alianza Ensayo, 2007.

Rivière Gómez, Aurora. *"Caídas, Miserables, degeneradas." Estudios sobre la Prostitución en el siglo XIX.* Madrid: Direccion General de la Mujer, 1994.

Roca i Girona, Jordi. *De la puereza a la maternidad. La construcción del género femenino en la postguerra española.* Madrid: Ministerio de Educación y Cultura, 1996.

Roseman, Sharon R. and Parkhurst, Shawn S. *Recasting Culture and Space in Iberian Contexts.* Albany: SUNY Series in National Identities, 2008.

Roura, Asumpta, ed. *Un inmenso prostíbulo. Mujer y moralidad durabte el Franquismo.* Barcelona: Editotrial Base, 2005.

Said, Edward, *Orientalism.* 25th anniversary edition. New York: Vintage Books, 1994.

Salas, Mary, Merche Comabella et al. *Españolas en la Transición. De excluidas a Protagonistas 1973–1982.* Madrid: Biblioteca Nueva, 1999.

Schissler, Hanna, ed. *The Miracle Years. A Cultural History of West Germany, 1949–1968.* Princeton, NJ: Princeton University Press, 2001.

Scicluna, Charles J. *The Essential Definition of marriage According to the 1917 and 1983 Codes of Canon Law. An Exegetical and Comparative Study.* New York: University Press of America, 1995.

Scott, Joan Wallach. *Gender and the Politics of History.* Columbia University Press, 1999.

Serrano, Carlos. *El nacimiento de Carmen. Símbolos, mitos y nación.* Madrid: Taurus, 1999.

———, ed. *Nations en quêde passé. La peninsula ibériqueXIX^{e}–XXe.* Paris: Université de Paris-Sorbonne, 2000.

Shaviro, Steven. *The Cinematic Body Theory Out of Bounds.* Minneapolis: University of Minnesota Press, 1993.

Shubert, Adrian. *Social History of Modern Spain.* London: Routledge, 1991.

Siegel, Carol, and Ann Kibbey, ed. *Forming and Reforming Identity.* New York: New York University Press, 1995.

Smith-Rosenberg, Carroll, and Charles Rosenberg. "The Female Animal: Medical and Ideological Views of Woman and Her Role in Nineteenth-Century America." *The Journal of American History* 60, no. 2 (Sept. 1973): 332–56.

Sobchack, Vivian. *The Address of the Eye. A Phenomenology of Film Experience.* Princeton, NJ: Princeton University Press, 1992.

Sobremonte Martínez, José Enrique. *Prostitución y Código Penal.* Valencia: Universidad de Valencia, 1983.

Solomon, Michael. *The Literature of Misogyny in Medieval Spain. The Arcipreste de Talavera and the Spill.* Cambridge: Cambridge University Press, 1997.

Sopeña Monsalve, Andrés. *El florido Pensil: Memoria de la Escuela Nacionalcatólica.* Barcelona: Grijalbo, 1994.

Suárez Fernández, Luis. *Crónica de la Sección Femenina.* Madrid: Asociación Nueva Andadura, 1993.

Taylor Allen, Ann. *Feminism and Motherhood in Western Europe, 1890–1970: The Maternal Dilemma.* New York: Palgrave Macmillan, 2005.

Threlfall, Monic. *Gender Politics and Society in Spain.* New York: Routledge, 2004.

Torres, Rafael. *La Vida amorosa en tiempos de Franco.* Madrid: Temas de Hoy, 1996.

Tranche, Rafael R., and Vicente Sánchez-Biosca. *NODO. El tiempo y la memoria.* Madrid: Cátedra/Filmoteca Española, 2002.

Triana-Toribio. *Spanish National Cinema National Cinemas.* New York: Routledge, 2003.

Tyler May, Elaine. *Homeward Bound. American Families in the Cold War Era.* New York: Basic Books, 1988.

Umbral, Francisco. *Y Tierno Galván subió a los cielos.* Barcelona: Seix Barral, 1990.

———. "Los cuerpos y los siglos." *Interviú. Especial 25 Aniversario,* May 15, 2001.

Unamuno, Miguel de. *La Tía Tula.* Bilingual edition. New York: Dover Publications; 2005.

Valiente Fernández, Celia. *Políticas públicas de géneroen perspective comparada: La mujer trabajadora en Italia y España (1900–1996).* Marid: Universidad Autónoma de Madrid, 1997.

Valis, Noël. *The Culture of Cursilería. Bad Taste, Kitsch, and Class in Modern Spain.* Durham, NC: Duke University Press, 2002.

Val Valdivieso, María Isabel, Magdalena S. Tomás Pérez, María Jesús Dueñas cepeda, and Cristina dela Rosa Cubo, eds. *La historia de las mujeres una revision historiográfica.* Universidad de Valladolid: Asociación Española de Investigación Histórica de las Mujeres, 2004.

Varderi, Alejandro, *Severo Sarduy y Pedro Almodovar. Del Barroco al Kitsch en la narrativa y el cine postmodernos.* Madrid: Editorial Pliegos, 1996.

Vázquez Montalbán, Manuel. *Crónica Sentimental de España.* Barcelona: Grijalbo, 1998.

Vertinsky, Patricia. *Disciplining Bodies in the Gymnasium: Memory, Monument, Modernism Sport in the Global Society, 55.* New York: Routledge, 2003.

Villar, Paco. *Historia y Leyenda del Barrio Chino. 1900–1992 Crónica y documentos de los bajos fondos de Barcelona.* Barcelona: Edicons La Campana, 1996.

Vincent, Mary, *Spain, 1833–2002: People and State.* New York: Oxford University Press, 2008.

Vinyes Ribas, Ricard. "Construyendo a Caín. Diagnosis y terapia del disidente: Las investigaciones psiquiátricas militares de Antonio Vallejo Nágera con presas y presos politicos." *Ayer* 44 (2001): 227–50.

———. *Irredentas.* Temas de Hoy, 2002.

Walker-Bynum, Carolyn. *Fragmentation and Redemption. Essays on Gender and the Human Body in Medieval Religion.* New York: Zone Books, 1992.

Weeks, Jeffrey. *Sexualidad.* México: Paidos, 1998.

Wiarda, Howard J., and Margaret MacLeish Mott. *Catholic Roots and Democratic Flowers: Political Systems in Spain and Portugal* Westport, CT: Praeger, 2001.

Willson, Perry. *Peasant Women and Politics in Facist Italy: The Massaie Rurali Section of the PNF.* New York: Routledge, 2002.

Yalom, Marilyn. *History of the Breast.* New York: Ballantine Books, 1998.

———. *A History of the Wife.* New York: Harper Perennial, 2002.

Yeğenoğlu, Meyda, *Colonial Fantasies. Towards a Feminist reading of Orientalism* Cambridge: Cambridge University Press, 1998.

Zambrano, María. *Delirium and Destiny. A Spaniard in Her Twenties.* Albany: SUNY, 1999.

———. *España, sueño y verdad.* Madrid: Ediciones Siruela, 1994.

Index